The Political Economy of Industrial Democracies

DOUGLAS A. HIBBS, JR.

The Political Economy of Industrial Democracies

Harvard University Press
Cambridge, Massachusetts, and London, England   1987

Library of Congress Cataloging-in-Publication Data

Hibbs, Douglas A., 1944–
    The political economy of industrial democracies.

    Includes index.
    1. Business cycles—United States.   2. Business
cycles—Europe.   3. Strikes and lockouts—United States.
4. Strikes and lockouts—Europe.   5. Industry and
state—United States.   6. Industry and state—Europe.
I. Title.
HB3743.H53   1987   339.5'09171'3   86-9799
ISBN 0-674-68580-6

For my colleagues in politics and economics

Contents

Acknowledgments

This collection of essays on political economy owes much to my assistants and collaborators. I am especially grateful to Henrik Madsen, Douglas Rivers, and Nicholas Vasilatos.

Henrik Madsen is the coauthor of Chapter 9. More important, during our years together at Harvard, Henrik was a rich source of knowledge and insight about North European politics and economics, and my work benefited greatly from his help.

Doug Rivers, who also worked with me at Harvard, contributed greatly to Chapters 5 and 7. Moreover, Doug's deep knowledge of theoretical reasoning, statistical analysis, and American political behavior enriched several more of the chapters.

Nick Vasilatos and I first began working together in the early 1970s, when he was an undergraduate and I was an assistant professor at MIT. Nick helped substantially with Chapters 5, 7, 8, and 10, and his programming skills contributed to virtually every chapter in this book.

Most of the research reported in this volume was financed by grants from the National Science Foundation. I am very grateful to the NSF for its generous support. I also wish to thank the Center for International Affairs at Harvard, which supported much of my work after 1978 in the form of released time from my usual teaching load, and the Political Science Department at Göteborg University, Sweden, which supported the preparation of this book.

Finally, I want the many secretaries who struggled over the years with my technical manuscripts—an especially demanding job in the days before text-editing computer programs—to know how much I appreciate their efforts.

The Political Economy of Industrial Democracies

Introduction

Politics and economics are intimately connected. In all industrial democracies economic policies and outcomes are sources of deep political cleavages and social conflicts, and economic fluctuations often affect critically the political fortunes of governing parties and politicians. For these reasons, economic policies are rarely, if ever, based entirely on technical, apolitical considerations. Rather, economic policies, and therefore economic outcomes, are shaped importantly by the larger political environment facing policy authorities.

This volume contains most of my articles published from 1976 to 1982 on the political economy of industrial democracies. The essays share three characteristics. First, they generally have a macrolevel orientation rather than a microlevel one. The focus is on the political and economic aspects of expansions, contractions, and inflations. The analyses are framed in terms of labor and capital, electorates and parties, and governments and oppositions. Only rarely is attention given to the behavior and experiences of voters and politicians or workers and managers, viewed explicitly as individual actors in the political economy. Second, the chapters deal with relations over time between political and economic phenomena, which are typically modeled dynamically by means of standard econometric and statistical techniques. Some readers will find many of the analytical frameworks quite demanding. But these modeling strategies have allowed me to address important questions in macropolitical economy that would have been difficult or impossible to confront by means of more accessible techniques. Third, and most important, nearly all the chapters were motivated in part by my persistent concern with class-based cleavages and political conflicts over macroeconomic and distributional policies and outcomes.

In preparing this book I have resisted the temptations to modify the essays in response to critics and, in general, to take advantage of hindsight. I have eliminated most of the repetitious material, improved awkward constructions, and deleted superfluous notes. In all other respects the essays appear here as originally published.

The book is divided into three parts: the political economy of industrial conflict, politics and economics in the United States, and comparative and European politics and economics.

Industrial Conflict: Fluctuations, Trends, and Consequences

Part I contains three chapters on strike activity in capitalist democracies. Chapter 1 deals with short-run fluctuations in postwar industrial conflict in ten countries in relation to fluctuations in the macroeconomy (wages, prices, profits, and unemployment), the degree of centralization of labor relations, and the political strength of Labor, Socialist, and Communist parties.

Descriptive empirical analyses of strikes were first undertaken at least one hundred years ago, and a number of statistically sophisticated analyses of strikes and the business cycle had been published before I began my own work in this area.[1] The novel features of this chapter therefore lie elsewhere. As I see it, the chapter makes three contributions to the literature. First, I try to incorporate an explicit conception of strike measurement, developed in earlier descriptive quantitative studies of strikes, into more rigorous statistical analyses of industrial conflict. Second, I tie traditional sociology of conflict orientations toward strike activity to the modern econometric approach to empirical analysis.[2] And, third, I systematically analyze

1. Michael Shalev reviews some early studies in "Trade Unionism and Economic Analysis—The Case of Industrial Conflict," *Journal of Labor Research*, 1 (Spring 1980), 133–173. On the more recent literature on economics and strikes, which uses powerful econometric techniques and modern economic theoretical perspectives, see John Kennan, "The Economics of Strikes," in Orley C. Achenfelter and Richard Layard, eds., *Handbook of Labor Economics* (Amsterdam: North-Holland, forthcoming).

2. For reasons that never made sense to me, modern statistical and econometric techniques of empirical analysis were once viewed as somehow embodying a "conservative" bias and were therefore believed to be incompatible with left-leaning, sociological, and conflict-oriented approaches to the study of strike activity. (The so-called behavioral revolution, which brought formalization and modern empirical measurement and statistical analysis techniques to my own field, political science, in the early

fluctuations in strike activity in relation to variations in important features of the party system.

In the original essay I did not satisfactorily treat the *political* economy of strikes. One of my conclusions was that neither the electoral strength of Labor and Socialist parties nor their outright control of national governments deterred short-run increases in strike activity during the period 1950–1969. Although this conclusion pertained to short-run, postwar strike fluctuations, I repeatedly emphasized that the evidence presented was at odds with the arguments of Ross and Hartman about the impact of political arrangements on longer-run strike trends.

In their classic comparative study of industrial conflict, published sixteen years earlier, Ross and Hartman wrote: "labor political action, labor parties, and labor governments have helped pave the way toward a renunciation of the strike."[3] One important reason was that "worker unrest is channeled off into the political sphere"; this phenomenon stemmed partly from the fact that "the [modern] state can influence the workers' economic welfare more powerfully through tax policy, public spending, economic planning, and social welfare legislation than the unions can affect it through collective bargaining."[4] I soon realized that to have given the impression that Ross and Hartman's arguments should be rejected wholesale was misguided.

Indeed, although there was no general "withering away" of the strike during the twentieth century, as Ross and Hartman suggested in their seminal study, political developments after the first third of the century profoundly affected the long-run trend of industrial conflict in democratic societies. Chapter 2 addresses this issue. In it I try to clarify the political conditions underlying the pronounced decline in strike activity over the long run in some countries and the long-term stability of industrial conflict levels in others. Beginning with the premise that strike activity is one manifestation of continuing struggle for power between classes over the distribution of resources (principally national income), I show that from before World War II to the postwar period strike activity declined in proportion to the success of Labor and Socialist parties in gaining control of national govern-

1960s, was also viewed for many years as an inherently "conservative" force.) However, formal reasoning and rigorous quantitative methodologies are now used by social scientists of all political stripes and theoretical orientations.

3. Arthur Ross and Paul Hartman, *Changing Patterns of Industrial Conflict* (New York: Wiley, 1960) p. 58.

4. Ibid., pp. 69 and 68.

ments. I argue, however, that the critical factor underlying international changes in the long-run equilibria of strike activity was not so much the political success of Labor and Socialist parties per se, but rather their effectiveness in socializing the consumption and final distribution (though not necessarily the production) of national income. The latter process represented a massive, politically induced circumvention of the private market and shifted the locus of distribution of national income, and hence the locus of distributive conflict, from the market, where capital interests enjoy a comparative advantage, to the electoral arena, where the political resources of the organized working class are more telling. Consequently, in the welfare states (largely the creatures of Labor and Social Democratic political action) the political process decisively shapes the final distribution of income, and strike activity and conflict between labor and capital in the economic marketplace have to a great extent been replaced by political competition and conflict between left- and right-wing parties in the electoral marketplace.

Soon after the initial publication of this essay, Michael Shalev argued in a thoughtful critique that my emphasis on changes in the distributional role of the state as the most important mediating link between the (acknowledged) association of Labor/Social Democratic political mobilization and declines in strike activity was too narrow.[5] Shortly thereafter, Shalev and Walter Korpi wrote a number of articles taking a somewhat broader theoretical view of variations in long-run equilibria in strike activity and emphasizing the importance of changes in the "distribution of power resources between the main classes."[6] According to Shalev and Korpi, "industrial conflict tends to lose its central role in the political economy of Western nations to the extent that the labor movement achieves access to political power and is thereby able to move the center of gravity of the manifestations of conflicts of interest between capital and labor from the industrial to the political arena."[7] This interpretation is quite close to mine,[8] yet by not focusing on the growth of the public economy alone it broadened

5. Michael Shalev, "Strikers and the State: A Comment," *British Journal of Political Science*, 8 (1978), 479–492.

6. Walter Korpi and Michael Shalev, "Strikes, Power and Politics in Western Nations, 1900–76," *Political Power and Social Theory*, 1 (1980), 299–332 and "Strikes, Industrial Relations and Class Conflict in Capitalist Societies," *British Journal of Sociology*, 30 (June 1979), 164–187.

7. Korpi and Shalev, "Strikes, Power and Politics," pp. 324–325.

8. Shalev and Korpi emphasized that they found my interpretation too narrow (and I am inclined to agree with them) and took pains to distinguish their own theory from it. Yet in another article published just two years after my own, Korpi advanced a theory

the scope of the argument and thereby enhanced a field that, as Shalev put it, "has long been starved of theoretical innovation."[9]

In Chapter 3 I analyze the consequences of strike activity in the manufacturing sector in France, Great Britain, Italy, and the United States for postwar wage inflation. In the first half I estimate several "excess demand" models of inflation and argue that international differences in the rate and extent of wage adjustment to price increases (in price expectations Phillips curve models) reflect, in part, variations in the power of organized labor in collective bargaining. In the second half of the chapter I estimate a number of "cost-push" wage models, show that strike activity is the most relevant indicator of labor militancy for analyses of wage inflation, and compare the relative contributions of militancy and institutionalized labor power in the four countries to the postwar wage formation process.

The main conclusion of Chapter 3 is that in a diverse group of industrial societies both labor power and labor militancy play an important role in perpetuating received rates of inflation. In the case of Italy, but not in that of the other countries, I find persuasive evidence that labor action not only helped perpetuate inflation (because of "real wage resistance") but also, and more important, made a direct and systematic contribution to the acceleration of inflation after the late 1960s (prices chasing accelerating wages). As informed observers would expect, labor action appeared to be less important for the inflationary process in the United States than in the other countries. Indeed, because I estimated the adjustment of manufacturing wages to bursts of price inflation to be incomplete in the United States, I went so far as to suggest that there might be a viable long-run conventional Phillips curve in this country. Subsequent events have demonstrated that this conclusion was much too strong, although the idea that real wages have greater downward flexibility in the United States than elsewhere is now firmly embedded in the comparative macroeconomics literature.[10]

---

that I find essentially indistinguishable from mine. He wrote: "A strong and stable control over the government makes it possible for the working class to use public policy to intervene in the distributional processes in society. It is thus no longer limited to fight for its share of production on the labor market." And with a strong Labor/Social Democratic party "industrial conflict can be expected to decrease and political struggles related to public interventions into the distributive processes in society to become the central arena for distributional conflicts"; Korpi, "Social Policy and Distributional Conflict in the Capitalist Democracies," *West European Politics*, 3 (October 1980), 309.

9. Shalev, "Strikers and the State," p. 491.

10. See, for example, Jeffrey Sachs, "Wages, Profits, and Macroeconomic Adjustment: A Comparative Study," *Brookings Papers on Economic Activity* (1979:2), 269–319.

I also argued in this essay that, except in the United States, some form of national wages or incomes policy was the only feasible route to lowering the high inflation rates of the 1970s. I assumed that policy officials would find it impossible, for political reasons, to create the prolonged period of high unemployment and idle capacity necessary to break the back of inflation through conventional policies of monetary and fiscal austerity. This assumption proved to be wrong. During the decade after the first OPEC oil price shock of 1973–74, most European countries relentlessly pursued restrictive macroeconomic policies designed to fight inflation. As a result, European inflation rates are generally much lower today than during the mid-1970s, and Europe has experienced a decade of nearly continuous economic stagnation.

Yet the main message of the chapter—that autonomous trade union action is a crucial feature of the postwar inflationary process—has, I think, stood up well to the test of time. Once commonly rejected as of no fundamental importance to an understanding of the problem of inflation,[11] trade union power and militancy now occupy a prominent place in comparative macroeconomic analysis.[12]

Politics and Economics in the United States

Part II consists of three chapters on politics and economics in the United States. During the postwar era of economic policy activism, American political authorities have frequently pursued restrictive macroeconomic policies, depressing real output and employment in order to fight inflation. As one who strongly believes that the nation's welfare is best served by policies designed to yield a low-unemployment, high-activity economy, I have been puzzled and concerned by this emphasis on the problem of inflation.

In Chapter 4 I examine one important aspect of the political environment of macroeconomic policy: the electorate's relative concern about inflation and unemployment, as reflected in opinion polls. After briefly reviewing the distributional consequences of inflations and recessions, I analyze the combinations of inflation, unemployment, and real income growth in the economy that typically gave rise to an

11. A forceful example is Harry Johnson, *Essays in Monetary Economics* (London: Allen and Unwin, 1967), chap. 3.

12. A good example is Michael Bruno and Jeffrey Sachs, *Economics of Worldwide Stagflation* (Cambridge, Mass.: Harvard University Press, 1985), chap. 8.

anti-inflation versus an anti-unemployment-oriented majority in the electorate during the first half of the 1970s.[13] Not surprisingly, the analysis shows that the public's relative aversion to inflation and unemployment responds to the prevailing economic situation. During big accelerations of prices, the electorate's relative concern about inflation rises sharply; when the economy goes into recession, public concern about unemployment increases. In all economic situations, however, downscale groups (lower income and occupational classes) in the electorate tend to be more unemployment averse (less inflation averse) than upscale groups. The reasons are that unemployment falls most heavily on the lower classes and that postwar inflations have generally redistributed income and wealth away from the rich.

Yet, despite large cyclical fluctuations and important intergroup differences in relative concern about inflation and unemployment, anti-inflation sentiment is a widespread and remarkably durable feature of American public opinion. Indeed, estimates presented in the final section of Chapter 4 indicate that even at relatively modest inflation rates—as low as 5 to 6 percent per year—a solid majority of the electorate is likely to favor disinflationary macroeconomic policies yielding extra unemployment and slower growth, unless unemployment is very high or is rising rapidly.

In Chapter 5 I discuss the same themes from a different vantage point. Building on a tradition launched by John Mueller and later extended significantly by Samuel Kernell,[14] I develop direct evidence on the political consequences of macroeconomic events by analyzing the responsiveness of political support for American presidents, as registered in the Gallup polls, to movements in inflation, unemployment, and other economic and political variables. The analyses are embedded in a dynamic nonlinear model of political support, which is based on the theory of quantal choice and on the idea that voters evaluate a president's cumulative, discounted performance relatively

13. Chapter 5 of Hibbs, *The American Political Economy: Macroeconomics and Electoral Politics in the United States* (Cambridge, Mass.: Harvard University Press, forthcoming), extends this line of research with data covering the early 1980s. Subsequent studies by Fischer and Huizanga and Peretz also analyze public opinion toward inflation and unemployment; Stanley Fischer and John Huizanga, "Inflation, Unemployment and Public Opinion Polls," *Journal of Money, Credit and Banking*, 14 (February 1982), 1–19; Paul Peretz, *The Political Economy of Inflation* (Chicago: University of Chicago Press, 1983), chaps. 4 and 5.

14. John Mueller, "Presidential Popularity from Truman to Johnson," *American Political Science Review*, 64 (March 1970), 18–34; Samuel Kernell, "Explaining Presidential Popularity," *American Political Science Review*, 71 (March 1977), 44–66.

rather than absolutely. The dynamic specification of the model, the main elements of which were novel at the time, allowed me to estimate the weights voters implicitly give current and past performance outcomes when making contemporaneous political evaluations of the president (political discounting), and to estimate the contributions of interparty and interadministration relative performance comparisons to movements through time in presidential approval ratings.[15] This latter feature of the model provides an explicit, endogenous account of the tendency of a new president's support to decline over time from early "honeymoon" levels, which earlier studies (including some of my own) had picked up with ad hoc dummy variables and time trend terms.

However, my main motivation for developing the model presented in this and related chapters (Chapters 7–10) was to investigate the responsiveness of the political support of important electoral groups to variations in nominal and real macroeconomic performance. I was particularly interested in the impact of inflation and unemployment on presidential support ratings, because macroeconomic policy conflicts so frequently center on the relative priority to be given to these two problems. The cross-group patterns in the estimation results reported in Chapter 5 are broadly consistent with what we know about the distributional consequences of recessions and inflations. The estimates indicate that the political support of blue-collar voters and Democratic partisans in the electorate is more sensitive to unemployment and less sensitive to inflation than is the political support of white-collar voters and Republican partisans.

Nonetheless, high inflation adversely affects political support for presidents among all groups. And because the effects of inflation

15. In my own and many others' studies of the dynamics of political support, voters are assumed to be backward looking, or "retrospective," when evaluating performance. Forward-looking behavior is accommodated only to the extent that voters believe that past performance is the best guide to future performance.

Recent papers by Henry Chappel and William Keech have explored a novel alternative to the retrospective tradition: voters are assumed to acknowledge the (short-run) Phillips curve tradeoff between real and nominal economic performance, and to weight the expected future consequences of the current economic situation when making contemporaneous political choices. Hence, by the reasoning of Chappel and Keech, voters may punish unsustainable expansions likely to yield higher future inflation and may accept, or even reward, recessions likely to yield lower future inflation. See Chappel, "Presidential Popularity and Macroeconomic Performance: Are Voters Really So Naive?" *Review of Economics and Statistics*, 65 (1983), 385–392; and Chappel and Keech, "A New View of Accountability for Economic Performance," *American Political Science Review*, 79 (March 1985), 10–27.

were estimated in the presence of real income growth rates, the results in Chapter 5, as in Chapter 4, imply that the electorate has a substantial "pure" aversion to inflation, which does not seem to hinge on actual erosion of standards of living by price increases. In view of the enormous costs of unemployment in the form of lost real output and underutilized human resources, and the relatively small costs of inflation, these results may seem surprising. But they leave little doubt that variations in inflation, along with movements in unemployment and real income growth, are an important source of fluctuations in mass support for American presidents.

Chapter 6 is a case study of the electoral consequences of macroeconomic performance. The 1980 elections represented a substantial victory for the Republican party. Ronald Reagan received more than 55 percent of the two-party, Carter-Reagan vote, and he was the first challenger to defeat an elected incumbent since Roosevelt beat Hoover in 1932. Moreover, the Republicans substantially increased their strength in Congress, gaining thirty-three seats (and a policy majority) in the House and twelve seats (and a numerical majority) in the Senate. Chapter 6 confronts the question of whether the Republicans' 1980 victories should be interpreted as a fundamental "shift to the right" of the electorate's preferences about the federal government's role in social and economic affairs, which signaled a dramatic erosion of the political base of American welfare state liberalism; or are more accurately seen as the predictable consequence of poor performance, in particular poor late-term economic performance, under Carter and the Democrats.

Evidence from data on economic performance under postwar presidential administrations, both from simple statistical models of the postwar association of election outcomes and the economy and from opinion surveys of 1980 voters, all support the second explanation. Reagan was elected because of the dismal late-term economic performance of the Carter administration, and not because of any widespread desire for a conservative shift in federal spending and taxing policy. For this reason, I argued that the president would be reelected only if there was a late-term economic expansion. As it turned out, President Reagan presided over one of the greatest election-year booms of the postwar era and defeated Walter Mondale in 1984 by a landslide.[16] Very few examples in American electoral history illustrate

16. I analyze the decisive contribution of cyclical macroeconomic performance to President Reagan's 1984 election success in *The American Political Economy*, chaps. 7 and 9.

more dramatically the electoral potency of cyclical macroeconomic performance.

Comparative and European Politics and Economics

Part III contains two comparative studies on politics and economics, and three studies of specific European countries. Chapters 7 through 9 deal with the impact of macroeconomic performance on *aggregate* mass political support for governing parties or chief executives. Chapter 7 is a comparative analysis; Chapters 8 and 9 focus on France and Sweden, respectively, although I have used the results for comparative purposes elsewhere.[17]

The political support models in these chapters have the same basic theoretical structure as the model discussed above for Chapter 5. All five try to assess voters' sensitivity to real economic performance (unemployment and real income growth) in relation to their sensitivity to nominal economic performance (changes and accelerations of the price level). Such relative sensitivities yield important information about the mass political base favoring expansionary policies geared to sustaining high employment, on the one hand, and the popular base underlying restrictive policies geared to producing disinflation, on the other. They therefore help illuminate an important aspect of the political environment constraining policy authorities in the industrial democracies.

The empirical results of Chapters 7, 8, and 9 generally conform to the impressions of informed observers about variations over time and

---

According to Michael Lewis-Beck, the simple statistical model for presidential voting outcomes presented in this essay came closer than other published models to forecasting the magnitude of Reagan's 1984 victory. A parallel model for House seat shifts, presented in the same article, forecast perfectly the Republicans' 1984 gain of fourteen seats. See Beck, "Election Forecasts in 1984: How Accurate Were They?" *PS*, 18 (Winter 1985), 53–62. However, my forecast that House Republicans would lose thirty-nine seats in 1982 was too big. The Republicans lost twenty-six seats.

17. A thoughtful analysis of my treatment of political dynamics and political change in Chapter 8 appears in Jean-Dominique Lafay, "Political Change and the Stability of the Popularity Function," *Political Behavior*, 6 (1984), 333–352. For my comparative analyses see "Inflation, Political Support, and Macroeconomic Policy," in *The Politics of Inflation and Economic Stagnation*, ed. Leon Lindberg and Charles Maier (Washington, D.C.: Brookings Institution, 1985), and "Macroeconomic Performance, Macroeconomic Policy and Electoral Politics in Industrial Democracies," in *Global Dilemmas*, ed. Samuel Huntington and Joseph Nye (Lanham, Md.: University Press of America, 1985).

across countries in the impact of real and nominal economic performance on mass political support. In all five countries analyzed, unemployment, real income growth performance, or both have considerable influence on political support for governments. Given the obvious social and economic costs of lower growth and extra unemployment, such political costs are hardly surprising. However, in several countries the relative importance of inflation on political support increased from the 1960s to the 1970s. This too comes as no surprise, in view of the big inflationary shocks of the latter decade. Finally, the empirical evidence also suggests that voters' sensitivity to unemployment fluctuations is more pronounced in Sweden than elsewhere, whereas sensitivity to inflation is greatest in Germany and the United States. This pattern is consistent with the preeminence of the full-employment issue in Swedish political life, which was nurtured by forty-four years of continuous Social Democratic government, and with the widely held view that the Weimar era hyperinflation left German society with an enduring distaste for inflation. Concerning the United States, one might conjecture (and it is only a conjecture) that the relative weakness of organized labor—everywhere the key producer group generating pressure and mobilizing (and creating) sentiment on behalf of high-employment policies—helps explain the American electorate's comparatively high aversion to inflation.

Chapter 10 reports class-specific analyses of the dynamics of political support in Great Britain.[18] In it I relax the unrealistic assumption, which is an implicit feature of all aggregate political support models, that voters respond more or less homogeneously to macroeconomic (and other performance) outcomes. The empirical estimates show that cross-class differences in the responsiveness of political support to movements in unemployment exhibit the same basic pattern in Britain as in the United States (see Chapter 5). Manual or blue-collar British workers are much more sensitive to unemployment, viewed absolutely and relative to inflation, than are nonmanual or white-collar voters.

18. The dynamic functional form of the model presented in this chapter, as in those discussed previously, supplies an endogenous account of (early term) political support trends. No "add-on" (or ad hoc) time trend terms appear in the equations. For helpful clarification of the theoretical and methodological issues, see William R. Keech, "Of Honeymoons and Economic Performance: Comment on Hibbs," *American Political Science Review*, 76 (June 1982), 280–281. I reply to Keech's observations in Hibbs, "More on Economic Performance and Political Support," *American Political Science Review*, 76 (June 1982), 282–284.

This is precisely the pattern one would expect from the incidence and distributional consequences of unemployment, as compared to inflation, across classes. It also drives home the continuing relevance of class to analyses of politics and economics in Britain. In fact Chapter 10 demonstrates that there is little evidence of a persistent decline in class-based partisan political support among the British electorate. Class-based political allegiances observed in survey data exhibit cyclical oscillations rather than steady downward trends. The analysis suggests that such oscillations are explained at least in part by the interaction of fundamental class-based allegiances to the parties, with cross-class differences in sensitivities to economic outcomes.

Chapter 11, which concludes Part III and the volume as a whole, deals mainly with political parties and macroeconomic *outcomes*. It begins by introducing a "partisan" or "party cleavage" framework for the analysis of politics and macroeconomics. The principal elements of the framework are:

1. A macroeconomic assumption that price stability and full employment pose conflicting goals, and that policy authorities therefore must often choose between containing inflationary pressures and achieving sustained low rates of unemployment.

2. A distributional assumption that low unemployment, even if it means higher inflation, improves the relative and absolute economic well-being of downscale groups as compared to upscale groups.

3. A behavioral assumption that downscale groups, who form the core constituency of "left" parties, are more averse to unemployment and less averse to inflation than are upscale groups, who form the core constituency of "right" parties.

4. A representational assumption that parties in office pursue macroeconomic policies broadly consistent with the economic interests and relative preferences of their class-defined core political constituencies; hence labor-oriented, working-class-based leftist parties typically attach higher priority to achieving full employment and lower priority to fighting inflation than do business-oriented, upper-middle-class-based rightist parties.

Most of the chapter is devoted to showing that such party differences in economic priorities and policies have an impact on macroeconomic outcomes, especially unemployment outcomes, observed cross-nationally (highly aggregated data for twelve industrial democracies) and over time (quarterly, time-series statistical models for

Britain and the United States). To my surprise, the arguments and evidence I presented quickly attracted quite a bit of attention and generated considerable controversy.[19] Although my main goal was to stimulate interest in political influences (especially class-linked political influences) on economic policies and outcomes, the study unquestionably had serious limitations, three of which seem to me to be particularly important. First, I took almost no account of international economic and political constraints on domestic macroeconomic policies and outcomes. Second, I assumed a more or less stable unemployment-inflation tradeoff, which, though reasonable at the time, was refuted by subsequent events. Finally, the empirical evidence pertained to patterns in macroeconomic outcomes rather than to movements in monetary, fiscal, and other policy instruments. Only policies, of course, are controlled directly by the authorities.

In subsequent work on the same topic, I have tried to make progress on these problems by incorporating international economic shocks into the analysis, basing unemployment-inflation policy choices on the more realistic "natural rate of unemployment" theory of the (short-run) Phillips curve, and abandoning the heavily empirical, time-series (ARIMA) methodology used in Chapter 11 in favor of more theoretically structured models for economic policies and outcomes, pursued by parties with different economic goals.[20]

By the early 1980s quantitative analyses of the consequences of variations in party strengths and party governments for a diverse range of economic and distributional policies and outcomes had become something of a light industry.[21] Even so, much more remains to be done. Fortunately, many of the best minds in social science are now concentrating on empirical political economy, and for this reason the field is advancing rapidly.

19. See, for example, James Payne, "Inflation, Unemployment, and Left-Wing Political Parties: A Reanalysis," *American Political Science Review*, 73 (March 1979), 181–185, and Hibbs, "Reply to Payne," *American Political Science Review*, 73 (March 1979), 185–190; Nathaniel Beck, "Parties, Administrations, and American Macroeconomic Outcomes," *American Political Science Review*, 76 (March 1982), 83–93, and Hibbs, "Reply to Beck," *American Political Science Review*, 77 (June 1983), 447–451. Parts of these exchanges regrettably have a polemical tone, for which I bear much responsibility.

20. See Hibbs, *The American Political Economy*, chaps. 8 and 9, and "Political Parties and Macroeconomic Policies and Outcomes in the United States," *American Economic Review, Papers and Proceedings*, 76 (May 1986), 66–70. The ARIMA modeling approach of the 1977 study is significantly extended in James Alt's recent paper, "Party Strategies, World Demand, and Unemployment in Britain and the United States," *American Political Science Review*, 79 (December 1985), 1016–40.

21. Francis Castles, ed., *The Impact of Parties* (Beverly Hills, Calif.: Sage, 1982), provides a good guide to the literature through 1982.

I

Industrial Conflict: Fluctuations, Trends, and Consequences

1

Industrial Conflict in Advanced Industrial Societies

Labor strikes have long held the interest of economic historians, social scientists, industrial relations specialists, and statisticians. The
reason is that secular movements and short-term fluctuations in strike
activity are an invaluable source of quantitative information about the
state of labor-capital relations, working-class militancy, and general
socioeconomic unrest. In part because strike participation was commonly viewed during the nineteenth century as a form of criminal
activity, but also because strikes are overt and dramatic expressions of
discontent, data on industrial disputes have been carefully compiled
over long periods in most industrial nations. The size, duration, and
frequency of strikes are of course not the only indices of working-
class grievances. Chronic absenteeism, high labor turnover rates, pil-
ferage, work slowdowns, outright sabotage, as well as various kinds
of political protest and rebellion, are also significant manifestations of
discontent; but, unlike strikes, these have not been recorded with any
regularity. Nevertheless, strikes remain an important instrument of
collective working-class economic action, and they pose a direct chal-

Reprinted from *American Political Science Review*, 70 (December 1976), 1033–58. Research for the original article was supported by National Science Foundation Grant GFS
33121. An earlier version was presented at the IXth World Congress of the International
Political Science Association, Montreal, Canada, August 19–25, 1973. This revision has
benefited greatly from the comments of Hayward Alker, Donald Blackmer, Daniel
Lerner, Benjamin Page, Adam Przeworski, Robert Jackman, Domenico Mastrangelo,
Peter Lange and Douglas Smith. I am also grateful to John Chandler, Everett Kassalow,
M. Lacroix, Arthur Neff, E. Paltig, and A. Suchinsky for providing advice on data
sources and supplying a variety of data series. Finally, I am pleased to acknowledge the
assistance of Robert Berrier, Rhonda Crane, Giustina Mastrangelo, James Short, Marie
Taylor, and Nicholas Vasilatos in data collection, analysis, editing, and typing.

lenge to the authority of management, capital, and, increasingly, government in industrial societies.

This chapter focuses on strike activity during the period 1950–1969 in ten advanced industrial societies: Belgium, Canada, France, Italy, Japan, the Netherlands, Norway, Sweden, the United Kingdom, and the United States. Two considerations motivated the selection of these nations for study. First, because working-class economic and political organizations have on the whole been free of direct repression in these societies since World War II, patterns of labor-management confrontation can be meaningfully compared. Second, reliable data on socioeconomic and political variables necessary for the empirical evaluation of theoretical arguments are available for each of these countries during most of the postwar period.

The chapter has three major sections. The first deals with issues of strike measurement and introduces a three-dimensional characterization of strike activity that forms the basis of subsequent statistical analyses. The next section examines trends in industrial conflict in the postwar period and is designed to dispose of the argument that strike activity and labor militancy are "withering away" in advanced industrial societies.[1] The third and most important part develops a number of theoretically plausible statistical models to explain short-term fluctuations in the volume of strikes. These models incorporate a variety of economic and political factors that are commonly believed to influence strike activity. The economic factors include (1) movements in real wages, which are given an expectation-achievement theoretical rationalization; (2) the demand for labor, as indexed by the unemployment rate; and (3) changes in the ratio of aggregate profits to total employee compensation, that is, changes in the relative shares of labor and capital in the national income. Among the most important political influences evaluated in these models are (1) the incentive of labor-oriented Socialist parties to discourage strike activity by their working-class constituencies, which is posited to be a function of the competitive position of Labor-Socialist parties in the political system; and (2) the relative size of Communist parties, which are viewed as significant agencies for mobilizing labor discontent. The fourth and last section reviews the evidence concerning the impact of economic and political factors on fluctuations in industrial conflict and develops some implications of the statistical results for labor militancy in advanced industrial societies and working-class rationality in the use of the strike weapon.

1. I have deleted this section of the original article; but see Chapter 2.

Strike Measurement

The International Labor Office (ILO) compiles and publishes data on three basic components of industrial conflict that are supplied by national labor ministries: number of strikes, number of workers involved (strikers), and number of worker-days lost. Annual data on these components are reported for economywide totals and for nine separate sectors of economic activity. Since strikes rarely occur in the agricultural sector (and those that do are not recorded with great accuracy), it is sensible to exclude agriculture from international and intertemporal comparisons. The mining sector has also been excluded from this analysis because of the rather special character of labor-capital relations in that industry.[2] Hence this study focuses on aggregate strike activity outside of agriculture and mining.

As in the earlier, seminal work of Forchheimer, Knowles, and Goetz-Girey and the more recent work of Shorter and Tilly, the basic industrial conflict components are used in conjunction with data on employment to form three theoretically distinct strike dimensions: size, duration, and frequency:[3]

Size: Strikers per strike

Duration: Worker-days lost per striker

Frequency: Strikes per 1,000 civilian wage and salary workers

---

2. The well-known political leftism of miners is paralleled by their atypical militancy in economic confrontations with management. See, for example, Clark Kerr and Abraham Siegel, "The Interindustry Propensity to Strike—An International Comparison," in *Industrial Conflict*, ed. Arthur Kornhauser, Robert Dubin, and Arthur Ross (New York: McGraw-Hill, 1954).

3. See K. Forchheimer, "Some International Aspects of the Strike Movement," *Oxford University Institute of Statistics Bulletin*, 10 (January 1948); K. G. J. C. Knowles, *Strikes—A Study in Industrial Conflict* (Oxford: Basil Blackwell, 1952); Robert Goetz-Girey, *Le Mouvement des grèves en France 1919–1962* (Paris: Editions Sirey, 1963); and Edward Shorter and Charles Tilly, "The Shape of Strikes in France, 1830–1960," *Comparative Studies in Society and History*, 13 (January 1971), 60–86.

Small proprieters, entrepreneurs, *rentiers*, and other self-employed persons are on the whole not relevant to industrial conflict but constitute a significant fraction of the civilian labor force in some nations and periods. Therefore, they have been excluded from the frequency ratio. The self-employed do of course occasionally strike (witness, for example, the strikes by independent French shopkeepers over the government's profit and price controls in 1973, or the strikes by independent truckers over fuel pricing issues in the United States). However, such events are not included in the industrial conflict data reported to the ILO and are in any case not germane to the line of analysis pursued here.

Each of these dimensions is suitable for cross-time, cross-country analysis; however, it is advantageous to array them into a three-dimensional solid or cuboid that represents the profile or "shape" of strikes in a particular nation during a particular period. Figure 1.1 displays two distinctive hypothetical strike shapes. Figure 1.1a depicts the profile shown by Shorter and Tilly to describe nineteenth- and early twentieth-century strikes in many industrial nations. The typical strike during this initial stage of industrialization was comparatively small in size (few strikers per strike), reflecting the small scale of early establishments; long in duration (many worker-days lost per striker), evidencing the bitter, protracted resistance that newly formed unions encountered from employers; and relatively low in frequency (few strikes per 1,000 workers), indicating the rather weak organization and mobilization of the labor force.

Figure 1.1b represents a "modern" strike profile that Shorter and Tilly suggest was more common in the mid-twentieth century. It shows a vastly increased average strike size, which was in part produced by the consolidation of industrial establishments; a somewhat higher frequency, corresponding to the heightened mobilization and organization of the working class; and a markedly shorter duration. Hence what might be called the "trench warfare" pattern of infrequent, long, but relatively small strikes that typified disputes between capital and newly organized labor in the nineteenth century seems to have been supplanted by a "guerrilla warfare" pattern of frequent, short, and relatively large "lightning" strikes in more recent decades.

Aside from the structural changes that undoubtedly contributed to this evolution of strike profiles (growth in firm size, the extension of

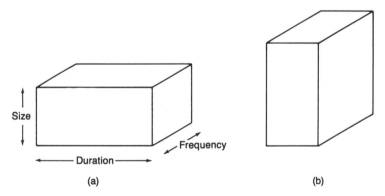

Figure 1.1. Hypothetical strike profiles.

labor organization, and so on), there appears to be a rational basis for labor's abandoning the trench warfare pattern of Figure 1.1a in favor of the guerrilla warfare approach of Figure 1.1b. Although the evidence on this score is slim, Knowles's study of industrial conflict in Great Britain and Peterson's analysis of work stoppages in the United States indicate that strike outcomes were more likely to be favorable to employers when conflicts were infrequent, long, and small, and more favorable to workers when strikes were frequent, short, and large.[4] Thus the long-term change in strike profiles may partly reflect a working-class learning process informed by the historical experience of labor-capital struggles.

Contemporary cross-national patterns provide some additional evidence that rational working-class behavior may underlie observed differences in aggregate strike shapes. For example, in France and Italy, where the most important unions are essentially Leninist organizations with relatively small memberships and slender financial resources, the guerrilla warfare strike profile of Figure 1.1b is pronounced. Organized labor in these nations could not well withstand long sieges or tests of strength against management; therefore, the relatively large, brief, and frequent lightning strike prevails.[5] The strike profiles of the United States and Canada, on the other hand, more nearly resemble the trench warfare pattern of Figure 1.1a. Unions in these countries have large dues-paying memberships and as a result command the substantial strike funds necessary to engage in comparatively long trials of strength against management.

Although comparative time-series analysis of strike profiles is potentially useful, my primary purpose here is to develop statistical models explaining short-run postwar fluctuations in overall strike

4. Knowles, *Strikes*, and Florence Peterson, *Strikes in the United States, 1880–1936* (Washington, D.C.: U.S. Department of Labor, Bureau of Labor Statistics, Bulletin no. 651, 1937).

5. The contrast between the traditional, war-of-attrition strike familiar to most Americans and the guerrilla warfare strategy described in the text is put into even sharper focus by the description of the latter pattern given by Blumenfeld: "Italian unions, which have no strike funds, have developed a whole range of disruptive activities. Among these are the 'chessboard' strike, involving only selected departments; the 'paybook' strike, in which every worker whose paycard carries an odd number engages in disputes on odd days of the week, while workers with even numbers fight out their claims on the even days; and strikes in which blue-collar workers lay down their tools in the morning but return to work after lunch, only to find that the white-collar clerks are out—thus stopping work for an entire day with the loss of only a half day's pay"; Yorick Blumenfeld, "Industrial Strife in Western Europe," *Editorial Research Reports*, 21 (June 1971), 409.

magnitudes. What we need is a single series that captures the net "damage" or impact of strikes. Perhaps the most suitable index of overall strike activity is the volume of the three-dimensional strike profile. The volume of any cuboid is of course the product of its three dimensions. Accordingly we calculate a quantity akin to the physical concept of volume:

$$
\begin{aligned}
\text{Strike volume} &= \text{worker-days lost per 1,000 wage and salary} \\
&\quad\text{workers} \\
&= \text{frequency} \times \text{duration} \times \text{size} \\
&= \frac{\text{strikes}}{1,000 \text{ workers}} \times \frac{\text{worker-days lost}}{\text{striker}} \times \frac{\text{strikers}}{\text{strike}}
\end{aligned}
$$

Worker-days lost from strikes per 1,000 wage and salary workers not only has substantial theoretical justification, being the volume of a three-dimensional profile that characterizes strike activity at any time or place, but also has obvious intuitive appeal as a comprehensive index of industrial conflict. Since it represents the net impact of a nation's overall strike profile it permits comparative, dynamic analyses that are not confounded by changes in a single conflict dimension. Erroneous conclusions about the "withering away" of industrial conflict, which can arise from focusing exclusively on one strike dimension and mistaking decreases in it for decreases in overall strike activity, are therefore avoided. Notice, for example, the reduction in strike duration but not in overall strike volume between Figures 1.1a and 1.1b.

Statistical Models of Industrial Conflict

A survey of the literature on industrial conflict suggests that most of the factors believed to influence intertemporal and international variations in strike activity can conveniently be partitioned into two broad categories. These are (1) the state of the economy, particularly movements in real wages, profits, and the demand for labor; and (2) the configuration of parties in the political system, especially the competitive position of labor-oriented parties on the non-Communist left and the extent of Communist party influence in the work force. This section briefly develops the relevant theoretical arguments, attempts to specify the appropriate structural equations, evaluates the capability of contrasting models to account for postwar (1950–1969) fluctuations in the volume of strikes in the ten-nation sample, and tests the stability of model parameters across institutionally diverse industrial relations systems.

Unemployment, Profits, and Real Wages

It has frequently been argued (though not without qualifications) that the strike is a more effective weapon during periods of general prosperity than during periods of widespread economic hardship. Indeed, there is considerable evidence that strike activity tends to follow the business cycle, increasing at cycle peaks and dropping off during business downturns.[6] Business cycle hypotheses and related propositions are best articulated in terms of unemployment, profits, and real wages.

The level of unemployment is perhaps the most sensitive indicator of general business conditions (countercyclical), and it is natural to expect working-class militancy to vary inversely with it. Low unemployment offers great strategic advantages to an aggressive labor force. A tight labor market means that management will have difficulty replacing potential strikers, who in any case can anticipate good prospects for securing permanent employment elsewhere if employers are able to replace them. Opportunities for temporary or part-time employment during a strike are also likely to be good. The situation is reversed when unemployment is high and there is an excess supply of labor. Strikebreakers are more easily recruited by employers, and alternative job opportunities for strikers are reduced.[7] Faced with

6. See Jean Bouvier, "Mouvement ouvrier at conjonctures économiques," *Le Mouvement Social* (juillet–septembre 1964), 3–30; Goetz-Girey, *Le Mouvement des greves en France;* Knowles, *Strikes;* F. S. O'Brien, "Industrial Conflict and Business Fluctuations: A Comment," *Journal of Political Economy,* 73 (1965), 650–654; Albert Rees, "Industrial Conflict and Business Fluctuations," in Kornhauser, Dubin, and Ross, *Industrial Conflict;* and Andrew Weintrab, "Prosperity versus Strikes: An Empirical Approach," *Industrial and Labor Relations Review,* 19 (January 1966), 231–238.

7. It is not necessary for employers actually to replace strikers with great regularity— it is the *psychological* threat that is important, and this is heightened during periods of high unemployment. For example, after the 1970–71 recession in the United States, the *Wall Street Journal* ran a front-page article on the "conciliatory mood" of U.S. workers. The story read in part: "across the country at large and small companies, workers are choosing to be more conciliatory when faced with the threat of losing their jobs. This is in sharp contrast to the labor scene of recent years [i.e., when unemployment was low], both union and corporate officials agree. Not long ago, they say, rank-and-filers . . . would probably have been angered by the thought of concessions . . . many

decreased product demand, capital is unlikely to be affected adversely by a prolonged work stoppage, and may even welcome an interruption of production in a period of receding profits and excessive inventories. Hence, potential strikers are more vulnerable and militancy is discouraged. Letting SV and U denote strike volume and the level of unemployment, respectively, we therefore would expect $\partial SV_t/\partial U_t < 0$.

The effect of profits on strikes is more problematic. From the perspective of working-class aggressiveness, the relevant quantity is returns to capital as a ratio of returns to labor, that is, aggregate business profits/total employee compensation. It seems reasonable to assume that when the profit ratio is increasing, workers will escalate their demands and press them more militantly. Other things being equal, this should produce an upward movement in the volume of strikes. However, management is more likely to yield to labor demands in such situations because of the severe opportunity costs of absorbing a strike when markets are expanding and profits are potentially high. As Hicks put it in his classic *The Theory of Wages*, "when trade is good, the cost of a strike to the employers will be immensely enhanced. Once an employer is making large profits, and expects those profits to continue in the near future, he is an easy mark for union demands. He will nearly always be prepared to make some concession in order to avoid a strike."[8] The net impact of changes in profits on strike activity is therefore uncertain. Letting ΔC denote the rate of change of the profit ratio, we have $\partial SV_t/\partial \Delta C_t \lesseqgtr 0$.

My specification of the influence of real wages on industrial conflict is based on expectation-achievement theory, which assumes that aggressive, violent, or protest behavior is caused in part by a gap between expectation and achievement. Variants of the theory have appeared in all branches of social science. For example, writing of civil violence, Gurr observes: "The fundamental cause of civil strife is deprivation-induced discontent: the greater the discrepancy between what men believe they deserve and what they think they are capable of attaining, the greater their discontent. The more intense and widespread discontents are in society, the more intense and widespread strife is likely to be."[9] Similarly, James Davies has argued that collec-

---

manufacturing executives have openly complained in recent years that too much control has passed from management to labor. With sales sagging . . . they feel safer in attempting to restore what they call balance" (January 26, 1972, p. 1, cited in Raford Boddy and James Crotty, "Class Conflict and Macropolicy: The Political Business Cycle," *Review of Radical Political Economics*, 7 [Spring 1974], 1–19).

8. Sir John Hicks, *The Theory of Wages* (New York: St. Martin's Press, 1963), p. 156.

tive disorder "is most likely to take place when a prolonged period of rising expectations and rising gratifications is followed by a short period of sharp reversal, during which the gap between expectations and gratifications quickenly widens and becomes intolerable."[10] In a statement of the theory closer to the topic of this study, the psychologists Krech and Crutchfield have written: "A wage rate is psychologically inadequate, no matter how large in absolute amount, if it results in a wide discrepancy between the worker's level of aspiration and his level of achievement."[11]

Although expectation-achievement theory has not received consistent support from empirical studies and tends to understate or ignore altogether the importance of structural factors for conflict behavior, the basic thesis provides a plausible theoretical framework within which to specify the impact of real wage movements on strike activity. Since labor-management conflict typically centers on proportional wage increases rather than on wage levels,[12] a reasonable functional form in the present context is:

$$SV_t = \beta_0 + \beta_1(\Delta R_{t-1} - \Delta R^*_{t-1}) + \text{other factors}. \tag{1.1}$$

$$\partial SV_t/\partial(\Delta R_{t-1} - \Delta R^*_{t-1}) < 0,$$

where SV = strike volume (worker-days lost per 1,000 workers),

ΔR = actual percentage rate of change of real wages,

ΔR^* = expected percentage rate of change of real wages.

9. "A Comparative Study of Civil Strife," in *Violence in America*, ed. Hugh Davis Graham and Ted Robert Gurr (New York: New American Library, 1969), p. 590.

10. James C. Davies, "The Curve of Rising and Declining Satisfactions as a Cause of Some Great Revolutions and a Contained Rebellion," in Graham and Gurr, *Violence in America*, p. 671.

11. David Krech and R. S. Crutchfield, *Theory and Problems of Social Psychology* (New York: McGraw-Hill, 1948), p. 542. Economists and industrial relations specialists also have used expectational explanations of worker unrest and militancy. See, for example, Joel Seidman, ed., *Trade Union Government and Collective Bargaining: Some Critical Issues* (New York: Praeger, 1970), particularly the essays by Jack Barbash and Clifford Wirtz.

12. Even the massive strikes of May–June 1968 in France (which were viewed largely as spontaneous "political" events in many popular and academic accounts) centered in the overwhelming majority of cases on traditional demands for wage increases and were called, promoted, and directed by the usual labor organizations. See Claude Durand, "Revendications explicites et revendications latentes," *Sociologie du Travail*, 4 (1973), 394–409, and George Ross, "French Working Class Politics After May–June 1968: A New Working Class?" (Paper delivered at the annual meeting of the American Political Science Association, New Orleans, September 1973). Such strikes of course have important political implications in the sense that they challenge state economic policies designed to hold down the rate of increase of wages and prices.

Strike volume in the current period is therefore hypothesized to be (partly) a function of the disparity between actual and expected real wage changes in the recent past. When ΔR_{t-1} exceeds ΔR^*_{t-1} strike activity should decrease, whereas if the gap between actual and expected real wage changes runs the other way, strike volume is anticipated to increase.[13]

As things stand ΔR^* is unobserved and Equation (1.1) is not estimable. Since attitudinal (survey) time-series data on labor force real wage expectations do not exist, we need a plausible model that specifies ΔR^* in terms of observed quantities. The theoretical and statistical literature on the formation of expectations (expectation-generating functions) presents several reasonable alternatives.[14] Consider first the so-called extrapolative expectations model:

$$\Delta R^*_t = \Delta R_{t-1} + \gamma(\Delta R_{t-1} - \Delta R_{t-2}). \tag{1.2}$$

The extrapolative expectations model asserts that the expected change in real wages in the current period equals the actual change in the previous period plus a correction to allow for the trend observed over the preceding period. If $\gamma > 0$, the labor force expects past trends to continue (extrapolative expectations), whereas if $\gamma < 0$ a reversal of past trends is anticipated (regressive expectations). If $\gamma = 0$, real wage expectations are static.

Collecting the hypotheses regarding unemployment, profit ratios, and the gap between actual and expected real wage increases yields the following theoretical model:

$$SV_t = \beta_0 + \beta_1(\Delta R_{t-1} - \Delta R^*_{t-1}) + \beta_2 U_t + \beta_3 \Delta C_t + \epsilon_t. \tag{1.3}$$

13. In the current period ΔR is likely to be influenced by SV; therefore, the model in (1.1) should be viewed as an abbreviated form of a larger system within which ΔR and ΔR^* are lagged endogenous variables.

14. See Kenneth J. Arrow and Marc Nerlove, "A Note on Expectations and Stability," *Econometrica*, 26 (April 1958), 297–305; Philip D. Cagan, "The Monetary Dynamics of Hyperinflation," in *Studies in the Quantity Theory of Money*, ed. Milton Friedman (Chicago: University of Chicago Press, 1956); Allan C. Enthoven and Kenneth J. Arrow, "A Theorem on Expectations and the Stability of Equilibrium," *Econometrica*, 24 (April 1956), 288–293; Josef Hadar, "On Expectations and Stability," *Behavioral Science*, 13 (November 1968), 445–454; Marc Nerlove, "Adaptive Expectations and Cobweb Phenomena," *Quarterly Journal of Economics*, 72 (May 1958), 227–240; and Steven J. Turnovsky, "Empirical Evidence on the Formation of Price Expectations," *Journal of the American Statistical Association*, 65 (December 1970), 1441–54.

Substitution of the extrapolative model of (1.2) for ΔR^*_{t-1} in (1.3) produces an estimating equation that is composed entirely of observed variables:

$$SV_t = \beta_0 + \beta_1\{\Delta R_{t-1} - [\Delta R_{t-2} + \gamma(\Delta R_{t-2} - \Delta R_{t-3})]\}$$
$$+ \beta_2 U_t + \beta_3 \Delta C_t + \varepsilon_t$$
$$SV_t = \beta_0 + \beta_1\Delta R_{t-1} - \beta_1\Delta R_{t-2} - \beta_1\gamma\Delta R_{t-2} + \beta_1\gamma\Delta R_{t-3}$$
$$+ \beta_2 U_t + \beta_3 \Delta C_t + \varepsilon_t$$
$$SV_t = \beta_0 + \beta_1(\Delta R_{t-1} - \Delta R_{t-2}) - \beta_1\gamma(\Delta R_{t-2} - \Delta R_{t-3})$$
$$+ \beta_2 U_t + \beta_3 \Delta C_t + \varepsilon_t. \tag{1.4}$$

A second model for expectations is the "adaptive" scheme. As initially formulated by Cagan and Nerlove, this model is:

$$\Delta R^*_t - \Delta R^*_{t-1} = (1 - \lambda)(\Delta R_{t-1} - \Delta R^*_{t-1}), \quad 0 < \lambda < 1. \tag{1.5}$$

The conventional adaptive model posits that expectations are revised linearly each period in proportion to some fraction of last period's forecast error. Hence, we form current expectations by adapting or modifying previous expectations in the light of previous experience. This implies, however, that if real wage increases are accurately anticipated in the past, expectations are static, that is, when $\Delta R_{t-1} = \Delta R^*_{t-1}$, $\Delta R^*_t = \Delta R^*_{t-1}$. For our purposes it seems more reasonable to allow for a systematic escalation of labor-force real wage expectations over time. Accordingly, the standard adaptive expectations model is modified to provide for a trend:

$$(\Delta R^*_t - \Delta R^*_{t-1}) = (1 - \lambda)(\Delta R_{t-1} - \Delta R^*_{t-1}) + \delta\Delta R^*_{t-1}$$
$$0 < \delta < 1, \quad 0 < (\lambda + \delta) < 1. \tag{1.6}$$

This model permits current expectations to escalate (or deescalate) by the trend factor $\delta\Delta R^*_{t-1}$ even if actual and expected real wage increases in the recent past are identical.

Rewriting the modified adaptive expectations model of (1.6) yields:

$$\Delta R^*_t = \Delta R^*_{t-1} + \Delta R_{t-1} - \lambda\Delta R_{t-1} - \Delta R^*_{t-1} + \lambda\Delta R^*_{t-1} + \delta\Delta R^*_{t-1}$$
$$\Delta R^*_t = (1 - \lambda)\Delta R_{t-1} + (\lambda + \delta)\Delta R^*_{t-1}, \tag{1.7}$$

which upon repeated substitution gives:

$$\Delta R_t^* = (1 - \lambda) \sum_{i=0}^{\infty} (\lambda + \delta)^i \Delta R_{t-i-1}. \tag{1.8}$$

The theoretical model for strike volume in (1.3) corresponding to the revised adaptive expectations scheme in (1.8) can now be written:

$$SV_t = \beta_0 + \beta_1 \left\{ \Delta R_{t-1} - \left[(1 - \lambda) \sum_{i=0}^{\infty} (\lambda + \delta)^i \Delta R_{t-i-2} \right] \right\}$$
$$+ \beta_2 U_t + \beta_3 \Delta C_t + \varepsilon_t. \tag{1.9}$$

The infinite, geometrically declining lag in ΔR_{t-i-2} means that (1.9) is not estimable in its present form. We can readily circumvent this problem by applying the so-called Koyck transformation. Lagging (1.9) one period and multiplying through by $(\lambda + \delta)$, we obtain:

$$(\lambda + \delta)SV_{t-1} = (\lambda + \delta)\beta_0$$
$$+ (\lambda + \delta)\beta_1 \left\{ \Delta R_{t-2} - \left[(1 - \lambda) \right. \right.$$
$$\left. \left. \sum_{i=0}^{\infty} (\lambda + \delta)^i \Delta R_{t-i-3} \right] \right\} + (\lambda + \delta)\beta_2 U_{t-1}$$
$$+ (\lambda + \delta)\beta_3 \Delta C_{t-1} + (\lambda + \delta)\varepsilon_{t-1}. \tag{1.10}$$

Subtracting this expression from (1.9) produces an empirical estimating function with finite lag:

$$SV_t = \beta_0(1 - \lambda - \delta) + (\lambda + \delta)SV_{t-1}$$
$$+ \beta_1(\Delta R_{t-1} - \Delta R_{t-2}) - \beta_1 \delta \Delta R_{t-2} + \beta_2 U_t$$
$$- (\lambda + \delta)\beta_2 U_{t-1} + \beta_3 \Delta C_t - (\lambda + \delta)\beta_3 \Delta C_{t-1}$$
$$+ [\varepsilon_t - (\lambda + \delta)\varepsilon_{t-1}]. \tag{1.11}$$

Our final expectation-achievement function has a theoretical basis somewhat different from that underlying the previous models. In this specification, strike activity is determined by the gap between actual real wage changes over *several* recent periods and the expected *long-run* increase in real wages.[15]

15. This model is adopted from Orley Ashenfelter and George E. Johnson, "Bargaining Theory, Trade Unions, and Industrial Strike Activity, *American Economic Review*, 59 (1969), 35–49. I am grateful to Robert Solow for helping me derive the implications of various lag functions that led to the interpretation given here.

$$SV_t = \beta_0 + \beta_1(\Delta R' - \Delta R^*) + \text{other factors,} \tag{1.12}$$

$$\frac{\partial SV_t}{\partial(\Delta R' - \Delta R^*)} < 0,$$

where $\Delta R'$ = actual real wage changes over several recent periods,

ΔR^* = the expected long-run increase in real wages.

Thus, the volume of strikes is hypothesized to increase or decrease depending on whether the rate of change of real wages during recent years has exceeded or fallen short of labor's long-run expectations.

The mechanisms for $\Delta R'$ and ΔR^* are as follows. Recent experience, $\Delta R'$, is defined simply as a finite moving average of previous real wage changes:

$$\Delta R'_t = \sum_{i=1}^{I} \alpha_i \Delta R_{t-i}$$

$$\Sigma \alpha_i = 1. \tag{1.13}$$

Long-run expectations, ΔR^*, are formed as the weighted sum of a constant (very long-term) increase parameter (L) and a finite moving average of previous real wage changes:

$$\Delta R^*_t = (1 - \rho)L + \rho \sum_{i=1}^{K} \phi_i \Delta R_{t-i}$$

$$\Sigma \phi_i = 1, \quad 0 < \rho < 1. \tag{1.14}$$

The theoretical expectation-achievement model in (1.12) can now be expressed in terms of observed variables by substitution of (1.13) and (1.14):

$$SV_t = \beta_0 + \beta_1 \left[\sum_{i=1}^{I} \alpha_i \Delta R_{t-i} \right.$$

$$\left. - \left((1 - \rho)L + \rho \sum_{i=1}^{K} \cdot \phi_i \Delta R_{t-i} \right) \right] + \text{other factors}$$

$$SV_t = [\beta_0 - \beta_1(1 - \rho)L] + \beta_1$$

$$\cdot \left[\sum_{i=1}^{N} (\alpha_i - \rho\phi_i)\Delta R_{t-i} \right] + \text{other factors.} \tag{1.15}$$

Rewriting, we have:

$$SV_t = \beta_0' + \beta_1 \sum_{i=1}^{N} \mu_i \Delta R_{t-i} + \text{other factors,} \qquad (1.16)$$

where $\beta_0' = \beta_0 - \beta_1(1 - \rho)L,$
$\mu_i = (\alpha_i - \rho\phi_i).$

The lag functions determining the behavior of (1.13) through (1.16) are likely to have the following properties. The weighted average of real wage changes defining $\Delta R'$ (recent experience) will depend heavily on the outcomes of the latest periods, perhaps peaking after a few lags, and the experience of more distant periods will be rapidly discounted. Hence the α_i coefficients forming $\Delta R'$ should be governed by a low-order polynomial lag distribution with a steep rate of decay. In contrast, it is reasonable to anticipate the moving average component of long-run real wage expectations (ΔR^*) to be weighted more equally by current and past experience, which implies a linear or quasigeometric lag distribution with a relatively slow rate of decay in the ϕ_i. The difference of these lag functions (μ_i) is therefore likely to exhibit an inverted U-shaped distribution, which is conveniently estimated by the polynomial distributed lag method of Shirley Almon.[16]

To this point, the discussion has developed three plausible models specifying the impact of unemployment, business profits, and real wage changes on the volume of strikes:

Expectation-Achievement Gap: Extrapolative Expectations

$$SV_t = \beta_0 + \beta_1(\Delta R_{t-1} - \Delta R_{t-2}) - \beta_1\gamma(\Delta R_{t-2} - \Delta R_{t-3})$$
$$+ \beta_2 U_t + \beta_3 \Delta C_t + \varepsilon_t,$$
$$\beta_1 < 0, \qquad 0 < \gamma < 1, \qquad \beta_2 < 0, \qquad \beta_3 < 0. \qquad (1.17a)$$

Expectation-Achievement Gap: Adaptive Expectations (with trend)

$$SV_t = \beta_0(1 - \lambda - \delta) + (\lambda + \delta)SV_{t-1}$$
$$+ \beta_1(\Delta R_{t-1} - \Delta R_{t-2}) - \beta_1\delta\Delta R_{t-2} + \beta_2 U_t$$
$$- (\lambda + \delta)\beta_2 U_{t-1} + \beta_3 \Delta C_t - (\lambda + \delta)\beta_3 \Delta C_{t-1}$$
$$+ [\varepsilon_t - (\lambda + \delta)\varepsilon_{t-1}],$$
$$0 < (\lambda + \delta) < 1, \qquad \beta_1 < 0, \qquad 0 < \delta < 1,$$
$$\beta_2 < 0, \qquad \beta_3 < 0. \qquad (1.17b)$$

16. Shirley Almon, "The Distributed Lag between Capital Appropriations and Expenditures," *Econometrica*, 33 (January 1965), 178–196.

Expectation-Achievement Gap: Long-Run Expectations
(polynomial distributed lag)

$$SV_t = \beta_0' + \beta_1 \sum_{i=1}^{N} \mu_i \Delta R_{t-i} + \beta_2 U_t + \beta_3 \Delta C_t + \varepsilon_t,$$

$$\beta_0' < 0, \qquad \beta_1 \Sigma \mu_i < 0, \qquad \beta_2 < 0, \qquad \beta_3 \lesseqgtr 0, \qquad (1.17c)$$

where ΔR = the percentage rate of change of real wages,
U_t = the percentage of the civilian labor force unemployed,
ΔC_t = the rate of change of aggregate profits/total employee compensation.

Table 1.1 reports the estimation results for Equations (1.17a) through (1.17c). Notice that the estimation strategy is to pool all observations (20-year time series, 10 nations), so that strictly speaking the functions should be indexed $SV_{nt} = f(\Delta R_{nt-i}, U_{nt}, \Delta C_{nt})$; $n = 1$ . . . 10, $t = 1950$ . . . 1969. Furthermore, all parameters except the constant term are constrained at this point to be invariant through time and space. This amounts to replacing the general intercept constant, β_0, with a series of country-by-country dummy variables, $\Sigma_{n=1}^{10}$ α_n, which pick up the net effects of nation-specific, time-invariant, structural-historical factors not captured explicitly (causally) in the equations.[17] Therefore, the models are geared to explaining fluctuations in strike activity in the presence of a location parameter or ignorance term that varies across countries.

The estimates for (1.17a) and (1.17b) in Table 1.1 indicate that neither the extrapolative expectations model nor the adaptive expectations model performs very well in this body of data. The coefficients of the real wage change (ΔR) terms are without exception statistically

17. A fixed, dummy variable approach to the pooled estimation problem is taken here in preference to the alternative random variables, "error components" approach because of computational ease, and also because an important assumption necessary to preserve the consistency of the latter method—that "specific ignorance" be independent of regressors—seems unreasonable. Extensive analyses of pooled estimation strategies are given by G. S. Maddala, "The Use of Variance Components Models in Pooling Cross Section and Time Series Data," *Econometrica*, 39 (March 1971), 341–358; Marc Nerlove, "Further Evidence on the Estimation of Dynamic Economic Relations from a Time Series of Cross Sections," *Econometrica*, 39 (March 1971), 359–382; and T. D. Wallace and Ashig Hussain, "The Use of Error Components Models in Combining Cross Sections with Time Series Data," *Econometrica*, 37 (January 1969), 55–72. Note also that the long-run increase expression $(1 - \rho)L$ in (1.15) is necessarily embedded within the nation-specific intercepts of (1.17c) and therefore is effectively "lost" for inferential purposes (that is, these parameters are underidentified).

Table 1.1. Strike volumes in ten advanced industrial societies, 1950–1969: Estimation results for Equations (1.17a) through (1.17c).

Equation	U_t	U_{t-1}	ΔC_t	ΔC_{t-1}	$\sum_{i=1}^{5} \Delta R_{t-i}$	$\Delta R_{t-1} - \Delta R_{t-2}$	$\Delta R_{t-2} - \Delta R_{t-3}$	SV_{t-1}	ΔR_{t-2}	R^2
(1.17a)	−74.2 (−5.1)	—	484.9 (0.5)	—	—	3.3 (0.5)	6.5 (1.1)	—	—	.52
(1.17b)	−47.8 (−1.7)	−39.1 (−1.4)	792.7 (0.8)	−573.2 (−0.6)	—	−7.3 (−0.8)	—	.006 (0.05)	−13.7 (−1.1)	.52
(1.17c)	−94.1 (−5.0)	—	452.5 (0.4)	—	−44.7 (−2.0)	—	—	—	—	.53

Sources: Strike data are from ILO, *Yearbook of Labor Statistics* (Geneva), various years. Unemployment and labor force data are from OECD, *Manpower Statistics 1950–1962* (Paris, 1964); *Labour Force Statistics 1958–1969* (Paris, 1972). Employee compensation and profits data are from OECD, *National Accounts Statistics.* Consumer price index data are from *U.N. Statistical Yearbook* (New York), various years. Money earnings data were provided by the Bureau of Labor Statistics, U.S. Department of Labor.

Note: The *t*-statistics for the regression coefficient estimates are in parentheses. Constant terms vary by country and are omitted. U_t is the % of the civilian labor force unemployed. R_t is average hourly money earnings deflated by the consumer price index. ΔR denotes the % rate of change: $[R_t - R_{t-1}/R_{t-1}] \cdot 100$. C_t denotes the ratio of profits to total employee compensation. ΔC is the rate of change: $[C_t - C_{t-1}]$. SV_t is the volume of strikes outside of agriculture and mining and is defined as total worker-days lost per 1,000 wage and salary earners.

insignificant and in several cases have the wrong sign. The extrapolative equation (1.17a) was estimated both linearly (by ordinary least squares) and nonlinearly (along the lines proposed by Marquardt)[18] with the constraint that the parameter γ lie in the interval 0 to 1. The adaptive expectations function (1.17b) was similarly estimated by ordinary least squares and by a nonlinear-instrumental variables procedure designed to preserve consistency in the presence of the lagged endogenous SV_{t-1} term and potentially autocorrelated disturbances.[19] The constraints imposed in this nonlinear regression were $0 < (\lambda + \delta) < 1$ and $0 < \delta < 1$. Despite great efforts to maximize the success of these models, it appears that strike activity in advanced industrial societies during the postwar period is not well explained by expectation-achievement gap functions of the extrapolative or adaptive variety.

The regression results in Table 1.1 do, however, provide evidence in favor of the long-run (polynomial distributed lag) expectation-achievement gap model of (1.17c).[20] This model asserts that if actual real wage increases over several recent years exceed labor's long-run expectations, the volume of strikes should decline. The significant negative estimate for the $\Sigma_{i=1}^{5} \Delta R_{t-i}$ lag coefficients clearly supports the long-run expectations hypothesis and suggests that labor has a "memory" extending many periods back through time in the sense that a change in real wages influences strike activity (negatively or positively) for several subsequent years.[21]

18. Donald W. Marquardt, "An Algorithm for Least Squares Estimation of Non-Linear Parameters," *Journal of the Society for Industrial and Applied Mathematics,* 11 (June 1963), 431–441.

19. Note that even if the disturbance of the original adaptive expectations function in (1.9) is "white noise," application of the Koyck transformation introduces a first-order moving average error process in the estimating equation (1.17b). As it turned out, however, the errors displayed negligible serial correlation in all equations, so that instrumental variables as well as the rather complicated estimation procedures required to secure efficiency in a pooled data model proved unnecessary. For a discussion of the estimation problems posed by autocorrelated disturbances and lagged endogenous variables, see Douglas A. Hibbs, Jr., "Problems of Statistical Estimation and Casual Inference in Time-Series Regression Models," in *Sociological Methodology 1973–74,* ed. Herbert Costner (San Francisco: Jossey-Bass, 1974), pp. 252–308.

20. The best-fitting model was a second-degree polynomial constrained to drop off to zero after a five-period lag. Similar results are reported by Ashenfelter and Johnson, "Bargaining Theory," and John H. Pencavel, "An Investigation into Industrial Strike Activity in Britain," *Economica,* 37 (1970), 239–256, for quarterly models of strike frequency in the United States and Great Britain respectively.

21. A plot of the lag distribution coefficients is presented in a later section, after several additional hypotheses are incorporated into the strike volume model. The real

The level of unemployment (U_t) consistently displays a significant and sizable negative coefficient as hypothesized. This indicates that the strategic considerations outlined earlier govern labor's use of the strike and that strikes should be viewed as tactical weapons in struggles against management and not as poorly timed, spontaneous protests. Moreover, this relationship suggests that labor grievances are, as Rees put it,[22] "durable" or at least "semi-durable," and that industrial conflict therefore represents a rational translation of working-class discontent into overt action.

The parameter for the rate of change in profit ratios (ΔC_t) is insignificant in all regressions. This probably reflects the contrasting effects attributed to profits earlier—increasing labor's demands and aggressiveness on the one hand, but decreasing capital's incentive to resist on the other. Thus, profits do not appear to have a very important influence on fluctuations in industrial conflict, and the profit term should therefore be deleted from a revised model.[23]

Industrial Relations Systems and Strike Dynamics

The validity of previous conclusions concerning the impact of real wages, unemployment, and profit ratios on strike activity rests in part on the assumption that the structural coefficients are more or less constant through time and space. Although there is little reason to suspect systematic shifts through time in these coefficients during the

---

wage data used here are average hourly earnings in the manufacturing sector deflated by the consumer price index. Movements in manufacturing wages are presumed to reflect closely economywide changes (cf. Orley Ashenfelter, George E. Johnson, and John H. Pencavel, "Trade Unions and the Rate of Change of Money Wages in United States Manufacturing Industry," *Review of Economic Studies*, 39 [January 1972], appendix). Analyses using total annual employee compensation per civilian labor force member produced results virtually identical to those in Table 1.1.

22. Rees, "Industrial Conflict and Business Fluctuations."

23. Although the profits result is theoretically plausible, the statistical insignificance of this variable may stem from excessive measurement error. Profits data are easily subjected to the artistry of corporate accountants, are well known to be "hidden" as costs via accelerated depreciation tax laws, and are difficult to determine for unincorporated businesses. Furthermore, a significant fraction of the labor force in all economically advanced societies is employed in nonprofit activities. The profits-to-wages ratio is also correlated with real wages and unemployment. However, excessive collinearity is not a problem here: the multiple R^2 of profits/wages with the remaining independent variables is .17.

postwar period, there is cause to question whether the parameters are equivalent cross-nationally, given the diversity of national institutional arrangements.

When considering the importance of institutional diversity in explaining cross-national differences in strike activity, industrial relations specialists have, not surprisingly, given great attention to contrasting systems of industrial relations. (Certain features of the political system are also considered important, but these are taken up later.) The usual argument is that centralized systems of collective bargaining, in which labor and management organizations impose real behavioral constraints on their respective clienteles (with or without government coordination), serve to diminish or contain the level of industrial conflict. As Ross and Hartman put it: "Just as unions in centralized systems eliminate improvident emotional gestures by the rank and file, likewise employer associations exclude reckless or primitive attitudes to which small businessmen in particular are subject . . . The knowledge that any strike will be large and expensive serves as a deterrent to both sides . . . Furthermore, employers within an industry do not have to worry about suffering a competitive disadvantage when all of them are subject to the same demands . . . At the same time unions tend to be less aggressive since different branches are not competing to make the best showing within an industry."[24]

There is less than unanimous agreement, however, that centralized labor-management bargaining systems contain strike activity quite as effectively as Ross and Hartman and others have suggested. Malles, for example, expresses doubt as to whether "there is any correlation at all between a particular type of industrial relations system and the incidence of industrial warfare."[25] Sturmthal has even argued that highly centralized labor organizations and bargaining structures can lead to heightened grass-roots unrest because of the "distance" created between the rank and file and the level at which decisions are made.[26]

24. Arthur M. Ross and Paul T. Hartman, *Changing Patterns of Industrial Conflict* (New York: Wiley, 1960), pp. 49–50.

25. Paul Malles, *Trends in Industrial Relations Systems of Continental Europe* (Ottawa: Economic Council of Canada, Task Force on Labour Relations, 1969).

26. Adolf Sturmthal, *Comparative Labor Movements: Ideological Roots and Institutional Developments* (Belmont, Calif.: Wadsworth Publishing, 1972).

Three modal types of collective bargaining systems are readily identified in the descriptive literature:

1. *Decentralized systems,* characterized by firm-level bargaining (as in Canada, Japan, and the United States) or by anarchic labor-management relations embedded within a formal superstructure of multiemployer bargaining that imposes few constraints on the principal actors (as in France and Italy).

2. *Centralized systems,* typified by industrywide bargaining or by multiemployer bargaining with industrywide constraints (as in Belgium until 1959, the Netherlands after 1963, and the United Kingdom throughout most of the postwar period).

3. *Highly centralized systems,* within which economywide bargaining, or industrywide bargaining with economywide constraints, prevails (as in Belgium after 1959, the Netherlands before 1964, Norway, and Sweden).

Simple calculation of strike volume means for each type of bargaining system leaves no doubt that during the postwar period the average level of strike activity covaried with the degree of centralization: mean worker-days lost per 1,000 wage and salary workers are 425, 172, and 67 for decentralized, centralized, and highly centralized systems, respectively. Our primary interest here, however, is the stability of the structural (regression) coefficients of real wages, unemployment, and profits across these diverse systems of industrial relations. Recall that the most successful equation in Table 1.1 was the long-run expectations model of (1.17c):

$$SV_t = \beta_0' + \beta_1 \sum_{i=1}^{5} \mu_i \Delta R_{t-i} + \beta_2 U_t + \beta_3 \Delta C_t + \varepsilon_t. \qquad (1.18)$$

Let D_1 denote a binary or dummy variable equal to unity for centralized collective bargaining systems and equal to zero otherwise, and let D_2 denote a dummy variable equal to unity for highly centralized bargaining systems and zero otherwise. (Decentralized systems represent the null case.) It is now possible to specify an alternative, unconstrained model that permits the parameters to vary across the three types of industrial relations systems (the intercept-constant, β_0', already takes a unique value for each country and so is not affected by this respecification):

$$SV_t = \beta_0' + \beta_1 \sum_{i=1}^{5} \mu_i \Delta R_{t-i} + \alpha_1 \sum_{i=1}^{5} \pi_i (\Delta R_{t-i} \cdot D_1)$$

$$+ \gamma_1 \sum_{i=1}^{5} \omega_i (\Delta R_{t-i} \cdot D_2) + \beta_2 U_t + \alpha_2 (U_t \cdot D_1)$$

$$+ \gamma_2 (U_t \cdot D_2) + \beta_3 \Delta C_t + \alpha_3 (\Delta C_t \cdot D_1)$$

$$+ \gamma_3 (\Delta C_t \cdot D_2) + \varepsilon_t. \tag{1.19}$$

Table 1.2 reports the estimation results for the respecified long-run expectations model of (1.19). Clearly, these estimates lend support to the earlier presumption of parameter equivalence across contrasting industrial relations systems. More formally, the joint hypothesis that all coefficients are common across bargaining systems, or

$$\beta_1 \Sigma \mu_i = \alpha_1 \Sigma \pi_i = \gamma_1 \Sigma \omega_i, \qquad \beta_j = \alpha_j = \gamma_j \qquad (j = 2,3),$$

may be evaluated by computation of the following F ratio:

$$F = \frac{[RSS_{(1.18)} - RSS_{(1.19)}]r^{-1}}{RSS_{(1.19)}(T - K)^{-1}},$$

where RSS = the residual sum of squares in the respective equations,

            r = the number of restrictions or constraints in (1.18),

     $T - K$ = the number of degrees of freedom of RSS (1.19).

Computation of this test statistic gives $F(8,113) = 0.9$, which is insignificant at any conventional level. Therefore, although the mean level of strike activity during the postwar period covaries strongly with the degree of centralization in collective bargaining, estimation of the unconstrained model yields results which do not challenge the earlier assumption that the structural parameters governing the impact of real wages, unemployment, and profits (the latter being of little importance) are approximately equivalent across institutionally diverse systems of industrial relations.

Table 1.2. Strike volumes in ten advanced industrial societies, 1950–1969: Estimation results for Equation (1.19).

$\sum\limits_{i=1}^{5} \Delta R_{t-i}$	$\sum\limits_{i=1}^{5} \Delta R_{t-i}D_1$	$\sum\limits_{i=1}^{5} \Delta R_{t-i}D_2$	U_t	U_tD_1	U_tD_2	ΔC_t	ΔC_tD_1	ΔC_tD_2	R^2
−49.3	−22.7	6.9	−102.9	119.7	67.6	994.3	−7140.4	374.4	.56
(−1.7)	(−0.4)	(0.1)	(−5.1)	(1.4)	(0.7)	(0.7)	(−1.4)	(0.2)	

Sources: See Table 1.1.
Note: The t-statistics for the regression coefficient estimates are in parentheses. Constant terms vary by country and are omitted. Variables are defined in Table 1.1 and in the text.

The Money Illusion Hypothesis

In addition to the presumption of parameter equivalence, the previous analyses tacitly assumed that labor's propensity to strike is influenced by changes in real wages as opposed to changes in money wages. Therefore, before incorporating certain features of the political system into the strike volume model it is important to dispose of the so-called money illusion thesis. The money illusion hypothesis holds that since movements in real wages are less perceptible than changes in money wages, working-class attention focuses largely on the latter; hence workers are deceived by increases in money wages alone. Knowles's study of strikes in the United Kingdom, for example, concludes (albeit with considerable hesitancy): "Arguments based on the level of real wages are relatively unimportant at the level of strikes, even though they may have some importance at the level of negotiation, since (a) a rise in real wages is less evident and 'tangible' than a rise in money wages, and (b) a fall in real wages, even where it is immediately apparent, is less likely than is a cut in money wages to be taken as a deliberate act of the employers . . . and therefore is less likely to meet with immediate resistance."[27]

Although it has been true historically that decreases in money wages have been vigorously resisted by labor, quantitative studies of postwar industrial conflict in Canada, Great Britain, and the United States indicate that movements in prices and money wages act essentially as mirror images with regard to strike activity.[28]

Since $\Delta R = \Delta W - \Delta P$—where ΔR, ΔW, and ΔP denote the percentage rate of change of real wages, money wages, and prices, respectively—we test the money illusion hypothesis simply by replacing $\Sigma \Delta R_{t-i}$ with $\Sigma \Delta W_{t-i}$ and $\Sigma \Delta P_{t-i}$ in a revised version of (1.17c). Accordingly we estimate the model (which omits the nonsignificant ΔC_t term):

$$SV_t = \beta_0' + \beta_1 \sum_{i=1}^{5} \pi_i \Delta W_{t-i} + \beta_2 \sum_{i=1}^{5} \omega_i \Delta P_{t-i} + \beta_3 U_t + \varepsilon_t. \quad (1.20)$$

Confirmation of the hypothesis requires that movements in money wages have a greater effect on strike activity than do movements in prices; that is, the (negative) sum of the lag coefficients for ΔW_{t-1}

27. Knowles, *Strikes*, p. 227.
28. See Ashenfelter and Johnson, "Bargaining Theory"; Pencavel, "Industrial Strike Activity in Britain."

should be significantly larger in absolute value than the corresponding (positive) sum of the ΔP_{t-1} lag coefficients. Table 1.3 reveals that,
if anything, just the reverse is true. The difference, however, is neither theoretically nor statistically important; the standard F-test of the
null hypothesis,

$$\beta_1 \Sigma \pi_i(\Delta W) = -\beta_2 \Sigma \omega_i(\Delta P),$$

yields $F(2,120) = .06$, which is insignificant at virtually any test level.

The evidence clearly demonstrates, then, that labor does not suffer
from a money illusion but, on the contrary, takes price changes as
well as money wage changes fully into account in the use of the
strike. This again suggests that strike activity is governed by a rational
and rather sophisticated calculus.

Strikes and the Political System

Beyond the economic factors appearing in the previous models, certain characteristics of the political system are also commonly believed
to influence the magnitude of industrial conflict. The most important
are the relative status in the political system of labor-oriented parties
on the non-Communist left, the presence of governments controlled
outright by Labor or Socialist parties, and the extent of Communist
party influence in the labor force.

It has often been noted in comparative studies of industrial conflict
that where Labor and Socialist parties are serious contenders for political power, the use of the strike weapon is restrained. The argument

Table 1.3. Strike volumes in ten advanced
industrial societies, 1950–1969: Estimation results
for Equation (1.20).

$\sum_{i=1}^{5} \Delta W_{t-i}$	$\sum_{i=1}^{5} \Delta P_{t-i}$	U_t	R^2
−44.5	53.3	−93.3	.53
(−2.0)	(1.4)	(−4.9)	

Sources: See Table 1.1.
Note: The t-statistics for the regression coefficients are
in parentheses. Constant terms vary by country and are
omitted. Variables are defined in Table 1.1 and in the
text.

that Labor parties act to discourage worker militancy is well summarized by Ross and Hartman: "Why is labor political action a deterrent to strikes? First, strikes are injurious to the political fortunes of the labor party. Middle-class votes must be attracted if the party is to be successful, but the middle-class voter is antagonized by strikes . . . Second, worker unrest is channeled off into the political sphere. Demands that would otherwise be made upon the employer are directed against the government instead."[29] There are numerous illustrations of this line of reasoning. For example, anticipating good prospects for a Labour party victory in the British general elections of 1964, Harold Wilson urged railway union leaders in the spring of 1963 to prevent a scheduled work stoppage because "such a strike would damage Labour severely in public eyes and jeopardize its position in the elections." The New York Times observed: "Fresh in every Labour politician's memory is the six-week London bus strike of 1958. The strike has been considered a major reason for Labour's overwhelming defeat by the Conservatives a year later."[30]

How might this argument be incorporated into a formal model of strike activity? First, an index is needed that permits specification of a plausible incentive function governing the inclination of Labor or Socialist parties to deter strike activity by their constituencies. It would then be possible to evaluate the success of Labor-Socialist parties in actually diminishing the volume of strikes by relating the incentive function to the variable SV_t.

In terms of the theoretical argument briefly outlined above, the incentive of Labor-Socialist parties to discourage strikes in order to attract the middle-class votes deemed necessary for electoral success is likely to hinge on their competitive position in the party system. Following Przeworski and Sprague,[31] two things are assumed with regard to party competition: (1) the goal of party competition is electoral victory, and victory is defined as becoming the largest party; and (2) the goal is perceived in terms of the outcome of the last election. Victory, then, may be as little as one-quarter of the vote in a multiparty system and greater than one-half the vote in a two-party system.

29. Ross and Hartman, Changing Patterns of Industrial Conflict, p. 69.

30. Cited in Everett M. Kassalow, Trade Unions and Industrial Relations: An International Comparison (New York: Random House 1969), p. 52.

31. Adam Przeworski and John Sprague, "Concepts in Search of Explicit Formulation: A Study in Measurement," Midwest Journal of Political Science, 15 (May 1971), 183–218.

For simplicity, parties are classified in four political blocs or *tend-ances:* Communist, Non-Communist Labor-Socialist, Center, and Right. The competitive position of Labor-Socialist parties can now be defined as the difference or distance between their percentage vote share and that of the largest *tendance* in the system:

$$LD_t = \max(V_{t-1}) - LV_{t-1}, \tag{1.21}$$

where LD_t = Labor-Socialist percentage vote share distance,
      LV_{t-1} = Labor-Socialist percentage vote share in the pre-ceding election,
      $\max(V_{t-1})$ = percentage vote share of the largest *tendance* in the preceding election.

It seems reasonable to suppose that the incentive of Labor-Socialist parties to dampen industrial conflict in hopes of attracting (or retain-ing) the marginal middle-class votes necessary to achieve (or main-tain) plurality status in the party system would depend nonlinearly on their vote share distance (LD_t). Figure 1.2 depicts a likely form for this relationship. It suggests that the incentive (LI_t) should be very large when Labor's distance from its principal rival(s) in the party system (LD_t) is small or nil but should quickly decline (asymptotically approaching zero) as the distance increases. In other words, Labor-Socialist party elites have substantial motivation to restrain working-class militancy when electoral victory is very close at hand, but this incentive subsides rapidly with small increments in LD_t (especially at the lower ranges), given the risk of unnecessarily antagonizing hard-

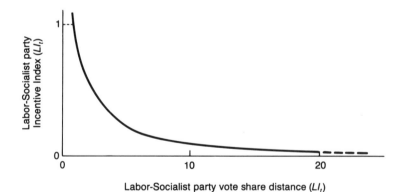

Figure 1.2.   Theoretical incentive function.

core supporters or losing them to more radical competitors on the left. The most appropriate formalization of the model depicted in Figure 1.2 is a slightly modified reciprocal function. Accordingly, the Labor-Socialist Incentive index is defined:

$$LI_t = 1 \text{ if } LD_t \leq 1, \qquad LD^{-1} \text{ otherwise.} \tag{1.22}$$

Finally, the theory at hand seems best articulated if we posit an inverse, linear relationship between the volume of strikes (SV_t) and the incentive index (LI_t):

$$SV_t = f(LI_t, \ldots) \ f \text{ linear}, \qquad \partial SV_t / \partial LI_t < 0. \tag{1.23}$$

In conjunction with the decrease in strike activity ascribed to sharply competitive Labor-Socialist parties, an additional influence on working-class militancy is often attributed to the presence of Labor governments. It is argued that, other things being equal, workers, or at least union leaders, are much more reluctant to see a Labor or Socialist government embarrassed by severe strike activity than a Conservative one. Consequently, "if the labor party comes into power, the deterrent effect is even stronger. The trade union officials, having invested heavily in the party, are disinclined to do anything that would have the effect of sabotaging its program . . . and will show maximum restraint in the use of the strike."[32]

We can evaluate this hypothesis straightforwardly by including in the model a Labor-Socialist Government dummy variable (LG_t) taking a value of unity when a Labor or Socialist party was in power and a value of zero otherwise. (Coalition governments are coded 1 only if Labor or Socialist parties had a plurality of key cabinet posts.) If workers as well as union elites in fact respond to the partisan character of the government in the way that this argument suggests, strike activity should be lower during Labor or Socialist administrations than during Centrist or Rightist ones. Hence we have:

$$SV_t = f(LI_t, LG_t, \ldots), \qquad \partial SV_t / \partial LG_t < 0. \tag{1.24}$$

The model or minimodel in (1.24) presumes that the effects of LI_t and LG_t operate continuously in time. Perhaps it is more plausible to assume that these influences are activated only in election years.

32. Ross and Hartman, *Changing Patterns of Industrial Conflict*, p. 69.

Unions, for example, might make a real effort to minimize industrial conflict during the crucial election-year period but are far less likely to relinquish the strike during the entire tenure of a Labor or Socialist administration. Similarly, party officials may find it infeasible (if not unnecessary) to attempt to discourage strikes in nonelection years no matter how close they are to "victory." These qualifications suggest a revision of (1.24) such that:

$$SV_t = f(LI_t \cdot E_t, LG_t \cdot E_t, \ldots), \tag{1.25}$$

where E_t is a dummy variable equal to unity in the year preceding an election and zero otherwise. The specification in (1.25) therefore constrains the effects of the Labor-Socialist Incentive Index (LI_t) and Labor-Socialist Governments (LG_t) to be zero in nonelection years.

Finally, the strike model should also incorporate a term representing Communist party influence in the labor force. Communist parties in most advanced industrial societies are of course no longer revolutionary in the traditional Marxist sense. Indeed the French and Italian parties and their union affiliates (by far the largest in Europe) have in recent years exhibited caution, if not moderation, in the use of the strike and related protest activities in order to avoid unnecessarily alienating less radical or militant segments of society.[33] However, despite the significant tactical variations exhibited by Communist movements during the postwar period in confronting dynamic sociopolitical environments, it seems clear that in contrast to other major political actors in industrial societies of the West, Communist parties remain important agencies for the mobilization of discontent and the crystallization of labor-capital cleavages. On the assumption that there is nearly always a certain reservoir of latent grievance or discontent which is not manifested in overt conflict unless mobilized and channeled by radical agencies on the left, it is anticipated that sizable Communist parties will have a systematic impact on strike activity beyond that attributable to the economic variables considered previously and opposite to that of Labor parties and Labor governments.

Using Communist party membership as a fraction of the civilian labor force (CP_t) to index the relative extent of Communist organizational mobilization, the preceding discussion suggests the function:

$$SV_t = f(CP_t, \ldots), \qquad \partial SV_t/\partial CP_t > 0. \tag{1.26}$$

33. See Donald L. M. Blackmer, "Italian Communism: Strategy for the 1970's," *Problems of Communism*, 21 (May–June 1972), 41–56, and Ross, "French Working Class Politics After May–June 1968."

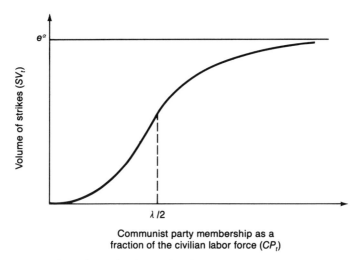

Figure 1.3. Hypothetical relationship between Communist party membership and volume of strikes.

The precise form of (1.26) is unspecified; it is unlikely that a conventional linear formulation will adequately capture the response of strike activity to variations in Communist membership. In particular, a plausible argument can be made that Communist parties cannot effectively mobilize labor discontent and thereby influence industrial conflict appreciably unless membership size (relative to the total work force) reaches a certain "critical mass" or threshold. Increments in CP_t above the critical threshold might lead to substantial increases in industrial conflict until an upper bound or "grievance exhaustion" point is reached beyond which further growth in party size has little or no additional effect on strike activity. A nonlinear relationship of this sort is shown in Figure 1.3 and is given formally by the function:

$$SV_t = e^{\alpha - \lambda/CP_t}. \tag{1.27}$$

Figure 1.3 and Equation (1.27) simply articulate the idea that beyond some initial threshold, strike activity moves rapidly upward with increases in Communist party size (the rate of response being greatest at the point of inflection $\lambda/2$) but then levels off, asymptotically approaching an upper bound or grievance exhaustion level e^α.

Combining the political hypotheses of this section with the most successful economic model developed previously yields the following equation for the volume of strikes:

$$SV_t = \beta_0' + \beta_1 \sum_{i=1}^{5} \mu_i \Delta R_{t-i} + \beta_2 U_t + \beta_3 LI_t \cdot E_t$$

$$+ \beta_4 LG_t \cdot E_t + e^{\alpha - \lambda/CP_t} + \varepsilon_t,$$

$$\beta \Sigma \mu_i < 0, \qquad \beta_2 < 0, \qquad \beta_3 < 0, \qquad \beta_4 < 0,$$

$$\alpha > 0, \qquad \lambda > 0. \tag{1.28}$$

Table 1.4 reports the estimation results for three versions of the basic model in (1.28). Clearly, both the Labor-Socialist Incentive index (LI_t) and the Labor-Socialist Government dummy (LG_t) exhibit negligible influence on strike activity. The estimated coefficients of these variables oscillate in sign across specifications, and the t-statistics are insignificant at any conventional test level. Moreover, this is true whether the hypothesized (negative) effects are permitted to operate in all years (1.28a) or are restricted to election years only (1.28b).

Interpretation of the Labor government (LG_t) result is straightforward: during the postwar period left-wing governments have been no more successful than center or right-wing governments in discouraging short-run upward movements in strike activity, notwithstanding the electoral ties of the former to the working class.[34] From the workers' point of view, the correspondence of interests with Socialist party elites is simply less than perfect. As Ernest Bevin put it when leading the strikes of dock and tramway workers in Britain just after the first Labour government came into office in 1923: "There is work to do in the industrial field as well as in the political arena. While it is true that the two are to some extent part of the same effort, we must not lose sight of the fact that governments may come and governments may go, but the workers' fight for betterment of conditions must go on all the time."[35] Subsequent Labour government leaders have been no more effective in deterring labor militancy and strikes than was the first Labour prime minister, Ramsay MacDonald.

The implication of the Incentive index (LI_t) result, unlike that of the Labor government dummy variable outcome, is not unambiguous.

34. Similar conclusions with regard to Great Britain are reached by John E. T. Eldridge, *Industrial Disputes: Essays in the Sociology of Industrial Relations* (London: Routledge & Kegan Paul, 1968), and Herbert A. Turner, *The Trend of Strikes* (Leeds: Leeds University Press, 1963). The results associated with the political party terms apply only to nations experiencing oscillations in Labor-Socialist rule. The effects of long-term leftist rule on labor militancy (for example, in Sweden, Norway, and Denmark, where the left has governed almost continuously during the postwar period) are absorbed by the country-specific constant terms. The consequences of such long-standing political and institutional differences are discussed in the next chapter.

35. Cited in Kassalow, *Trade Unions and Industrial Relations*, p. 50.

Table 1.4. Strike volumes in ten advanced industrial societies, 1950–1969: Estimation results for Equation (1.28).

Equation	$\sum_{i=1}^{5} \Delta R_{t-i}$	U_t	LI_t	LG_t	$e^{\alpha CP_t -}$	$LI_t^* E_t$	$LG_t^* E_t$	R^2
(1.28a)	−58.6	−89.1	−62.1	81.9	0.08	—	—	.58
	(−2.8)	(−4.9)	(−0.4)	(0.9)	(27.1)			
(1.28b)	−60.1	−89.4	—	—	0.08	16.9	−80.8	.58
	(−2.8)	(−4.9)			(27.1)	(0.1)	(−0.6)	
(1.28c)	−59.2	−89.3	—	—	0.08	—	—	.58
	(−2.8)	(−5.0)			(27.2)			

Sources: Electoral data and Communist party membership data are primarily from U.S. Department of State, Bureau of Intelligence and Research, *World Strength of Communist Party Organizations*, annual volumes for 1950–1970. See Table 1.1 for the sources of other variables.

Note: The t-statistics for the regression coefficient estimates are in parentheses. Constant terms vary by country and are omitted. ΔR and U_t are defined in Table 1.1. LI_t denotes the Labor-Socialist Incentive Index and equals unity when LD_t is $\leq l$ and LD_{t-1} otherwise, where LD_t = max vote share minus the Labor-Socialist vote share. LG_t and E_t are Labor-Socialist Government and election-year dummy variables, respectively. CP_t is Communist party membership per 1,000 civilian workers.

For example, it is possible that the incentive function presented in Figure 1.2 and in Equation (1.22) is poorly specified, or that its definition in terms of vote share distances in (1.21) is too simple. However, alternatives to the incentive function developed in the text, elaborations of the basic specification in (1.24), and analyses permitting the coefficients to vary across subsets of countries produced results no better than those reported in Table 1.4.[36] Thus, it is plausible that

36. Several of these alternatives are worth mentioning. First, since the translation of electoral votes into legislative seats is by no means direct (see Douglas W. Rae, *The Political Consequences of Electoral Laws*, rev. ed. [New Haven: Yale University Press, 1971], for an exhaustive analysis), the incentive function of Labor-Socialist party elites in (1.22) was also defined in terms of seat shares as opposed to vote shares. Second, Equation (1.23) was revised to incorporate the capability as well as the motivation of party elites to discourage strike activity; capability was measured in terms of the size of the Labor-Socialist political constituency (voters). Third, the Labor-Socialist vote share distance in (1.21), as well as the seat share variant described in the first point above, was modified to include (a) the vote or seat share of the U.S. Democratic party— following Greenstone's argument (J. David Greenstone, *Labor in American Politics* [New York: Alfred A. Knopf, 1969]) that American labor and the Democrats have become interpenetrated in a way that is at least partially equivalent to party-union alliances in much of Western Europe—and (b) the vote or seat share of the French Communist party (PCF) during the period of the left alliance. As noted in the text, none of these modifications led to empirical outcomes significantly different from those reported in Table 1.4.

Labor-Socialist party attempts to discourage strike activity are indeed governed by a model akin to that outlined previously, but that such attempts, on the whole, have been unsuccessful.

This apparent failure of party elites to reduce the use of the strike may stem less from the unresponsiveness or irresponsibility of top union leadership than from the fundamental radicalism and militancy of the rank and file. In Great Britain, where there is a close, organic relationship between trade union and Labour party elites, the vast majority of strikes during the last decade have been unsanctioned, "illegal" conflicts typically led by left-wing shop steward militants.[37] Although the British case is probably the best documented, wildcat strikes, contract rejections, and other manifestations of grass-roots rebelliousness have also become serious issues in Canada, the United States, and continental Europe.[38] Strikes, then, not only are weapons in disputes with private capital but also can serve as instruments of rank-and-file rebellion against union authority and, in some situations, state authority. Hence, the conclusions of Ross and Hartman's influential study that "labor political action, labor parties, and labor governments have helped pave the way toward renunciation of the strike" and that political action is "more in line with the middle-class orientation of workers in advanced industrial societies"[39] seem to be seriously at odds with the empirical data.

37. J. F. B. Goodman, "Strikes in the United Kingdom: Recent Statistics and Trends," *International Labour Review*, 95 (May 1967), 465–481; and Michael Silver, "Recent British Strike Trends: A Factual Analysis," *British Journal of Industrial Relations*, 11 (March 1973), 66–104. The situation was reversed, however, after passage of the Industrial Relations Act of 1971, which was bitterly resented by the British trade union establishment and which stimulated the normally moderate Trades Union Congress (the peak union organization) to join the shop stewards in pressing the militant position. Consequently, nearly 80 percent of the worker days lost in strike activity in the years after 1971 were due to "official" disputes. A detailed analysis is given by Gerald Dorfman, "An End to Producer Group Politics in Britain? The Industrial Relations Act of 1971" (Paper delivered at the annual meeting of the American Political Science Association, New Orleans, September 1973). The dynamics underlying differential responsiveness of union leadership and the rank and file to the wider political interests of Labor-Socialist parties is of course an important problem, which the simple models developed here cannot address with any authority.

38. See John S. Greenbaum, "The Rebellious Rank and File," *Personnel*, 49 (March–April 1972), 20–25; Stuart M. Jamieson, *Times of Troubles—Labour Unrest and Industrial Conflict in Canada 1900–66*, (Ottawa: Economic Council, Task Force on Labour Relations, 1968); Seidman, *Trade Union Government and Collective Bargaining;* and Stanley Weir, "Rebellion in American Labor's Rank and File," in *Workers' Control*, ed. Gary Hunnius, G. David Garson, and John Case (New York: Vintage Books 1973).

39. Ross and Hartman, *Changing Patterns of Industrial Conflict*, p. 58.

Although the results in Table 1.4 give no evidence that Labor-Socialist parties and governments have a significant impact on short-run fluctuations in strike activity, they do substantiate the anticipated effect of Communist party influence in the labor force. However, the initial specification of a critical mass/grievance exhaustion model, represented by the function $SV_t = e^{\alpha - \lambda/CP_t}$, . . . , produced coefficient estimates that were statistically insignificant, unstable in sign, and unreasonable in magnitude. (A standard nonlinear algorithm in conjunction with reasonable initial parameter guesses was used.) An alternative, unbounded exponential function of the form $SV_t = e^{\alpha CP_t}$ . . . , which preserves the idea that strike activity should increase (decrease) rapidly and nonlinearly with growth (decline) in Communist mobilization, proved to be far more successful in describing the relationship of industrial conflict to Communist membership over the range of variation observed in the latter variable in this body of data. The highly significant estimates[40] for this revised exponential model (reported throughout Table 1.4) support the original proposition that sizable Communist parties are associated with levels of industrial conflict that cannot be attributed to such economic factors as changing rates of increase in real wages ($\Sigma \Delta R_{t-i}$) or fluctuations in the demand for labor (U_t).

Conclusions

The evidence developed above supports several tentative conclusions.

Patterns in the fluctuation of industrial conflict suggest that the working class exercises considerable sophistication in the use of the strike weapon. The pronounced inverse relationship between the volume of industrial conflict and the rate of unemployment demonstrates that on the whole strikes are timed to capitalize on the strategic advantages of a tight labor market. What Hobsbawm has called "the common sense of demanding concessions when conditions are favorable" indeed seems to prevail.[41] Moreover, labor does not ap-

40. The t-statistics in this nonlinear model should be interpreted with caution, since strictly speaking they have meaning only in terms of the linearized equation at the solution point. There is no question, however, that the exponential form given in Table 1.4 outperforms all reasonable alternative functions.

41. E. J. Hobsbawm, "Economic Fluctuations and Some Social Movements since 1800," *Economic History Review*, 2d ser., 5 (1952), 1–25.

pear to be misled by a "money illusion." The empirical results clearly show that price changes are no less important than money wage changes in their effects on strike activity. Industrial conflict therefore responds to movements in real wages rather than to those in money wages, which is further and rather persuasive evidence that rational behavior underlies observed strike fluctuations.

The real wage function that proved to be most successful empirically was a polynomial distributed lag in $\Sigma_{i=1}^{5} \Delta R_{t-i}$ (graphed in Figure 1.4). The general form of this lag distribution was deduced from a formal specification of a long-run expectations variant of the basic expectation-achievement hypothesis, although the lag function does not depend in any essential way on this particular theoretical rationalization. Even without the precise shape or exact coefficient values of this lag distribution, it can be said that labor militancy appears to be governed, in part, by a "memory" persisting several periods back, in the sense that a change in real wages affects strike activity over a number of subsequent years. More specifically, the estimates indicate that an equilibrium reduction of 1 percent in the rate of change of real wages is associated with a strike volume increase on the order of 59 worker-days lost per 1,000 workers, which is distributed nonlinearly over about five periods.

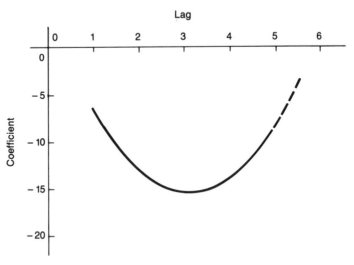

Figure 1.4. Distribution of real wage lag coefficients. (From Table 1.4 and Equation 1.28c.)

Finally, the analyses reveal that the Labor-Socialist party elites are, on the whole, unable to deter short-run increases in strike activity despite their strong incentive to do so (especially when the prospects of electoral victory are good) and notwithstanding their political ties to organized labor. Similarly, industrial conflict exhibits no consistent tendency to drop off during the tenure of governments controlled by Labor or Socialist parties. The empirical evidence for the postwar period suggests, therefore, that left-wing parties and governments relying upon symbolic, electorally expedient appeals to political solidarity, which are not accompanied by tangible rewards to labor (wages, hours, fringe benefits, and so on), have had little success in discouraging working-class militancy. In contrast, strike activity does appear to vary (nonlinearly) with the relative size of Communist party membership. This result lends support to the earlier proposition that Communist parties in advanced industrial societies remain important agencies for the mobilization of latent discontent and the crystallization of labor-capital cleavages.

Extensions of the simple single-equation strike models presented in this chapter have obvious implications for public policy. One of the most important problems confronting industrial nations during the postwar period is the tradeoff that appears to exist between unemployment and the rate of wage-price inflation (the so-called Phillips curve). If labor militancy or strike activity in the current period influences wage movements in current and subsequent periods independently of market conditions, then this phenomenon implies a lagged reciprocity between strikes and wage changes and, more important, means that strike activity affects, perhaps crucially, the unemployment-inflation dilemma. This relationship seems clear enough intuitively, although conventional economic formulations of the problem rarely consider labor aggressiveness explicitly.[42] In any case, an adequate treatment of the economic and political dimensions of these linkages is beyond the scope of this study and requires empirical analyses not yet completed.

---

42. The studies by Hines and by Ashenfelter, Johnson, and Pencavel are important exceptions to the restrictive treatment of the employment-inflation problem found in the majority of empirical economic research. See A. G. Hines, "Trade Unions and Wage Inflation in the United Kingdom 1893–1961," *Review of Economic Studies*, 31 (October 1964), 221–252; and Orley Ashenfelter, George E. Johnson, and John H. Pencavel, "Trade Unions and the Rate of Change of Money Wages in United States Manufacturing Industry," *Review of Economic Studies*, 39 (January 1972), 27–54. Also see Chapter 3 in this book.

2

On the Political Economy of Long-Run Trends in Strike Activity

Outbursts of strike activity in many industrial societies during the late 1960s and early 1970s focused considerable attention on relations among labor, capital, and the state in advanced capitalist systems and led to many inquiries into the sources of the "new" labor militancy. The events of May–June 1968 in France, the "hot autumn" of 1969 in Italy, and the nationwide strikes of the coal miners in 1972 and 1974 in the United Kingdom (the first since the great General Strike of 1926) are the most dramatic examples, but sharp upturns in strike activity in Canada (1969, 1972), Finland (1971), the United States (1970) and smaller strike waves in other nations also contributed to the surge of interest in labor discontent.

Recent attempts to reevaluate the potential of advanced industrial societies to generate severe social conflicts are perhaps a useful corrective to the dominant theoretical perspectives of postwar social science, which has stressed the integration of the working class into the socioeconomic fabric of modern capitalist nations. Sociologists wrote of the *embourgeoisement* of blue-collar workers; political scientists and

Reprinted from *British Journal of Political Science*, 8 (1978), 153–175. The original article was a revised, abbreviated version of my monograph *Long-Run Trends in Strike Activity in Comparative Perspective* (Cambridge, Mass.: Center for International Studies, MIT, 1976). The research was supported by the National Science Foundation. I am grateful to Marilyn Shapleigh and Nicholas Vasilatos for able research assistance on all phases of the project; to Agnes Page and Suzanne Planchon for expert manuscript typing; and to Frank Lerman, Andrew Martin, Charles Meyers, Stuart Scheingold, Theda Scopol, Michael Shalev, Charles Tilly, Jorgen Westerstahl, and members of the State and Capitalism seminar at Harvard University for comments on the earlier version.

political sociologists argued about, but in the main subscribed to, the idea of "the end of ideology"; and among industrial relations specialists the thesis of the "withering away of the strike" (most prominently associated with the work of Arthur Ross and Paul Hartman) was widely accepted.

One of the aims of this chapter is to show that when industrial conflict is analyzed over the long run—that is, viewed in historical perspective—the thesis of a *general* withering away of the strike is at odds with the empirical evidence, and that the emphasis on a *new* labor militancy is to a great extent misplaced. The first section analyzes quantitative trends in the overall magnitude of industrial conflict in eleven nations since the turn of the century. Next I present my own theory of the long-run evolution of industrial conflict. Strike activity is viewed as one manifestation of persistent class-linked conflict over the distribution of the national product. I shall argue that trends in industrial conflict have been shaped primarily by changes in the political economy of distribution and not by cultural, sociological, or purely economic factors.[1] The core of the argument is that major changes in the volume of industrial conflict during the twentieth century are explained largely by the effectiveness of Social Democratic and Labor parties in socializing the consumption and *final* distribution of national income, thereby shifting the distributional struggle away from the private marketplace, where allocation takes place through collective bargaining and industrial conflict, to the public arena, where labor and capital compete through political negotiation and electoral mobilization. The concluding section briefly reviews recent economic and political developments in highly developed welfare states and speculates about the implications of trends in the public-sector share of national income for political and industrial conflict over the distribution of the national product.

Twentieth-Century Trends in Aggregate Strike Activity

Perhaps the most important comparative, quantitative investigation of strike activity is Ross and Hartman's *Changing Patterns of Industrial Conflict*. One of the principal conclusions of this influential empirical

---

1. Economic variables do, of course, have an important influence on short-run fluctuations in strike activity. See Chapter 1 and the studies cited there.

study was that industrial conflict had withered away in the industrialized world during the twentieth century. Although Ross and Hartman acknowledged that the decline in strike activity was most pronounced in the Northern European countries—Denmark, Netherlands, the United Kingdom, Germany, Norway, and Sweden—they believed they had identified a general trend that by the 1950s was apparent in virtually all capitalist democracies: "There has been a pronounced decline in strike activity throughout the world. Man-days of idleness in the late 1950's are fewer than in the late 1940's or the late 1930's, despite the increases in population and union membership."[2]

The analyses that follow will show that this conclusion is simply erroneous. It is true, of course, that the bloody, violent clashes between labor and capital that characterized the early union-recognition strikes are now rare and, in this sense, strikes have become more "civilized." Over the long run, however, it is also clear that the gross magnitude of strike activity exhibits no *general* secular decline: strike activity has increased in some nations, oscillated about a more or less constant average level (stationary mean) in a few countries, and declined by varying degrees in others.

Figure 2.1 presents time-series graphs of strike volumes (worker-days lost in strike activity per 1,000 nonagricultural civilian employees) during the twentieth century in eleven countries: Belgium, Canada, Denmark, Finland, France, Italy, the Netherlands, Norway, Sweden, the United Kingdom, and the United States. The sample of nations includes all major Western industrial societies except Germany (whose partitioning makes long-run time-series analyses a problem). The exact time range of the strike series varies by country according to the availability of data; in some nations data on all components of strike activity were not collected systematically until the second quarter of the century; countries occupied by the Germans during World War II have gaps for the late 1930s and early 1940s; and for Italy there is a long gap corresponding to the period of Fascist repression of organized labor.

It is clear from the graphs that in most countries strike activity exhibits great year-to-year fluctuation. Strike action normally fell sharply during major business contractions and increased during

2. Arthur M. Ross and Paul T. Hartman, *Changing Patterns of Industrial Conflict* (New York: Wiley, 1960) pp. 4–5.

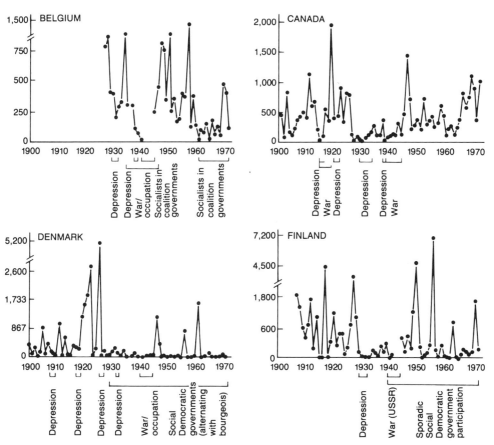

Figure 2.1.   Strike volume in eleven nations, 1900–1972. (From Nicholas Vasilatos and Douglas Hibbs, "Strike Data Codebook" [Mimeo, Harvard University, 1974].)

periods of economic recovery. (Major depressions are also identified in the graphs in Figure 2.1.)[3] Although there are some exceptions to the pattern, widespread unemployment typically demoralized workers and their leaders and led to great declines in union membership. The strikes that were called during depressions were usually desper-

3. Depressions are defined as periods in which unemployment increased and gross national product and industrial production decreased for two years in succession. The primary source used to identify depression periods was B. R. Mitchell, *European Historical Statistics 1750–1970* (New York: Columbia University Press, 1975).

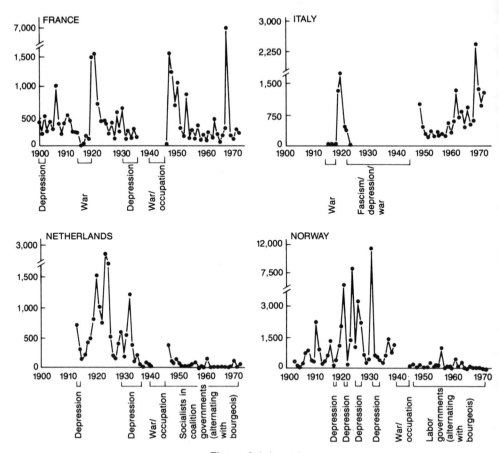

Figure 2.1 (cont.).

ate actions by unions in response to wage cuts and as often as not were provoked by management to weaken labor organizations. Industrial conflict also declined markedly in combatant (and some neutral) nations during World Wars I and II (see Figure 2.1). In part this trend was due to legal prohibitions against wartime strikes, but more important was the voluntary commitment of unions in virtually all combatant countries to give maximum support to the war effort. (Such pledges were usually accompanied by government protection against attacks by capital on established labor organizations.) Wartime strikes in most countries were sporadic, usually unauthorized by

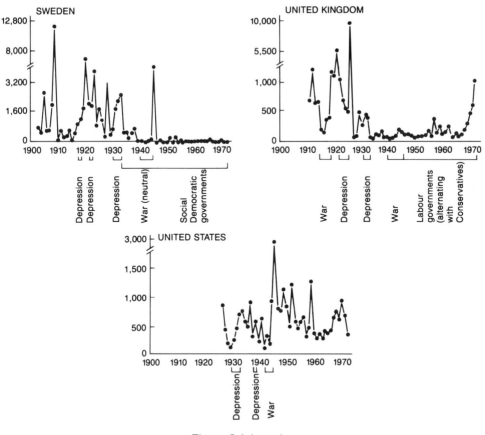

Figure 2.1 (cont.).

trade union leaders, and very short-lived. Most nations experienced strike explosions toward the end or just after the end of the wars as labor sought to defend its wartime organizational gains, to resolve the shop-floor grievances that had accumulated over the long period of "discipline," and to preserve real wages in the face of war-generated upward movements in prices.

Table 2.1 reports regression estimates of the average percentage change per year in strike volume and strike participation in each of the eleven countries. Various schemes for estimating the long-run strike trends were explored (including the conventional least-squares linear trend model and the Box-Jenkins ARMA trend model), but the most satisfactory proved to be the simple log trend (exponential) model:

$$Y_t = Y_0(1 + g)^t, \qquad \log Y_t = \log Y_0 + t \log(1 + g),$$

where Y denotes strike volume and g denotes the average annual percentage rate of change (reported in Table 2.1). The trend estimates in Table 2.1 merely summarize what is apparent from visual inspection of the graphs in Figure 2.1.

There simply is no evidence of a general decline or withering away of strike activity in industrial societies during the twentieth century. In five of the eleven countries—Canada, Finland, France, Italy, and the United States—strike activity has either increased or fluctuated (often markedly) about a constant mean or equilibrium level. Industrial conflict has declined significantly in Belgium and the United Kingdom but has decreased to truly negligible levels only in Denmark, the Netherlands, Norway, and Sweden. Hence the withering away of the strike is a rather limited phenomenon, confined largely to the smaller democracies of Northern Europe. Moreover, to the extent that strike data are relevant in judgments about the state of class relations, the long-run trend results cast considerable doubt on macrosociological arguments claiming that the working class has been integrated into the social structure of advanced capitalist nations.

At the same time, historical trends in strike activity lead one to question the existence of the "new" labor militancy, an assumption currently popular in many social scientists' interpretations of contemporary industrial relations. Most strike outbursts of the late 1960s and early 1970s simply do not represent significant departures from long-standing patterns in industrial conflict. The events of May–June 1968 in France must of course stand as an exception to this generalization. The 1968 strike wave was unquestionably the most severe in recorded French labor history[4] (the strike volume of that year was nearly three

---

4. In fact the strike wave of 1968 in France was not recorded in the usual way at all; the figures for worker-days lost shown in the graph for France in Figure 2.1 were derived from careful unofficial calculations by M. Durand and Y. Harft, "Panorama statistique des grèves," *Sociologie du Travail*, 4 (1973), 356–375.

times that of the great general strike of 1920) and it surely merits the hundreds of studies devoted to it.[5] It should be recognized, however, that France has a long history of periodic strike explosions—for example, 1906, 1919–20, 1936, and 1947–48—of which 1968 is the most dramatic example.[6]

Recent upturns in strike activity in other nations are not exceptional when viewed from the perspective of the long-run record of labor relations. In Italy, the "hot autumn" of 1969 represented the peak of that nation's postwar industrial conflict, but Italian strike activity has fluctuated about a distinct upward trend since the early 1950s. It is obvious from the time-series graphs for the remaining countries that recent movements in strike volume are quite consistent with past patterns in strike activity, and thus do not require a search for unusual factors or the development of special explanations.

The log trend analyses discussed earlier and reported in Table 2.1 clearly do not yield a very satisfactory characterization of long-run trends in industrial conflict. Although the trend coefficients are significant by conventional statistical criteria, the log trend equations account for very little of the variation in strike volume and strike participation. (R^2s are not reported in Table 2.1, but they were in the neighborhood of .20.) The reasons are apparent from the time-series graphs. First, strike activity fluctuates greatly about estimated trends or, in the trendless cases, about equilibrium (mean) levels. Second, and for the purposes of this study more important, in nations where industrial conflict has decreased substantially, the decline occurred suddenly in the late 1930s—or just after World War II—rather than gradually by so many percent per year as the trend coefficients imply. For example, in Sweden strike volume does not drop off more or less continuously by 9 or 10 percent per annum from the early 1900s as the trend estimate in Table 2.1 suggests. On the contrary, the withering away of the strike in Sweden is apparent only by the late 1930s and is particularly marked during the postwar era.[7] Long-run changes in

5. An excellent source for references on the events of May–June 1968 is Laurence Wylie et al., *France: The Events of May–June 1968, A Critical Bibliography* (Pittsburgh: Council for European Studies, 1973).

6. See Edward Shorter and Charles Tilly, *Strikes in France 1830–1968* (Cambridge: Cambridge University Press, 1974).

7. Figure 2.1 shows that the dramatic decline in strike activity in Sweden, as in other countries, took place after the Social Democrats assumed political power. I return to this important point later.

Table 2.1. Twentieth-century trends in strike volume in eleven countries.

Country	Average percentage change in strike volume per year (g)
Belgium (1927–40, 1945–72)	−3.50
Canada (1901–72)	Negligible
Denmark (1900–72)	−4.88
Finland (1907–41, 1945–72)	Negligible
France (1900–35, 1946–72)	Negligible
Italy[a] (1916–23, 1949–72)	+6.87
Netherlands (1913–40, 1946–72)	−10.15
Norway (1903–39, 1945–72)	−6.88
Sweden (1903–72)	−9.65
United Kingdom (1911–72)	−2.66
United States (1927–72)	Negligible

Source: Nicholas Vasilatos and Douglas Hibbs, "Strike Data Codebook" (Mimeo, Harvard University, 1974).

a. With the exception of Italy, data on strikes are restricted to the nonagricultural sectors of economic activity.

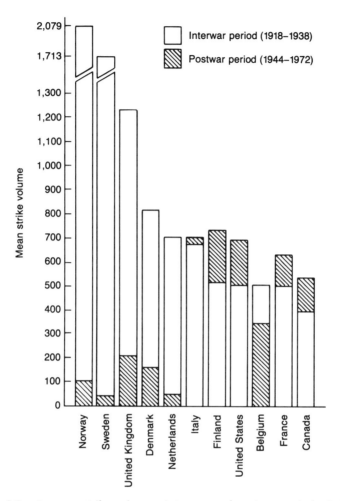

Figure 2.2.   Average strike volumes, interwar and postwar periods. Interwar data are incomplete for some nations; 1945 is excluded for Sweden. (From Vasilatos and Hibbs, "Strike Data Codebook.")

aggregate levels of industrial conflict are therefore probably better summarized by contrasting pre– and post–World War II mean scores.

Figure 2.2 shows a histogram of interwar (1918–1938) and postwar (1944–1972) average strike volumes (worker-days lost per 1,000 non-agricultural, civilian employees) for the eleven countries. For example, Norway's interwar mean strike volume was over 2,000, whereas its postwar mean was only about 100; Canada's interwar mean volume was about 400, but its postwar mean was well over 500. The histogram merely provides a graphic illustration of patterns identified in the previous discussion of the time-series data. In the interwar period Norway, Sweden, the United Kingdom, Denmark, and the Netherlands had the highest levels of industrial conflict in the Western world. By the end of World War II, however, strike activity had declined dramatically in these nations—in most cases to negligible levels. This contrasts sharply with the record for most of the other countries. Elsewhere industrial conflict has either oscillated about the same average level for approximately three-quarters of a century or has actually increased somewhat during the postwar era.

Industrial Conflict and the Political Economy of Distribution

What explains the long-run patterns of strike trends, summarized in Figure 2.2? This issue has swollen the literature on the evolution of class relations in industrial capitalist societies. However, the arguments are familiar and need no review here.[8] I shall therefore proceed directly to a discussion of my own theory.

My principal assumption is that at the macrotheoretical level strikes are most usefully viewed as instruments of collective working-class action and that *strike activity is one manifestation of an ongoing struggle for power between social classes over the distribution of resources, principally (though not exclusively) national income.* The core of the argument is that *long-run changes in the volume of industrial conflict are largely explained by changes in the locus of the struggle over distribution.* Strike activity has

8. The classic summary and critical review of the sociological and industrial relations literature on strike activity is J. E. T. Eldridge, "Explanations of Strikes: A Critical Review," in *Industrial Disputes: Essays in the Sociology of Industrial Relations*, (London: Routledge & Kegan Paul, 1968). The recent books by Geoffrey K. Ingham, *Strikes and Industrial Conflict: Britain and Scandinavia* (London: Macmillan, 1974), and Richard Hyman, *Strikes* (Glasgow: Fontana/Collins, 1975), cover similar ground in greater detail.

declined dramatically in nations where Social Democratic or Labor parties assumed power in the 1930s or just after World War II and created the modern "welfare state." In these countries an enormous fraction of the national income now passes through the public sector, and the "social wage," in the form of collective consumption and personal transfers, looms large in relation to the private "market wage" in determining the economic security and well-being of a great part of society. The *political process* dominates the final allocation (though not necessarily the initial production) of the national product. Put somewhat differently, political competition and conflict between left-wing and right-wing parties in the electoral arena (the political marketplace) have to a great extent replaced industrial bargaining and conflict between labor and capital in the private sector (the economic marketplace) as the process shaping the final distribution of national income.[9]

By comparison, in countries governed more or less continuously by bourgeois parties of the center and right, the state budget or public economy remains comparatively small, the *private market* continues to dominate the *allocation* as well as the *production* of resources, and labor's economic well-being hinges primarily on market outcomes. The economic marketplace is therefore the primary locus of distributional conflict in these nations, and, consequently, the average level of strike activity has been relatively constant for three-quarters of a century or more.

The evidence in favor of this interpretation of long-run changes in the overall volume of industrial conflict is, I think, compelling. It is clear from the data presented in Figures 2.1 and 2.2 that nations experiencing a sustained decline or withering away of strike activity during the postwar era are largely those where Social Democratic and

---

9. Cf. Shorter and Tilly, *Strikes in France 1830–1968*, especially chaps. 1, 12, and 13; David Snyder and Charles Tilly, "Hardship and Collective Violence in France 1830 to 1960," *American Sociological Review*, 37 (1972), 520–531; and especially Walter Korpi, "Industrial Relations in Sweden" (Swedish Institute for Social Research, August 1975; subsequently published as "Sweden: Conflict, Power and Politics in Industrial Relations)," *Industrial Relations in International Perspective: Essays on Research and Policy*, ed. Peter B. Doeringer [London: Macmillan, 1981]). Although I read Korpi's unpublished paper after this article was drafted, the theory sketched here is in broad agreement with his analysis of the evolution of Swedish industrial relations. However, Korpi, Shorter and Tilly, and Snyder and Tilly attribute much more importance than I do to working-class political power per se, as opposed to its instrumental consequences for the political economy of distribution. See the following discussion.

Labor parties based on the working class and trade unions success-fully mobilized mass political support in the electoral arena, gained control (or at least shared control) of the state, and sharply expanded the scope of collective consumption and distribution. This historical development in the political economy of distribution in these societies represented a massive shift of political power away from business interests and their middle-class allies to the "organized working class." Some idea of the close association between the evolution of strike activity and the shift of political power between the social classes is given by Figure 2.3, which shows a scatter diagram of the interwar to postwar change in average strike volume and the interwar to postwar change in the average percentage of cabinet (executive) posts held by Socialist, Labor, and Communist parties. (The years in which Socialist/Labor parties were continuously in power or alter-nated regularly in power with bourgeois parties are identified on the graphs in Figure 2.1.)

The variables in Figure 2.3 clearly exhibit a strong linear association (the correlation is $-.96$); at one extreme lie the countries in which center and right-wing governments have ruled continuously throughout the twentieth century (the United States, Canada); at the other extreme lie the nations in which Social Democratic and Labor parties have dominated postwar governments (Norway and Swe-den).[10] Countries in which left-wing parties have shared or alternated in power with bourgeois parties during the postwar period fall in an intermediate position with respect to the decline in the volume of strikes.

What is crucial for explaining long-run trends in strike activity, however, is not the assumption of political power by Social Demo-cratic parties per se, but rather the change in the locus of the distribu-tion of the national income produced by the welfare state policies of Social Democratic regimes. By socializing the consumption and distri-bution (though typically not the production) of an enormous fraction

10. A discussion of the reasons underlying international differences in the electoral success and executive political power of Socialist, Labor, and Communist parties is beyond the scope of this essay. It should be noted, however, that the "politicization" of the strike is most pronounced in France and Italy, where the state is heavily involved in establishing wages and conditions of work in the private sector and, also, where left-wing parties have commanded a sizable share of the vote for thirty years or more but have been largely frozen out of positions of executive power. I return to this point later.

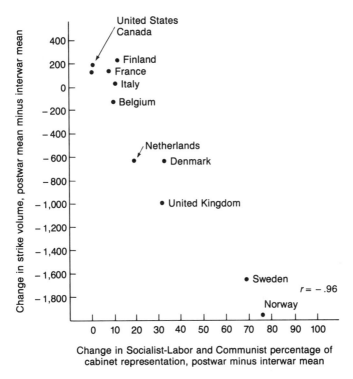

Figure 2.3. Change in average strike volume and in average Socialist-Labor and Communist percentage cabinet representation, interwar to postwar period. (From Vasilatos and Hibbs, "Strike Data Codebook.")

of the national product, Social Democratic and Labor governments engineered a massive circumvention of the private market. The principal locus of the distribution of national income was shifted from the private sector, where property and capital interests enjoy a comparative advantage, to the public sector, where the political resources of the organized working class are more telling.

Although the public sector's share of GNP increased in virtually all countries during the postwar period, and early welfare state measures were in some cases introduced by the right in order to retard the development of the labor movement (for example, the social insurance legislation initiated by Bismark and Lloyd George), the most dramatic increases in public-sector expenditure were primarily the result of Social Democratic and Labor government policies.[11] Consider the historical experience of the two cases that lie near the opposite ends of the range of variation in the political power of the working class and the extent of the public sector's allocation of the national income—Sweden and the United States. Between 1938 and 1972, the fraction of GNP passing through the public sector (exclusive of expenditures for defense and nationalized industries) in Sweden, which has been governed almost continuously by the Social Democrats since the early 1930s, grew from less than one-fifth to almost one-half— that is, nearly tripled. In contrast, from 1938 to 1972 general, nondefense, government expenditure in the United States, which of course has never experienced Socialist or Labor party rule, increased from just under one-fifth to only about one-quarter of GNP. The experience of other nations falls at various points within the bounds set by these two cases.

Some empirical support for the historical model sketched here for long-run changes in the *volume* of strike activity is given in Figure 2.4, which displays simple correlations between the growth of Social Democratic and Labor party power (percentage of cabinet representation), the change in the locus of the distribution of national income (growth of the public sector's share of GNP), and change in strike volume (worker-days lost per 1,000 nonagricultural civilian employees) from the interwar to postwar period in nine countries.[12]

Postwar *levels* of strike activity are also explained well by this highly abstracted model of the causal relations among working-class political power, the importance of the public sector for the allocation of na-

11. In the United Kingdom, for example, the public-sector share of GNP (exclusive of defense) expanded in three waves: (1) 1944–1948, from less than 20 percent to 35 percent as a result of the postwar Labour government's creation of the welfare state and nationalization; (2) 1964–1968, from 35 percent to 45 percent, during the second postwar Labour government; and (although it is beyond the time frame of this study) (3) 1973–1975, from 45 percent to 55 percent, as the third Labour government tried to deliver on its side of the social contract. See the analysis in the *Economist*, 21 (February 1976).

12. I was unable to find data on general government expenditure in Belgium and Italy before the Second World War; therefore, the correlations in Figure 2.5 are based on nine rather than eleven countries. Sources of the government expenditure data were: Statistical Office of the United Nations, *National Income Statistics* (New York, 1950), and Harry T. Oshima, "Share of Government in G.N.P. for Various Countries," *American Economic Review*, 47 (1957), 381–390; OECD, *National Accounts of OECD Countries 1961–1972* (Paris, 1974). Sources of the data for the other variables are given in earlier footnotes.

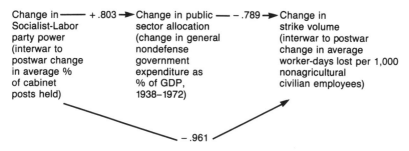

Figure 2.4. Politics and long-run changes in strike activity.

tional income, and the volume of strike activity. Figure 2.5 reports the simple correlations among the indicators, for eleven countries.

Clearly, postwar levels as well as interwar to postwar changes in aggregate strike activity vary inversely with the extent to which national income is ultimately distributed via the political process. In nations such as Denmark, Norway, the Netherlands, and Sweden, where by 1972 the public-sector share of GNP was nearly 50 percent, where the average tax rate for blue-collar workers was in the 30–35 percent range, and where the marginal tax rate approached 60 percent, the political arena is the key locus of distributional outcomes, and therefore industrial conflict stands at comparatively low levels. By contrast, in countries with relatively high strike volumes (such as Canada, Italy, and the United States), the fraction of GNP passing through the public sector was on the order of 25 to 30 percent by 1972, the average tax rate for manufacturing workers was 15 percent or less, and the marginal tax rate was in the 23–28 percent range. In these societies the bulk of the national income is allocated in the private sector, and therefore the economic marketplace remains the most important arena of conflict over distributional outcomes.

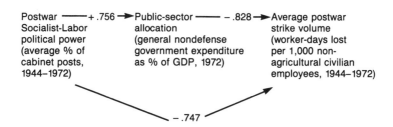

Figure 2.5. Politics and postwar levels of strike activity.

My basic argument is summarized from a slightly different perspective in Table 2.2, which shows how the loci of distributional conflict and the character of strike activity vary by the degree of state economic intervention and the market orientation of the state's politicoeconomic goals. In nations where state intervention is comparatively low (passive) and the market is supported, the private sector is the primary arena of conflict over distributional outcomes, "business unionism" is the dominant orientation of organized labor, and strike activity is relatively high and has shown no tendency to decline over the long run. Canada and the United States are examples of this pattern. Strike activity also stands at comparatively high levels and shows no signs of declining in countries where the state has intervened actively in the labor market in order to support the market—that is, has actively participated in setting private-sector wages, hours, and conditions of work without socializing the consumption and distribution of a very large fraction of the national income. The distinctive feature of industrial relations in societies falling in this category is the *politicization* of the strike. The state is an important actor in the system of industrial relations, and therefore the strike is frequently used as a form of political action to exert pressure on the government, either to grant concessions to labor unilaterally or to coerce a favorable settlement from recalcitrant employers.[13] France and Italy are the exemplary cases. Only in societies where the state has actively (and successfully) pursued market-modifying policies has there been a massive displacement of conflict over distributional issues to the electoral arena and, as a result, the withering away of the strike in the private marketplace. This historical configuration is of

13. Notwithstanding the larger political visions of many left-wing trade union leaders, most workers are probably mobilized for strike activity not by slogans about the workers' seizure of political power but by the narrower economic incentives usually associated with American "business unionism." As Val Lorwin (*The French Labor Movement* [Cambridge, Mass.: Harvard University Press, 1966], p. 215) put it in his study of French labor relations: "When they received wage adjustments, workers, including most union members, showed little determination to press for the institutional content of agreements about which their leaders talked." Even the massive strikes of May–June 1968 in France (which were viewed largely as spontaneous "political" events in many popular accounts) centered in the overwhelming majority of cases on traditional demands for wage increases and came to an end in the wake of sizable wage concessions from the government and employers. See Durand and Harft, "Panorama statistique des grèves," and George Ross, "French Working Class Politics after May–June 1968: A New Working Class?" (Paper delivered at the annual meeting of the American Political Science Association, New Orleans, September 1973).

Table 2.2. Strike activity and the state.

State political/ economic goals (ideology)	State intervention	
	Active (high)	Passive (low)
Market supporting (bourgeois)	Primary locus of distributional conflict: private sector (with state intervention) Implications for strike activity: "politicization" of the strike, little or no decline in strike volume Exemplars: France, Italy Long-run strike trend: negligible or upward Postwar average strike volume: 670 Government revenue as % of GNP, 1972: 35.4%[a] Average tax rate, 1972: 11%[b]	Primary locus of distributional conflict: private sector Implications for strike activity: "business unionism," little or no decline in strike volume Exemplars: Canada, U.S. Long-run strike trend: negligible or upward Postwar average strike volume: 557 Government revenue as % of GNP, 1972: 28.7%[a] Average tax rate, 1972: 15%[b]
Market modifying (Social Democratic)	Primary locus of distributional conflict: public sector/political process Implications for strike activity: "withering away" of the strike; displacement of distributive conflict to political marketplace Exemplars: Denmark, Norway, Sweden Long-run strike trend: downward from late 1930s Postwar average strike volume: 103 Government revenue as % of GNP, 1972: 44.8%[a] Average tax rate, 1972: 31.3%[b]	Null cell

a. Excluding defense and state enterprises.
b. Mean for manufacturing production workers with two children.

course best illustrated by the experience of the Scandinavian social democracies.[14]

Although it is clear that the political arena becomes decisive for distributional outcomes when the share of national income passing through the public sector reaches great proportions, it may not be obvious why this should necessarily lead (as historically it has) to a sharp decline in industrial conflict in the private marketplace. Even if labor's economic security and well-being depends to a large extent on the "social" or "political" wage, why should trade unions give up struggling over the "market" wage? There are at least three (related) reasons.

First, for broad segments of welfare state societies, public consumption (collective goods) and the social wage are simply acceptable, indeed preferable, substitutes for private consumption and the market wage. The system of collective consumption and distribution is after all the *raison d'être* of Social Democratic parties, and their electoral success has derived from its popular appeal.

Second, the high and steeply progressive tax system of welfare state societies means that the marginal rate of taxation even for average-wage employees is high enough to discourage great efforts on behalf of nominal (money) market wage increases. For example, Calmfors reports that by the early 1970s in Sweden rapid inflation and high marginal tax rates (about 60 percent for an average wage earner) made it impossible for most wage earners to obtain any increase in post-tax real wage income from upward movements in nominal wage rates.[15] Data for the late 1960s in Great Britain analyzed by Jackson, Turner, and Wilkinson point to a similar conclusion.[16] Although I am not aware of comparable quantitative analyses for other countries, the published data on marginal tax rates for average-income workers in industrial nations suggest that the disincentive has been equally strong in such welfare states as Denmark, Norway, and the Netherlands.

14. Headey has argued that a similar configuration of factors underlies trade union acceptance of incomes policies. See Bruce W. Headey, "Trade Unions and National Wages Policies," *Journal of Politics*, 32 (1970), 407–439.

15. In some situations investigated by Calmfors the tax system had perverse effects: increases in money wages lead to *decreases* in aftertax real wages. See Lars Calmfors, "Inflation in Sweden," in *Worldwide Inflation: Theory and Recent Experience*, ed. L. B. Krause and W. S. Salant (Washington, D.C.: Brookings Institution, 1977).

16. D. Jackson, H. A. Turner, and Frank Wilkinson, *Do Trade Unions Cause Inflation?* (Cambridge: Cambridge University Press, 1972). In fact Jackson et al. found that *very large* increases in money wages were necessary for workers to realize modest net-of-tax increases in real wages.

Finally (and to some extent this is the prior point writ large), it simply was rational for trade unions to commit scarce organizational resources to the arena of activity likely to yield the highest marginal payoff. After working-class-based Social Democratic and Labor parties had mobilized enough support in one electoral arena to assume political power and push through the welfare state, it made sense for organized labor to seek to maximize its objectives (in particular, the economic well-being of its constituency) in the political rather than the industrial marketplace. Put another way, the political marketplace and the private marketplace can be viewed as alternative arenas for the maximization of goals. Once the Social Democrats began to reshape fundamentally the political economy of distribution, the political process offered labor the greater marginal return on activity. Political pressure and bargaining were emphasized at the expense of industrial militancy, and strike activity in the market declined dramatically.[17]

Distributional Conflict in the Welfare State: Recent Developments and Some Speculations about the Future

A number of recent developments in advanced welfare state societies suggest that the assumptions upon which the central argument of this essay rests are collapsing. Mass electoral opposition to further expansion of public expenditure has increased sharply in several welfare states; trade unions have pressed for, or acquiesced in, bargains with the state that reduce personal taxes in exchange for restraint in market wage bargaining; and, in Great Britain at least, strike activity may have *increased* as increasing numbers of workers have felt the bite of high direct taxation, and labor has fought to preserve accustomed rates of increase in net, real, market wages.

If people, and in particular the working class, continued to prefer public consumption and distribution to private consumption and allocation by the market, or at least were indifferent to the two, discon-

17. Although most union energy in the United States is still committed to private market activity, the process outlined in the text has occurred to a limited extent, though not enough to make a great impact on the volume of industrial conflict. As a result of labor's favorable experience with the Democratic party during and since the Roosevelt era, there has been a perceptible shift in the allocation of American unions' organizational resources toward the political arena.

tent with the political economy of the welfare state of the sort just identified should not arise. I suspect that such discontent among the working class has much to do with changes in the composition and interclass *re*distributive impact of public consumption and transfers, but until more empirical work along these lines has been completed this remains a conjecture.[18] What is clear, however, is that once the public sector's share of the national product approaches 50 percent or more, serious resistance to further extension of the welfare state begins to appear even within the traditional political constituency of Social Democratic and Labor parties.

The evidence of working-class discontent with high taxes and public expenditure in the welfare state is worth reviewing at great length. Contrary to my "long-run" argument that industrial conflict declined in proportion to the success of Social Democratic and Labor parties in socializing the distribution of national income, two studies of labor militancy and wage bargaining in the United Kingdom argue that just the opposite has been true in recent years. Jackson, Turner, and Wilkinson have presented evidence showing that when wage inflation pushed blue-collar workers into high direct-tax brackets for the first time in the mid-1960s, real net-of-tax market wages stagnated. As a result, they argue, the trade unions militantly pursued even higher money wage settlements, which led to a sharp increase in Britain's strike rate. In other words, the expansion of public expenditure and increases in the rate of personal taxation brought on by the, inflation of nominal wage levels reduced labor's net real wage and prompted greater militancy in market wage bargaining. Although I have detected no sign of this effect in my own models of British strike fluctuations, Johnson and Timbrell's econometric study of postwar wage formation in Britain does report results consistent with this argument.[19] Johnson and Timbrell conclude that labor's struggle to achieve *net-of-tax* real gains in *market* wages explains both the upturn in British strike activity and the escalation of wage inflation.[20]

18. Jackson, Turner, and Wilkinson (*Do Trade Unions Cause Inflation?*) have already completed some suggestive research on the British case. They found that since the 1960s "the combined effect of income movements and changes in tax policy was to increase post-tax inequality between earned incomes" (p. 79) and that "the ratio of benefits-received to taxes-paid was falling" (p. 83) for most employee and wage-earner households.

19. J. Johnson and M. Timbrell, "Empirical Tests of a Bargaining Theory of Wage Rate Determination," *Manchester School of Economic and Social Studies*, 41 (1973), 140–167.

20. The conclusion is controversial. For an alternative account of the recent wage explosion that does not rely on the private consumption/tax effect argument, see the next chapter.

The argument connecting growth in social spending and in direct taxation to strike activity is controversial and the evidence appears to be limited to the British case. Perhaps more revealing are recent government-coordinated quasi–incomes policy bargains in Denmark, Great Britain, Norway, and Sweden in which trade unions have tacitly agreed to exercise restraint in wage bargaining in return for reductions in personal taxation. One of the aims of these bargains is to increase net real personal income without incurring the inflationary pressures of large nominal wage settlements.

Some of the tax reductions have been fictitious; indirect taxes were raised (in Sweden and Great Britain, for example) to compensate for the loss of direct tax revenue. But public spending and social benefits were also cut back. Although personal tax reductions were generally skewed to the advantage of low-wage earners, net market income has nonetheless increased at the expense of public consumption, subsidies, and transfers. As a result outcomes in the private market have a greater impact on the final distribution of personal income. One might therefore interpret labor's participation in such incomes policy bargains as an implicit preference for strengthening the hand of the private market and weakening the impact of the state on the distributional process.

In the Scandinavian social democracies the sharpest challenge to the established system of public-sector distribution has come not from strike action or quasi–incomes policy bargains involving reduced direct taxation and social expenditure, but rather from electoral mobilization by anti–welfare state, "new bourgeois" flash political movements. The most dramatic example is the spectacular rise of Mogen Glistrup's Progress party in Denmark. Capitalizing on growing dissatisfaction with the performance and financial burdens of the welfare state, Glistrup's party burst upon the political scene just before the 1973 election and, running on a program of drastic reductions in the state bureaucracy, social expenditure, and taxation, became the second largest party in the Danish Folketing virtually overnight.[21] The Progress party's success was a severe shock to what had been a very stable two-bloc Danish party system, and subsequent govern-

21. For an extensive analysis, see Ole Borre, "The General Election in Denmark, January 1975: Toward a New Structure of the Party System," *Scandinavian Political Studies*, 10 (1974), 211–216; and Jerrold Rusk and Ole Borre, "The Changing Space in Danish Voter Perceptions 1971–1973," *European Journal of Political Research*, 2 (1974), 329–361.

ments of the left as well as of the right responded to the drift in public sentiment by reducing taxation and state expenditure.[22]

A new bourgeois flash political party, akin to the Glistrup movement in Denmark, also appeared in Norway in 1973. This new anti–welfare state party was organized by Anders Lange—an activist in the old right-wing movements of the 1930s—around a platform similar to Glistrup's, calling for a radical rollback of public expenditure and taxation. Although "Anders Lange's Party" (ALP) had neither the initial support nor the staying power of Glistrup's Progress party in Denmark, it did reflect considerable discontent with the established parties and the political economy of collective consumption and distribution over which they presided.

The archetype of the modern welfare state is Sweden. However, in contrast to the recent political experience of Denmark and Norway, the two-bloc Swedish party system has exhibited great stability. Sweden has not experienced a new bourgeois, anti–welfare state movement similar to the Glistrup phenomenon in Denmark or the smaller Anders Lange party in Norway. Undoubtedly this is because Sweden is the only highly developed welfare state in which the traditional bourgeois parties have been in opposition for the entire postwar era.[23] Responsibility for growth of the bureaucracy, public expenditure, and taxation therefore rests wholly with the Social Democrats. Consequently, the "old bourgeois" party bloc stands as a viable alternative to the welfare state, and popular discontent with the system of collective consumption and distribution has been channeled through the established right-of-center parties.

22. In September 1974 Prime Minister Paul Hartling's Agrarian-Liberal minority government introduced a 7 billion kroner cut in income taxes and government expenditure that was passed in parliament with the support of Radical Liberals, Conservatives, Center Democrats, Christian People's party, Single Taxers, and some members of the Progress party. I am tempted to infer, without support from survey evidence, that the decline in "new bourgeois" electoral support in the 1975 election was associated with this significant policy change. In any case, public sentiment continues to run strongly against further extensions of the Danish welfare state: according to the *New York Times* (28 September 1975), polls taken in 1975 indicate that 63 percent of the public felt that the burden of taxation was excessive and that the welfare state had gone too far. The minority Social Democratic government, which assumed office after the 1975 election, acknowledged this by submitting a budget that further reduced social spending.

23. See, for example, the analyses by Henry Valen and Stein Rokkan, "Norway: Conflict Structure and Mass Politics in a European Periphery," in *Electoral Behavior: A Comparative Handbook*, ed. R. Rose (New York: Free Press, 1974), pp. 315–370; and Olof Petersson, "The 1973 General Elections in Sweden," *Scandinavian Political Studies*, 9 (1974), 219–228.

Survey evidence reported by Särlvik suggests that such discontent is widespread and has increased significantly in recent years.[24] These survey results show that the proportion of the Swedish mass public advocating a reduction in social welfare benefits grew from 41 percent to 60 percent between 1968 and 1973. The growth of opposition to welfare policies was apparent among the supporters of all political parties, but was particularly pronounced among Social Democratic voters.

This "shift to the right" on the social welfare issue coincided with a gradual (albeit small) erosion of electoral support for the Socialist bloc, which began in 1970, continued into the 1973 election, and culminated in the first outright (and inevitable) defeat of the Social Democrats in forty-four years in the September 1976 election.[25]

The appearance of new bourgeois flash political parties in Denmark and Norway, the decline of Social Democratic electoral support in Sweden, and survey data showing increased public hostility to high taxation and social spending suggest that the political base of the welfare state is eroding. It is likely that inflation and economic stagnation, rather than discontent with the welfare state per se, played at least some part in the defeat of the Social Democrats in Sweden and the remarkable success of the Glistrup movement in Denmark, and was surely a major factor in the British Labour government's recent attempts to reduce public expenditures and divert resources to the private sector. Nonetheless, costs in the form of high levels of taxation have apparently begun to exceed perceived benefits from state transfers and collective consumption for a sizable fraction of the working class in many welfare states. Perhaps it is not coincidental, then, that the most dramatic expression of popular opposition to public expenditure and taxation occurred in Denmark, where the average tax rate for manufacturing workers is the highest in the Western industrial world, and disposable income (inclusive of transfers) as a percentage of gross earnings the lowest.[26]

24. Bo Särlvik, "Recent Electoral Trends in Sweden," in *Scandinavia at the Polls*, ed. K. Cerny (Washington, D.C.: American Enterprise Institute, 1977).

25. A Bourgeois coalition led by the Center party won the 1976 election. (The Social Democrats returned to power in 1982.)

26. I base this statement on data for manufacturing production workers with average incomes, reported in OECD, *Revenue Statistics in OECD Member Countries 1965–1972* (Paris, 1975), appendix, tables 2, 3, and 6. See also Douglas Hibbs and Henrik Madsen, "Public Reactions to the Growth of Taxation and Government Expenditure," *World Politics*, 33 (April 1981), 413–435.

It seems likely that developments in the political arenas of advanced welfare states will ensure that the leveling off of the share of the national income passing through the public sector, already visible in Great Britain and the Scandinavian social democracies, will be long-lived. The share of national income allocated in the private market may even increase significantly, particularly if the distributional impact of a further growth in the public sector continues to be viewed as disadvantageous by a significant fraction of the politically dominant "organized working class." If the private sector's allocation of national income does increase appreciably in the welfare state societies, we are likely to observe a renaissance of industrial conflict (which now stands at negligible levels) as the economic marketplace regains some of its former importance as the locus of distributional outcomes.

3

Trade Union Power, Wage Inflation, and Labor Militancy: A Comparative Analysis

Broadly speaking, two views have dominated the literature on post-war wage and price inflation: "demand-pull" and "cost-push."[1] Admittedly, the distinction is somewhat artificial, probably more so now than in the past. Indeed, the empirical results of excess demand models of inflation are easily rationalized in cost-push or "sociological" terms—a point I pursue further in the main body of this chapter. Conventional, demand-pull inflation models imply that the percentage rate of change of money wages depends essentially on the level of, and in some models the rate of change of, excess demand for labor. Historically, one of the principal theoretical controversies in the demand-pull literature (and one that has obvious policy implications) was whether there is a stable, long-run tradeoff between the demand for labor (usually proxied by a nonlinear function of the measured unemployment rate) and the rate of wage and/or price inflation. The neo-Keynesian position was that there is a long-run unemployment-inflation tradeoff (although this view was later abandoned in the light

Reprinted from the Center for International Studies, MIT, Monograph Series, C/77-6, April 1977 (subsequently published in Italian in *MICROS*, 3 [March 1984], 27–42). This is one of a series of papers from my project on industrial conflict and its consequences, supported by the National Science Foundation. I am grateful to Nicholas Vasilatos for able research assistance, to Henry Brady and Hartojo Wignjowijoto for comments on an earlier draft, to Marilyn Shapleigh for editorial advice, and to Suzanne Planchon for typing the manuscript.

1. A third view should also be acknowledged: the monetarist, quantity theory. Models representing the quantity theory framework are not examined here. However, see the comparative study by W. F. Nordhaus, "The Worldwide Wage Explosion," *Brookings Papers on Economic Activity* (1972:2), 439, who concludes that "the strict monetarist hypothesis is rejected whenever the evidence is sufficient."

of experience), whereas the traditional neoclassical stance was that any such tradeoff is merely a short-run, transitory phenomenon due to lags in adjustment between expected and actual rates of inflation.

International factors aside, cost-push theories of wage inflation usually take a social conflict or collective bargaining orientation to wage formation and point to the influence of sociological variables—especially trade union militancy or labor aggressiveness. At the core of the cost-push view is the idea that trade union action exerts significant upward pressure on the rate of change of wages *independently* of excess demand for labor, that is, independently of market forces. Wage settlements following outbursts of strike activity (such as May–June 1968 in France, the "hot autumn" of 1969 in Italy, and nationwide strikes of coal miners in 1972 and 1974 in Great Britain) as well as the poor performance of conventional models in explaining the general wage inflation experienced by most Western industrial societies since the late 1960s appear to have enhanced the status of labor militancy, cost-push theories among orthodox economists.[2]

The main body of this chapter examines various demand-pull and cost-push models of wage inflation against annual postwar data on hourly compensation of manufacturing employees in four industrial societies: Italy, France, Great Britain, and the United States.[3] My principal purpose is to show that the "power" and "militancy" of trade unions play an important role in the dynamic process of wage determination in a diverse group of industrial societies. Contrary to the usual practice, I shall summarize my main assumptions, arguments, and conclusions here rather than at the end:

1. The existence of a long-run unemployment/wage inflation tradeoff (Phillips curve) requires money illusion on the part of labor and/or trade union weakness in wage bargaining.

2. Being persuaded on a priori grounds by the neoclassical-accelerationist position that widespread money illusion is implausible, I argue that less than full wage adjustment to nontrivial episodes of price inflation is most likely due to the weakness of organized labor in collective bargaining.

3. The empirical results show that the long-run coefficient of adjustment of manufacturing wage changes to price changes is less than

2. See, for example, G. L. Perry, "Determinants of Wage Inflation around the World," *Brookings Papers on Economic Activity* (1975:2), and the discussion in the second and third major sections of this chapter.

3. Throughout this chapter I use "wages" and "compensation" interchangeably, although they are of course distinct. All empirical results pertain to the latter.

unity only in the United States; that is, only in the United States is there any evidence of a nonvertical long-run Phillips curve.

4. Both the rate at which wages adjust to prices and the long-run magnitude of the adjustment coefficient are interpreted as a reflection of trade union power in wage bargaining. Rank ordering of the countries along these lines is consistent with the qualitative judgment of industrial relations specialists about the comparative power of the various trade union movements—particularly the comparative weakness of organized labor in the United States.

5. In all four countries trade union militancy (which should be distinguished from trade union power), as measured by strike activity, exerts sizable effects on the rate of change of manufacturing wages independently of market forces. However, in most cases trade union action has not systematically contributed to accelerating wages and prices, except perhaps in recent years, when "real wage resistance" has persisted in the face of changes in relative prices in favor of food and fuel producers.

6. Outside the United States (and other countries with relatively weak trade union movements) wage and price stability probably cannot be achieved without union acquiescence in some form of incomes policy—unless, of course, political authorities are willing to run the economy at a *very* low (and politically infeasible) level of activity. The postwar experience suggests that, barring major political changes, such union cooperation is not likely to be forthcoming in any of the countries examined here, with the partial exception of Great Britain; even there it has taken the conjunction of a Labour government facing an extraordinary economic crisis to elicit voluntary trade union restraint.

Excess Demand Models

Simple Phillips Curve

The point of reference for most contemporary treatments of wage inflation is A. W. Phillips's seminal 1958 study of the relation between unemployment and the rate of change of money wages in the United Kingdom over the period 1861–1957. Phillips employed somewhat unorthodox statistical procedures in his analysis, but his plots of the percentage rate of change of wages against the unemployment rate revealed a nonlinear, inverse association (convex toward the origin) that was replicated in many subsequent studies and is now widely known as the "Phillips curve." Phillips rationalized his empirical results with an excess demand argument that most work in this tradition has adopted:

> When the demand for labour is high and there are very few unemployed we should expect employers to bid wage rates up quite rapidly, each firm and each industry being continually tempted to offer a little above the prevailing rates to attract the most suitable labour. . . . On the other hand it appears that workers are reluctant to offer their services and less than prevailing rates when demand for labour is low and unemployment is high so that wage rates fall only very slowly. The relation between unemployment and the rate of change of wage rates is therefore likely to be highly nonlinear.[4]

Phillips also noticed a tendency for wages to respond to *changes* in the unemployment rate. Although he acknowledged the implications of this association for labor bargaining power, Phillips interpreted this relationship primarily in demand-pull terms as well: "Thus in a year of rising business activity, with demand for labour increasing and the percentage unemployment decreasing, employers will be bidding more vigorously for the services of labour than they would be in a year during which the average unemployment was the same but the demand for labour was not increasing."[5]

With U denoting the unemployment rate, the simple or "naive" Phillips curve model therefore takes the form:

$$w' = f(U, \Delta U), \tag{3.1a}$$

which, following conventional practice, is specified to be linear in $1/U$ and ΔU.

$$w'_t = b_0 + b_1(1/U_t) + b_2\Delta U_t, \tag{3.1b}$$

where w' = the percentage rate of change of wages (hourly compensation of employees in manufacturing) computed as 100 times the first backward difference of the natural logs,
   U = the civilian unemployment rate,
   ΔU = the first backward difference of U.

---

4. A. W. Phillips, "The Relation between Unemployment and the Rate of Change of Money Wage Rates in the United Kingdom, 1861–1957," *Economica*, 25 (1958), 283.
5. Ibid.

For purposes of comparison with the more realistic models introduced below, estimates of the simple Phillips curve model are reported in the first column of Tables 3.1 through 3.4. It will come as no surprise to those familiar with the contemporary wage determination literature that the simple excess demand, Phillips curve hypothesis does a poor job of explaining the postwar wage inflation. In all four countries the $\bar{R}^2$s are low, the regression standard errors relatively high, and ΔU_t has the wrong sign (positive). The level unemployment rate term, $1/U_t$, is properly signed (positive) in all regressions but reaches conventional statistical significance only in the equation for Italy.

The most obvious empirical shortcoming of the naive Phillips model is that no account is taken of movements in prices. Phillips did not ignore prices altogether; rather, he advanced a threshold hypothesis in which price changes affected the wage bargain only when they threatened to reduce real wages, that is, only when the rate of change of prices was greater than the rate of change of wages ($p' > w'$). Since in Phillips's sample real wages rarely fell over a sustained period, a price term was not explicitly incorporated into his wage equation.

Phillips Curve with Contemporaneous Price Changes

Among the first to build price changes directly into the wage equation was Lipsey.[6] However, Lipsey's most important contribution was his attempt to tie the inflation-unemployment (Phillips curve) tradeoff to conventional supply and demand economic analysis. Lipsey developed an argument showing that (1) the proportional rate of change of money wages is a linear function of the ratio of excess demand to total labor supply, and (2) the unobserved excess demand ratio is approximated by a negatively sloped, nonlinear function of the observed unemployment rate, U.

Lipsey's disequilibrium wage adjustment model was generally taken to be a strong theoretical rationalization of the empirical Phillips curve.[7] Lipsey also developed an ingenious explanation—which cen-

6. R. G. Lipsey, "The Relationship between Unemployment and the Rate of Change of Money Wages in the United Kingdom, 1862–1957: A Further Analysis," *Economica*, 27 (1960), 1–31.

7. Objections on theoretical grounds were, of course, raised. See, for example, Bernard Corry and David Laidler, "The Phillips Relation: A Theoretical Explanation," *Economica*, 34 (1967), 189–197. The accelerationist argument is treated in the next section.

Table 3.1. Italy: Manufacturing average hourly compensation (w') regressions, annual data, 1954–1972.

	(1)	(2)	(3)	(4)	(5)	(6a)	(6b)	(7)
Constant	-2.272	-1.019	1.697	23.055	—	3.333	3.463	2.55
	(-0.54)	(-0.45)	(0.83)	(3.35)		(2.90)	(3.76)	(1.20)
$1/U_t$	46.904	15.349	10.533	-2.421	—	0.518	—	—
	(2.96)	(1.50))	(1.30)	(-0.36)		(0.10)		
ΔU_t	0.442	—	—	—	—	—	—	—
	(0.50)							
$\sum_{i=1}^{2} U_{t-i}$	—	—	—	—	—	—	—	0.043
								(0.20)
p'_t	—	1.649	—	—	—	—	—	—
		(4.52)						
$\sum_{i=0}^{2} p'_{t-i}$	—	—	1.226	0.591	—	0.942	0.931	1.041
			(3.18)	(1.67)		(3.38)	(3.60)	(3.33)
$\Delta R/Y_t$	—	—	—	-0.104	—	—	—	—
				(-0.81)				
R/Y_t	—	—	—	-0.160	—	—	—	—
				(-3.02)				
Strike volume, $t-1$ (worker-days lost per worker in manufacturing)	—	—	—	—	—	1.910	1.953	2.108
						(3.99)	(4.34)	(3.85)
$\bar{R}^2$	.273	.690	.774	.888	—	.914	.917	.910
DW	1.85	2.00	1.85	2.18	—	1.99	2.01	1.94
SER	3.474	2.381	2.302	1.986	—	1.750	1.749	1.823
GLS[a]	$r_1 = +.500$	$r_1 = +.281$	—	$r_1 = -.372$	—	$r_1 = -.383$	$r_1 = -.406$	$r_1 = -.415$

Note: t-statistics are given in parentheses.
a. r_1 is an autoregressive coefficient from a generalized least-squares estimation.

Table 3.2. France: Manufacturing average hourly compensation (w') regressions, annual data, 1951–1972.

	(1)	(2)	(3)	(4)	(5)	(6a)	(6b)	(6c)	(7)
Constant	7.260	6.851	6.640	—	—	0.715	0.643	—	-1.741
	(1.35)	(3.77)	(3.17)			(0.31)	(0.40)		(-0.53)
$1/U_t$	2.421	-1.404	-1.411	—	—	-0.469	—	—	2.012
	(0.65)	(-1.05)	(-1.01)			(-0.04)			(0.59)
ΔU_t	0.834	—	—	—	—	—	—	—	—
	(0.13)								
Dum 68	—	—	—	—	—	7.399	7.433	7.989	7.820
(= 1, 1968)						(3.05)	(3.31)	(4.60)	(3.29)
$\sum\limits_{i=0}^{2} U_{t-i}$	—	—	—	—	—	—	—	—	2.012
									(0.59)
p'_t	—	0.889	—	—	—	0.664	0.663	0.681	—
		(6.34)				(5.40)	(5.64)	(6.38)	
$\sum\limits_{i=0}^{2} p'_{t-i}$	—	—	0.927	—	—	—	—	—	0.683
			(4.95)						(3.12)
Strike volume, $t-1$ (worker-days lost per worker in manufacturing)	—	—	—	—	—	4.236	4.233	4.134	6.593
						(2.97)	(3.06)	(3.12)	(1.82)
Strike frequency (strikes per 10,000 workers economy-wide)$_t$	—	—	—	—	—	2.381	2.389	2.698	2.571
						(2.69)	(2.85)	(7.87)	(1.87)
$\bar{R}^2$	0.0	.645	.632	—	—	.826	.836	.845	.714
DW	1.93	1.72	1.91	—	—	2.00	2.00	1.99	1.86
SER	4.347	2.633	2.681	—	—	1.782	1.729	1.689	1.787
GLS^a	$r_1 = +.600$	—	—	—	—	$r_1 = +.196$	$r_1 = +.198$	$r_1 = +.200$	$r_1 = +.613$

Note: t-statistics are given in parentheses.

a. r_1 is an autoregressive coefficient from a generalized least-squares estimation.

Table 3.3. Great Britain: Manufacturing average hourly compensation (w') regressions, annual data, 1951–1972.

	(1)	(2)	(3)	(4)	(5)	(6a)	(6b)	(7)
Constant	5.306 (1.57)	4.521 (2.46)	2.948 (1.41)	9.815 (1.09)	2.092 (1.04)	-2.874 (-2.32)	-2.699 (-1.84)	-5.287 (-2.67)
$1/U_t$	4.432 (0.92)	-1.327 (-0.54)	-0.763 (-0.34)	1.221 (0.42)	1.157 (0.48)	6.721 (4.54)	6.637 (4.07)	6.694 (2.76)
ΔU_t	0.504 (0.36)	—	—	—	—	—	—	1.941 (1.45)
$\sum_{i=1}^{2} u_{t-i}$	—	—	—	—	—	—	—	—
Dum 68 (=1, 1968–72)	—	—	—	—	—	—	1.013 (0.24)	—
Dum 68 × $(1/U_t)$	—	—	—	—	—	—	-2.585 (-0.27)	—
p'_t	—	0.843 (4.30)	—	—	—	0.683 (7.41)	0.669 (5.59)	—
$\sum_{i=0}^{2} p'_{t-i}$	—	—	1.207 (4.17)	1.080 (3.44)	1.090 (3.90)	—	—	0.710 (4.33)
$\Delta R/Y_t$	—	—	—	0.417 (1.08)	—	—	—	—
R/Y_t	—	—	—	-0.371 (-0.82)	—	—	—	—
$\Delta T/L_t$	—	—	—	—	0.935 (1.78)	—	—	—
Strike volume, $t-1$ (worker-days lost per worker in manufacturing)	—	—	—	—	—	4.332 (3.62)	4.064 (2.51)	4.040 (3.85)
Strike frequency, $t-1$ (strikes per 10,000 workers in manufacturing)	—	—	—	—	—	2.080 (4.85)	2.080 (3.45)	1.161 (1.63)
$\bar{R}^2$	0.0	.451	.640	.662	.683	.911	.899	.938
DW	2.07	1.87	1.96	2.00	1.79	1.83	1.86	1.98
SER	2.514	1.90	1.754	1.785	1.646	1.152	1.220	.996
GLS[a]	$r_1 = +.720$	$r_1 = +.26$	—	$r_1 = -.100$	—	$r_1 = -.565$	$r_1 = -.555$	$r_1 = -.600$

Note: t-statistics are given in parentheses.

a. r_1 is an autoregressive coefficient from a generalized least-squares estimation.

Table 3.4. United States: Manufacturing average hourly compensation (w') regressions, annual data, 1951–1972.

	(1)	(2)	(3)	(4)	(5)	(6a)	(6b)	(6c)	(7)
Constant	2.471	1.816	1.753	1.991	2.100	-1.181	-1.190	—	-2.807
	(1.39)	(2.15)	(1.90)	(1.40)	(2.56)	(-1.48)	(-1.56)		(-1.01)
$1/U_t$	12.330	8.343	8.283	8.874	7.400	2.988	—	—	—
	(1.63)	(2.44)	(2.29)	(2.03)	(2.07)	(1.00)			
ΔU_t	0.034	—	—	—	—	—	—	—	—
	(0.13)								
$\sum_{i=1}^{2} U_{t-i}$	—	—	—	—	—	—	—	—	0.026
									(0.11)
P'_t	—	0.583	—	0.563	0.514	0.464	0.467	0.496	—
		(5.83)		(3.42)	(4.56)	(6.01)	(6.32)	(5.91)	
$\sum_{i=0}^{2} p'_{t-i}$	—	—	0.620	—	—	—	—	—	0.336
			(3.44)						(4.55)
$\Delta R/W_t$	—	—	—	-0.064	—	—	—	—	—
				(-0.57)					
R/W_t	—	—	—	-0.021	—	—	—	—	—
				(0.21)					
$\Delta T/L_t$	—	—	—	—	0.413	—	—	—	—
					(1.98)				
Strike frequency, $t-1$ (strikes per 10,000 workers in manufacturing)	—	—	—	—	—	3.514	4.050	3.062	5.520
						(4.18)	(6.23)	(14.74)	(3.47)
$\bar{R}^2$	.074	.684	.654	.647	.714	.855	.865	.822	.793
DW	2.13	2.06	2.06	2.11	2.08	2.03	2.07	2.09	2.17
SER	1.323	.792	.828	.875	.779	.674	.673	.687	.709
GLS[a]	$r_1 = +.484$	$r_1 = +.196$	$r_1 = +.203$	$r_1 = +.246$	$r_1 = +.275$	$r_1 = -.141$	$r_1 = -.191$	—	$r_1 = -.300$
	—	$r_2 = +.349$	$r_2 = +.355$	—	—	$r_2 = -.060$	$r_2 = -.094$	—	—

Note: t-statistics are given in parentheses.

a. r_1, r_2 are autoregressive coefficients from a generalized least-squares estimation.

tered on the consequences of aggregating individual market tradeoff curves across markets—for the aggregate association observed by Phillips between the rate of change of wages and the rate of change of unemployment, U'.[8]

The empirical form of Lipsey's model is simply the naive Phillips curve equation with a term for contemporaneous price changes:

$$w'_t = b_0 + b_1(1/U_t) + b_2 p'_t + b_3 U'_t, \qquad (3.2)$$

where p' = the percentage rate of change of prices (computed by the log-difference method described previously) and all other terms are as defined earlier.

Since the Phillips curve argument does not depend heavily on U'_t and this term was insignificant in all regressions (studies using this class of models typically find $b_3 = 0$), the results reported in the second column of Tables 3.1 through 3.4 are based on equations omitting the term for the rate of change of unemployment. The estimates for this model yield little evidence in favor of the conventional Phillips curve argument. The coefficient of the unemployment or excess demand term $1/U_t$ has a perverse (that is, wrong) sign in the equations for France and Great Britain and is insignificant in the regression for Italy. Moreover, the coefficient of the contemporaneous price change term p'_t is not significantly different from unity in the regressions for France and Great Britain and is significantly *greater* than unity in the equation for Italy.[9] This result alone is sufficient to deny the Phillips curve thesis, for it implies that the wage bargain is struck in real rather than money terms, and therefore there cannot be a tradeoff between the nominal phenomenon of money wage inflation and a real quantity such as the unemployment rate.[10] This point

8. Lipsey used the proportional rate of change of the unemployment rate (U') in his study rather than the simple rate of change (U) used in Equation (3.1). Phillips appears to have had the latter in mind, but I found that it made little difference: regressions using U'_t produced results very similar to those reported in column 1 of Tables 3.1 through 3.4.

9. A similar estimate of the elasticity of manufacturing wages with respect to prices for postwar Italian data is reported by P. Sylos-Labini, *Trade Unions, Inflation, and Productivity* (Lexington, Mass.: Lexington Books, 1974), who surprisingly does not comment on its implications. As it turns out (see the following sections), the *long-run* elasticity is on the order of 1.0.

10. I am inclined to pay greater attention to the coefficient of p' than to that of U in evaluating the Phillips curve thesis, since it can be argued with some justification that during the estimation period unemployment and other measures of aggregate demand did not vary enough to permit a sharp estimate of the excess demand coefficient. For all of the countries treated in this chapter, the coefficient of variation of p' is substantially greater than that of U.

is pursued further in the next section. Only for the United States do the estimates for Equation (3.2) support the (wage) inflation-unemployment tradeoff view. The results in column 2 of Table 3.4 show a significant positive parameter estimate for $1/U_t$ and an estimate for p_t' (0.58) that is many standard errors less than unity.

Price Expectations Phillips Curves

The Phillips-Lipsey tradeoff model implies that high rates of inflation yield long-term benefits in the form of lower unemployment. This view is plausible on theoretical grounds only if one of the following conditions is satisfied:

1. Workers value, at least to some extent, nominal wage increases alone; that is, a significant fraction of the labor force suffers from "money illusion."

2. Other things being equal, labor organizations are not powerful enough relative to management to obtain full wage adjustment to price increases.

Among economists, the tradeoff debate has hinged largely on the plausibility of the first condition. For example, Tobin summarizes the theoretical foundation of the Phillips curve thus: "The Phillips curve idea is in a sense a reincarnation of the original Keynesian idea of 'money illusion' in the supply of labor. The Phillips curve says that increases in money wages—and more generally, other money incomes—are in some significant degree prized for themselves, even if they do not result in equivalent gains in real income."[11]

Economists working in the strict neoclassical tradition attack this idea, pointing out that even though wages are set in money terms, the wage determination process is essentially a bargain for real wages conditioned by the forecasts of buyers and sellers of labor of the behavior of prices over the contract period. Hence Friedman, Phelps, and others argued that any steady rate of inflation will eventually be anticipated fully by economic actors and that wage adjustment to

11. J. Tobin, "Unemployment and Inflation: The Cruel Dilemma," in *Prices: Issues in Theory and Public Policy*, ed. Almarin Phillips and Oliver E. Williamson (Philadelphia: University of Pennsylvania Press, 1968), p. 106. J. M. Keynes, *The General Theory of Employment, Interest and Money* (London: Macmillan Press, 1936), pp. 14–15, wrote: "The workers . . . resist reductions of money wages . . . whereas they do not resist reductions of real wages . . . Every trade union will put up some resistance to a cut in money-wages, however small. But since no trade union would dream of striking on every occasion of a rise in the cost of living, they do not raise the obstacle to any increase in aggregate employment which is attributed to them by the classical school."

expected price inflation will be complete; that is, the *long-run* elasticity of wages with respect to prices will be unity.[12] In this view the Phillips curve is merely a short-run, "statistical" phenomenon stemming from lags in adjustment between expected and actual rates of price (and/or wage) inflation. In Friedman's words: "There is always a temporary trade-off between inflation and unemployment; there is no permanent trade-off. The temporary trade-off comes not from inflation per se, but from unanticipated inflation, which generally means a rising rate of inflation. The widespread belief that there is a permanent trade-off is a sophisticated version of the confusion between 'high' and 'rising' that we all recognize in simpler forms. A rising rate of inflation may reduce unemployment, a high rate will not."[13]

The position of neoclassical, "expectations" theorists is, then, that the wage equation should be specified in the form:

$$w'_t = b_0 + b_1(1/U_t) + b_2 p^{*'}_t, \tag{3.3a}$$

where $p^{*'}$ = the expected rate of price inflation. b_2 can be interpreted as the parameter of money illusion. If $b_2 = 0$, Equation (3.3a) reduces to the simple Phillips curve model introduced earlier. For $0 < b_2 < 1$ we have what essentially is the Phillips-Lipsey model of the previous section, in which the long-run tradeoff between (wage or price) inflation and unemployment is steeper (less favorable) than the short-run Phillips curve. Friedman, Phelps, and other strict expectations theorists assert that $b_2 = 1$. There is no money illusion in the labor market, and the long-run Phillips curve is a vertical line crossing the U axis at the "natural rate" of unemployment. The only possible long-run tradeoff is therefore between the rate of change of *real* wages $(w' - p')$ and the unemployment rate and/or between the rate of *acceleration* of inflation and the unemployment rate.[14]

12. Milton Friedman, "The Role of Monetary Policy," *American Economic Review*, 58 (1968), 1–17; E. Phelps, "Phillips Curves, Expectations of Inflation and Optimal Unemployment over Time," *Economica*, 34 (1967), 254–281; E. Phelps, "Money Wage Dynamics and Labor Market Equilibrium," *Journal of Political Economy*, pt. 2, 76 (July/August 1968), 678–711.

13. Friedman, "The Role of Monetary Policy," p. 11.

14. If Equation (3.3a) is evaluated at steady state (that is, at $p' = p^{*'}$), $b_2 = 1$ implies: $(w' - p') = f(U)$. Any tradeoff is therefore between changes in real wages and unemployment (excess demand).

Passing a price function through (3.3a) illustrates the acceleration argument. Suppose p' follows the simple markup scheme $p' = w' - x'$, where x' = rate of change of labor productivity, and it is implicitly assumed that any asymmetry in the system

Since price expectations are not measured directly, empirical testing of (3.3a) requires that $p^{*\prime}$ be specified in terms of observable variables. The conventional practice is to use some function of actual price changes, p'. For annual data the hypothesis

$$p_t^{*\prime} = p_t'$$
(3.3b)

is not unreasonable. Expectations may be fully embodied in actual price changes averaged over a twelve-month period. This hypothesis was effectively tested by the estimation of Equation (3.2). The results (in the second column of Tables 3.1 through 3.4) provided strong support for the neoclassical or strict expectations argument. The hypothesis $b_2 = 1$ was rejected only for the United States.

A second model for price expectations is the unconstrained, finite autoregressive scheme:

$$p_t^{*\prime} = \sum_{i=0}^{} a_i p_{t-i}',$$
(3.3c)

in which expectations are generated by the weighted, finite sum of current and lagged price changes.

The third model tried in this study incorporates the adaptive expectations hypothesis:

$$p_t^{*\prime} - p_{t-1}^{*\prime} = (1 - a)(p_t' - p_{t-1}^{*\prime})$$

$$p_t^{*\prime} = (1 - a) \sum_{i=0}^{\infty} a^i p_{t-i}'$$

$$p_t^{*\prime} = \frac{1 - a}{1 - aL} p_t',$$
(3.3d)

where L is a lag operator.

In the adaptive model, price expectations are revised linearly each period in proportion to some fraction of last period's forecast error.

(which is necessary for the existence of a conventional tradeoff) occurs in the wage equation. Hence we have: $p' = (b_0 - x') + b_1(1/U) + b_2 p^{*\prime}$, which for $b_2 = 1$ implies: $dp'/dt = (1/p)(d^2p/dt^2) = f(U)$. The tradeoff is therefore between the rate of acceleration of inflation and the employment rate and requires that workers be continually "surprised" by new bursts of inflation ($p' > p^{*\prime}$).

The "natural rate" of unemployment is given by the root of the equation: $p' - p^{*\prime} = 0 = (b_0 - x') + b_1(1/U) = -b_1/(b_0 - x')$.

The model implies that expectations are governed by an exponentially weighted moving average of observed price changes.

Estimation of the price expectations Phillips curve models using the finite autoregressive and the adaptive schemes for $p^{*\prime}$ rendered essentially the same results; therefore, estimates of only the former scheme are reported in the third column of Tables 3.1 through 3.4.[15] The results for France, Great Britain, and the United States do not differ appreciably from the estimates of the Phillips-Lipsey model shown in column 2. The unemployment term again has the "wrong" sign in the regressions for France and Great Britain, and, more important, the sum of the price change coefficients is just about unity. However, in the case of Great Britain the sum of the autoregressive price coefficients (1.2) exceeds the contemporaneous price coefficient of Equation (3.2) (0.843) by a large enough margin to yield an increase in $\bar{R}^2$ and a decrease in standard error of the regression. The price expectations model estimates for the United States are essentially the same as those of the static Phillips-Lipsey equation: the parameter of the inverse of the unemployment rate is positive and significant, and the elasticity of wages with respect to prices is on the order of 0.6.[16]

The estimate of the sum of the price change coefficients for Italy represents the most important departure from previous results. The coefficient of contemporaneous price changes, $p_t^\prime$, in Equation (3.2) was 1.65, that is, substantially larger than unity. This, of course, implies that every burst of price inflation is followed by a sizable increase in real wages—an implausible result.[17] The sum of the coefficients of the $p_{t-1}^\prime$ in column 3 of Table 3.1 shows that the *long-run* elasticity of wages with respect to prices in Italy is not significantly different from 1.0. The time path of the price coefficients—substantially greater than unity at time (t), negative at times ($t - 1$) and ($t -$

15. I tested the adaptive price expectations version by estimating the implied nonlinear equation: $w_t^\prime = b_0(1 - a) + aw_{t-1}^\prime + b_1(1/U_t) - b_1a(1/U_{t-1}) + b_2(1 - a)p_t^\prime$. The estimate of b_2 was approximately unity in the regressions for Italy, France, and Great Britain. I experimented with lags of various lengths in the finite autoregressive expectations models; the tables report the best-fitting equation.

16. I ran a number of additional experiments for the United States to test the idea (which appears from time to time in the literature) that the coefficient of adjustment is closer to unity once a critical threshold in observed rates of price inflation is reached. I could find little support for this appealing hypothesis.

17. Adding the rate of change of labor productivity to the contemporaneous price change model for Italy does not appreciably alter this result: the parameter estimate of $p_t^\prime$ is 1.6 and the productivity term is insignificant. Adding productivity to the equations for the other countries did not yield anything worth reporting either.

2)—does indicate, however, that in the Italian system prices are more or less continually chasing wages.[18] Clearly there is little evidence of neo-Keynesian money illusion.[19]

Why is the United States the only industrial society of the four considered here to exhibit a viable Phillips curve?[20] I doubt that it is because workers and/or union leaders in the United States, unlike their Italian, French, and British counterparts, suffer from money illusion. In other words, I think it is unlikely, particularly in the manufacturing sector, that a sizable fraction of the labor force in any industrial society is fooled by (or prizes to a significant degree) money wage increases alone. A more plausible model would specify that the elasticity of *target* wages with respect to *expected* prices is unity, or very nearly so, at least in industrial labor markets. If this idea has merit, then international variation in the rate and equilibrium magnitude of the adjustment of *observed* wages to price inflation reflects to some extent differences in the power of trade unions to obtain target wage increases, rather than money illusion in labor markets.[21]

18. The period-by-period price coefficients are: $p'_t = 1.89$, $p'_{t-1} = -0.18$, and $p'_{t-2} = -0.48$.

19. As in other studies of wage inflation, there is some danger that the price coefficients reported here suffer from (simultaneous equations) bias. It is unlikely that this accounts for the pattern of results, but the only way to sort the matter out definitively would be to employ a correctly specified "large" econometric model in which wages, prices, and employment were jointly endogenous. I take heart in the fact that according to Ezio Tarantelli, economist at the University of Florence and consultant to the Bank of Rome, prices also "chase wages" in the bank's econometric model of Italy.

20. I do not mean to imply that the U.S. Phillips curve has been stable over the postwar period; there is a great deal of evidence that it has not. See, for example, the comparative analysis by R. J. Gordon, "Wage-Price Controls and the Shifting Phillips Curve," *Brookings Papers on Economic Activity* (1972:2), 385–421.

21. I am not saying that if trade unions did not exist the elasticity of wages in relation to prices would be zero. This is an absurd argument. Trade union power presumably makes a difference on the margin; but the margin may be important enough to determine whether there is a viable Phillips curve tradeoff. If equations in the form of (3.3) were estimated for a large number of countries (or sectors or industries—see note 22), then analyses of the following sort in principle could be undertaken: $a_i = A + g(X_{ki})$, where a_i = the long-run elasticity of observed wages with respect to prices in the ith country (sector or industry), A = pure "market" component, $g(X_{ki})$ = union "power" component, and X_{ki} = a vector of variables measuring the (relative) wage bargaining power of trade unions.

A similar model might be specified for the rate of wage adjustment, which might exhibit greater international (intersectoral, interindustry) variation. Obviously the job of identifying and measuring X_{ki} and specifying g would not be trivial. Until serious studies along these lines are undertaken, the argument in the text will remain largely speculative.

Recall that the pattern of results for the elasticity of wages with respect to prices across the four countries was:

Italy
full wage adjustment to price inflation in the long run;
"prices chasing wages" in the short run

Great Britain and France
full and more or less instantaneous (annual) wage adjustment to price inflation

United States
less than full long-run wage adjustment;
viable Phillips curve

If one adopts the hypothesis that wage adjustment dynamics in part reflect the power of organized labor in collective bargaining, these results imply that (in the manufacturing sector at least) trade unions are most powerful in Italy, strong in Great Britain and France, and comparatively weak in the United States.[22] Without attempting to discuss or reference the voluminous literature here, I think it is accurate to say that this rough rank ordering is consistent with the qualitative assessment of most industrial relations specialists about the comparative strength in wage bargaining of organized labor in these countries.[23]

Perhaps the best way to illustrate international differences in trade union power is to contrast briefly the situation in the two polar cases—Italy and the United States. In Italy it is extremely difficult for employers, even if hard pressed, to dismiss workers. Moreover, the wages of most workers (nearly all in the manufacturing sector) are pegged to the cost of living, and escalator wage adjustment (*scala mobile*) takes place every three months. More dramatic examples of institutionalized trade union power are difficult to find. By contrast, in the United States there are virtually no constraints on employers' rights to discharge workers for economic reasons, and only the

22. My interpretation of these results is compatible with intranational, cross-sectional studies finding that the elasticity of wages with respect to prices is higher in strongly unionized industries than in weakly organized sectors. See G. Pierson, "The Effect of Union Strength on the U.S. Phillips Curve," *American Economic Review*, 57, (1968), 456–467; J. Vanderkamp, "Wage and Price Level Determination: An Empirical Model for Canada," *Economica*, 33 (1966), 194–212; and R. L. Thomas, "Wage Inflation in the UK: A Multi-Market Approach," in *Inflation and Labour Markets*, ed. D. Laidler and D. Purdy (Manchester, England: Manchester University Press).

23. Note that in Italy and France, where the state is an important actor in the (private- as well as public-sector) labor market—that is, it is involved in setting wages, hours, and conditions of work—trade union power to a great extent consists in the ability to induce concessions from the government.

strongest and most innovative unions have tried (with limited success) to bargain for cost-of-living wage escalator clauses. Wage adjustment takes place almost wholly via periodic contract renegotiation. It is hardly surprising, therefore, that the response of wages to price inflation in the United States is both less rapid and less complete than in Italy.

Sociological Cost-Push Models

It was noted at the beginning of this chapter that the excess demand class of wage inflation models is easily rationalized from a cost-push or collective bargaining theoretical perspective.[24] The empirical results presented in the previous section were to some extent interpreted from this point of view. The purpose of this section is to determine whether explicit indicators of union aggressiveness or labor militancy have significant influence on the rate of change of wages independently of price movements and unemployment—in other words, whether autonomous trade union actions exert significant upward pressure on money wages, or whether discrete expressions of union militancy merely represent a form of ritualized conflict ratifying outcomes that market forces would have produced in any case. A variety of direct and proxy measures have appeared in the sociological cost-push literature; the principal ones are:

1. the level and rate of change of profits
2. the rate of change of the proportion of the labor force in trade unions
3. subjective (ad hoc) estimates of labor militancy
4. strike activity

The relevant models and empirical results are presented below.

Profit-Augmented Wage Change Models

Among the first to challenge Phillips-type excess demand models of wage inflation and to propose an alternative collective bargaining theory in which profits played a central role was Kaldor. Kaldor ar-

---

24. A more sustained argument along these lines is given by A. Rees, "The Phillips Curve as a Menu for Policy Choice," *Economica*, 37 (1970), 227–238.

gued that "the rise in money wages depends on the *bargaining strength* of labor; and bargaining strength, in turn, is closely related to the prosperity of industry, which determines both the eagerness of labour to demand higher wages and the willingness and ability of employers to grant them."[25] By prosperity Kaldor clearly meant the rate of change of profits: "The rise in wages is prompted by the rise in profits."[26]

Kaldor's rather casually formulated theory was followed by a series of empirical studies testing the impact of profits and the rate of change of profits on the rate of wage inflation.[27] These studies produced rather mixed results; hence the thesis that movements in profits are an important influence on wage changes remains problematic.

Comparative results for a profits-augmented manufacturing wage inflation model are reported in the fourth column of Tables 3.1 through 3.4 and are based on the equation:

$$w'_t = b_0 + b_1(1/U_t) + \sum_i a_i p'_{t-i} + b_2 \frac{(R/Y_t)}{(R/W)} + b_3 \frac{(\Delta R/Y_t)}{(\Delta R/W)} \quad (3.4)$$

where R/Y = manufacturing profits as a percentage of gross income produced (Italy, Great Britain),

R/W = manufacturing profits as a percentage of employee compensation (United States),

and all other terms are as previously defined.

The regression estimates give little or no support to the profits thesis.[28] The profit level term R/Y is significant but has the wrong sign

25. N. Kaldor, "Economic Growth and the Problem of Inflation," *Economica*, 26 (1959), 293.

26. Ibid., p. 294.

27. W. G. Bowen, *The Wage-Price Issue: A Theoretical Analysis* (Princeton: Princeton University Press); R. G. Lipsey and M. D. Stueuer, "The Relation between Profits and Wage Rates," *Economica*, 28 (1961), 137–155; R. J. Bahatia, "Unemployment and the Rate of Change of Money Earnings in the United States, 1900–1958," *Economica*, 28 (1961), 286–296; G. L. Perry, "The Determinants of Wage Rates Changes and the Inflation-Unemployment Tradeoff for the United States," *Review of Economic Studies*, 31 (1964), 287–308; and R. L. Bodkin, *The Wage, Price, Productivity Nexus* (Philadelphia: University of Pennsylvania Press, 1966). There is no unique measure of the level of profits. Profits as a percentage of stockholders' equity, the ratio of profits to wage income, and the ratio of profits to total income produced are all acceptable indicators. The various measures generally point in the same direction.

28. Because I was unable to find manufacturing profits data for France, no results are reported in column 4 of Table 3.2.

(negative) in the equation for Italy; elsewhere the level of profits and the rate of change of profits variables have negligible, perversely signed coefficients and very small t-statistics.[29]

Contrary to Kaldor's argument, these results indicate that in the presence of unemployment and (especially) price inflation variables, the profits terms have no systematic influence on the rate of wage inflation. Either union bargaining strength and militancy have no appreciable effect on wage movements or profits variables are poor proxies for these concepts. Evidence presented later in this chapter suggests the latter is true.

Wage Inflation and Trade Union Mobilization

Perhaps the most forceful and influential argument that trade unions affect the rate of change of wages independently of the demand for labor was made in a series of papers by A. G. Hines.[30] In his celebrated 1964 article on wage inflation in the United Kingdom over the period 1893–1961, Hines showed that one measure of union aggressiveness—the rate of change in the percentage of the labor force unionized—accounted for a sizable fraction of the variation in the rate of change of wages. Indeed, in the interwar and early postwar years, it appeared to be the most important explanatory variable.[31] Hines rationalized the use of changes in the density of unionization as a proxy for labor aggressiveness with the assumption that militancy is simultaneously manifested in union recruiting drives and pressure on wage rates: "a successful membership drive [is] a necessary accompaniment of success in the wage bargain."[32]

Hines's thesis implies a model of the form:

$$w'_t = b_0 + b_1(1/U_t) + \sum_i a_i p'_{t-i} + b_2 \Delta T/L_t, \qquad (3.5)$$

29. Models in which the profits terms were lagged performed no better. Notice also the large, implausible constants in the equations for Italy and Great Britain.

30. A. G. Hines, "Trade Unions and Wage Inflation in the United Kingdom, 1893–1961," *Review of Economic Studies*, 31 (October 1964), 221–252, and "Wage Inflation in the United Kingdom, 1948–1962: A Disaggregated Study," *Economic Journal*, 79 (March 1969), 66–89.

31. Hines's last postwar observation was 1961. The importance of this will become clear in the following discussion. Similar results were reported by O. C. Aschenfelter, G. E. Johnson, and J. H. Pencavel, "Trade Unions and the Rate of Change of Money Wages in United States Manufacturing Industry," *Review of Economic Studies*, 39 (1972), 127–154, a study of manufacturing wage changes in the United States during the period 1914–1963.

32. Hines, "Trade Unions and Wage Inflation," pp. 67–68.

where T/L = trade union membership (T) as a percentage of the labor force (L). Since union membership data for France and Italy are very unreliable, and, more important, the meaning of unionization in these countries is not comparable to that in other Western labor movements,[33] Equation (3.5) was estimated only for Great Britain and the United States. The results appear in column 5 of Tables 3.3 and 3.4.

The regression estimates yield only weak support for the trade union mobilization hypothesis: the coefficient of $\Delta T/L$ is properly signed in both regressions but is insignificant in the equation for Great Britain and only marginally significant in the U.S. model.

Why do these estimates contrast so sharply with the impressive results of the studies by Hines and by Ashenfelter et al.? The reason undoubtedly is that by the mid or late 1950s union mobilization was more or less complete and the small observed fluctuations in the density of union membership no longer served as a very good proxy for variations in labor militancy in wage bargaining. Models incorporating what I think are more direct indicators of labor militancy are introduced in the next section.

Strike Activity and Wage Inflation

Outbursts of strike activity since the late 1960s in Italy, France, Great Britain, and several other countries have led to renewed attempts to incorporate labor aggressiveness explicitly into models of wage inflation. The most recent effort is Perry's comparative study.[34] Perry called attention to the increased militancy over wage issues in the late 1960s and early 1970s, formulated a "battle over income shares" interpretation of labor unrest, and, on the argument that the shares hypothesis could not be captured by a continuous variable, introduced dummy variables for the years of wage explosions in the equations for the seven countries in his sample. Although the "shares" dummy variables generally increased the fits and enhanced the forecasting

33. In Great Britain, the United States, and most other Western systems union "members" include all workers covered by contract who merely pay dues, typically via an automatic checkoff (payroll deduction) method. In contrast, "members" of the largest (Communist) unions in France and Italy are usually militant activists (although in recent years French and Italian Communist trade unions have tried to become mass organizations). The strength of French and Italian unions is probably judged better by the number of workers they can mobilize for an activity rather than by the number of their official members.

34. G. L. Perry, "Determinants of Wage Inflation around the World," *Brookings Papers on Economic Activity* (1975:2).

performance of his wage models, Perry's approach is purely ad hoc and is therefore of limited scientific value.[35]

A more more straightforward measure of trade union militancy or aggressiveness in wage bargaining is strike activity. A number of earlier studies incorporated strike indicators into wage determination models and the results typically supported the militancy hypothesis.[36] The principal exception, and an important one, is the comparative study by Ward and Zis. They concluded from their analysis of postwar wage inflation in six countries that "the evidence . . . does not seem to support strongly the cost-push [strike] hypothesis."[37] Actually, Ward and Zis's conclusion is somewhat misleading: their regressions showed one or more strike indicators to be significant variables in three of the six countries. Moreover, the Ward and Zis study suffers from at least three important limitations:

1. An explicit scheme for strike measurement is never introduced, and there is heavy reliance on the arbitrary index developed by Galombos and Evans.[38]

2. Data on the strike indicators pertain to economywide aggregates, whereas the wage data are for the manufacturing sector.[39]

35. Predictably, the arbitrary character of Perry's test of the militancy-shares hypothesis was pointed out during the discussion of his paper. See the comments by Ackley and Nordhaus in the same issue. For an earlier attempt to build subjective estimates of trade union militancy into wage inflation models, see L. A. Dicks-Mireau and J. C. Dow, "The Determinants of Wage Inflation in the United Kingdom: 1946–1956," *Journal of the Royal Statistical Society*, 72 (1959).

36. See Aschenfelter, Johnson, and Pencavel "Trade Unions and The Rate of Change of Money Wages" (United States); K. G. Knight, "Strikes and Wage Inflation in British Manufacturing Industry 1950–1968," *Bulletin of Oxford University Institute of Economics and Statistics*, 34 (August 1972), 281–294; Sylos-Labini, *Trade Unions*, (Italy); J. Taylor, "Incomes Policy, the Structure of Unemployment and the Phillips Curve: The United Kingdom Experience: 1953–70," in *Incomes Policy and Inflation*, ed. M. Parkin and M. T. Sumner (Manchester, England: Manchester University Press, 1972); J. Taylor, *Unemployment and Wage Inflation with Special Reference to the USA* (London: Longman Press, 1974) (Great Britain, United States); and R. Swidinsky, "Trade Unions and the Rate of Change of Money Wages in Canada, 1953–1970," *Industrial and Labor Review*, 25 (1972). An extended qualitative discussion of the British case is provided by D. Jackson, H. A. Turner, and F. Wilkinson, *Do Trade Unions Cause Inflation?* (Cambridge: Cambridge University Press, 1972).

37. R. Ward and G. Zis, "Trade Union Militancy as an Explanation of Inflation: An International Comparison," *Manchester School*, March 1966, p. 55.

38. P. Galombos and E. W. Evans, "Work-Stoppages in the United Kingdom, 1951–1964: A Quantitative Study," *Bulletin of the Oxford University Institute of Statistics*, 28 (1966); see K. G. J. C. Knowles, "Work-Stoppages in the United Kingdom: A Comment," in the same journal for a thorough critique of the Galombos and Evans indices.

39. This is also true of other studies of strikes and wage inflation; see the sources cited in note 36.

3. Only contemporaneous strike activity appears in the wage equations, yet strike-induced wage increases are often not fully observed until a year or more has elapsed.

The first objection raised above suggests that it is important to
develop a conceptual scheme for strike measurement before under-
taking empirical analysis. The International Labor Office compiles
and publishes data on three basic components of industrial conflict
that are supplied by the national labor ministries: the number of
strikes, the number of workers involved (strikers), and the number of
worker-days lost in strike activity. Annual data on these components
are reported for economywide totals and for nine separate sectors of
economic activity. Here we are interested only in manufacturing
strike activity.

As in Chapter 1,[40] the basic industrial conflict variables are used in
conjunction with data on manufacturing wage and salary employment to form three theoretically distinct dimensions of strike activity:
the average *size* of strikes (that is, the number of workers involved per
strike), the average *duration* of strikes (that is, worker-days lost per
worker involved), and a labor force–adjusted measure of strike *frequency* (that is, the number of strikes per number of manufacturing
employees). Cost-push models incorporating these strike dimension
variables as the indicators of labor militancy in wage bargaining were
estimated in the following general form:

$$w'_t = b_0 + b_1(1/U_t) + \sum_i a_i p'_{t-i} + \sum_{ji} c_{ji} S_{jt-i}, \tag{3.6}$$

where S_j = manufacturing sector strike dimension variables. Regression experiments based on Equation (3.6) were tried for various combinations of strike variables and time lags. On a priori grounds I
expected strike volume (worker-days lost per number of manufacturing employees) and strike frequency (the number of strikes per number of manufacturing employees) to have the biggest effects on movements in wages—strike volume because it is the most comprehensive
indicator of labor militancy, and strike frequency because it represents the number of aggressive labor actions of whatever duration

40. See K. Forchheimer, "Some International Aspects of the Strike Movement,"
Oxford University Institute of Statistics Bulletin, 10 (January 1948); K. G. J. C. Knowles,
Strikes—A Study in Industrial Conflict (Oxford: Basil Blackwell, 1952); and Edward
Shorter and Charles Tilly, "The Shape of Strikes in France, 1830–1960," *Comparative
Studies in Society and History*, 13 (January 1971), 60–86. See also the text in Chapter 1 on
the method used to compute strike volume in Figure 1.1.

and size.[41] Strike size depends largely on the scale of firms or, more important, on the scale of the bargaining unit; therefore, it was not anticipated to exhibit any systematic influence on wage inflation. Increases in strike duration beyond a certain (and probably rather low) threshold are unlikely to influence the wage settlement substantially and in most cases probably reflects the stubbornness of the parties in accepting the inevitable outcome. So I did not expect duration to be a very strong predictor of wage charges either.

Although the logic of these a priori hunches may be faulty, they were strongly supported by the empirical results: the coefficient estimates in column 6a of Tables 3.1 through 3.4 show that in each of the four countries strike volume or strike frequency or both had sizable and significant effects on the rate of wage inflation. In every case the strike equations yield a substantially higher corrected multiple correlation and a lower standard error of the regression than do the rival models discussed earlier. With the exception of the strike frequency variable in the regression for France, a one-year lag on the strike terms produced the best fits.[42] Because official statistics on French strike activity in 1968 have never been published, the model for France includes a dummy (binary) variable to pick up the effects of the great May–June 1968 general strike. The coefficient of the dummy variable implies that the 1968 strike wave produced an increase in manufacturing hourly wages between 7 and 8 percent greater than what would have otherwise been expected.[43]

The excess demand term, $1/U$, remained insignificant in the equations for Italy and France and dropped to insignificance in the U.S. regression.[44] Hence the inverse of the unemployment rate variable was deleted from the equations for these countries. (Estimates for the revised wage models are reported in columns 6b and 6c of the tables.) In the strikes model for Great Britain, however, the $1/U$ term (for the first time) achieves significance; that is, net of strike volume and

41. The occurrence of a strike depends of course to a certain extent on the behavior of both labor and management (and/or government), but the vast majority of strikes are labor initiated.

42. Frequency data for the manufacturing sector were not available for France; therefore, the economywide frequency is used as a proxy.

43. This estimate appears to be right on target. The agreement that ended the 1968 workers' strike, the Protocole de Grenelle, provided for wage increases of 4.5 to 5 percent on June 1, and another 2.5 to 3 percent on October 1.

44. Since large fractions of the Italian and French labor forces were until recent years employed in agriculture, a nonagricultural unemployment rate variable was also tried in the equations for these countries; however, this alternative measure of the demand for labor did not yield significantly different results.

strike frequency, the level of excess demand for labor appears to exert significant influence on the rate of wage inflation. It has been suggested that the breakdown of the unemployment–wage inflation connection in Great Britain, which was first noticed in the late 1960s, was due in part to upward adjustments in unemployment compensation initiated by the Labour government in the latter part of 1966.[45] However, the results for model 6b in Table 3.3 show that the location and slope of $1/U_t$ are stable over the post-1967 period. The reason for the revival of the $1/U_t$ term is, I believe, that the usual inverse association between unemployment and labor militancy[46] broke down in Great Britain in the mid-1960s (perhaps because of the change in unemployment compensation emphasized by Feldstein and others). Thus Great Britain experienced steadily increasing strike activity in the face of rising measured unemployment. Only after the effects of strike activity are netted out does the excess demand–wage inflation linkage in Great Britain show up in the regressions.[47] This implies that the tightness of labor markets (level of aggregate demand) has contributed to the postwar British inflation.

The coefficients of the rate of change of prices are generally smaller in the strike equations than in the expectations models discussed earlier. These results are not surprising in view of the sizable correlations among the strike and price variables (discussed in more detail later). What they suggest is that the more or less complete adjustment of wages to prices observed in the pure expectations models for France and Great Britain, as well as the partial adjustment estimated for the United States, depends importantly on labor militancy as well as on trade union "power." In other words, trade union strike action has been an essential mechanism for the adjustment of wages to prices in these countries.

In contrast, the results of the strike equations for Italy show that the sum of the price coefficients is still essentially unity—indeed, as noted earlier, prices typically are chasing wages.[48] This implies that full wage adjustment in Italy does not hinge directly on the incidence

45. See M. Feldstein, "The Economics of the New Unemployment," *Public Interest*, 33 (1973), 3–42.

46. On this point see Chapter 1 and the sources cited therein.

47. The correlation between measured unemployment and strike activity is strongly positive during the latter postwar years in Great Britain. The conclusion in the text is readily demonstrated by means of standard specification error algebra.

48. That is, the p'_t coefficient is substantially greater than 1.0 and the p'_{t-2} coefficient is sizable and negative.

of strike activity, which squares with the observations made earlier about the power of Italian trade unions.

Since strike activity is known to be influenced by current and lagged values of unemployment and prices, perhaps the strike terms in Equation (3.6) merely register the effects of these omitted economic variables. To guard against this possibility, quasi-reduced form regressions, including appropriately lagged unemployment and price inflation terms, were estimated.[49] The results appear in column 7 of Tables 3.1 through 3.4. Although the t-statistics of the strike variables are generally smaller in these regressions, it is clear that the strike activity coefficients are very robust in the face of a rather severe test.[50] It seems very unlikely, then, that the estimated influence of labor militancy on wage inflation merely reflects the effects of present or past states of aggregate economic activity.

Just how important are the labor militancy terms relative to the macroeconomic variables in explaining wage inflation? There are several ways to approach this question. One method is to look at the "beta" or standardized regression coefficients. (The square of these coefficients gives the proportion of the variance of the rate of change of wages that can be uniquely attributed to a particular variable.) Beta coefficients for each term in the best strike-augmented wage equation are reported in Table 3.5.[51] Although the beta coefficients of the strike terms are somewhat smaller than those of the macroeconomic variables, they are sizable and show that a nontrivial proportion of the variation in wage inflation is due to fluctuations in strike activity. However, this much was already fairly clear from earlier results—the strike wage equations exhibited substantially higher $\bar{R}^2$s than alternative models.

A better way of assessing the relative importance of labor militancy is to compute the products of ordinary regression coefficients and the

49. Because previous research indicates that the untransformed unemployment rate, U, is the best predictor of strike activity, this variable is used in the regressions. The time index on U corresponds to the time index, and the index lagged one period, of the strike variable(s). For example, if the strike variable appears in the original equation at time $(t - 1)$, U_{t-1} and U_{t-2}, enter the quasi-reduced form regression. The price inflation variables are specified at time (t), $(t - 1)$, and $(t - 2)$.

50. Since strike activity responds to prior movements in real wages rather than to those in money wages, quasi-reduced form regressions in which real wage change terms replaced the price terms were also estimated. Again, the strike activity coefficients were robust.

51. The best strike models from Table 3.1 are (3.6b) for Italy, (3.6c) for France, (3.6a) for Great Britain, and (3.6c) for the United States.

Table 3.5. Relative importance of unemployment, prices, and strike activity in structural models of wage inflation (based on results of Equations 3.6–3.6c).

Country	F_t	F_{t-1}	V_{t-1}	$1/U_t$	p'_t	p'_{t-1}	p'_{t-2}
Italy							
beta coefficient	—	—	0.411	—	0.576	0.152	−0.302
$b_i\bar{X}_i$ (1955–64)	—	—	1.38	—	4.91	1.23	−2.12
$b_i\bar{X}_i$ (1965–74)	—	—	3.27	—	7.87	1.77	−3.54
France[a]							
beta coefficient	0.375	—	0.319	—	0.644	—	—
$b_i\bar{X}_i$ (1955–64)	4.51	—	0.900	—	3.09	—	—
$b_i\bar{X}_i$ (1965–74)	5.03	—	1.03	—	3.69	—	—
Great Britain							
beta coefficient	—	0.529	0.392	0.460	0.578	—	—
$b_i\bar{X}_i$ (1955–64)	—	1.28	1.27	4.48	2.04	—	—
$b_i\bar{X}_i$ (1965–74)	—	3.80	2.18	2.98	4.55	—	—
United States							
beta coefficient	—	0.406	—	—	0.591	—	—
$b_i\bar{X}_i$ (1955–64)	—	3.45	—	—	0.716	—	—
$b_i\bar{X}_i$ (1965–74)	—	3.71	—	—	2.30	—	—

Note: F = strike frequency; V = strike volume; p' = percentage rate of change of prices; U = employment rate; $b_i\bar{X}_i$ = regression coefficient × mean.
a. Excludes contribution of 1968 strike wave.

means of the associated variables over the time intervals of interest. The second and third rows of Table 3.5 show the resulting estimates, that is, the average impact of unemployment, prices, and strike activity on the rate of wage inflation, for two periods: 1955–1964 and 1965–74.

Again, it is obvious from the $b_i\bar{X}_i$ quantities that the strike variables have contributed importantly to the rate of increase of manufacturing wages during the postwar period. Contrary to what I had expected, though, there is no general sign that the strike terms have had greater relative effects on the upward movement of wages during the later period (1965–1974) than during the earlier one (1955–1964). However, the relative effects of the strike activity variables do exhibit a cross-national pattern that reinforces previous remarks concerning the role of labor militancy versus trade union power in the wage inflation process. The best way to reveal the pattern is to take the ratio of the strike activity average wage inflation effects to the average impact attributed to the macroeconomic terms, that is, to calculate $b_i\bar{X}_i$ (strikes)/$b_i\bar{X}_i$ (macroeconomy).

Table 3.6 gives the results, which are based on the data in Table 3.5. The average impact ratios indicate that in both subperiods strike activity was more important than the macroeconomic variables in explaining wage inflation in the United States and less important in Italy. France and Great Britain fall between these extreme cases, although the French ratio implies that, as in the United States, strikes were more important than the macroeconomy in generating upward movements in manufacturing wages, whereas the British ratio, as in the case of Italy, implies the reverse.[52]

Since the impact ratios are essentially the ratio of strike effects to price effects,[53] if one accepts the interpretation presented earlier that the price coefficients reflect in part the power of trade unions in wage bargaining, then the ratios give a rough quantitative estimate of the influence of labor militancy relative to union power on wage inflation. Hence the country rank order in Table 3.6 is in *inverse* relation to trade union power: the greater the effect of (reliance on?) strike activity in wage determination, the less the power of trade unions, and vice versa.[54] Table 3.6 therefore implies that Italy > Great Britain > France > United States with respect to the relative power of trade unions in wage bargaining.

Cross-national differences aside, the influence of strike activity on wage movements may cause surprise. It is often pointed out, for example, that working time lost from illness is substantially greater than time lost from industrial disputes. Of course, time lost from sickness does not lead to upward movements in wages; time lost from strikes does. In a more serious vein, there are at least two reasons why strike activity exerts sizable effects on the rate of inflation.[55] First, wage settlements obtained by one union or unionized sector often become the wage bargaining targets of other unions, either in an absolute sense, or in a relative sense as other groups of workers

52. Unless the contribution of unemployment (excess demand) is excluded from the calculation of macroeconomic effects in Britain.

53. With the partial exception of Great Britain, where the strike model includes $1/U_t$.

54. The results in Table 3.6 are of course not altogether independent of the pattern in the price coefficient estimates. To a certain extent the table is just another way of making the earlier point about international differences in trade union power. (As one reviewer of this essay pointed out, it probably would have been better to view labor power and labor militancy as independent features of industrial relations rather than as competing dimensions, as I implicitly do here.

55. Taylor, *Unemployment and Wage Inflation*, covers similar ground.

Table 3.6. Average impact ratios from strike-augmented wage equations
(ratio of strike effects to macroeconomic price effects).

Country	1955–1964	1965–1974
United States	4.81	1.61
France	1.75	1.64[a]
Great Britain	0.39	0.79
	(1.25)[b]	(1.31)[c]
Italy	0.34	0.54

Note: For method, see text.
a. 1968 strike wave not included in strike effects.
b. Excluding $1/U_t$ from macroeconomic effects.
c. Excluding $1/U_t$ from macroeconomic effects.

attempt to maintain established wage differentials. This has been
emphasized in Eckstein and Wilson's "key industries" theory of wage
movements in the U.S. manufacturing sector.[56] Wage settlements in
one industry or sector of the economy therefore have proportional
effects elsewhere through parity bargaining. Second, wage rates ne-
gotiated in unionized plants (strike-induced or not) are known to
influence nonunion wage settlements. If employers of unorganized
workers did not raise wages in line with the pattern established by
union settlements, they would risk losing workers and, perhaps more
important, expose themselves to the threat of unionization. This
threat is particularly important in the United States, where nearly half
of the manufacturing labor force remains unorganized.

The estimation range for the wage regressions in Tables 3.1
through 3.4 was not taken beyond the year 1972, so that the 1973–
1975 observations could be used for forecasting. Actual, fitted, and
forecast values of manufacturing wage changes in the four countries
are plotted in Figures 3.1 through 3.4. Clearly, the fitted data points
from the strike equations track the actual wage change observations
rather well, reflecting the relatively high multiple correlations reported earlier. More important, the forecasting performance of the
strike models is also reasonably good, especially in view of the fact
that the forecast range coincides with exogenous inflationary shocks
of unprecedented magnitude—the extraordinary rise in food prices
and the OPEC-induced quadrupling of petroleum prices. No doubt

56. O. Eckstein and T. Wilson, "Determination of Wages in American Industry,"
Quarterly Journal of Economics, 76 (1962), 1379–1414.

Table 3.7. Forecast errors from expectations and strike-augmented wage equations, 1973–1975 (percentage per year).

	Expectations (Eq. 3.3)	Strikes (Eq. 3.6)
Italy		
Average error	−2.08	−0.78
RMSE	4.61	4.37
France (1973–74)		
Average error	1.04	2.13
RMSE	1.59	3.01
Great Britain		
Average error	−3.42	−1.03
RMSE	3.73	1.52
United States		
Average error	0.83	1.19
RMSE	1.68	1.34

Note: RMSE = root mean square error.

this is why the strike models for all countries except the United States (where the impact of international oil price increases was less severe than in Europe) generate comparatively large forecast errors in either 1973 or 1974; the 1975 forecasts are uniformly more accurate.[57]

A better way to evaluate the predictive performance of the strike-augmented wage equations is to make comparisons with the forecasts of an alternative model. The leading rival model is, of course, the price expectations Phillips curve of Equation (3.3). Table 3.7 reports the average and root mean square errors (RMSEs) forecast for each model. The strike models are clearly superior to the price expectations equations for Italy, Great Britain, and, in terms of RMSE, the United States. Only in the case of France does the expectations equation yield lower average and RMSE forecast errors. Perhaps the pure expectations model is a better approximation of the wage formation process in that country. My own belief (or, more accurately, prejudice) is that the particular forecast range (1973–74) and the fact that economywide strike frequency had to serve as a proxy for manufacturing strike frequency in the regressions for France underlies this outcome. Indeed, I was somewhat surprised that the strike equations generally

57. Because strike data for France were not available for 1975, it was not possible to generate a 1975 forecast.

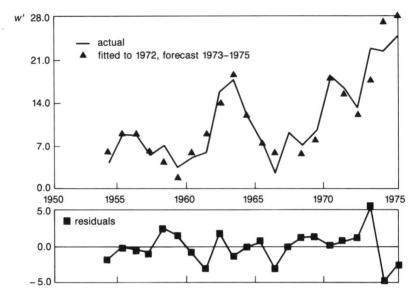

Figure 3.1.   Italy: Actual, fitted, and forecast values of manufacturing money wage changes, 1954–1975. (From Equation 3.6b.)

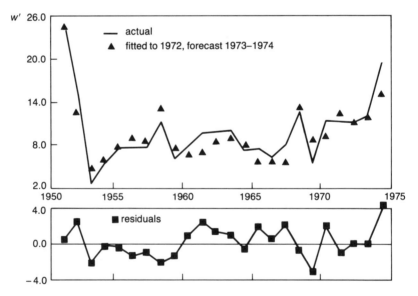

Figure 3.2.   France: Actual, fitted, and forecast values of manufacturing money wage changes, 1951–1974. (From Equation 3.6c.)

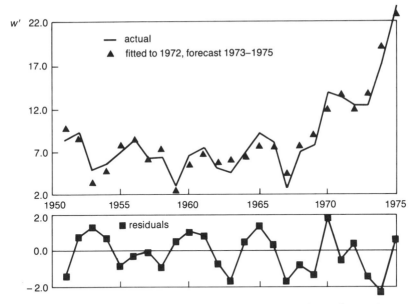

Figure 3.3.   Great Britain: Actual, fitted, and forecast values of manufacturing wage changes, 1951–1975. (From Equation 3.6a.)

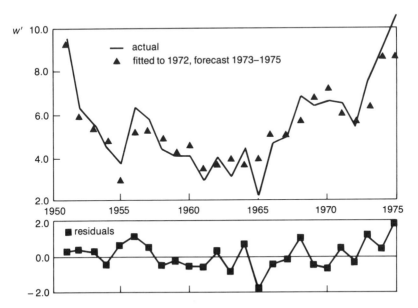

Figure 3.4.   United States: Actual, fitted, and forecast values of manufacturing wage changes, 1951–1975. (From Equation 3.6c.)

outperformed the pure expectations equations for three of the four countries in forecasting over the period 1973–1975. The major inflationary impulse during these years came from international prices, which would seem to give considerable (short-run) predictive advantage to autoregressive price expectation models. Therefore, I take the forecasting performance of the strike equations to be rather strong evidence that labor militancy should be incorporated into structural models of wage inflation.

Implications for the Acceleration and Stability of Wages and Prices

Do the strike model regressions yield any evidence that labor militancy has contributed to the *acceleration* of wages and prices experienced by all four countries since the late 1960s? Insofar as the *domestic labor market* is concerned, a steady or declining rate of inflation can be maintained if the rate of change of money wages does not exceed the rate of change of prices plus the rate of change of labor productivity. In other words, barring changes in employment, nonlabor costs, and the factor distribution of income, a sustained escalation of the rate of inflation will occur when the rate of change of real wages chronically runs ahead of the rate of change of labor productivity.

Consider the following simple system. The rate of change of money wages is determined by the strike-augmented wage model discussed in the previous section:

$$w'_t = b_0 + b_1(1/U_t) + \sum_i a_i p'_{t-i} + \sum_{j,i} c_{ji} S_{t-i}. \tag{3.7}$$

Short-run price changes are assumed to follow the markup scheme:

$$p'_t = (w' - x')_{t-1} + m'_{t-1}, \tag{3.8a}$$

where x' = the rate of change of labor productivity,
  m' = the rate of change of nonlabor costs, principally raw materials,
  and other terms are as defined earlier.

Substituting for w' in the pricing model gives:

$$p'_t = b_0 + b_1(1/U_{t-1}) + \sum_i a_i p'_{t-i-1}$$
$$+ c_{ji} S_{t-i-1} - x'_{t-1} + m'_{t-1}. \tag{3.8b}$$

Moving $a_0 p'_{t-1}$ to the lefthand side and subtracting $(1 - a_0) p'_{t-1}$ from both sides of the equation yields an expression for the rate of acceleration of prices, $\Delta p'$:

$$\Delta p'_t = b_0 + b_1(1/U_t) - (1 - a_0) p'_{t-1} + a_1 p'_{t-2} + \cdots$$
$$+ a_k p'_{t-k-1} + \sum_{i,j} c_{ji}S_{t-i-1} - x'_{t-1} + m'_{t-1}. \tag{3.8c}$$

It will prove useful to rewrite the price acceleration function as follows:

$$\Delta p'_t = S^* + Z + m'_{t-1}, \tag{3.8d}$$

where $\quad S^* = \sum_{i,j} c_{ji}S_{t-i-1}$
$$Z = b_0 + b_1(1/U_t) - (1 - a_0) p'_{t-1} + \ldots + a_k p'_{t-k-1} - x'_{t-1}.$$

It is now clear that labor militancy can be pinpointed as a source of *accelerating* prices if S^* (the strike activity wage change effect) is nonzero and $(S^* + Z) > 0$.[58] For example, suppose $\sum_i a_i = a_0$ and $m' = b_0 = b_1 = 0$, which leads to a price acceleration function:

$$\Delta P'_t = S^* + Z$$
$$= \sum_{i,j} c_{ji}S_{t-i-1} - (1 - a_0) p'_{t-1} - x'_{t-1}. \tag{3.8e}$$

(The French and U.S. acceleration expressions would take this form.) Equation (3.8e) implies that trade union strike activity contributes to the acceleration of prices to the extent that the strike activity wage effect on average exceeds the sum of price changes not compensated for by the price adjustment coefficient, a_0, *and* the rate of change of labor productivity, x'. Put another way, labor militancy underlies accelerating prices if S^* pushes real wages up faster than x'.

The relevant data for assessing the direct contribution of strike activity to accelerating prices over the period 1963–1975 appear in Table 3.8. To smooth out cyclical fluctuations in wages, prices, productivity, and so on, the data have been averaged over three subpe-

58. $(S^* + Z) > 0$ does not necessarily lead to accelerating prices, $\Delta p' > 0$. Two other outcomes are possible: $R/Y < 0$ (falling profit share) or $U > 0$ (falling employment, rising unemployment). Also note that the argument concerning $(S + Z)$ and p' does not hinge on the precise form of the price markup scheme (3.8a). Related pricing equations—for example, the "normal" average cost model—would yield similar results for p' averaged over several periods.

Table 3.8. Average rates of change of wages, prices, labor productivity, and strike-induced inflationary impulses, 1963–1975.

Country	$\bar{w}'_{t-1}$	$\bar{p}'_{t-1}$	$\bar{r}'_{t-1}$	$\bar{x}'_{t-1}$	$(\bar{r}' - \bar{x}')_{t-1}$	$\overline{\Delta p}'_t$	$\bar{S}*$	$\bar{Z}$	$\bar{S}* + \bar{Z}$
Italy									
1963–67	11.09	5.59	5.50	7.07	−1.58	−0.71	2.29	−3.54	−1.25
1968–72	11.92	3.98	7.95	5.04	2.91	0.70	3.69	−1.49	2.19
1973–75	19.45	10.74	8.70	7.68	1.02	3.19	3.67	−2.47	1.20
France									
1963–67	8.12	3.60	4.52	5.51	−0.99	−0.42	4.63	−6.65	−2.02
1968–72	9.74	4.75	4.99	5.95	−0.96	0.67	6.63	−7.46	−0.83
1973–75	14.33	8.42	5.91	4.53	1.37	1.82	7.25	−7.23	0.03
Great Britain									
1963–67	6.71	3.54	3.16	4.24	−1.08	−0.32	3.16	−4.12	−1.03
1968–72	8.88	5.50	3.37	3.53	−0.16	0.88	5.76	−5.49	0.27
1973–75	13.92	10.18	3.73	3.57	0.17	4.95	8.09	−7.36	0.73
United States									
1963–67	3.65	1.65	2.01	4.27	−2.27	0.31	3.23	−6.29	−3.06
1968–72	6.20	4.41	1.79	1.98	−0.19	0.10	3.93	−5.39	−1.46
1973–75	7.32	6.58	0.74	1.33	−0.59	1.83	3.57	−5.84	−2.27

Note: $\overline{\Delta p}'$ = the first difference of p', the mean rate of acceleration of inflation; $\bar{w}'$ = mean rate of change of manufacturing hourly compensation; $\bar{p}'$ = mean rate of change of consumer prices; $\bar{r}'$ = mean rate of change of real manufacturing hourly compensation; $\bar{x}'$ = mean rate of change of manufacturing labor productivity; for $\bar{S}*$ and $\bar{Z}$, see text.

riods: 1963–1967 (a period of decelerating prices in all countries except the United States), 1968–1972 (a period of accelerating prices in all four countries), and 1973–1975 (the period of the OPEC-induced inflationary burst).

The data presented in Table 3.8 show that during the first subperiod, 1963–1967, the rate of price inflation was falling in Italy, France, and Great Britain and rising by just under .33 percent per year in the United States (see column 6 of the table). However, in *all* countries the rate of change of real wages lagged behind the rate of change of labor productivity (the lag was dramatic in the United States—see column 5), and everywhere $\bar{S}* + \bar{Z}$ was less than zero. Clearly, there is no evidence that labor militancy contributed to the steady acceleration of prices in the United States over the period 1963–1967.

For the second period, 1968–1972, the picture is mixed. Prices accelerated substantially in Italy, France, and Great Britain, modestly in the United States. $\bar{S}* + \bar{Z}$ is negative in France and the United States (as is $r' - x'$), which again implies that labor militancy did not generate the acceleration. In Great Britain $\bar{S}^* + \bar{Z}$ is greater than zero, but too small to explain fully the sharp rise in the rate of inflation.[59] However, the data in columns 5 and 9 of the table show that in Italy labor militancy was on average pushing up real wages much more rapidly than was the rate of growth of labor productivity. There is good reason to conclude, therefore, that the most important source of price acceleration in Italy during this period was trade union cost-push.

The 1973–1975 average annual rate of price acceleration was enormous: nearly 5 percent in Great Britain, more than 3 percent in Italy, and almost 2 percent in France and the United States. In view of the dramatic increases in the international prices of food and fuel since 1973, it comes as no great surprise that the data in Table 3.8 indicate that the general acceleration of prices cannot be attributed to labor militancy. For the United States the estimated net effect of strike activity on price acceleration, $\bar{S}^* + \bar{Z}$, is negative. In other words, the pressure on manufacturing money wages from trade union strike action was apparently not great enough in the United States to keep real wages growing as fast as labor productivity. $\bar{S}^* + \bar{Z}$ is positive for France and Great Britain, but it is not large enough to account for much of the price acceleration, especially the recent acceleration of British consumer prices.[60] In Italy the evidence again points to a different conclusion. Both $r' - x'$ and $\bar{S}^* + \bar{Z}$ are greater than 1.0, which suggests that strike-induced wage escalation was a significant component of the post-OPEC burst of inflation.

Admittedly, the calculations in Table 3.8 might yield conservative estimates of average strike-induced inflationary impulses. Wages and productivity pertain to the manufacturing sector, whereas prices are based on economywide consumer indices.[61] Since the prices of manufactured goods have generally increased less than the consumer price indexes in recent years, the strike activity inflation effects may be somewhat understated. Taken as a whole, however, the evidence strongly implies that only in Italy has trade union strike action systematically contributed to increasing rates of inflation over the period 1968–1975.[62] In order to explain the general acceleration of wages and

59. Also notice that $(r' - x')$ is negative.

60. Notice, however, that $r' - x'$ is substantially greater than zero in France.

61. Consumer prices are of course more relevant for modeling wage determination.

62. Italian unions are not only powerful but also among the most militant. For example, the postwar average of worker-days lost in strike activity per worker is higher for Italy than for any other major industrial, capitalist society. (See Chapter 2.)

prices in the late 1960s and 1970s one must look to other factors; macropolicy mismanagement, deficit financing of the Vietnam War, changes in the relative prices of fuel and agricultural commodities, and so on.

Although the results of this study indicate that manufacturing labor militancy has not been an important proximate cause of escalating rates of inflation,[63] the data in Tables 3.5 and 3.8 show that the combined effects of union power and union militancy effectively index manufacturing wages to prices in all four countries.[64] Two implications follow. First, any received rate of price inflation tends to be perpetuated. Second, and perhaps more important, inflationary shocks requiring *real* adjustments, such as changes in the relative prices of fuel and food redistributing income to the producers of oil and agricultural commodities, can generate accelerating inflation rates *if* both labor and capital are in the short run unwilling to accept the real income loss. Therefore an "imported" inflation can lead to a "home-grown" inflation as a result of what Hicks has called "real wage resistance."[65] Until the principal domestic actors acknowledge the shift in the terms of trade and settle the problem of allocating the decline in real income, increasing inflation is almost an inevitable interim outcome, particularly if political authorities attempt to maintain a steady level of output and employment and "validate" the inflation by expanding the money supply.[66]

If the perpetuation and in some circumstances the escalation of inflation are influenced by trade union action, what can be done to bring about wage and price stability? Perhaps nothing should be

63. Except in Italy to the extent noted above.

64. That is, the combined effects of price adjustment and strikes keep the rate of change of real wages positive. The only exceptions in the period 1950–1975 are 1969 in France (real wages fell by about 0.5 percent following a 13 percent increase the previous year) and 1974 in the United States (a decline of about 1 percent).

65. J. R. Hicks, "What is Wrong with Monetarism?" *Lloyds Bank Review* (October 1975), 51. As G. D. N. Worswick put it in testimony before the British House of Commons' Public Expenditure Committee: "If all of us just took the rise in the price of oil on the chin that would be one thing, but most of us do not; we say, 'Our income is unchanged and prices have risen. We wish to restore our real income'" (cited in M. H. Miller, "Can a Rise in Import Prices Be Inflationary and Deflationary?" *American Economic Review*, 66 [1976], 510).

66. A rough formalization of this idea has been worked out by Miller (see note 66), who builds on the work of J. D. Sargan, "Wages and Prices in the United Kingdom," in *Econometric Analysis for National Economic Planning*, ed. P. E. Hart, G. Mills and J. K. Whittaker (London: Butterworths, 1964).

done. As Tobin and others have observed, inflation is not the worst way of resolving group rivalries and social conflict.[67] Moreover, much if not all of the pain attributed to the recent inflation is actually due to the massive *real* income loss caused by the shift in *relative* prices in favor of producers of food, fuel, and raw materials. Had the real loss absorbed by urban, industrial societies (or sectors of society) taken place around a stable price level, the pain would not have been any less unpleasant.

A "do-nothing" posture may be viable in the United States. Inflation has been running at below double-digit figures (except for 1974), and trade unions are comparatively weak. In France, Italy, and Great Britain, however, inflation has reached almost ruinous proportions. For social as well as economic reasons it must be brought under control.

The results presented earlier showed that outside the United States there is little evidence of a Phillips curve and that the impact of strike action on wages is largely independent of market forces. Yet there is little doubt that if political authorities were willing to run the economy at *very* low levels of activity for a prolonged period the power of unions to obtain wage increases equal to or in excess of the rate of price inflation would be broken. This of course amounts to killing the patient to cure the disease. In any case policies of this sort are simply not politically feasible in modern capitalist democracies.[68]

If it is necessary to do something about inflation, and if orthodox deflationary macroeconomic policies are unlikely to be effective or politically acceptable, the only alternative is probably some form of national wages or incomes policy. In a democratic society the success of a national wages policy hinges on the voluntary cooperation of the trade unions. Headey's study of the postwar experience shows that two conditions are critical for trade union cooperation:[69]

1. Whether or not the state directly coordinates the wages policy, the government must command the confidence of the unions. In practice this means that trade-union-based (Socialist, Labor, Communist) political parties must control (or share in the control of) the government.

---

67. J. Tobin, "Inflation and Unemployment," *American Economic Review,* 62 (1972), 1–18.

68. Events since the late 1970s have proved this remark to be completely wrong.

69. B. Headey, "Trade Unions and National Wages Policies," *Journal of Politics,* 32 (1970), 407–439.

2. The trade union movement must be centralized to the degree
   that the peak organizations exercise effective control over the
   principal bargaining demands and strike decisions of the major
   constituent unions.

None of the countries treated in this study entirely satisfies
Headey's conditions. However, the British Labour government has
been able to sell wage restraint—indeed, severe wage restraint—to
the trade unions for two successive years, even though the Trade
Union Congress (TUC, the peak labor organization) does not exercise
the kind of centralized authority outlined above.[70] To be sure it took
an extraordinary domestic economic crisis, external pressure from the
international economic community, and the promise of tax relief to
low-wage groups to elicit the union's cooperation. Although a national wages policy probably does not have a long-run future in Britain, it has helped to alleviate the short-run, post-OPEC crisis. Perhaps this is all one should expect.

Even a policy of short-run restraint designed to reverse the post-
1972 wage and price acceleration is not feasible in France and Italy
unless the left opposition is brought into the government. The economic situation is particularly acute in Italy, where annual wage increases have exceeded 20 percent for four consecutive years. The
Italian Communist party (PCI) pressed for participation in the government for several years (the "historic compromise"), but the ruling
Christian Democrats rejected PCI overtures. If the Christian Democrats continue to oppose PCI government participation, trade union
wage pressure is unlikely to abate, and Italy may slide from economic
crisis into economic catastrophe.

---

70. In August 1975 the trade unions agreed to hold weekly wage increases to £6—a
rise of about 10 percent. Wage restraint was even greater the following year: the
August 1976 agreement held wage increases to an average of 4.5 percent. The increase
in both years was substantially less than the rate of inflation. It is clear that a Conservative government could never have pulled this off.

II

Politics and Economics in the United States

4

The Mass Public and Macroeconomic Performance: Dynamics of Public Opinion toward Unemployment and Inflation

The Rise of the Economy as a Public Issue

Not since the Great Depression of the 1930s and the immediate post-war reconversion scare has the state of the economy occupied such a salient place among the mass public's concerns. The time series of Gallup poll data in Figure 4.1 shows that once the American withdrawal from Vietnam was completed, the economy outstripped all other issues as a source of popular concern. In every year from 1972 to 1977 more than 70 percent of the mass public identified an economic issue as "the most important problem facing this country today."

In view of recent macroeconomic policies and outcomes this comes as no surprise. The extraordinarily tight labor markets accompanying the Vietnam war boom and the Johnson administration's attempt to obscure the war's true cost through a policy of hidden deficit finance (abandoned too late with the 1968 tax surcharge) left the incoming Nixon administration facing accelerating rates of inflation. Predictably, the new Republican government pursued a contractionary macroeconomic plan to check the inflation.[1] Real federal expenditure was

Reprinted from *American Journal of Political Science*, 23 (November 1979), 705–731. I am grateful to Nicholas Vasilatos for able research assistance, to Christine Aquilino and Suzanne Planchon for expert manuscript typing, and to Robert E. Hall for sharing his knowledge of macroeconomics. David Cameron, Robert Jackman, William Keech, Robert Keohane, and Mette Sorensen gave helpful comments on earlier drafts. The research was supported by National Science Foundation Grants SOC 76-14635 and SOC 77-20693.

1. I tried to show just how "predictable" or characteristic this was in an earlier article, "Political Parties and Macroeconomic Policy," *American Political Science Review*, 71 (December 1977), 1467–87 (reprinted as Chapter 11 in this volume).

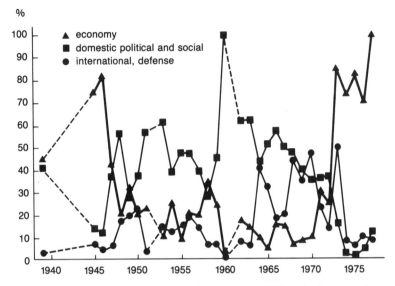

Figure 4.1. Aggregate responses to the question "What is the most impor-
tant problem facing this country today?" 1939–1977. Question wording is
approximate. Includes multiple responses; other responses omitted. (From
George Gallup, *The Gallup Poll, Public Opinion: 1935–1971*, 3 vols. [New York:
Random House, 1972], and American Institute for Public Opinion, *The Gallup
Opinion Index*, various issues.)

reduced by 0.6 percent in 1969 and grew by only 2.9 percent in 1970
(as compared with the postwar average of 6.2 percent). Dr. Arthur
Burns—Nixon's appointee as chairman of the Federal Reserve—accommodated the administration's fiscal policy by decreasing the real
money supply (deflated M1) by 1.7 percent in 1969 and by 0.2 percent
in 1970. (The postwar average is +0.5 percent per annum.) The plan
worked, producing the 1970–71 recession, which helped lower the
rate of inflation by more than 2 percentage points—from 5.7 percent
per year in 1969 to 3.4 percent in 1971.[2]

Although the policy of restraint was jettisoned in 1972 in a successful attempt to stimulate an election-year boom,[3] a new crisis soon

2. The numbers are averages of annualized quarterly rates based on log differences.
The wage and price controls of 1972 also probably had a short-run impact on the
inflation rate.

3. Nixon was painfully aware of the contribution of the 1960–61 recession to his
defeat by Kennedy, never forgave Eisenhower for failure to pump up the economy on
his behalf, and shamelessly used the levers of macroeconomic policy to ensure there
would be no repetition of 1960 in 1972. E. Tufte reviews this and other evidence of an
"electoral business cycle" in great detail in *Political Control of the Economy* (Princeton:
Princeton University Press, 1978).

rocked the economy. This time the shock was largely exogenous: dramatic increases in the world prices of food and raw materials and the OPEC-induced quadrupling of the price of petroleum in 1973 led to unprecedented double-digit rates of inflation throughout 1974. The Ford administration responded to the crisis by launching the "Whip Inflation Now" media campaign and, more tangibly, by cutting back the rate of growth of real government spending. Dr. Burns again accommodated the Republican administration's policy of restraint, proclaiming that the shortage was "of oil not money,"[4] and real M1 declined on the average by a crushing 4.8 percent during 1974–75. Of course many questioned the logic of fighting an inflation initiated largely by an international shift in the terms of trade by inducing a domestic recession. In any case, the consequence was the most severe contraction in postwar U.S. history. Unemployment stood at nearly 9 percent by the middle of 1975. Inflation declined from the double-digit rates of 1974 to the 5 to 7 percent per annum range in 1975 and 1976.

The severity of the recession prompted the Ford administration to pursue moderately expansionary policies in late 1975 and 1976,[5] but the administration's basic priorities were not fundamentally altered: President Ford declared to a cheering Wall Street audience in 1976 that "after all, unemployment affects only 8 percent of the people while inflation affects 100 percent."[6]

The Gallup data in Figure 4.1 were organized so as to show that the economy has become the dominant public issue in recent years, but it is clear that unemployment and inflation were the variables preoccupying both policymakers and the mass public.[7] Moreover, macroeconomic policy toward unemployment and inflation generates intense controversy and conflict among key political actors and interest groups and therefore cannot be explained adequately from a purely technical economic perspective. Although there is no fixed, stable tradeoff between unemployment and inflation in the macroeconomy,

4. Quoted in *Business Week*, May 22, 1978, p. 109.

5. The electorate was treated to an $18 billion rebate of income and corporate taxes in the second quarter of 1975. The administration proposed adding another $10 billion to the tax cut stimulus in early 1976 and planned to justify the cuts by an equivalent $28 billion reduction in federal expenditure late in the year—too late to be felt before the November election.

6. Quoted in J. Tobin, "Inflation Control as Social Priority" (Paper presented to the Conference on the Political Economy of Inflation and Unemployment in Open Economies, Athens, 1976).

7. Other economic issues, such as the balance of payments and the distribution of income, were mentioned infrequently in the Gallup surveys.

most economists and politicians recognize that full employment and price stability pose conflicting goals, in that it is difficult to make substantial progress on one problem without running risks with respect to the other.

The policy tradeoff has been particularly apparent since the long expansion of 1961–1969 came to an end in the 1970–71 recession. The Nixon and Ford administrations consistently attempted (with some success) to shave points off the rate of inflation by inducing high levels of unemployment. The financial community, corporate spokesmen, and the Republican party leadership generally endorsed the deflationary policies, whereas the trade unions and most elements of the Democratic party leadership attacked them, arguing that unemployment rather than inflation was "domestic enemy number 1."[8] Groups on both sides of the policy debate of course acknowledge the evils of inflation *and* unemployment. Trade union leaders express concern about inflation, and business elites are not entirely insensitive to the hardships imposed by high rates of unemployment. The conflict is over *relative* priorities in macroeconomic policy.

This chapter reports disaggregated analyses of the dynamics of popular aversion to unemployment and inflation. If, as I believe, it is true that domestic economic policy is to some extent responsive to and/or constrained by public opinion toward salient economic issues, then these analyses will help illuminate the political environment conditioning government macroeconomic policies—in particular, deflationary policies oriented to price stabilization versus expansionary policies geared to moving the economy toward full employment.

The Public's Relative Aversion to Inflation and Unemployment

Survey data on the public's concern about inflation, unemployment, and other economic, social, and political issues have been available since the late 1930s, but we have direct evidence on the mass public's relative aversion to unemployment and inflation only for

8. For a more detailed discussion see D. A. Hibbs, "Economic Interest and the Politics of Macroeconomic Policy," Center for International Studies, MIT, Monograph Series, C/75-14, January 1976. The shift in the Carter administration's macroeconomic priorities announced in November 1978 as this was being written signaled a similar policy for 1979. I return to this at the end of the chapter.

recent years.[9] At intermittent quarters since August 1971, surveys undertaken by the Survey Research Center at the University of Michigan have explicitly asked national samples of American households: "Which of the two problems—inflation or unemployment—do you think will cause the more serious economic hardship for people [may have the more serious consequences for the country] during the next year or so?"[10] This is an ideal question for our purposes here because it encourages people to acknowledge (implicitly) the difficult choice that has been at the heart of recent macroeconomic policy debates. The question appeared in surveys taken in August–September 1974 and in every quarter from 1975 to the end of the series. Unfortunately, the question appeared in only one survey in 1972 and 1974 and was not asked at all in 1973. Nonetheless, we have a time series spanning the critical period 1971–1976 that makes it possible to identify the sources of fluctuations in the public's relative aversion to inflation and unemployment.

Figure 4.2 shows the aggregate responses to the inflation/unemployment question (the percentage responding that inflation is the more serious problem) along with the actual rates of inflation and unemployment in the macroeconomy.[11]

Obviously, the opinion data respond to the prevailing macroeconomic situation. In late 1971 and early 1972 the conjunction of recessionary levels of unemployment and a modest rate of inflation produced a popular majority more averse to unemployment than to inflation. However, by the summer of 1974, when inflation was raging at nearly 12 percent per annum, nearly three-quarters of the public saw inflation as the more important macroeconomic problem. The situation was reversed six months later. The inflation rate was cut in half, unemployment increased to its highest level since the Great Depression, and about two of every three people expressed greater aversion to unemployment. As the economy moved from severe re-

9. The Gallup series discussed earlier include virtually all public issues among the response alternatives and often confuse the "high cost of living" with "rising prices," that is, the price level and standards of living with the rate of inflation.

10. The alternative wording, shown in brackets, was used in the 1971:3–1972:1 surveys. I assume throughout that the respondents' views of the social welfare are coincident with their enlightened self-interest.

11. Respondents designating both problems as equally serious—typically about 10 percent of the samples and never more than 16.5 percent—were divided evenly between the inflation- and unemployment-averse groups. A negligible fraction of respondents answered "don't know," "neither," or otherwise indicated ignorance of or indifference toward the issue and were excluded from the computations.

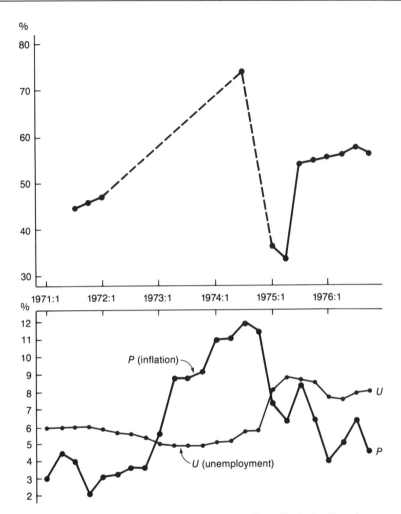

Figure 4.2. *Top:* Aggregate percentages responding "inflation" to the question "Is inflation or unemployment the more serious problem?" 1971:3–1976:4 (see text for exact wording of question). *Bottom:* Actual unemployment and inflation rates, 1971:1–1976:4.

cession into stagnation in late 1975 and 1976, popular concern about inflation grew sharply and hovered about the 55 percent mark for the next eighteen months.

Public sensitivity to inflation perplexes most economists because such concern is difficult to justify fully in economic terms. What matter most from an economic point of view are real quantities such as output and employment, not the nominal price level. On the other hand, politicians (particularly Republican politicians) have been surprised by the extent of public aversion to unemployment. President Ford's remark cited earlier is a prominent illustration. The aggregate opinion data in Figure 4.2 suggest that both views misjudge popular thinking. Before developing a statistical model of microlevel fluctuations in the opinion data, it will therefore be useful to review briefly some facts and conjectures about the "costs" of inflation and unemployment.[12]

The Costs of Inflation and Unemployment

Nothing in neoclassical economic theory adequately explains high levels of public concern about inflation. The principal economic costs of anticipated inflation are the resources devoted to economizing cash balances and fixed interest rate assets. Surely this is a trivial matter, particularly when viewed in relation to the costs of unemployment. The menu of costs associated with unanticipated inflation is longer and more interesting, but in my view it does not provide a convincing explanation of the public's aversion to rising prices. The existing empirical evidence suggests that the aggregate wage and salary income share is not eroded by inflations and that rising prices have no dramatic effects on the size distribution of income.[13] Unanticipated price increases do of course arbitrarily redistribute wealth from nominal creditors to nominal debtors, and the aggregate amounts involved are probably large. But at the microlevel a great deal of "canceling" must also take place. People lose on some accounts (fixed-price assets) and gain on others (fixed-price liabilities). One of the major inflation-induced wealth redistributions is intergenerational: from the old and

12. Because extensive reviews of the literature on this topic are available elsewhere, the next section develops briefly only important points useful in analyzing the mass opinion empirical results presented there. Recent reviews include G. Ackley, "The Costs of Inflation," *American Economic Review: Papers and Proceedings*, 68 (May 1978), 149–154; M. Feldstein, "The Private and Social Costs of Unemployment," ibid., pp. 155–158; S. Fischer and F. Modigliani, "Aspects of the Costs of Inflation" (Paper presented to the Conference on the Economic Crisis of the 1970s, Baden, Austria, September 1977); and D. Laidler and M. Parkin, "Inflation: A Survey," *Economic Journal*, 85 (December 1975), 741–809.

13. A. L. Blinder and H. Y. Esaki, "Macroeconomic Activity and Income Distribution in Postwar United States," *Review of Economics and Statistics*, 65 (November 1978), 604–609.

retired, who are likely to be net creditors, to the young and economically active, who are likely to be net debtors.[14] In theory, the aged poor—retirees whose welfare depends on Social Security—are perhaps the most exposed to inflation. Since 1974, however, Social Security has been indexed to inflation, thus limiting the adverse affects of rising prices on this group.

To the extent that state revenue is raised by direct taxation based on progressive nominal schedules, inflation increases the effective rate of income taxation (inflationary fiscal drag) unless authorities take compensatory action. However, at the federal level discretionary tax cuts have neutralized the potential gross transfer to the state: effective federal tax rates have increased little if at all since 1960, fluctuating in the aggregate around 11 percent of adjusted personal income.[15]

Since the income, wealth or tax effects of inflation do not appear large enough to explain widespread public aversion to rising prices, less tangible subjective and psychological factors are probably more important than objective costs. As Okun has argued, sustained high rates of inflation may undermine "the foundations of habit and custom," forcing people "to compile more information and to try to predict the future—costly and risky activities that they are poorly qualified to execute and bound to view with anxiety."[16] Empirical evidence does indicate that high rates of inflation are associated with high variability of the inflation rate, and variability presumably heightens uncertainty about the future stream of prices.[17] It is also possible that people fail to credit inflation-induced windfall gains, for example on fixed interest liabilities such as home mortgages, against the losses incurred on such money-valued assets as pension and life insurance reserves. Perhaps more important, the connection between rising wages and rising prices apparently is not well understood by the mass public.[18] There is some evidence that inflation tends to be

14. G. L. Bach and J. B. Stephenson, "Inflation and the Redistribution of Wealth," *Review of Economics and Statistics,* 61 (February 1974), 1–13.

15. E. M. Sunley, Jr., and Joseph A. Peckman, "Inflation Adjustment for the Individual Income Tax," in *Inflation and the Income Tax,* ed. Henry J. Aaron (Washington, D.C.: Brookings Institution, 1976).

16. A. Okun, "Inflation: Its Mechanics and Welfare Costs," *Brookings Papers on Economic Activity* (1975:2), 351–390.

17. Ackley, "The Costs of Inflation," and B. Klein, "The Social Costs of the Recent Inflation: The Mirage of Steady 'Anticipated' Inflation," *Journal of Monetary Economics,* suppl. ser. 3 (1976), 185–212.

18. G. Katona, *Psychological Economics* (New York: Elsevier, 1975).

viewed as an arbitrary tax that erodes the purchasing power of nominal income increases that people believe they deserve to enjoy fully.

After 1973 the most important factor contributing to popular concern about inflation was probably the decline in real income experienced by consumers of food, raw materials, and especially petroleum as a result of the shift in the terms of trade in favor of the producers of these commodities. It is likely that many people blamed rising prices for the shrinkage of their real income, even though the immediate post-OPEC inflationary burst was to a large extent merely the mechanism of a change in relative prices. Had the real loss absorbed by the oil-consuming nations taken place about a stable price level, the pain would not have been any less unpleasant, but inflation could not have been held responsible. However, if people were confused it is understandable: as James Tobin has pointed out, neither President Ford, nor his economic advisers, nor the Federal Reserve authorities, and very few outside economists told the public that anti-inflationary policies could not restore the former terms of trade or the real income loss.[19] The following sections present new empirical evidence on many of these conjectures about the sources of popular aversion to inflation.

It is no mystery why people are averse to high and rising unemployment rates; after all, unemployment is a real quantity representing lost real output and underutilized human resources. The measured unemployment rate is just that—a *rate*—and a far larger fraction of the labor force experiences bouts of actual unemployment over any given interval than the average percentage numbers might suggest. In any given twelve-month period the fraction is likely to be about three times the average "official" rate. Moreover, in addition to households touched directly by some form of unemployment or underemployment, an even larger number will be aware of unemployment among relatives, friends, neighbors, and, of course, fellow workers.

The data reported in Figure 4.2 indicate, as one would expect, that the mass public's relative concern about inflation and unemployment is influenced by the macroeconomic situation. However, even if a long time series of survey results were available, it would not be wise to confine the analysis of opinion fluctuations to such highly aggregated observations. It is well known that the likelihood of suffering unemployment varies sharply across socioeconomic and demo-

19. Tobin, "Inflation Control as Social Priority."

graphic groups. For example, at any given aggregate rate of unemployment the incidence of joblessness generally has a negative, monotonic relationship with occupational status.[20]

Figure 4.3 displays responses to the inflation/unemployment question by the occupation of household heads for three comparatively homogeneous periods. The figure clearly shows that lower status, unemployment-prone blue-collar occupational groups are less averse to inflation (more averse to unemployment) than are upper status, unemployment-sheltered white-collar groups, although the group differences are not as dramatic as one might expect from the substantial interoccupational variation in the incidence of unemployment.[21] The relationship holds under a wide range of macroeconomic situations, although of course all groups become much more inflation conscious during periods of sharply rising prices (the curve shifts upward) and much more unemployment averse during serious recessions (the curve is displaced downward). The large shifts in inflation/unemployment aversion common to all groups associated with changes in the macroeconomy suggest that people probably react to aggregate, economywide movements in unemployment (and/or inflation) as well as to the particular rates experienced by their socioeconomic group.

The group at the right end of the horizontal scale of Figure 4.3 consists of people actually unemployed at the time of the surveys. Their relative aversion to inflation is startling. Although the unemployed are a heterogeneous group, one surely would have expected them to view unemployment as a more serious problem than inflation by a wide margin. In the period 1975:3–1976:4 a slightly large proportion of unemployed respondents expressed greater sensitivity to inflation than (employed) laborers and service workers; the fraction of the unemployed more averse to inflation exceeded that of all blue-collar workers in 1971:3–1972:1. (Too few unemployed people were interviewed in the 1975:1–1975:2 surveys to permit reliable calcula-

20. In principle the rate of inflation might also vary significantly across groups. The conventional consumer price index is based on a standardized "basket" of goods and services consumed by urban wage and clerical workers. We took considerable trouble to compute occupation- and age-specific price indices, but they did not differ appreciably from the national CPI. See N. Vasilatos and D. A. Hibbs, "Public Opinion toward Unemployment and Inflation in the United States, 1970–1976: Technical Report" (Harvard University, 1977).

21. For example, during the period 1970–1976 the average unemployment rate of laborers and service workers was about 4.6 times that of managers and officials. The occupational dispersion of the opinion distributions is modest by comparison.

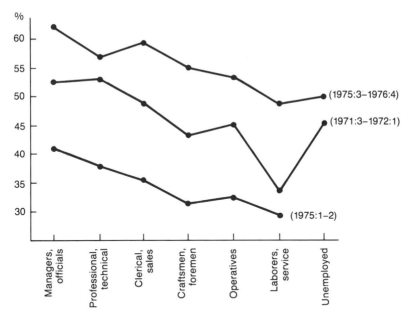

Figure 4.3. Percentages responding "inflation" to the inflation/unemployment question, by occupation or employment status of household head.

tions of the opinion distribution.) These results imply that for many individuals fear of future unemployment, the memory of past unemployment, or the aggregate social costs of unemployment are more powerful influences than the pain of contemporaneous personal experience. One of the reasons must be that unemployment no longer poses an economic disaster for many of those affected directly. In the 1930s the unemployed often went hungry. Today most suffer a temporary reduction in income. In other words, the private (individual) cost of unemployment is much lower now than in the past. Nonetheless, the distribution of opinion among the unemployed suggests that there is considerable confusion in the mass public about the relative costs of inflation.

A Disaggregated Dynamic Model of Short-Run Opinion Fluctuations

I pointed out earlier that aggregate public concern about rising prices and employment responds to the actual rates of inflation, unemployment, and possibly real income growth. However, it was also clear that relative aversion to unemployment and inflation varies across subgroups of the population because the likelihood of experiencing unemployment and of being adversely affected by inflation also varies across groups. Ignorning the possible wealth effects of inflation, which I am unable to measure, the earlier discussion implies a model of the form:

$$Y_{jt}^* = b_{11}g_{11}(L)U_{jt} + b_{12}[U_{jt} - g_{12}(L)U_{jt-1}]$$
$$+ b_{21}g_{21}(L)P_{jt} + b_{22}[P_{jt} - g_{22}(L)P_{jt-1}]$$
$$+ b_3g_3(L)R_{jt} + b_4(P \cdot R)_{jt}, \tag{4.1}$$

where $Y^* =$ an (unobserved) unemployment-to-inflation aversion index,

$U =$ the (official) rate of unemployment,

$P =$ the rate of price inflation,

$R =$ the rate of change of real personal income per household,

$g(L) =$ a lag function in the lag operator L, such that $g(L)X_t = \Sigma_k g^k L^k X_t = \Sigma_k g^k X_{t-k}$ and all variables are measured for groups $j = 1, 2, \ldots, J$ (defined by region, age, and occupation of household heads) at times (quarters) $t = 1, 2, \ldots, T$.[22]

The model is specified in terms of a latent aversion index, Y^*. Its connection to the observed survey opinion data is developed in the next section. For the moment let us assume that Y^* is a continuous variate that gets large as aversion to inflation increases (aversion to unemployment decreases) and gets small as concern about inflation declines (concern about unemployment rises).

The expected signs of the coefficients of U and P in Equation (4.1) are unambiguous. U_{jt} reflects the probability that a member of population group j will experience unemployment in the neighborhood of time t or will be aware of unemployment among others with similar social attributes. Both direct and vicarious exposure to unemploy-

---

22 All rates of change are formed: $[\ln(X_t) - \ln(X_{t-1})] \cdot 400$, the annualized quarterly percentage rate of change. Estimation of Equation (4.1) and of the extensions ahead involves merging survey opinion data (the lefthand side) with external sources of data for the economic experience variables (the righthand side) for subgroups defined by j at times t.

ment increase anxiety about the unemployment problem relative to inflation, and therefore $b_{11} < 0$ is a strong prior hypothesis. Since Figure 4.3 indicates that people may also be sensitive to movements in the economywide unemployment rate, an alternative to Equation (4.1) in which the aggregate unemployment rate, U_t, replaced the group-specific rates, U_{jt}, on the righthand side of the model, was tried in the empirical analyses reported below.

Although the term for the rate of inflation, P, is indexed for j as well as for t, the price indices of age-and-occupation-defined groups turned out to be indistinguishable from the overall consumer price index (see note 20). The conventional regional CPI was therefore used in the regressions reported below. It was clear from the earlier discussion that $b_{21} > 0$ is likely, even though in the presence of the real income growth rate term (R) this outcome might be interpreted on purely economic grounds as evidence of an "irrational" popular aversion to inflation. Subjective reasons why people might find rising prices distasteful even when real income is not affected adversely were reviewed in the previous section.

The per household personal income data are available in published form only on an annual basis by occupation of household heads; therefore, I used Newton's divided difference interpolation technique to impute quarterly variation to the observed annual nominal rates of change. The quarterly rate of change of real per household income, R, is simply the quarterly rate of change of nominal income less the quarterly rate of change of consumer prices. Notice that R does not vary over the full range of the group index j.[23]

The sign of b_3 in Equation (4.1), that is, the impact of the growth rate of real income per household on public concern about inflation, is indeterminate a priori. If people believe inflation is the major threat to real income, the b_2 should be negative: downward movements in R generate high aversion to inflation, and upward movements in R produce diminished concern about inflation. However, if recession and unemployment are viewed as more important threats to real income growth, then upward movements in R should decrease public concern about the unemployment issue (and hence increase concern about the inflation issue), and conversely, which implies $b_3 > 0$.

---

23. Annual data on personal income by occupation *and* age and other attributes of the household head can be obtained from the Bureau of the Census's March Current Population Survey data tapes, but the cost of doing this was beyond the resources of this project.

The $(P \cdot R)$ interaction term, which takes a nonzero value only when $R < 0$, tests the important proposition that, whatever the marginal effect of R alone, the conjunction of high inflation and falling real income sharply (and nonadditively) increases popular aversion to inflation. As the earlier discussion indicated, the events of 1974–75 appear to give strong support to this conjecture; the anticipated sign of b_4 is therefore negative.

Thus far the discussion has assumed implicitly that only *contemporaneous* economic experience influences the current distribution of opinion on the inflation/unemployment question. However, common sense as well as social theory suggests that current opinion is likely to respond to the experience of several (perhaps many) past periods, particularly since all variables are observed quarterly. Therefore, U, P, and R are specified as distributed lags defined by the $\mathbf{g}(L)$ operators. In principle it is possible to estimate expressions of the form $\mathbf{g}(L)X_t$ by experimenting with the order and length of the lag functions and allowing all coefficients to take a free form. Although this option is appealing in the absence of strong a priori beliefs about the relative impact of past experience on current opinion, it is simply not empirically feasible in view of the high collinearity among the time-series observations on the righthand-side economic variables. In practice, therefore, it is necessary to impose some restrictions on the pattern of the lag coefficients so that they are generated by a smaller number of underlying parameters. A number of lag function schemes are available, but the most plausible hypothesis in the present case is that the effects of U, P, and R are greatest at the current period and decline rapidly thereafter. The most suitable model is a geometric distributed lag function, which assumes:

$$\mathbf{g}(L)X_t = (1 - \mathbf{g}) \sum_{k=0}^{\infty} \mathbf{g}^k X_{t-k} \tag{4.2}$$

for all memory/discount lag sequences.

Equation (4.2) expresses the idea that public opinion toward inflation and unemployment responds to a moving average of prior economic experiences with exponentially decaying weights. Relatively large values of the $\mathbf{g}$ coefficients imply that past economic outcomes weigh heavily on people's current opinions on the inflation/unemployment issue; that is, in forming current opinions people have long memories of past experiences. Equivalently, small values of the $\mathbf{g}$

parameters imply that people greatly discount or have short memories of prior experiences. In this case recent economic outcomes dominate the current distribution of opinion toward macroeconomic issues, perhaps because people are forward looking and the best guide to the immediate future is the recent past.

The earlier discussion of the aggregate opinion data suggested that public aversion to inflation and unemployment may respond to the rate of price acceleration and the rate of change of unemployment as well as to current and past levels of these variables. Put more generally, it is reasonable to conjecture that people become accustomed to, or develop expectations about, the rates of inflation and unemployment. If, for example, the contemporaneous inflation rate exceeds what people expect, the public's relative aversion to inflation may rise. Conversely, if inflation decelerates sharply and runs behind the "customary" rate, concern about inflation, other things being equal, may decline. The same holds for the difference between the expected and currently realized unemployment rate, but with opposite effects on the opinion index Y^*.

The hypothesis that public opinion toward inflation and unemployment is also sensitive to sudden deviations of contemporaneous U and P outcomes from their customary levels is represented in Equation (4.1) by the terms $[U_{jt} - \mathbf{g}(L)U_{jt-1}]$ and $[P_{jt} - \mathbf{g}(L)P_{jt-1}]$. The customary or expected performance indices $\mathbf{g}(L)U_{jt-1}$ and $\mathbf{g}(L)P_{jt-1}$ are again assumed to be based on an exponentially weighted moving average of past experience, which is identical to the distributed lag memory/discount function defined by Equation (4.2), although the theoretical motivation here is somewhat different.[24] The anticipated coefficient signs are of course $b_{12} < 0$, $b_{22} > 0$.

Equation (4.1) is not estimable in its present form because Y^* is unobserved and because the $\mathbf{g}(L)X$ functions imply infinite lags. These and other estimation issues are taken up in the next section.

Individual Qualitative Response and Grouped Estimation

Although the ideas summarized in Equation (4.1) will be evaluated against survey data on population subgroups observed through time,

24. If expectations (in the usual economic sense) are adaptive, then the deviations of contemporaneous U and P levels from the customary levels represent *unanticipated* unemployment and inflation.

it is important that the empirical results be consistent with an underlying model of *individual* qualitative response. For simplicity let Equation (4.1) be written stochastically for the ith individual at time t as:

$$Y_{it}^* = X_{it}b + v_{it},\tag{4.3}$$

where Y^* = the unobserved unemployment-to-inflation aversion index,

Xb = a matrix of righthand variables and associated
parameters,

v = a stochastic disturbance.

Furthermore, let the *observed* individual survey responses to the
inflation/unemployment question be designated by the binary variable Y_{it}: Y_{it} = 1 for "inflation" responses, 0 for "unemployment"
responses.

Now consider the following qualitative response model.[25] Assume
that the observed binary variable Y is an ordered quantal response
crudely reflecting the underlying continuous aversion index Y^* such
that: Y_{it} = 1 if $Y_{it}^* > c$,   0 if $Y_{it}^* \leq c$, where c is a "critical threshold."
It follows that the probability of observing an "inflation" response for
individual i at time t is:

$$P(Y_{it} = 1) = P(X_{it}b + v_{it} > c) = P(v_{it} > c - X_{it}b),\tag{4.4}$$

and $1 - P_{it}$ gives the probability of an "unemployment" response. In
other words, people express greater concern about inflation than
about unemployment (Y = 1) when $Xb + v(Y^*)$ exceeds some critical
threshold c. The probability of an "inflation" response therefore
hinges on the value of $c - Xb$ and the distribution of the random
variable v.

The critical threshold, quantal response structure means the probability function for Y may be regarded as a cumulative distribution
function. If v is normal, the probabilities are given by the cumulative
normal distribution function. It is much more convenient, however,

25. This class of models originated in biometrics. The scheme presented here owes
much to J. R. Ashford, "Quantal Responses to Mixtures of Poisons under Conditions of
Simple Similar Action—The Analysis of Uncontrolled Data," *Biometrika*, 45 (June 1958),
74–88; idem, "An Approach to the Analysis of Data for Semi-Quantal Resources in
Biological Assay," *Biometrics*, 15 (December 1959), 573–581; and P. S. Hewlett and R. L.
Plackett, "The Relations between Quantal and Graded Responses to Drugs," *Biometrics*, 12 (March 1956), 72–78.

to assume that v satisfies the logistic distribution, which differs trivially from the normal.[26] Assuming v logistic with mean zero and scale parameter $\sigma^2 \cdot 3/\pi^2$ implies the probability function:

$$P(Y = 1) = P(v > c - Xb) = 1 - \frac{e^{(c-Xb)/s}}{1 + e^{(c-Xb)/s}}$$

$$= 1 - L^*[(c - Xb)/s] = L^*[(Xb - c)/s], \qquad (4.5)$$

where $s = \sigma\sqrt{3}/\pi$,
$\quad L^* = $ the logistic operator,
$\quad L^*(z) = \exp(z)/[1 + \exp(z)]$,

and the subscripts it have been dropped for convenience.

It is apparent from (4.5) that the response probabilities monotonically approach 1 as Xb gets large (for example, as the rate of inflation gets large relative to the rate of unemployment) and monotonically approach 0 as Xb gets small (as unemployment gets large relative to inflation, for example).[27]

Summing (4.3) and (4.4) over individuals and taking averages for j groups alters nothing fundamentally, but Equation (4.5) now gives the distribution of cell probabilities rather than binary outcomes.[28] The model can be estimated by maximum likelihood or, since we observe proportions instead of binary responses, by generalized (weighted) least squares. Because the latter estimator is reasonably efficient and a great deal cheaper computationally, it was employed in most of the regression experiments.[29]

Manipulating Equation (4.5) gives:

$$L^{*-1}P = \ln\left(\frac{P}{1 - P}\right) = \frac{Xb - c}{s} = Xb^*, \qquad (4.6)$$

26. See N. I. Johnson and S. Kotz, *Continuous Univariate Distributions*, vol. 2 (Boston: Houghton Mifflin, 1970), chap. 22.

27. The same probability function could have been derived for deterministic Y^* and stochastic threshold(s) c_{it} by assuming the c_{it} to distributed as the logistic.

28. Indeed, because the same individuals were not observed repeatedly through time, the only way to preserve the dynamic features of the model is to analyze population groups (stratified by appropriate socioeconomic attributes) over time. In principle, however, the model should be broadly consistent with individual choices.

29. See J. Berkson, "Maximum Likelihood and Minimum Chi Square Estimates of the Logistic Function," *Journal of the American Statistical Association*, 50 (March 1955), 131–162.

which expresses the log odds corresponding to the conditional probability P (the "logit") as a linear function of the model parameters.[30] The lefthand side of (4.6) involves the true probabilities P, but only sample proportions $\hat{P}$ are observed in the grouped survey data. Rewriting (4.6) to conform to the situation faced in empirical estimation yields:

$$\ln\left(\frac{\hat{P}}{1-\hat{P}}\right)_{jt} = X_{jt}b^* + \ln\left(\frac{\hat{P}}{1-\hat{P}}\right) - \ln\left(\frac{P}{1-P}\right)_{jt}$$
$$= X_{jt}b^* + e_{jt}. \tag{4.7}$$

Assuming independent samples from a binomial population,[31] the asymptotic distribution of $\hat{P}_{jt}$ is normal with mean P_{jt} and variance $[n^{-1}P(1-P)]_{jt}$, where n is the number of observations used to form P_{jt}. It follows that e has mean zero and variance $[nP(1-P)]_{jt}$, which implies the generalized least-squares (GLS) estimator:[32]

$$b^* = (X^TV^{-1}X)^{-1}X^TV^{-1}y, \tag{4.8}$$

where $y = \ln[\hat{P}/(1-\hat{P})]$, and V^{-1} is diagonal with typical element equal to $n \cdot P(1-P)_{jt}$.

All parameters in the substantive model are identified except the constant threshold structure. If Xb is specified with an intercept term, b_0, the constant in b^* estimates the ratio $b_0-c/(\sigma\sqrt{3}/\pi)$. If b_0 is assumed zero in the substantive model, then the critical threshold c can be deduced for $\sigma = 1$.

Estimation Results

Equation (4.1) gives the most general form of the estimation models, except that the logit, $\ln[\hat{P}(1-\hat{P})]$, appears in place of Y^* on the lefthand side of the GLS regression equations for the reasons just

30. Proof: Let $Xb = z$. Hence $P = L^*(z) = \exp(z)/[1 + \exp(z)]$, and $1 - P = 1/[1 + \exp(z)]$. Therefore, $P/(1 - P) = \exp(z)$, and $\ln[P/(1 - P)] = z$.
31. Strictly speaking this is not correct, since many of the surveys were reinterviews of some of the same respondents. The (unknown) time variances are probably smaller.
32. See Berkson, "Maximum Likelihood and Minimum Chi Square Estimates," or the more recent exposition by H. Theil, "On the Estimation of Relationships Involving Qualitative Variables," *American Journal of Sociology*, 76 (July 1970), 103–154. Notice that Equation (4.8) amounts to estimating Equation (4.7) by ordinary least squares after weighting all observations by $[n \cdot \hat{P}(1 - \hat{P})]_{jt}^{1/2}$.

reviewed. Several estimation strategies were entertained, but the most convenient one involved searching over the relevant values of g (0 to 1) by "brute-force" choosing the estimates minimizing chi square or the sum of squared GLS residuals.[33] Although in theory the model is specified with an infinite lag structure, this method is feasible because the weighting function $g(L) = (1 - g)\Sigma_k g^k$ approaches zero after finite lag (k) for g between 0 and 1.

Obviously it was necessary to impose a priori restrictions on the memory/discount parameters, g. Experiments were undertaken assuming a common lag distribution parameter, $g_{11} = g_{12} = g_{21} = g_3 = g$, and for the less restrictive case where the constraints $g_{11} = g_{12}$ and $g_{21} = g_{22}$ were imposed. The result of these regression experiments was that the assumption of a homogeneous memory parameter (g) for the U, P, and R terms proved to be consistent with the data. This is a credible result because there is no reason to believe that the weights people give to past economic experiences in forming current opinions, or the weights placed on past outcomes in developing views of customary economic performance, vary substantially for unemployment, inflation, or the growth rate of real income.

Table 4.1 reports the GLS conditional logit coefficient estimates for representative values of the parameter g.[34] The basic estimation equa-

33. The appropriate goodness-of-fit test for the validity of the logit specification is the chi square statistic obtained from differences between the observed relative frequencies and the estimated probabilities. The smaller the chi square statistic, the better the fit of the model. In the present case, chi square is the quadratic form of the GLS residuals: $X^2 = (y - Xb^*)^T V^{-1}(y - Xb^*)$.

34. Each observation is defined over the index jt, where j refers to the joint characteristics occupation, age, and region of household head, and the periodicity of t is quarterly.

The unemployment rate generally varies over the full range of j and t although aggregate, economywide series were also used. For reasons discussed previously, the rate of inflation varies across regions and over time only. Similarly, real income per household varies across occupations and time, but not over the age and region of the groups. The regions are defined by the standard census classification: Northeast, North, Central, South, and West. Neither the unemployment nor the opinion survey sample sizes would sustain a finer geographic disaggregation.

The age variable has three values: under age 21, age 25–64, and over age 64 and outside the labor force (that is, retired).

The occupation categories are: (1) managers, officials, and businessmen; (2) professional, technical, and kindred; (3) clerical and sales; (4) craftsmen and foremen; (5) operatives; (6) laborers and service workers; and (7) students. The observed unemployment and real income experience of all white-collar occupations (weighted averages) were imputed to the student category on the assumption that the white-collar class is the target or reference group of student respondents. So that the sensitivity of retired

Table 4.1. Weighted least-squares logit coefficient estimates, 1971:3–1976:4.
$N = 56$, $T = 12$, $N \cdot T = 672$

	Values of g		
	0.55	0.65	0.75
Constant	−0.325	−0.262	−0.128
	(0.07)	(0.07)	(0.08)
Age 25	0.233	0.220	0.201
	(0.07)	(0.07)	(0.07)
Age 65	−0.070	−0.060	−0.048
	(0.05)	(0.05)	(0.05)
$g(L)U_{jt}$	−0.042	−0.043	−0.045
	(0.01)	(0.01)	(0.01)
$[U_t - g(L)U_{t-1}]$	−0.485	−0.480	−0.463
	(0.03)	(0.03)	(0.03)
$g(L)P_{jt}$	0.115	0.117	0.114
	(0.01)	(0.01)	(0.01)
$[P_{jt} - g(L)P_{jt-1}]$	−0.020	−0.013	−0.007
	(0.01)	(0.01)	(0.01)
$g(L)R_{jt}$	0.012	−0.0003	−0.015
	(0.01)	(0.01)	(0.02)
$(P \cdot R)_{jt}$	−0.007	−0.006	−0.006
	(0.002)	(0.002)	(0.002)
Chi square (663 d.f.)	600.7	598.2	606.1

$$g(L)X_t = (1 - g) \sum_k g^k X_{t-k}$$

Note: Numbers in parentheses are asymptotic standard errors. See text on gaps in estimation range.

people to unemployment and inflation could be estimated, they were assigned the regional average rates of unemployment. The unemployed were excluded from all regressions.

Finally, the logit in $[P/(1 - P)]$ is not defined for $P = 0, 1$; therefore, following the suggestion of Berkson, "Maximum Likelihood and Minimum Chi Square Estimates," observations where $P = 0$ were set equal to $n/2$, and observations where $P = 1$ were set equal to $(1 - n/2)$. Only a small fraction of the observations were manipulated in this way, and the estimation results were not affected appreciably by the procedure. For further discussion of the data see Vasilatos and Hibbs, "Public Opinion toward Unemployment and Inflation."

tion is 1 with two additional dummy variables. The first binary variable identifies respondents less than 25 years of age (excluding students) who were in the labor force: *age 25* = 1 if < 25 years old and in the labor force and 0 otherwise. The second identifies respondents 65 years or older not working full time, which essentially means retirees: *age 65* = 1 if > 64 years old and not working full time and 0 otherwise. These variables are designed to pick up the wealth effects of inflation, which I am unable to measure directly. For reasons mentioned previously, inflation typically redistributes wealth to the young away from the old; therefore, the expected signs of the coefficients are: b (*age 25*) < 0; b (*age 65*) > 0.

It was clear from the numerous regression experiments performed (only three of which are reported in Table 4.1) that the memory coefficient **g** lies in the vicinity of 0.5–0.8. The optimal value of **g** appeared to be 0.65, yielding the smallest chi square statistic and hence a superior fit to the observed data. A lag parameter of 0.65 implies that 35 percent of the total impact on $\ln[\hat{P}/(1 - \hat{P})]$ of each level economic variable occurs contemporaneously (that is, at time t, lag $k = 0$), about 82 percent of the impact is felt after a year, and 97 percent after two years (7–8 quarters).[35] The same temporal distribution of lag weights governs the formation of customary or expected economic performance in the acceleration, rate of change terms of the model. Fluctuations in public opinion toward inflation and unemployment therefore appear to be viscous rather than volatile in the sense that the recent past exerts considerable influence on the public's current reactions to macroeconomic issues.

The estimated coefficients of both the group-specific unemployment rate, $\mathbf{g}(L)U_{jt}$, and deviations of the current aggregate unemployment rate from the customary level, $[U_t - \mathbf{g}(L)U_{t-1}]$, were significant and negatively signed as anticipated. In other words, the regression experiments showed that popular aversion to inflation versus unemployment is sensitive to the level of unemployment experience of particular groups and to changes in the unemployment rate prevailing in the macroeconomy. Therefore, as the economy moves into recession or expansion—that is, when $(U_t - \mathbf{g}(L)U_{t-1})$ is sizable—the distribution of opinion is dominated by the dynamic development of the aggregate economy. However, when the economy settles down to a steady unemployment path, the unemployment experience of particular groups influences the observed opinion dis-

35. This is obvious from evaluating $(1 - 0.65) \Sigma_k 0.65^k$ for $k = 0, 1, \ldots, 7$.

tribution. But the relative size of the logit coefficient estimates indicates that the rate of change of unemployment has a much greater impact than does the level of unemployment on the public's relative aversion to inflation. I return to this important (and somewhat discouraging) point in the final section.

The parameter estimates for the inflation terms indicate that only the rate of inflation, $g(L)P_{jt}$, has a sizable and significant effect on popular concern about rising prices. The term for accelerations (or decelerations) in the rate of change of prices, $[P_{jt} - g(L)P_{jt-1}]$, was generally insignificant and incorrectly signed and hence apparently has no affect on the public's aversion to inflation beyond what would be predicted from recent inflation rates alone.[36] Perhaps it was too much to expect the mass public to be sensitive to the second as well as to the first derivative of the price level.

However, the coefficient estimate of $g(L)P$ is obtained in the presence of the growth rate of real personal income per household, R. In other words, the public is averse to inflation per se; people find rising prices distasteful even when money income fully adjusts to cost of living increases. But the parameter of the $(P \cdot R)$ interaction term (which takes a nonzero value only if $R < 0$) suggests that sensitivity to inflation is nonetheless greatest when rising prices are accompanied by declining real income. The $(P \cdot R)$ estimate is of course dominated by the experience of 1974: in that year aggregate per household real personal income fell by 4.6 percent and inflation raged at an annual rate of 11–12 percent. There is little doubt that people (erroneously) blamed the inflation for at least some of the real loss. As I mentioned earlier, officials in the Ford administration actively promoted this misconception.

Aside from the consequences of the (unusual) conjunction of high inflation and falling real income, R alone seems to have no systematic impact on popular concern about inflation. This result suggests that the public has no uniform tendency to view either inflation or recession as the primary threat to the real income stream.

The major surprises in Table 4.1 are the signs of the parameters of the binary variables for retirees (*age 65*) and the young (*age 25*). Contrary to what I expected from the literature on the effects of inflation on intergenerational transfers of wealth, retirees are not more averse to inflation than one would predict from movements in their real income or the rates of inflation and unemployment. In fact, although

---

36. Neither this nor any of the other parameter estimates was influenced appreciably by collinearity among the independent variables.

it is never quite significant, the *age 65* coefficient consistently has a negative sign, which implies that retirees have a special aversion to unemployment. However, this result has a sensible explanation. Retirees in the surveys were old enough to have experienced the Great Depression. The negative *age 65* parameter therefore may reflect the *generational memory* of this event, which apparently was traumatic enough to counteract the immediate economic self-interest of the aged.

The large positive parameter estimate for working respondents less than 25 years old, which means there is a higher incidence of aversion to inflation among this group than anticipated, is more difficult to rationalize. Perhaps the young worry less about unemployment and more about inflation than expected because they have fewer family and financial obligations than older household heads and their spouses. Or, the young may have been particularly susceptible to the anti-inflation rhetoric of the Nixon-Ford years because their objective economic experiences and points of reference were more limited than those of older, experienced workers. Nonetheless, the *age 25* coefficient is anomalous.

Implications

Since the lefthand variable of the estimation model is the logit, $\ln[\hat{P}/(1 - \hat{P})]$, it is difficult to judge the impact of the independent variables on the distribution of opinion toward the inflation/unemployment issue by inspection of the parameter estimates. Therefore, it is useful to simulate predicted opinion distributions (aggregate percentages more concerned about inflation) for reasonable combinations of the unemployment and inflation variables.

Figures 4.4 and 4.5 graph the predicted percentage more concerned about inflation, obtained by aggregating the underlying micro opinion predictions, for combinations of the rate of inflation and the level unemployment rate, and the rate of inflation and changes in the unemployment rate.[37] Figure 4.4 shows the simulated percentages for

37. To generate the predictions, I reestimated the best fitting model in Table 4.1 after deleting the insignificant price acceleration and real income growth rate terms. The reestimated equation is:

$$\ln[\hat{P}/(1 - \hat{P})]_{jt} = -0.26 + 0.22 \, age \, 25 - 0.06 \, age \, 65 - 0.04 \, \mathbf{g}(L)U_{jt}$$
$$- 0.48[U_t - \mathbf{g}(L)U_{t-1}] + 0.12\mathbf{g}(L)P_{jt} - 0.006 \, (P \cdot R)_{jt},$$

where $\mathbf{g} = 0.65$.

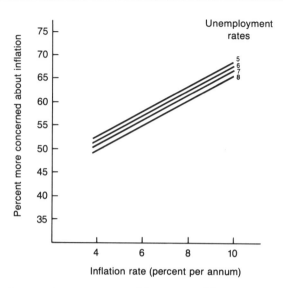

Figure 4.4. Aggregate percentages of the mass public more concerned about inflation than about unemployment at various inflation/unemployment configurations (change in unemployment fixed at zero).

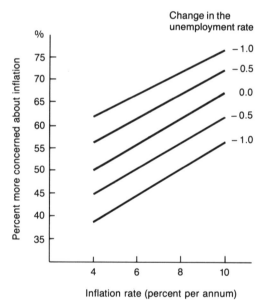

Figure 4.5. Aggregate percentages of the mass public more concerned about inflation than about unemployment at various inflation/change in unemployment configurations (unemployment level fixed at 7 percent).

inflation rates of 4, 6, 8, and 10 percent per annum and occupation by age by region unemployment rates consistent with economy-wide unemployment rates of 5, 6, 7, and 8 percent. The change in unemployment has been held at zero.[38] It is obvious from Figure 4.4 that, relative to steady-state unemployment levels, only the inflation rate has a major impact on the distribution of opinion. Even at the comparatively low inflation rate of 4 percent, the level unemployment effects do not exceed 3 percent. By comparison, moving from a 4 percent per annum inflation rate to a 10 percent per annum rate increases popular aversion to inflation by 15 percentage points or more at all plausible unemployment rates. Moreover, at all *stable* unemployment rates a solid majority of the public is likely to be more averse to inflation than to unemployment if the rate of inflation runs higher than 6 percent per annum.

However, the simulation predictions illustrated in Figure 4.4 are based on the assumption that unemployment had converged to some stable level. Figure 4.5 graphs the effects of *changes* in the unemployment rate on the opinion distribution, in conjunction with several plausible inflation rates. When simulating the results the unemployment level was held at 7 percent.[39] In these experiments the inflation rate effects are similar to those reported in Figure 4.5: moving from a 4 percent rate to a 10 percent rate increases aggregate public concern about inflation on the order of 14 to 17 percentage points. What are new in Figure 4.5 are the effects associated with changes in the unemployment rate. Public aversion to inflation decreases by a little more than 4 percentage points for every 0.5 percentage point increase in the unemployment rate. The precise impact depends on the prevailing rate of inflation, but only slightly. Hence, a 2 percentage point increase in unemployment when inflation is running at 4 percent per annum decreases aggregate public aversion to inflation by about 23 percentage points. The decline is closer to 20 points if the prevailing inflation rate is 10 percent per annum.

Believing as I do that the social welfare is best served by a major policy assault on unemployment, I find it discouraging that when the

---

38. Since the logit model is nonlinear, the results in Figure 4.4 would change nonadditively if the third dimension, $U_t - g(L)U_{t-1}$, were varied. However, the level U effects are so small that the third variable may be safely ignored. Moreover, as the figure shows, the two dimension effects are nearly linear, additive. The same is true of the results in Figure 4.5.

39. Because the unemployment level has such small effects, varying the fixed 7 percent rate would not noticeably perturb the results in Figure 4.5.

unemployment rate is stable (albeit high) an expansionary policy is not likely to command great public support if the inflation rate stands at 6 percent per annum or higher. In view of the "new" deflationary monetary policy announced on November 1, 1978, in reaction to the acceleration of the inflation rate to the neighborhood of 8 percent, this point apparently was not lost on the Carter administration. The main casualty, at least in the short-to-medium run, will of course be the administration's earlier commitment to achieving a sustained low rate of unemployment.

5

The Dynamics of Political Support for American Presidents among Occupational and Partisan Groups

Introduction and Review of the Political Support Model

This chapter investigates the dynamic response of political support for American presidents among occupational and partisan groups to economic and noneconomic performance. The analysis is based on the model developed in my comparative study of the response of aggregate political support to economic conditions (see Chapter 7) and focuses on quarterly Gallup poll approval ratings from 1961–1979. Gallup presidential approval ratings of course are not electoral outcomes, although they do correlate quite highly with the vote share received by incumbents running for reelection and, surprisingly, with the vote share of nonincumbent nominees of the president's party.[1] The Gallup ratings also have proved to be good predictors of the success of the president's party in midterm congressional elections.[2] Even more important, the Gallup approval data provide the best available time-series index of presidents' mass political support between elections, when policies are made and pursued and the substantive winners of elections are revealed. Neustadt observed more than twenty years ago that a president's standing in the approval

Reprinted from *American Journal of Political Science*, 26 (May 1982), 312–332. The original article was written with the assistance of R. Douglas Rivers and Nicholas Vasilatos. The research was supported by National Science Foundation Grant SOC 78-27022 and by the Center for International Affairs at Harvard University. Christine Aquilino and Elizabeth Welch typed various versions of the manuscript.

1. Lee Sigelman, "Presidential Popularity and Presidential Elections," *Public Opinion Quarterly*, Winter 1979, pp. 532–534.

2. Edward Tufte, "Determinants of the Outcomes of Midterm Congressional Elections," *American Political Science Review*, 69 (September 1975), 812–826.

polls greatly contributes to his public prestige, which in turn "is strategically important to his power."[3] This insight has been supported by subsequent quantitative work indicating that variations over time in congressional support for a president's legislative initiatives are systematically influenced by his Gallup approval ratings.[4]

Most previous time-series analyses of political support or electoral outcomes have assumed, at least implicitly, that voters respond homogeneously to performance outcomes. However, voters' responses to economic conditions and to other salient social and political issues are likely to vary significantly because of differences in the objective, concrete interests at stake, and perhaps also because of partisan attachments, which may influence voters' perceptions and interpretations of politically relevant information. Hence, changes in political support generated, for example, by movements in inflation and unemployment or by the escalation of the Vietnam war and the unfolding of the Watergate scandal are not likely to have been uniform within the electorate. Political elites of course realize that they do not face an undifferentiated mass public; they know that conscious policy shifts, as well as unanticipated events, yield political rewards and penalties that often vary sharply across electoral groups.

In investigating the sources and magnitudes of differences in voters' responses to economic and noneconomic events within the framework of a dynamic model of political support, I allow the relative importance (regression weights) placed on performance variables to vary across occupational and partisan groups. Occupation (of the household's chief wage earner) was selected as a dimension of disaggregation because it is preeminent in sociological analyses of political behavior and, more important, because the incidence of unemployment and other distributional consequences of macroeconomic fluctuations vary dramatically across the occupational hierarchy. Partisanship was selected because it divides the electorate into as homogeneous a set of political groups as we are likely to obtain with a single variable in the American setting.[5] If economic performance is as important to the electorate as survey data indicate,[6] cleavages

3. Richard E. Neustadt, *Presidential Power* (New York: Wiley, 1960).

4. George C. Edwards, *Presidential Influence in Congress* (San Francisco: W. H. Freeman, 1980).

5. Ideally, analysis would be based on *joint* disaggregation along several dimensions. However, the presidential approval time-series data are not published in this form.

6. See the Gallup poll time-series data on the relative importance of economic issues reported in Chapter 4.

among voters concerning economic priorities should be clearly revealed by analysis of data on partisan groups. Moreover, party identification is probably the dimension of disaggregation most relevant to the thinking of elected political officials, and elected officials determine macroeconomic policy.

Since the basic political support model used here is discussed in detail in Chapter 7, I shall review the model only briefly. Three features distinguish it from many others applied to similar empirical data on mass political support for elected officials in capitalist democracies.

1. People are assumed to evaluate an administration's performance *relatively* rather than *absolutely*. In particular, the model expresses voter approval as a weighted average of two relative performance comparisons: (a) the cumulative performance of the incumbent party in relation to the cumulative past performance of the current opposition party, and (b) the cumulative performance of the current administration in relation to the cumulative performance of all previous administrations regardless of partisan composition.

2. Although past as well as current performance influences voters' contemporaneous political judgments, the present relevance of information conveyed by past performance decays over time; therefore, the importance attached to past performance outcomes (Z_{t-k}) in the model declines at rate g^k, where g is a decay-rate parameter lying between zero and one.

3. Although public opinion surveys typically force people to make discrete, qualitative responses—in the present case, whether respondents approve or disapprove of the incumbent president's performance—in principle, voters' approval of an incumbent is not a discrete "yes or no" phenomenon, but instead falls on an underlying continuum ranging from strongly positive to strongly negative. Therefore, the dependent variable in the model is the logit $\ln[P'_{jt}/(1 - P'_{jt})]$, with P'_{jt} being the proportion of group j expressing approval of the president's performance at time t. The logit, or natural logarithm of the odds ratio $P/(1 - P)$, yields a good approximation to an unobserved, continuously valued support index. (See Chapters 7 and 10.)

The theoretical political support model is defined by the following equation:

$$Y^*_{jt} = w_j LR^q_{jt} + (1 + w_j)SR^q_{jt} + a_{jq} + u_{jt}, \tag{5.1}$$

where $Y^* =$ the latent index of approval for the president represented by the logit, $\ln[P'_{jt}/(1 - P'_{jt})]$,

LR^q = interparty comparisons during the qth administration,

SR^q = interadministration comparisons of the qth administration with previous administrations,

a_q = administration-specific constants,

w = the weight defining the relative contribution of
LR and SR, $0 \leq w \leq 1$.

The interparty comparisons are generated by:

$$LR^q_{jt} = b_j \cdot D_t \sum_{k=0}^{\infty} g^k Z_{t-k} D_{t-k}, \qquad (5.2a)$$

where Z = a vector of performance variables (specified later)
with associated coefficients b,

g = the rate of decay of the lag weights, $0 \leq g \leq 1$,

D_t = +1 if the Democrats control the presidency at time
t, −1 if the Republicans control the presidency at
time t.

In Equation (5.2a) the product of the terms $D_t D_{t-k}$ ensures that LR represents the *difference* between the cumulative, discounted performance record of the incumbent party with respect to Z and the cumulative, discounted performance record of the current opposition party with respect to Z during earlier periods when the opposition controlled the presidency. However, the weights applied to previous performance outcomes (Z_{t-k}) decline at rate g^k because, as mentioned earlier, the present relevance of past performance decays over time. For example, if the Democrats controlled the presidency for the two most recent periods, the Republicans for the previous two periods, and the Democrats for two periods before that, Equation (5.2a) implies:

$$LR^q_{jt} = b_j(Z_t + g Z_{t-1} - g^2 Z_{t-2} - g^3 Z_{t-3}$$
$$+ g^4 Z_{t-4} + g^5 Z_{t-5} - \ldots). \qquad (5.2b)$$

The interadministration comparisons are given by:

$$SR^q_{jt} = \sum_{q=1}^{Q} A_{qt} b_j \cdot \sum_{k=0}^{\infty} g^k Z_{t-k} D^*_{qt-k}, \qquad (5.3a)$$

where $A_{qt} = +1$ during the qth administration, 0 otherwise,
$D_{qt}^* = +1$ during the tenure of the qth administration,
-1 otherwise.

The dummy variables A_{qt} and D_{qt-k}^* ensure that SR is based on the *difference* between the qth administration's cumulative, discounted performance and the cumulative, discounted performance of all previous administrations, regardless of partisan composition. For example, if the qth administration has been in office for two periods, the SR component of the political support model is given by:

$$SR_{jt}^q = b_j(Z_t + gZ_{t-1} - g^2Z_{t-2} - g^3Z_{t-3}$$
$$- g^4Z_{t-4} - g^5Z_{t-5} - \ldots). \tag{5.3b}$$

Working through Equations (5.1)–(5.3) shows that when a new administration assumes office its initial support depends significantly on the situation inherited from previous governments. The worse (better) the performance of earlier administrations, the higher (lower) will be the new president's initial approval rating. This is particularly true when a new presidential administration represents a change in the party in power. For example, if the performance vector Z consists of inflation and unemployment, and hence coefficients in b_j are negative, the model implies that the first-period support for the new presidential-party administration is given by:

$$Y_{jt}^* = (-b_jZ_t + b_jgZ_{t-1} + b_jg^2Z_{t-2} + b_jg^3Z_{t-3}$$
$$+ \ldots) + a_{jq} + u_{jt}. \tag{5.4}$$

However, as time goes on and the situation inherited by the new administration is discounted or "forgotten" (that is, as k becomes large and g^k becomes small), the administration's support will depend entirely on its own cumulative performance record. The tendency of a new president's approval rating to decline from early "honeymoon" levels, which earlier studies have picked up with ad hoc dummy variables and time trend terms, is therefore an endogenous feature of the theoretical model in Equations (5.1)–(5.3). Finally, although the lag functions in Equations (5.2) and (5.3) extend to the distant ("infinite") past, observations on the performance variables (Z) are available for at least 32 periods before the first observation on the Gallup approval data (1961:1); therefore, the model may be estimated using finite lags without affecting the consistency of the estimates.

Empirical Results

As Equations (5.1)–(5.3) indicate, the political support model is non-linear by virtue of the parameters w and g; therefore, I performed the regressions by using a standard nonlinear least-squares algorithm. The regression experiments are based on quarterly observations spanning the period from Kennedy through Carter (1960:1–1979:4).

For the reasons reviewed earlier, the dependent variable in the regressions is the logit $\ln[P'_{jt}/(1 - P'_{jt})]$, where P_{jt} is the proportion of the jth group in quarter t responding "approve" to the Gallup survey question "Do you approve or disapprove of the way [the incumbent] is handling his job as president?" The independent, performance variables (Z) include the rate of unemployment, the rate of inflation of consumer prices, and the rate of change of per capita real personal disposable income.[7] Three noneconomic variables that characterize the recent political life of this country also appear among the performance variables. First, the regressions include a term for the number (in thousands) of Americans killed in action in Vietnam, to pick up the war-induced deterioration of presidential approval ratings. Second, the equations include a Watergate variable to capture the decline in Nixon's approval rating associated with that scandal. The variable was formed by summing the number of Watergate "events" in each quarter, weighted on a scale of 1 to 3 according to how strongly the president was incriminated personally by the event in national press reports. Third, in view of the unique visibility of the president when public attention is focused on international affairs, the regressions include a "Rally-Round-the Flag" variable taken from John Mueller's work and extended through the Nixon, Ford, and Carter administrations. "Rally" points are dramatic, sharply focused international events involving the United States that typically give a brief boost to presidential support ratings. The rally variable is simply the number of such events in each quarter.[8]

7. All rates of change are formed by taking quarter-on-quarter differences of the logs and are expressed at annual rates: $\ln[Z_t/(Z_{t-1})] \cdot 400$. The inflation rate and the real income growth rate variables were adjusted downward and upward, respectively, by the magnitude of the unfavorable shifts in relative prices following the OPEC supply shocks of 1973:4–1976:4 and 1979:1–1979:4. The idea (tested and described more fully in Douglas A. Hibbs, Jr., and Nicholas Vasilatos, "Macroeconomic Performance and Mass Political Support in the United States and Great Britain," in *Contemporary Political Economy*, ed. D. A. Hibbs, Jr., and H. Fassbender [Amsterdam: North-Holland, 1981], pp. 31–48) is that domestic officials are not held responsible for unfavorable macroeconomic shocks beyond their control.

8. Mueller arbitrarily scored the first period of each administration as a rally point. This was not done here. See John E. Mueller, "Presidential Popularity from Truman to Johnson," *American Political Science Review*, 64 (March 1970), 18–34.

The regression estimates for the occupation/labor force and partisan population subgroups are reported in Tables 5.1 and 5.2. To facilitate interpretation of the results and to limit computational costs, equations were estimated for tripartite occupational and partisan group disaggregations. The tables show that there is considerable intergroup variability in the coefficients; in some cases the differences are quite large, which, as I argue later, has important political implications.[9]

The g *and* w *Parameters*

The g and w parameters in Tables 5.1 and 5.2 define the rate of decay of the distributed lag coefficients for the performance variables and the relative contribution of interparty and interadministration performance comparisons to group presidential approval ratings, respectively. When g is zero or nearly so, the model collapses to the static specification used in much of the existing empirical work, in which only very recent performance outcomes affect political support. The nonlinear least-squares estimates of g in the tables vary between 0.70 and 0.86 across groups. The occupational and partisan group weighted averages for g are about 0.81, which means that the American public is not quite as myopic as some analyses of political support have implied. A value of g of about 0.81 indicates that performance outcomes of many past periods affect voters' current approval rating of the president. The assumption in the model that political support is based on cumulative, relative performance is therefore not merely an appealing theoretical fiction: assuming that g is zero, and hence that only current and absolutely evaluated performance outcomes matter, yields inferior predictions of actual fluctuations in the political support data.

If a performance variable Z is held at some equilibrium value Z^* indefinitely, the ultimate impact on the political support index is, on average, $Z^* \cdot b(z)/(1 - g)$, where $b(z)$ is the contemporaneous impact of Z estimated by the relevant regression coefficient in the tables. The proportion of the ultimate impact of Z felt by the kth lag is given by $1 - g^{k+1}$. Hence for an average g of 0.81, about 57 percent of the total impact of a sustained movement in Z is felt after one year (4 quarters), 81 percent after two years (8 quarters), and about 97 percent after four years (16 quarters). The implications of these results for short-run

9. I have not reported pooled results in which the parameters are assumed to be common across groups. However, the null hypothesis of no variability in parameters across groups is rejected at virtually any test level.

Table 5.1. Occupational groups, nonlinear least-squares estimates, 1961:1–1979:4.

		Blue-collar (T = 71)	White-collar (T = 71)	Nonlabor force (T = 62)[a]	Means[a] of approval proportions
Constants (a_q)					
Kennedy	a	0.597	0.475	0.250	0.702
	(s.e.)	(0.029)	(0.032)	(0.045)	
Johnson	a	0.479	0.385	0.342	0.540
	(s.e.)	(0.030)	(0.030)	(0.038)	
Nixon	a	0.465	0.928	0.733	0.497
	(s.e.)	(0.019)	(0.024)	(0.054)	
Ford	a	0.812	1.126	0.344	0.461
	(s.e.)	(0.065)	(0.047)	(0.057)	
Carter	a	0.127	0.434	0.468	0.487
	(s.e.)	(0.065)	(0.054)	(0.060)	
Lag weight rate of decay					
	g	0.853	0.786	0.712	—
	(s.e.)	(0.009)	(0.012)	(0.025)	
LR/SR weight					
	w	0.782	0.699	0.586	—
	(s.e.)	(0.025)	(0.021)	(0.113)	

					Means[b] of independent variables
Noneconomic terms					
Vietnam, killed in action (in 1,000s)					
	b	−0.064	−0.059	−0.055	0.605
	$b/1 - g$	−0.437	−0.274	−0.191	
	(s.e.)	(0.002)	(0.003)	(0.005)	
Rally events					
	b	0.254	0.23	0.234	0.329
	(s.e.)	(0.009)	(0.041)	(0.016)	
Watergate scandal events					
	b	−0.016	−0.018	−0.017	1.18
	(s.e.)	(0.001)	(0.0008)	(0.0015)	
Economic terms					
Inflation rate					
	b	−0.02	−0.031	−0.037	4.823
	$b/1 - g$	−0.138	−0.147	−0.13	
	(s.e.)	(0.002)	(0.003)	(0.0059)	

Table 5.1   (cont.).

	Blue-collar $(T = 71)$	White-collar $(T = 71)$	Nonlabor force $(T = 62)^a$	Means[a] of independent variables
Unemployment rate				
b	−0.014	−0.014	−0.005	5.48
$b/1 - g$	−0.093	−0.065	−0.019	
(s.e.)	(0.001)	(0.002)	(0.0042)	
Growth rate of per capita real personal disposable income				
b	0.017	0.019	0.014	2.39
$b/1 - g$	0.115	0.088	0.049	
(s.e.)	(0.001)	(0.002)	(0.0024)	
Fit: correlation of actual and fitted proportions	0.96	0.94	0.92	—

Note: Dependent variable: $\ln(P'_{jt}/1 - P'_{jt})$; (s.e.) = asymptotic standard errors.

a. Generally the presidential approval question is not asked in the third quarter of election years; therefore, data for these periods are missing. Data for the non–labor force group are missing throughout 1970–1973. Data on the blue- and white-collar groups are missing for 1970:3 and 1971:3. Data for the lag functions of the performance variables extend back to 1953:1 (see discussion in text).

b. Computed for the regression estimation range.

"political business cycle" theories are obvious.[10] Clearly, an administration that implemented macroeconomic policies under the assumption that the public's political evaluations were based only on conditions during the most recent year or half-year would be miscalculating. Perhaps this is one reason why short-run electoral policy cycles have not been a systematic feature of the postwar American political economy.

The nonlinear estimates of the w parameter in the tables vary between about 0.6 and 0.8, with the weighted group averages falling in the vicinity of 0.7. This indicates that, net of the a_q intercept terms, about 70 percent of a given president's approval ratings are based on interparty rather than on interadministration performance comparisons. However, after about 24 quarters (six years) 0.81^k is negligible in magnitude and LR is therefore effectively equal to SR. Since SR is based on a president's own past performance record, a president

10. For an explanation of the "political business cycle," see Chapter 6, note 7.

Table 5.2. Partisan groups, nonlinear weighted least-squares estimates, 1961:1–1979:4, $T = 72$.

	Democrats	Republicans	Independents
Constants (a_q)			
Kennedy a	1.272	−0.431	0.128
(s.e.)	(0.033)	(0.032)	(0.037)
Johnson a	0.961	−0.379	−0.061
(s.e.)	(0.028)	(0.032)	(0.036)
Nixon a	0.014	1.824	0.600
(s.e.)	(0.020)	(0.027)	(0.019)
Ford a	0.195	1.506	1.049
(s.e.)	(0.050)	(0.050)	(0.027)
Carter a	0.487	−0.069	−0.157
(s.e.)	(0.059)	(0.048)	(0.076)
Lag weight rate of decay			
g	0.834	0.700	0.860
(s.e.)	(0.010)	(0.015)	(0.009)
LR/SR weight			
w	0.652	0.617	0.800[a]
(s.e.)	(0.020)	(0.029)	
Noneconomic terms			
Vietnam, killed in action (in 1,000s)			
b	−0.064	−0.059	−0.056
$b/1 - g$	−0.388	−0.197	−0.402
(s.e.)	(0.002)	(0.004)	(0.002)
Rally events			
b	0.204	0.297	0.264
(s.e.)	(0.009)	(0.012)	(0.010)
Watergate scandal events			
b	−0.022	−0.015	−0.017
(s.e.)	(0.0007)	(0.001)	(0.0007)
Economic terms			
Inflation rate			
b	−0.017	−0.044	−0.017
$b/1 - g$	−0.100	−0.146	−0.124
(s.e.)	(0.002)	(0.004)	(0.002)
Unemployment rate			
b	−0.017	−0.010	−0.017
$b/1 - g$	−0.104	−0.034	−0.120
(s.e.)	(0.002)	(0.003)	(0.002)
Growth rate of per capita real personal disposable income			
b	0.022	0.024	0.021
$b/1 - g$	0.133	0.082	0.148
(s.e.)	(0.001)	(0.002)	(0.016)
Fit: correlation of actual and fitted proportions	0.99	0.96	0.93

Note: Dependent variable: $\ln[P'_{jt}/(1 - P'_{jt})]$; (s.e.) = asymptotic standard errors.
a. Searched manually in the interval 0–0.8.

surviving into a second term is unlikely to be helped or hurt significantly by the record of his predecessors (of his own or the opposition party). During a second term a president's approval rating is based almost entirely on a distributed lag of his own previous performance, as well as on his own unique appeal and other unmeasured factors (including partisanship effects) that are embedded jointly in the a_q intercept constants.

Noneconomic Events

The noneconomic performance terms in the model—Americans killed in action in Vietnam, international rally events, and the Watergate scandal events—all enter the regressions in Tables 5.1 and 5.2 with properly signed, statistically significant, and sizable parameter estimates. Escalation of American losses in Vietnam and the unfolding of the Watergate scandal obviously contributed to the deterioration of Johnson's and Nixon's approval ratings, and rally events were sources of upward movements in public support for all presidents.

Where it is appropriate two coefficients are reported for the performance variables in Tables 5.1 and 5.2: the ordinary regression coefficient b giving the contemporaneous response of the dependent variable to a unit change in an independent variable, and the steady-state or long-run coefficient $b/(1 - g)$ giving the ultimate response of the dependent variable to a sustained unit change in an independent variable. Since the lag rate-of-decay parameter g varies across groups, the pattern across groups of the long-run $b/(1 - g)$ coefficients occasionally deviates from the intergroup pattern of the contemporaneous b coefficients.

The coefficients in Tables 5.1 and 5.2 pertain to the impact of the performance variables on the logits $\ln[P'_{jt}/(1 - P'_{jt})]$. However, practical political interest centers on sources of variation in the survey proportions, P'_{jt}, which are not obvious from direct inspection of the tables because P'_{jt} is a nonlinear function of the latent variable $\ln[P'_{jt}/(1 - P'_{jt})]$. Therefore, to give an idea of the practical political consequences of fluctuations in the noneconomic variables, I have computed the implied changes in the percentage of each group ($P'_{jt} \times 100$) expressing approval of the president following reasonable movements of the independent variables (Table 5.3).

The estimated contemporaneous response to a unit increase in Americans killed in action in Vietnam (an increase of 1,000) shown in Tables 5.1, 5.2, and 5.3 is small and does not sharply distinguish

Table 5.3. Gallup poll approval percentages for responses of occupational and partisan groups to noneconomic events.[a]

| | Variable, magnitude, and duration | | | | | | |
| | Vietnam killed-in-action[b] | | | Rally events[b] | | Watergate scandal | |
Group	1,000 per period sustained 1 quarter (Johnson & Nixon)	1,000 per period sustained indefinitely (5–6 years) (Johnson & Nixon)	Increase in battle fatalities from 1,240 to 4,800 per quarter, 1966–1968 (Johnson)	1 event in 1 quarter (all presidents)	3 events in 1979:4, 2 events 1980:1 (Carter)	1 event tied directly to Nixon (+3)	Change in Nixon's average approval rating, due to Watergate, 1972:2–1974:3
Blue-collar	−1.6	−10.4	−14.3	+6.3	+24	−1.2	− 9.6
White-collar	−1.5	− 6.8	−11	+5.7	+17	−1.3	− 9.2
Non-labor force	−1.4	− 4.7	− 9.8	+5.8	+22	−1.2	−10.0
Democrats	−1.5	− 8.7	−14.6	+4.8	+22	−1.5	−14
Republicans	−1.2	− 4.0	− 8.4	+5.4	+20	−0.9	− 7.7
Independents	−1.4	− 9.7	−13	+6.6	+25	−1.3	−13

a. At 50 percent approval, the response to a unit movement in the independent variables is 25 (0.25 for proportions) times the relevant regression coefficient in Tables 5.1 and 5.2.

b. The responses to Vietnam and rally events exhibited little variability across presidents. Rally events had somewhat smaller effects during Kennedy's administration, because his approval percentages deviated more (upward) from 50 percent in most groups.

groups, but a casualty rate of this magnitude sustained indefinitely yields sizable political effects and reveals clear group differences. Among the occupational groups, blue-collar workers were the most sensitive to the war and those outside the labor force were the least sensitive. Continued indefinitely (which, given the values of lag decay coefficient g, means 20 to 24 quarters, or five to six years), Table 5.3 indicates that a killed-in-action rate of 1,000 per quarter yields a decline of more than 10 points in the blue-collar approval percentage but a decline of less than 5 percentage points in the non–labor force group. Presidential support among white-collar workers falls by about 6.8 percentage points at this casualty rate (Table 3.3, column 1, entries 1 and 2). Of course, American losses in Vietnam climbed much higher than 1,000 per quarter. For example, during 1966 battle deaths averaged 1,200 per quarter and rose steadily thereafter, peaking at 4,800–4,900 per quarter during the first half of 1968 following the Tet offensive. Simulation experiments with the political support equations indicate that as a consequence of this dramatic increase in the fatality rate, by the third quarter of 1968 President Johnson's Gallup approval rating was depressed 14.3 percentage points among blue-collar workers, 11 points among white-collar workers, and 9.8 points among voters outside the labor force.[11]

Perhaps the response of the non–labor force group is comparatively small because these voters were largely retirees whose children were too old to have been threatened by the war. We do know that the results in Table 5.3 for the white- and blue-collar groups are consistent with evidence from surveys showing that the working class generally expressed greater opposition to the war than did the middle class. And, more important, these results also square with data indicating that the children of lower-status workers suffered a disproportionate share of casualties.[12]

11. These estimates were derived from comparison of the approval percentages simulated without the 1966–1968 increase in battle fatalities (holding fatalities fixed at the 1966 mean of 1,240 per quarter) with the approval percentages generated by the actual historical data. Several other Vietnam variables were tried in the regression equations—for example, draft rates, bombing activity, and war casualties as opposed to fatalities—but these additional measures of the war's intensity added little to the information already embodied in the killed-in-action variable.

12. For survey data on opposition to the war see Warren E. Miller et al., *American National Election Studies Data Sourcebook 1952–1978*, (Cambridge, Mass.: Harvard University Press, 1980), tab. 3.53; and William L. Lunch and Peter W. Sperlich, "American Public Opinion and the War in Vietnam," *Western Political Quarterly*, 32 (March 1979), 21–44. For a review of evidence on the socioeconomic distribution of American casual-

Although American battle fatalities in Vietnam typically were higher during President Johnson's administration than during President Nixon's, the political support of Democratic partisans (and Independents) was considerably more sensitive to the Vietnam conflict than was that of Republican partisans. Again, the political effects of a killed-in-action rate of 1,000 per quarter sustained only one period are small. However, when sustained indefinitely (five to six years), this fatality rate yields declines of about 9 to 10 percentage points in the approval ratings of Democrats and Independents, though it lowers the approval rating of Republicans only about 4 percentage points (see Table 5.3). The great increase in battle fatalities between 1966 and mid-1968 had more dramatic effects on President Johnson's poll ratings: simulations of the equations suggest that by 1968:3 the war depressed his approval rating 14.6 percentage points among his fellow Democrats, 13 points among Independents, and 8.4 points among Republicans (see Table 5.3).

Perhaps surprisingly, the difference between the magnitudes of the responses of Democrats and Republicans to Vietnam war fatalities exceeds the difference between the responses of blue- and white-collar workers in both the Johnson and Nixon administrations. Voters' reactions to the war apparently were not influenced greatly by the "perceptual filter" of party identification. Moreover, stratification of the electorate into occupational groups is somewhat less effective than a partisan-based stratification in revealing intergroup cleavages surrounding the Vietnam war. Undoubtedly this is true because the Democratic coalition of urban, less-educated, lower-income, black, unionized, and blue-collar voters better identifies those segments of the American electorate directly affected by the war's human toll than does a simple occupational classification.[13]

Since it makes no sense to think of international crises producing the rally effect as being repeated indefinitely, Tables 5.1 and 5.2 show estimates only of the initial, contemporaneous boost to presidential

ties, see Robert E. Berney and Duane E. Leigh, "The Socioeconomic Distribution of American Casualties in the Indochina War: Implications for Tax Equity," *Public Finance Quarterly*, 2 (1974), 223–235. For voting patterns in referenda on the war, see Harlan Hahn, "Correlates of Public Sentiment about War: Local Referenda on the Vietnam War," *American Political Science Review*, 64 (December 1970), 1186–98.

13. For a very useful compilation of the national election studies data on the partisan balance within a great many social groups over the period 1952–1978, see Miller, "American National Election Studies," tab. 2.34.

approval indices of a single rally event (b). The parameter estimates in the regression tables suggest that Republicans and Independents are somewhat more responsive than Democrats to the rally phenomenon, and that white-collar workers are slightly less responsive than other occupational/labor force groups. But the differences are not very large: Table 5.3 indicates that on average a rally event boosts a president's quarterly approval rating by about 5 to 6.5 percentage points in the various occupational and partisan groups.

Although rally events are not frequent (about 1.2 per year is the long-run average) and only rarely has more than one occurred in a quarter, President Carter experienced five distinct events related to the crises over Iran and Afghanistan during 1979:4 and 1980:1.[14] This unprecedented cluster of rally events produced a dramatic reversal of the president's approval time series, which in the face of accelerating prices and declining real disposable income had fallen by the third quarter of 1979 to a level not seen since the Watergate scandal. The estimates in Table 5.3, based on simulation experiments with the political support equations, suggest that by 1980:1 the crisis increased Carter's support by 17 or more percentage points in nearly all groups. Although such a sequence is unlikely to be repeated, these estimates do illustrate the upper bounds of the impact of international crisis events on political support for the president. The political benefits of rally events are of course transitory, but they were large enough to help at least one severely weakened and vulnerable president to survive the primary season and to gain his party's renomination, though not reelection.

The last noneconomic term in the model represents the Watergate scandal, which ultimately drove President Nixon from office. The coefficient estimates in Tables 5.1 and 5.2 reinforce the view that partisanship significantly colored the electorate's response to the Watergate events: the interoccupation differences in the Watergate coefficients are small, but the difference between the coefficients for Democrats and Republicans is sizable. Nonetheless, computations in Table

14. In 1979:4 the seizure of hostages in Teheran (November 4); the burning of the American embassies by Muslim extremists in Pakistan (November 21) and Libya (December 2); and the UN Security Council's condemnation of the hostage seizure and call for the hostages' release (December). In 1980:1 the grain embargo and other measures taken against the Soviet Union in retaliation for the invasion of Afghanistan (December 26, 1979); and the president's appeal for draft registration in a televised message to Congress (January 23).

5.3 show that a single Watergate revelation (one event incriminating Nixon personally and scored +3 on the importance scale) would not have affected Nixon's approval rating by more than a percentage point or so. The president's problem was that the scandal escalated far beyond this level as one revelation followed another. The press-weighted Watergate variable averages about 15 in 1973 and peaks at 24 in 1973:2 during the Senate hearings. Simulation of the approval rating trajectories implied by the model with and without the Watergate events indicates that between 1972:2 and 1974:3 Nixon's aggregate approval percentage was lowered by about 10 percentage points.[15] As noted earlier, the disaffection induced by Watergate was less than this among Republicans but considerably higher among Democrats and Independents (see Table 5.3, last column).

Macroeconomic Performance

It is natural to expect political responses to macroeconomic performance to vary across groups because the burdens and rewards conferred by fluctuations in aggregate economic conditions are unevenly distributed within the electorate.[16] The regression parameter estimates for the macroeconomic variables in Tables 5.1 and 5.2 are broadly consistent with what we know about the distributional consequences of economic configurations. Among occupational/labor force groups, blue-collar workers exhibit relatively greater sensitivity to sustained movements in unemployment and real income growth and relatively less sensitivity to the inflation rate than do white-collar workers or retirees (Table 5.1, $b/(1 - g)$). In other words, compared to white-collar workers or those outside the labor force, the political support of blue-collar workers is more responsive to the economy's real performance than to its nominal, inflation performance. The political support of voters outside the labor force (primarily retirees) shows considerable responsiveness to movements in the rate of inflation, but it is quite unresponsive to the movements in the rate of unemployment. Since this group is not touched directly by unem-

15. This estimate is smaller than many press reports at the time suggested, but prices also accelerated dramatically (following the OPEC petroleum shock of 1973:3) during this period. This combination of circumstances illustrates the advantage of estimating such effects by simulating a multivariate model including important variables that covary.

16. For a review of the distributional consequences of macroeconomic outcomes see Chapter 4 and the sources cited there.

ployment fluctuations and is adversely affected by inflation, these results are not surprising.

Because most political conflicts surrounding macroeconomic policies center on inflation and unemployment, it is useful to examine the relative magnitude of the associated coefficients across groups. Taking the ratio of the inflation and unemployment parameters gives what are known as the marginal rates of substitution (MRS), that is, the implicit rates at which voters are willing to substitute unemployment for inflation:

	Occupation		
	Blue-collar	White-collar	Non–labor force
MRS (inflation/unemployment)	1.5	2.2	7.1

The coefficient ratios, or marginal rates of substitution, indicate that maintaining a given level of the political approval index among blue-collar workers would require that a 1.0 percentage point increase in the inflation rate be accompanied by a decrease of about 1.5 percentage points in the unemployment rate, whereas for white-collar workers the decrease in unemployment would have to be about 2.2 percentage points.[17] For voters outside the labor force the implied preference (indifference) curve is much steeper: for this group's political approval index to remain unchanged, a unit increase in the inflation rate requires a decrease in the unemployment rate of more than 7 percentage points. Equivalently, blue-collar, white-collar, and non–labor force voters would be indifferent to a 1.0 percentage point increase in unemployment if the inflation rate declined by 0.68 (1/1.5), 0.45 (1/2.2), and 0.14 (1/7.1) points, respectively.

Across partisan groups the effects of the macroeconomic variables also have the expected relative magnitudes, but they reveal sharper cleavages than the corresponding results for blue- and white-collar workers. The political approval indices for Democrats and Independents are far more responsive to movements in unemployment and the real income growth rate, and less responsive to movements in the inflation rate than is the approval index of Republicans.

Again, it is useful to examine the marginal rates of substitution between inflation and unemployment implied for the various groups:

17. For some comparative results for Britain see Chapter 10.

	Partisan group		
	Democrats	Republicans	Independents
MRS (inflation/unemployment)	0.96	4.3	1.0

The ratio of the inflation parameter to the unemployment parameter for Democrats and Independents is about 1.0, indicating they are indifferent to equivalent, offsetting movements in the inflation and unemployment rates. However, in order for Republicans to be indifferent to a 1.0 percentage point increase in inflation, the unemployment rate would have to fall more than four times as much. Alternatively, if the unemployment rate rose by one point, the Republican approval index would remain unchanged if inflation fell by only 0.23 points (1/4.3). Among occupations, only the non–labor force group implicitly reveals a steeper, more inflation-averse preference curve.

Table 5.4 reports the percentage point changes in Gallup poll political approval responses to increases of 2.0 points in the inflation, unemployment, and real income growth rates that are maintained 1 quarter, 8 quarters, and indefinitely. The estimates in Table 5.4 indicate that the responses to transitory, 1-quarter changes in the macroeconomy are small. However, if sustained for two years (8 quarters) or longer the political penalties and rewards generated by movements in the economy variables are sizable.

The intergroup pattern of the responses is almost identical to that of the logit model regression coefficients just discussed. Relatively great sensitivity to inflation is exhibited by Republicans and especially by voters outside the labor force, and relatively great sensitivity to real economic fluctuations (unemployment and the real income growth rate) is exhibited by Democrats, Independents, and blue-collar workers. Thus the sharpest cleavages over macroeconomic performance are between voters in and outside the labor force and between Republicans and other voters.[18]

18. Without political approval data disaggregated jointly by both occupational/labor force status and partisanship (and other dimensions), it is impossible to make more precise statements. The results here, however, are broadly consistent with Weatherford's microanalysis of the effect of "personal financial conditions" and social class controlling for party on reported electoral behavior in the 1956, 1958, and 1960 elections. See Stephen M. Weatherford, "Economic Conditions and Electoral Outcomes: Class Differences in the Political Response to Recession," *American Journal of Political Science*, 22 (1978), 917–938.

Table 5.4. Gallup Poll approval percentages for responses of occupational and partisan groups to macroeconomic performance[a].

| | Variable and duration of 2 percentage point increase | | | | | | | | |
| | Inflation rate | | | Unemployment rate | | | Real income growth rate | | |
Group	1 quarter	8 quarters	Indefinitely	1 quarter	8 quarters	Indefinitely	1 quarter	8 quarters	Indefinitely
Blue-collar	−1.0	−4.8	−6.6	−0.7	−3.2	−4.4	+0.8	+3.9	+5.4
White-collar	−1.5	−6.1	−7.2	−0.7	−2.7	−3.2	+0.9	+3.6	+4.2
Non-labor force	−1.8	−6.0	−6.4	−0.3	−0.9	−0.9	+0.7	+2.3	+2.4
Democrats	−0.7	−3.3	−4.3	−0.7	−3.4	−4.4	+0.9	+4.3	+5.6
Republicans	−1.9	−6.0	−6.3	−0.4	−1.4	−1.5	+1.1	+3.3	+3.5
Independents	−0.8	−4.2	−6.0	−0.8	−4.1	−5.9	+1.0	+5.0	+7.2

a. See notes to Table 5.3.

Summary and Conclusions

The first section of this chapter reviewed a dynamic model of political choice in which rational voters forced to make discrete judgments apply relative rather than absolute evaluation standards. It was shown that past as well as current economic and noneconomic events influence voters' contemporaneous political judgments, but that past outcomes are discounted backward in time, undoubtedly because the present relevance of earlier performance decays over time. Although the model does not include arbitrary time trends or permit arbitrary parameter changes, which are common features in empirical analyses of presidential approval data, it generates predictions fitting the observed survey data remarkably well: the correlations between the actual survey proportions and those implied by the logistic model equations range from 0.92 to 0.99 (Tables 5.1 and 5.2). Moreover, the time paths of the actual and fitted approval proportions suggest no obvious, important errors in the functional form or specifications of the model.

The empirical results in the second section have implications extending beyond the boundaries of presidential approval dynamics that may be of broader interest to students of political behavior and political parties. Among the performance variables appearing in the equations, the perceptual screen of party identification appears to have influenced significantly voters' responses only to the Watergate events. The intergroup pattern of the Watergate parameter estimates and the simulation-based trajectories of the decline in Nixon's approval ratings produced by the scandal leave little doubt that partisanship was an important factor mediating voters' responses. But this is the only instance in which partisan perception, rather than objective partisan-group interest, appears to account for intergroup patterns in the estimated effects, although it is not possible to draw definitive conclusions on this point without time-series data disaggregated jointly by partisanship and other characteristics.

However, perhaps more than critics of American political life on the left and right have acknowledged, division of the electorate along partisan lines corresponds to objective cleavages among voters over important substantive issues and events. The responses across groups to the escalation of American losses in Vietnam and to movements in inflation, unemployment, and the growth rate of real income reveal sharp partisan differences which are difficult to attribute to the perceptual screen of party identification and which generally are more pronounced than the corresponding interoccupational differences. The political support of Democrats (and Independents) exhibited relatively great sensitivity to unemployment and real income growth as well as to the Vietnam battle fatalities, whereas the support of Republicans (and retirees) was less sensitive to the Vietnam losses and more sensitive to inflation. These results are broadly consistent with what we know about the objective distributional consequences of macroeconomic fluctuations and the socioeconomic incidence of Vietnam casualties, but they have no obvious, purely "partisan" explanation.

As Fiorina and others have argued, then, partisan alignments are not simply formations of voters united by psychological affinities long removed from concrete events; rather, they also may be realistically viewed as cleavage formations reflecting diverging objective interests over major political and economic issues.[19]

19. Morris Fiorina, "An Outline for a Model of Party Choice," *American Journal of Political Science*, 21 (1977), 601–628.

6

President Reagan's Mandate from the 1980 Elections: A Shift to the Right?

The 1980 elections obviously represented a substantial victory for Ronald Reagan and the Republican party. Mr. Reagan received 55.3 percent of the two-party vote (50.8 percent of all votes cast) and was the first challenger to defeat an elected, incumbent president since Roosevelt beat Hoover in 1932. The Democratic party's share of the popular vote for the House of Representatives fell 3 percentage points (from 54.3 percent in 1978 to 51.4 percent) and its share of seats 7.6 percent (from 276 to 243)[1] in the House. Democratic losses (Republican gains) were even heavier in the Senate: 12 seats (from 58 to 46). As a result the Republicans now enjoy their first Senate majority since 1954.[2] Among the victims of the debacle were seven well-known lib-

Reprinted from *American Politics Quarterly*, 10 (October 1982), 387–420.

1. Three formerly Democratic House seats were vacant at the time of the election; Democratic House strength on election day was therefore 273.

2. In statistical terms, the magnitude of the Democrats' losses in the Senate was the most unusual feature of the 1980 elections. The only other double-digit shifts in the party distribution of Senate seats since World War II were in 1946, when the Democrats lost 12 seats and the Republicans gained 13, and in 1958, when the Democrats gained 16 seats and the Republicans lost 12. The next-largest shift was in 1948, when the Democrats gained and the Republicans lost 9 seats. However, the Democrats were more exposed than the Republicans in 1980: they held 24 of the 34 seats up for election. And even though the Republicans won 22 of the 34 Senate races, they received only 47 percent of the nationwide senatorial vote.

By comparison, neither the presidential nor the House vote results were particularly unusual. Reagan's two-party vote share was just about equal to the postwar mean of 55 percent for presidential winners. The 3 percent decline in the Democrats' share of the popular vote for the House was within one standard deviation of the mean loss in presidential years for the party losing the presidency (the postwar mean is −1.84 percent with a standard deviation of 3 percent), as was the Democratic loss of 33 House seats (the postwar mean seat decline for the losing party in presidential elections is about 18 with a standard deviation of 26.)

eral Democratic senators: McGovern (South Dakota), Bayh (Indiana), Culver (Iowa), Magnuson (Washington), Durkin (New Hampshire), Nelson (Wisconsin), and Church (Idaho).

There are two ways to interpret the 1980 election outcomes. One interpretation, more popular among journalists and Republicans in or close to the administration than among academic specialists, is that the election results reflect a fundamental "shift to the right" of the electorate's preferences concerning the Federal government's role in domestic social and economic affairs.[3] According to this view, the election signaled a dramatic erosion of political support for federal economic intervention and social-welfare efforts that began with Franklin Roosevelt's New Deal legislation in the 1930s and reached maturity with Lyndon Johnson's Great Society programs in the 1960s.

An alternative interpretation is that the 1980 election outcomes represent the predictable consequences of poor performance—particularly poor macroeconomic performance—under Carter and the Democrats. The 1980 election results therefore should be seen as a referendum on the incumbents' (mis)handling of economy and perhaps of other problems.[4] Ironically, it follows from this view that the 1980 political successes of Ronald Reagan and François Mitterrand have common origins. Both the American Republican and the French Socialist candidates (and their respective parties) were the political beneficiaries of the restrictive economic policies embraced by the Carter and Giscard d'Estaing governments to fight inflation.[5] According to this view, then, any president and incumbent party going before the electorate with the record of Carter and the Democrats would have been in deep political trouble, and virtually any credible challenge to the president and the in-party—whether from the left or from the right—would have been successful. Hence the 1980 election results represent neither an ideological watershed nor a rejection of

3. For examples of this view see N. Podhoretz, "The New American Majority," *Commentary*, 71 (January 1981), 19–28, and (in a piece written just before the election) R. M. Scammon, quoted in B. J. Wattenberg, "Is It the End of an Era?" *Public Opinion*, October–November 1980, pp. 2–12.

4. The first extended development of the idea that the election results often represent rational, retrospective performance judgments by the voters appears in V. O. Key, *The Responsible Electorate* (New York: Vintage 1966). For a more modern treatment of this idea see M. Fiorina, *Retrospective Voting in American National Elections* (New Haven: Yale University Press, 1981).

5. For evidence on the political support for French presidents in response to economic outcomes see Chapter 8. The parallels between the Reagan and Mitterand (and Thatcher) victories are discussed in S. M. Lipset, ed., *Party Coalition in the 1980s* (San Francisco: Institute for Contemporary Studies, 1981).

liberal social policies, but rather a repudiation of the Carter administration's poor performance.

These alternative interpretations of the 1980 election have significant implications for the support that President Reagan's economic and fiscal program is likely to command among voters during the next few years. If Carter and the Democrats were defeated because of a substantial ideological shift in the electorate away from welfare-state liberalism, then President Reagan's program of substantial reductions in federal social expenditures and taxation is squarely consistent with the new distribution of voter preferences and consequently should enjoy sustained widespread support by the mass public. On the other hand, if the Democrats' defeat in 1980 stems primarily from the high inflation, high unemployment, and low growth experienced during the later part of the Carter administration, then President Reagan's "economic recovery" program must significantly improve America's macroeconomic performance (and not simply reduce federal social expenditures and redistribute income away from lower-income groups) in order to remain politically viable in the years ahead. As will be seen, evidence concerning the sources of the Republicans' victory as well as events since Mr. Reagan's inauguration supports the latter view.[6]

The Economy and the 1980 Elections: Evidence from Statistical Data and Models

The macroeconomic history of the Carter administration looks like the stylized "political business cycle" run backward.[7] Having inherited a

6. In addition to the arguments and evidence presented in the text see P. Abramson, J. H. Aldrich, and D. W. Rhode, *Change and Continuity in the 1980 Elections* (Washington, D.C.: Congressional Quarterly Press, 1981); W. D. Burnham, "The 1981 Earthquake: Realignment, Reaction, or What?" in *The Hidden Election: Politics and Economics in the 1980 Presidential Campaign*, ed. T. Furgeson and J. Rodgers (New York: Pantheon, 1981); S. M. Lipset, "France's Warning to the Reagan Administration," *Journal of Contemporary Studies*, Fall 1981, pp. 35–38; A. Ranney, *The American Election of 1980* (Washington, D.C.: American Enterprise Institute, 1981); and G. Orren and E. J. Dionne, "The Next New Deal," *Working Papers*, May/June 1981, pp. 25–36.

7. The "political business cycle" model of Nordhaus, Tufte, and others holds that presidents exploit the (assumed) myopia of voters for electoral gains by engineering unsustainable booms (such as unrealistically low unemployment and high real income growth) just before elections, postponing the inevitable austerity until the elections are safely over. See W. Nordhaus, "The Political Business Cycle," *Review of Economic Studies*, 42 (1975), 169–190, and E. Tufte, *Political Control of the Economy* (Princeton: Princeton University Press, 1978), chaps. 1 and 2.

7.7 percent rate of unemployment from the Ford administration—a hangover from the terrible 1974–75 recession—the Carter administration pursued stimulative macroeconomic policies throughout 1977 and into 1978. The policies succeeded and helped reduce unemployment by almost 2 percent between the end of 1976 and the beginning of 1979. However, inflation accelerated steadily in 1977 and 1978 and ratcheted upward even more in 1979 after the second big round of OPEC petroleum price increases. This prompted the Carter administration in late 1978 to abandon the liberal Democratic goal of moving the economy toward full employment and to implement restrictive monetary and fiscal policies designed to put downward pressure on the inflation rate. The policy shift created an election-year recession, but because of the sluggish response of wages and prices to economic slack, the inflation rate declined only slightly during the last two quarters of 1980 from its midyear peak. Consequently, President Carter and the Democrats went before the electorate in 1980 with the worst of all possible situations—high inflation, increased unemployment, and falling real income and output.

It is no surprise that President Carter was the first elected incumbent to be defeated in a reelection bid since 1932: Carter had the worst election-year economic record since Hoover. In 1980, for example, for the first time since 1932 the year-on-year growth rate of real output and income was actually *negative*. This is one important reason why President Carter's Gallup poll approval rating plummeted in July 1980 (the trough of the 1980 recession) to 21 percent—the lowest level recorded since the Gallup organization began polling in the 1930s, during the Roosevelt administration.

The Carter administration's economic performance record is compared more systematically with that of other postwar administrations in Table 6.1. Because we know that mass political support for the president (as registered in the Gallup polls) is influenced by the unemployment rate, the consumer price index inflation rate, and the growth rate of per capita real personal disposable income, these variables are shown in the table. The combined economic record displayed in column 4 is simply the sum of the real income growth rate *minus* the inflation and unemployment rates ($R - P - U$). Averaged over all voters, these three economic variables have been shown in empirical work to have approximately equal weight on support for the president, with inflation and unemployment of course being negatively signed (see Chapter 5).

The entries on the left in each of the columns in Table 6.1 show the

Table 6.1. Election-year and cumulative economic performance records of postwar presidential administrations.

Administration (election year)	(1) Unemployment rate (U)		(2) CPI inflation rate (P)		(3) Growth rate of per capita real personal disposable income (R)[a]		(4) Combined economic record (R − P − U)	
	Election year	Cumulative weighted avg.[b]	Election year	Cumulative weighted avg.[b]	Election year	Cumulative weighted avg.[b]	Election year	Cumulative weighted avg.[b]
Truman (1952)	3.02	3.59	2.26	3.22	1.07	1.80	−4.21	−5.01
Eisenhower I (1956)	4.12	4.32	1.46	1.36	3.12	2.63	−2.46	−3.05
Eisenhower II (1960)	5.54	5.51	1.50	1.36	0.82	1.03	−6.22	−5.84
Kennedy-Johnson I (1964)	5.16	5.46	1.31	1.14	5.51	4.72	−0.96	−1.87
Johnson II (1968)	3.56	3.75	4.12	3.75	2.85	2.60	−4.83	−4.90
Nixon I (1972)	5.58	5.56	3.27	3.67	3.38	3.14	−5.47	−6.09
Nixon II-Ford (1976)	7.67	7.48	5.56	6.36	2.27	1.37	−10.97	−12.47
Carter (1980)	7.15	6.55	12.67	10.33	−3.25	−0.78	−23.08	−17.66

a. Nominal per capita personal disposable income deflated by the consumer price index. All growth rates are formed by taking first (quarterly) differences of the natural logarithms and are expressed at annual rates.

b. The weighted average records are defined over the 15 preelection quarters of each administration, from the last performance outcome backward to the first using a decay-rate discount parameter of 0.8:

$$\left(1 \Big/ \sum_i g^i\right) \sum_i g^i X_{t-i-1}; \quad i = 0, 1, 2, \ldots 14.$$

$g = 0.8$ is based on the empirical estimate for presidential election outcomes presented in the text.

election-year economic record. Although the sustainable unemployment rate and the core inflation rate have shown an upward trend in the postwar American economy, it is obvious that Carter's record was an especially poor one. Compared with the election-year records of other administrations, Carter's inflation and real income growth rate performances were by far the worst, and his election-year unemployment rate was more favorable only than Ford's in 1976. The Carter administration's combined election-year record, shown in column 4, registers the least favorable score by a wide margin.

Since political support is based on an administration's cumulative performance and not just on its election-year record,[8] each column of the table also shows the weighted average of the economic performance outcomes for the 15 preelection quarters of each presidential term, starting from the quarterly outcome nearest to the election (the July–September quarter) and going backward to the first.[9] However, the message conveyed by the cumulative weighted average performance records does not differ substantially from that of the raw election-year records. Cumulatively from 1977:1 to 1980:3, Carter's real income and inflation records were the worst and his unemployment record the second worst of any postwar administration. Given his administration's dismal combined cumulative record of −17.7, it would have been surprising had Carter *not* lost the election. The only other sitting president to be defeated in a reelection bid—Ford in 1976—also had a distinctively poor macroeconomic record. With the exception of Carter's combined records, both the election-year and cumulative combined performance score of the Ford administration (−11 and −12.5, respectively) are substantially less favorable than the others.

8. Also see the regression results reported later in this chapter.

9. The cumulative weighted averages for each variable (X) in Table 6.1 are computed: $(1/\Sigma_{i=0}^{14} g^i) \Sigma_{i=0}^{14} g^i X_{t-i-1}$, where $i = 0, 1, 2, \ldots, 14$, and $g = 0.8$ is the lag rate-of-decay parameter estimate in Equation (6.2). For time t equal to the election quarter, this expression yields the weight sequence $0.198(t - 1)$, $0.161(t - 2)$, $0.130(t - 3)$, $0.105(t - 4)$, $0.085(t - 5)$, $\ldots$, $0.010(t - 15)$, which means that preelection quarter outcomes are weighted the most heavily by voters and that the weights applied to earlier outcomes back to the first in each administration decline geometrically. Note that $(1/\Sigma_{i=0}^{14} g^i)$ is simply a normalizing constant ensuring that the weights sum to 1.0; hence the weighted sums yield true performance averages for each administration.

In the cumulative performance calculations, the growth rate of per capita real income has been adjusted upward and the CPI inflation rate adjusted downward along the lines described in Chapter 7, to take account of the (small) direct unfavorable effects of the OPEC shocks during 1973–74 and 1979–80, which were beyond the control of domestic political authorities.

The impression conveyed by the statistical data in Table 6.1—that the economic record suffices to explain the Democrats' losses in 1980—is reinforced by predictions of several statistical models. In Chapter 5 I reported evidence indicating that a president's approval rating in the Gallup poll responds systematically to unemployment, inflation, and the growth rate of real income, and that the collapse of the economy during the last two years of the Carter administration accounted for the deterioration of Carter's Gallup ratings. Although Gallup approval ratings are not electoral outcomes, they do correlate highly with the vote shares received by incumbents running for re-election, as well as with the vote shares of nonincumbent nominees of the president's party. For all presidential elections from 1952 through 1976 the linear equation best describing the relationship between the two-party percentage of the vote received by the incumbent party's nominee (V) and the preelection quarterly Gallup percentage approval rating of the president ($Approve$) is:[10]

$$V_t = 33.3 + 0.373\ Approve_t, \qquad\qquad (6.1)$$
$$\ (6.33)\quad (0.11)$$

$R^2 = 0.68$, $SER = 4.2$ (standard errors in parentheses).

President Carter's preelection, 1980:3, Gallup approval rating was 33.3 percent. By Equation (6.1) the predicted two-party vote share for Carter in the 1980 election therefore is 45.7 percent [33.3 + (0.373 × 33.3)]—only 1.1 percent away from his actual two-party share of 44.6 percent and nearly two full standard errors lower than the 1952–1976 mean presidential vote share of 53.3 percent received by nominees of the incumbent party.

A second, more straightforward way of assessing the predictability of Carter's defeat from the economic record of his administration is to examine the 1980 presidential election outcome in light of the historical association between the vote share received by the incumbent party's candidate and macroeconomic performance. Because the structure of the American political economy has changed profoundly from the prewar to the postwar period, the analysis is confined to elections from 1952 onward. However, since the political effects of

10. The estimates in Equation (6.1) indicate that Gallup approval ratings exhibit wider swings than do presidential voting outcomes: people find it easier to approve or disapprove of a president's performance than to give or deny the incumbent party their presidential vote. For more evidence on the connection between Gallup poll ratings and presidential election outcomes, see L. Siegelman, "Presidential Popularity and Presidential Elections," *Public Opinion Quarterly*, Winter 1979, pp. 532–534.

unemployment, inflation, and the growth rate of real personal disposable income cannot be estimated reliably from only eight presidential election observations, the estimation equation includes only real income growth performance.[11]

The following equation best describes the association of the two-party vote share (in percentage points) of the incumbent party's candidate for president (V) and the (geometrically) weighted average of the (OPEC-adjusted) annualized quarter-on-quarter percentage rate of growth of real personal disposable income per capita (R) cumulated over the 15 preelection quarters in each administration:[12]

$$V_t = 45.7 + 3.30 \left[\sum_{i=0}^{14} 0.8^i \; R_{t-i-1} \left(1 \Big/ \sum_{i=0}^{14} 0.8^i \right) \right],$$
$$\quad (3.27) \;\; (1.49) \;\; (0.19) \tag{6.2}$$

$R^2 = 0.63, \qquad SER = 5.09$ (standard errors in parentheses).

11. Preliminary analyses undertaken here and a great many other studies have found the growth rate of per capita real income (or output) to be the single best predictor of election outcomes.

12. By virtue of the lag weight rate-of-decay parameter g, Equation (6.2) is nonlinear; therefore, a standard nonlinear least-squares algorithm was used for estimation. Nonlinear estimation of Equation (6.2) is equivalent to ordinary least-squares estimation of $V_t = \beta_0 + \beta_1 R_t^*$, where R^* is formed: $R_t^* = \sum_{i=0}^{14} g^i R_{t-i-1}(1/\sum_{i=0}^{14} g^i)$, and $0 \le g \le 1$. Forming an R^* variate for every value of g in the interval zero to one, running an ordinary least-squares regression with each R^* so formed, and choosing the equation yielding the minimum standard error of regression (best fit) would give estimates of β_0, β_1, and g identical to those reported in the text.

If the best-fitting least-squares regression is based on $g = 0$, then $R_t^* = R_{t-1}$ and election outcomes respond only to the preelection quarter (July–September) record. $g = 1$ means: $R_t^* = (1/15) \sum_{i=0}^{14} R_{t-i-1}$, implying that election outcomes respond to an arithmetic average of real income growth during the presidential administration. The value of g producing the best fit was $g = 0.8$, which means R_t^* is based on a cumulative geometrically weighted average of the R_{t-i-1}, $i = 0, 1, 2, \ldots , 14$, with the lag weight sequence given in note 9.

Equation (6.2) is similar in spirit to the model developed by Tufte, *Political Control of the Economy*, tab. 5-6, which uses the election-year change in per capita real personal disposable income and the net advantage of the incumbent's party's candidate in the average number of "good" versus "bad" points about the candidates mentioned by respondents in the election surveys conducted by the Survey Research Center at the University of Michigan. The problem with the latter variable (which exhibits a correlation of 0.91 with the nationwide presidential vote over the period 1948–1976) is that it comes too close to being a survey-based measure of intention to vote for the candidate of the incumbent party. It is not an exogenous measure of performance or voter preferences. To say, for example, that Carter did badly in 1980 (in part) because voters on average perceived fewer good points (or more bad points) about him than Reagan, supplies little independent information useful for explaining the election result. Finally, concerning the real income variable, the *cumulative* weighted average quarter-on-quarter real income growth rate used in Equation (6.2) does a better job empirically than election-year income changes in explaining presidential voting outcomes.

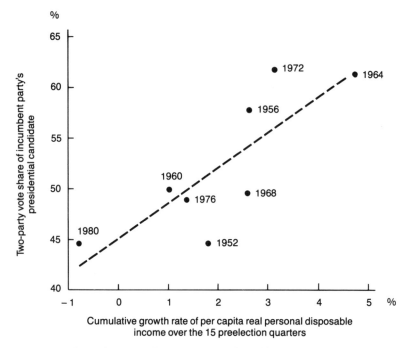

Figure 6.1. Cumulative real income growth performance and the vote for the incumbent party's presidential candidate, 1952–1980.

Figure 6.1 shows a scatterplot of the vote share and cumulative real income growth rate data along with the regression line implied by Equation (6.2). The regression line prediction for President Carter's two-party vote share is 42.5 percent, which is 2.1 percent below the 44.6 percent he actually received. The regression results reinforce the point that any incumbent candidate with a cumulative real income growth rate record as poor as Carter's would be expected to lose—and lose badly. The regression line in Figure 6.1 also yields large overpredictions (negative residuals) for the Democratic (incumbent party) candidates in 1968 and especially in 1952. Clearly the U.S. involvement in the Vietnamese and Korean civil wars—each of which ultimately became extremely unpopular and neither of which is taken account of by the simple economic performance model of Equation (6.2)—helped produce a vote for the incumbent party's presidential candidate lower than would have been anticipated from the real income growth rate record alone. Indeed, the regression line shown in Figure 6.1 suggests that had the United States not become involved in the Korean and Vietnamese conflicts during the Truman and Kennedy–Johnson presidencies, respectively, the Democrats might well have won both the 1952 and 1968 elections. (Prominent Republican campaign appeals in 1952 and 1968 were Eisenhower's pledge to "go to Korea" and Nixon's "secret plan" to end the Vietnam war, respectively.) In other words, on the basis of the incumbent party's cumulative real income growth rate record alone, Stevenson in 1952 and Humphrey in 1968 perhaps "should" have been winners.[13]

The main conclusion to be drawn from Equation (6.2), however, is that the incumbent party's presidential candidate typically can expect to receive about 45.7 percent of the vote plus a percentage equal to approximately 3.3 times the administration's geometrically weighted cumulative growth rate record for per capita real personal disposable income. Therefore, barring major noneconomic developments salient to the electorate (such as the military involvement in Korea and Vietnam), postwar candidates of the incumbent party could anticipate receiving a comfortable majority of the presidential vote—say 52 percent—if during the 15 preelection quarters the annualized quarter-on-quarter per capita real income growth rate was maintained at about 1.6 percent $[(52 - 45.7)/3.3 = 1.7]$. Because voters weight performance outcomes close to the election date much more heavily than outcomes earlier in the term (as note 9 shows, for $g = 0.8$ the weight given to the outcome in the preelection quarter is nearly twenty times larger than weight given to the outcome during the first quarter of the administration), a strong election-year economic record will compensate for truly miserable performance during the first couple of years of an administration. Conversely, miserable performance near the election will neutralize a very favorable record earlier in the term. In any case, not one postwar candidate of the incumbent party was successful when the cumulative, geometrically weighted average real income growth rate was under 1.7 percent. President Carter's problem was that the disastrous 1979–80 performance swamped the favorable growth record of 1977–78. Nixon's first election bid in 1960 was unsuccessful because the strong performance of 1959 was insufficient to neutralize the political consequences of the 1958 and, especially, the 1960 recessions during the Eisenhower administration. In President Ford's case, even though election-year outcomes are weighted more

13. Given the small number of observations in the regression, however, neither of these observations represents, in strict statistical terms, a highly significant deviation from the expected outcomes.

heavily than the earlier record, the favorable 1976 growth rate was simply not great enough to overcome the political fallout from the deep recession of 1974–75, which at the time was the worst contraction in postwar U.S. history.

A parallel statistical analysis of the expected popular vote for the president's party in on-year congressional elections also yields results indicating that nothing was unusual about the Democrats' 1980 losses. Following Edward Tufte, a sensible measure of congressional election outcomes is the standardized vote loss or gain (*SVL*) of the president's party, which is defined as the nationwide House vote percentage for the party of the president in the *t*th election *minus* that party's average popular vote percentage in eight prior congressional elections. Equation (6.3) reports the results for the regression of the standardized vote loss on the (OPEC-adjusted) cumulative growth rate of per capita real personal disposable income:[14]

$$SVL_t = \underset{(0.83)}{-3.57} + \underset{(0.29)}{1.19} \left[\sum_{i=0}^{14} \underset{(0.12)}{0.56^i} R_{t-i-1} \left(1 \Big/ \sum_{i=0}^{14} 0.56^i \right) \right], \quad (6.3)$$

$R^2 = 0.78, \qquad SER = 1.56$ (standard errors in parentheses).

Equation (6.3) indicates that each percentage point change in the cumulative growth rate record for per capita real personal disposable income typically has been associated with a change of 1.2 percent in the national vote for the incumbent party's House candidate. Given a "swing ratio" (the change in party seat shares accompanying a given change in House popular vote shares) that for recent on-year congressional elections has been estimated to fall between about 2.0 and 2.5,[15] each sustained percentage point change in the annualized,

---

14. In Equation (6.3) the (OPEC-adjusted) per capita real personal disposable income growth rate, *R*, is cumulated over the 15 quarters preceding each presidential-year congressional election. Cumulating *R* over the 7 preelection quarters from the last midterm congressional election yields very similar results. For evidence indicating that the effect of changes in per capita real disposable income on the postwar congressional vote is strongest for incumbents of the in-party outside the South, see J. R. Hibbing and J. R. Alford, "The Electoral Impact of Economic Conditions: Who Is Held Responsible?" *American Journal of Political Science*, 25 (1981), 423–439.

Because of the staggered election system, it makes less sense to analyze an equation such as (6.3) for Senate voting outcomes.

15. See estimates in R. L. Calvert and J. A. Ferejohn, "Presidential Coattails in Historical Perspective," *California Institute of Technology Social Science Working Papers*, 343 (January 1981), tab. 1.

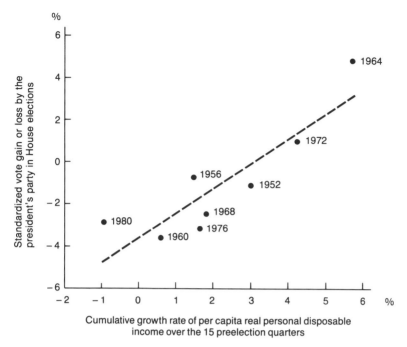

Figure 6.2. Cumulative real income growth performance and the vote for House candidates of the president's party, 1952–1980.

quarter-on-quarter real income growth rate translates into a 2.4–3.0 point shift in the percentage of House seats going to the party controlling the presidency. For example, in the case of the Democrats in 1980 each sustained percentage point decline in the real income growth rate had an implicit political price tag (political shadow cost) of between 10 and 13 House seats. Furthermore, the constant in Equation (6.3) of −3.6 implies that in order for the president's party to obtain a House vote share in a given on-year election equal to its long-run average (the mean of eight prior House elections), the cumulative, weighted average real income growth rate must be in the vicinity of 3 percent [3.6 = 1.2 × 3.0].

In 1980 the Democrats were saddled with a cumulative real income growth rate record of −0.94 percent (given $g = 0.56$). As illustrated in Figure 6.2, this yields via Equation (6.3) an expected standardized vote loss of about 4.7 percent ($SVL = -4.7$). In fact the Democrats' standardized (and actual) vote loss was just under 3 percent in 1980, which, in light of the Carter administration's economic record, was perhaps a fortunate result.[16] Nonetheless, it is clear that in the 1980 House races a sizable aggregate shift in the popular vote against Democratic candidates was to be expected from economic conditions during the Carter years.

The Economy and the 1980 Elections: Evidence from the Surveys

Some readers may find arguments based on statistical relations among aggregate electoral and economic data less than completely convincing. However, the evidence from survey interviews of large numbers of individual voters is fully consistent with the conclusions drawn from the aggregate statistical models presented above.

As in 1976, there is little doubt about the preeminent status of macroeconomic issues with voters in the 1980 election. For example, Gallup poll data show that in 1980 more than three-quarters of the public mentioned one or more economic issues as "the most important problem facing the country today." In contrast, only about 12 percent of Gallup respondents identified other domestic social and political issues, or international issues, as among the nation's most important problems. (See Chapter 4, Figure 4.1.) Interviews conducted by the CBS News/*New York Times* survey organization with more than 12,000 actual voters in selected precincts as they left the polls tell a similar story.

Table 6.2 shows data from the CBS News/*New York Times* interviews on the issues most important to Reagan voters. Clearly, neither social and "moral" questions—the Equal Rights Amendment and abortion—nor international issues—the crises in Iran and U.S. international prestige—weighed heavily on the minds of many Reagan supporters. This implies that the influence of antifeminist groups and the "right-to-life" and "moral majority" movements in the general election was quite small,[17] notwithstanding all the publicity their ac-

16. On the other hand, the swing ratio in 1980 was on the high side: Each percentage point shift in the popular vote was translated into a loss of about 2.5 percentage points in the Democrats' House seat share [2.5 = 7.6/3.0].

17. The fact that the ERA and abortion issues contributed little to Reagan's appeal comes as no surprise in view of the fact that public opinion on these questions diverged sharply from the Republican candidate's strong, well-publicized positions. For example, 1980 Gallup polls reported that only 31 percent of the public opposed the Equal Rights Amendment and only 18 percent favored making abortion "illegal under all

Table 6.2. Issues underlying the support for Reagan in the 1980 election, on the basis of the question "Which [of the listed] issues were most important in affecting how you voted today?" (two responses permitted).

Issue	Percentage responding
Inflation and the economy	40
Balancing the federal budget	26
Jobs and unemployment	20
U.S. prestige around the world	19
Reducing federal income taxes	13
Crisis in Iran	9
ERA and the abortion issue	5

Source: CBS News/*New York Times* 1980 Election Day Poll, reported in *National Journal,* August 11, 1980, p. 1877.

tivities received and all the money such groups raised.[18] Instead, the great economic issues of inflation and unemployment and the fiscal issue of the federal deficit (undoubtedly because many people see deficit spending as an important cause of inflation) dominated the attention of Reagan voters. The only issue directly touching a right-wing ideological chord—the question of federal tax reduction—was designated as an important influence by only 13 percent of the Reagan voters, putting it in fifth place among the significant issues.

These data are compatible with other survey results showing that government spending and service programs continue to enjoy widespread public support. For example, in the National Opinion Research Center's 1980 General Social Survey only 33 percent of the public thought that "the government should provide fewer services . . . in order to reduce spending." Overwhelming majorities held the view that we are spending either "too little" or "about the right

circumstances." These distributions have been quite stable since the mid-1970s. See the *Gallup Opinion Index,* Report no. 183 (December 1980), 2–3.

The University of Michigan Survey Research Center's National Election Study data also show that domestic economic concerns had a much greater influence on voting decisions in 1980 than did the crisis in Iran and other issues. See A. H. Miller and M. P. Wattenberg, "Policy and Performance Voting in the 1980 Election" (Paper presented to the annual meeting of the American Political Science Association, September 1981).

18. According to the Federal Election Commission, the various New Right organizations raised more money nationally for the 1980 elections than did the entire Democratic party. See F. Fitzgerald, "The Triumphs of the New Right," *New York Review of Books,* November 19, 1981, pp. 19 ff.

amount" on such major social program areas as health (92 percent), education (90 percent), solving the problems of big cities (76 percent), drug addiction (92 percent), improving the conditions of blacks (74 percent), and crime (94 percent).[19] Similarly, the January 1981 CBS News/*New York Times* poll found that 72 percent of the public would like to see federal spending "increased or kept about the same" for benefits to college students; 72 percent also held this view for unemployment compensation, 77 percent for controlling pollution, 75 percent for mass transit, 81 percent for highways, and 89 percent for Social Security cost-of-living benefits.[20] Only the food stamp program—whose abuses had been well publicized during the Carter administration—did not attract strong majority support in the CBS News/*New York Times* poll: 47 percent of the public thought spending on this program should be decreased and 47 percent thought spending should remain the same or be increased.

The personal qualities selected by Reagan voters as reasons for their choice also reveal little evidence of ideological voting in 1980. Table 6.3 shows the pertinent data from the CBS News/*New York Times* election-day survey. The most striking feature of these data is that only 11 percent of Reagan voters listed his conservatism as a reason for their choice. Rather, voters' sense that it was "time for a change" and their perception that Reagan was "a strong leader" were identified as the decisive factors. In light of the economic mismanagement of 1979–80 and Jimmy Carter's tendency to appear vacillating and ineffective, it is hard to argue that such judgments were inaccurate or unreasonable. Small wonder, then, that when the public was

19. Only a residual "welfare" category did not receive majority support, reflecting Americans' distaste for the welfare concept. Forty-one percent thought we were spending "too little" or "about the right amount" in this area. But the lack of strong majority support for welfare spending predates the 1980 election by many years. In 1976, for example, 37 percent of GSS respondents felt that too little or about the right amount was being spent on "welfare." See *General Social Surveys, 1972–1980: Cumulative Codebook* (Roper Center, 1980), 71–74, and *Public Opinion*, February–March 1981, p. 27).

20. See the report on this survey by A. Clymer, "Democrats Favored in House, Poll Shows," *New York Times*, April 25, 1982, p. 36. Nor did tax limitation referenda fare well in 1980. Efforts to reduce property taxes in Arizona, Michigan, Nevada, Oregon, South Dakota, and Utah failed by varying margins. The only property tax reduction measure to pass was Proposition 2½ in Massachusetts, although a postelection statewide poll taken in April 1981 indicated that respondents who had voted for the proposition by a 55–45 percent margin would defeat it by 48–44 percent if given the chance to recast their vote—many of them because they thought local officials were not implementing the measure responsibly. See *Public Opinion*, February–March 1981, p. 40, and, for comparable information about 1978 referenda, *Public Opinion*, November–December 1978, pp. 26–28.

Table 6.3. Qualities underlying Reagan's personal appeal in the 1980 election, on the basis of the question "Which [of the listed] qualities best describe your choice?" (two responses permitted).

Quality	Percentage responding
It's time for a change	38
He's a strong leader	21
He's my party's candidate	12
He's a real conservative	11
He impressed me during the debate	10
I like his vice-president	9
He has honesty and integrity	9
His experience in government	6

Source: CBS News/*New York Times* 1980 Election Day Poll, reported in *National Journal,* August 8, 1980, p. 1877.

asked to evaluate comparatively the performance of the last eight presidents (Roosevelt to Carter) in the January 1981 Harris poll, only 2 percent thought Carter "was best on domestic affairs" and fully 44 percent thought he "was least able to get things done."[21] In any case, there is no sign from the data in Tables 6.2 or 6.3 that support for Reagan reflected a dramatic surge in conservative political orientations among voters.

Recent trends in the ideological distribution of the electorate identified by various national surveys confirm this interpretation. Table 6.4 reports the relevant data. Although the various surveys used different question wordings and scales to assess the electorate's ideological orientation, the data in Table 6.4 show clearly that there was no great ideological shift in 1980. The National Election Studies, conducted by the University of Michigan's Survey Research Center (SRC), indicate considerable stability in the distribution of ideological orientations since 1972. Relative to earlier years, the only distinguishing feature of

21. Not surprisingly, Ford received the second least favorable ratings. Five percent considered him "best on domestic affairs" and 13 percent considered him "least able to get things done"; *Public Opinion,* February–March 1981, p. 38.

The SRC National Election Study data show that Ronald Reagan was not very positively evaluated during the 1980 campaign. A. H. Miller and M. P. Wattenberg ("Policy and Performance Voting in the 1980 Election") report that for the period since 1952, when the National Election Studies began, Reagan was evaluated less favorably than any other successful presidential candidate. But his opponent, Jimmy Carter, was seen even less favorably.

Table 6.4.   Recent trends in the ideological distribution of the electorate (percentages).

Survey	Year				
	1972	1974	1976	1978	1980
SRC National Election Studies					
Liberal	19	21	16	20	17
Neutral–moderate	27	26	25	27	20
Conservative	27	24	25	28	29
Gallup polls					
Liberal	27	—	20	—	19
Middle-of-the-road	34	—	47	—	49
Conservative	39	—	33	—	31
General Social Surveys					
Liberal	—	31	29	28	26
Moderate	—	40	40	38	41
Conservative	—	30	31	34	34

Sources: Warren E. Miller et al., *American National Election Studies Sourcebook 1952–1978* (Cambridge, Mass.: Harvard University Press, 1980), p. 95, and Interuniversity Consortium for Political and Social Research, University of Michigan, *Election Study Codebooks* (various years) for SRC surveys; Roper Center, *General Social Surveys, 1972–1980 Cumulative Codebook* (1980) for GSS data; *Public Opinion*, February–March 1981, p. 20, for Gallup data.

Note: Ideological scales and wording of questions vary.

1980 in the SRC data is the 5–7 percent shift out of the neutral-moderate group into a residual nonideological category (not shown in the table). The Gallup polls suggest a decline of perhaps 8 percentage points among the electorate viewing themselves as liberal and conservative, and a corresponding growth in the percentage of middle-of-the-roaders. The General Social Surveys show a gradual decline in the share of self-identified liberals and a growth in the share of conservatives of 4–5 percentage points from 1974 to 1980—hardly evidence of a major change in the political composition of the electorate. Survey evidence favoring the idea that the 1980 election represents a realignment of ideological commitments is therefore almost nil.

The implications of Equation (6.2) and Figure 6.1, tying Carter's defeat to his administration's economic performance, are supported by other survey results bearing more directly on the 1980 presidential contest. The data in Table 6.5 show the division of the vote among

Table 6.5. Family financial situation and the vote for the president, 1976 and 1980, on the basis of the question "Compared to a year ago, would you say that your family is financially better off today, about the same, worse off today, or not sure?".

	Financial position		
	Better	Same	Worse
1976			
% share between candidates			
Carter	30	51	77
Ford	70	49	23
Number in sample	3,262	6,924	3,908
% share of sample	23	49	28
1980			
% share among candidates[a]			
Carter	53/59	46/50	25/28
Reagan	37/41	46/50	64/72
Anderson	8	7	8
Number in sample	1,841	4,602	3,911
% share of sample	18	44	38

Source: CBS News/New York Times election-day interviews with voters as they left the polls, reported in the New York Times, November 9, 1980.

a. The second numbers in the Carter and Reagan entries for 1980 are two-party vote shares, excluding Anderson.

voters who reported their family financial situation as having become better, stayed the same, or become worse over the election year.[22] Since data are available for both 1976 and 1980, and since Jimmy Carter was a candidate in both elections, the survey results reveal the outcomes of a quasi-experiment.

In both elections the economy was the dominant issue. In 1976 Carter was the challenger attacking Ford's economic record. The challenge was successful, and in 1980, as the incumbent, Carter had to defend his record against the major challenge from Reagan and the nuisance factor posed by Anderson's independent candidacy.[23] Table

22. Mr. Reagan put a similar question to viewers of the October 28, 1980, Reagan-Carter debate when, in his closing statement, he encouraged voters to ask themselves, "Are you better off than you were four years ago?"

23. Anderson voters, who found both Reagan and Carter unappealing, appear to have hurt neither major party candidate relative to the other; therefore, their numbers may be ignored for the most part for the purpose of this analysis.

6.5 shows great symmetry across the two elections in the success of challengers and incumbents among voters with various economic experiences prior to the election. Among survey respondents reporting a stable family financial situation during the year preceding the election, both the 1976 and 1980 vote split evenly between the challenger and the incumbent. As the challenger in 1976, Carter received more than three-quarters of the votes from those perceiving a deterioration in their economic situation, but he won less than one-third of the votes from those claiming an improvement in their economic situation. As the challenger in 1980, Reagan did about the same. He attracted more support among voters feeling better off financially than Carter had in the previous election (41 percent versus 30 percent), but he did somewhat more poorly than Carter had among voters feeling worse off (72 percent versus 77 percent). From another perspective, in 1980 Carter as incumbent was somewhat more successful than Ford had been in 1976 with voters who perceived their families as being worse off financially (28 versus 23 percent), but was less successful with voters who felt better off economically (59 versus 70 percent).

The principal lesson to be drawn from Table 6.5, however, is that Reagan's success in 1980 among voters reporting various economic experiences is about what one would expect of a credible challenger in an election in which, as in 1976, the economy was the most salient issue. Since both the cumulative and election-year economic records of the Carter administration in 1980 were less favorable than the Nixon-Ford records in 1976 (see Table 6.1), fewer voters felt better off (18 versus 23 percent) and more voters felt worse off (38 versus 28 percent) during the Carter-Reagan contest than during the Ford-Carter race. And this is the main reason that Reagan defeated Carter by a (relative) margin larger than Carter's victory over Ford four years earlier.

Implications for President Reagan's Mandate and the Republican Party's Political Future

Statistical models and survey data strongly indicate that the Republican victory in 1980 was based on dissatisfaction with the Carter administration's management of the economy and a concomitant desire for change, rather than on any conservative tide or ideological shift to the right in the electorate. The voters did not reject welfare-state liberalism; they punished Carter and the Democrats for economic mismanagement. Jimmy Carter was the first elected incumbent to be defeated since Herbert Hoover because the economic record of his administration during periods just before the election was the worst since Hoover's. Indeed, there was more justice in the electorate's verdict in 1980 than in 1932, because the macroeconomic knowledge and policy tools available to the Carter administration were much more developed than those at the disposal of political authorities fifty years ago.

As Orren and Dionne recently noted, there is considerable irony in the fact that Carter's defeat has been interpreted as a sign of the political collapse of welfare-state liberalism. For in the context of his times, Jimmy Carter was probably the least liberal Democratic president in this century, and he lost the election not because of his liberalism but because he pursued conservative anti-inflationary policies that produced an election-year recession on top of severe inflation. The victim of this irony was one of the most enduring public perceptions in American political life: the idea that the Democrats are the party of prosperity and high employment. Thanks to the legacy of the Great Depression, which was sustained by the 1953–54, 1957–58, and 1960 recessions during the Eisenhower years, the 1969–70 recession during Nixon's first term, and by the terrible 1974–75 contraction during the Nixon-Ford administration, when Jimmy Carter was elected president in 1976 the Democratic party enjoyed its traditional advantage over the Republicans as the party voters saw as best equipped to manage the economy.[24] The 1976 SRC National Election Study, for example, showed that among voters who saw a difference in the parties' effectiveness managing the economy (not quite half the electorate), Democrats were considered better able to handle the unemployment problem by a factor of nearly 4 to 1 (36.4 percent to 9.5 percent). The Democrats also led the Republicans as the party seen as likely to handle inflation better, 28 percent to 19 percent. Four years and one Carter-induced recession later, these Democratic advantages were gone. In the 1980 preelection SRC survey the Republicans enjoyed a 2-to-1 (31 to 15 percent) advantage over the Democrats as the

24. Indeed, the last big contractions under the Democrats were in 1893–94 and 1895–96, during Grover Cleveland's presidency. Out of the 41 times from 1951 to 1980 that the Gallup poll asked "Which political party—Republican or Democratic—do you think will do a better job of keeping the country prosperous?" the Democrats led the Republicans 37 times. The Democratic advantage averaged 9 percentage points in the 1950s, 24 points in the 1960s, and 17 points in the 1970s. By the fall of 1980 the Democratic lead on the prosperity issue had vanished. See *Gallup Opinion Index*, 1980, p. 8.

party seen as likely to handle inflation better, and were also viewed as the party better able to handle unemployment (23 versus 19 percent).[25]

By featuring his economic and fiscal plan as a "program for economic recovery"[26] President Reagan struck a responsive political chord. Indeed, the packaging and promotion of the president's program after the 1980 election exhibited political deftness not seen in Washington since Lyndon Johnson's successes with his Great Society legislation in the mid-1960s. The president's program included a substantial reduction of federal civilian expenditure and a significant reduction in federal personal taxation rates, skewed toward the upper-income groups. These changes were designed to yield a shift in the composition of aggregate output and consumption away from the public sector to the private sector, and a shift in the distribution of income away from low- and middle-income groups (especially the working poor) to the higher-income classes.[27] But the president had no mandate for these distributional changes in the political economy. In order to remain politically viable, the program must, as advertised, also produce a sustained economic recovery. On this foundation rested the electorate's considerable initial goodwill toward the president. If the Reagan program does generate higher growth, lower unemployment, and lower inflation, or is at least correlated in time with a sharp improvement in America's macroeconomic performance, the president probably will succeed in crystallizing a popular base for "Reaganomics" that might well last a generation or more. But tangible economic improvement there must be. As Lawrence J. DeNardis, a freshman Republican congressman from Connecticut who backed the Reagan program, put it less than eight months into his term: "My constituents are willing to wait a respectable period of time. But a little edge is beginning to emerge. If this doesn't work, they're going to hang me."[28]

Congressman DeNardis's problem—and, more significantly, the problem of the Reagan administration and the Republican party as a

25. Percentages were computed from the marginal distributions in the 1976 and 1980 SRC National Election Study codebooks. The question was "Do you think (inflation, the problems of unemployment) would be handled better by the Democrats, by the Republicans, or about the same by both?"

26. I refer here to the president's February 18, 1981, budget package (Executive Office of the President/Office of Management and Budget, 1981).

27. See the distributional analyses by the Congressional Budget Office.

28. Quoted in S. Roberts, "2 Republican Legislators Threaten Wall Street with Tighter Controls," *New York Times*, September 10, 1981, p. 13.

whole—is that Reaganomics at the time of this writing (May 1982) has produced a near catastrophe in the American macroeconomy. Under Chairman Paul Volker's leadership and with the administration's encouragement, the Federal Reserve pursued a truly Draconian monetary policy in 1981–82. The combination of extremely tight money and credit and unprecedented current and projected future budget deficits[29] led to skyrocketing interest rates. The consequence is the most severe recession since the 1937–38 contraction during the Great Depression. Since President Reagan's inauguration the unemployment rate has risen 2 full percentage points—from 7.4 percent in January 1981 to 9.4 percent in April 1982—which is the highest level recorded since 1941. Real income and output have been stagnant or declining. Real personal disposable income per capita was virtually the same in the first quarter of 1982 as it was in the first quarter of 1981 ($3,225 in 1967 dollars), and real GNP was 2.2 percent lower in the first quarter of 1982 than it was when Reagan assumed office. The recent trajectory of aggregate output is especially frightening: real GNP fell 5.4 percent in the fourth quarter of 1981 and another 5.2 percent in the first quarter of 1982. The only bright spot has been inflation, particularly as measured by the much maligned consumer price index, which rose by 10.3 percent over 1981–82 (compared to an increase of 13.5 percent in Carter's last year) and by an annual rate of only 3.1 percent during the first quarter of 1982.[30]

However, if empirical studies of the impact of economic performance on presidential and congressional voting outcomes are a reliable guide to the future, the administration's real income (and unemployment) record will be far more important to voters than its inflation record, and therefore President Reagan and the Republicans are in serious trouble. Certainly this is the message from the polls. President Reagan's approval ratings in the Gallup polls, after peaking at 67–68 percent in March–April 1981, have eroded steadily, falling to

29. The deficits, current and projected, fundamentally are generated by the fact that the sharp defense outlay increases and tax-cut-induced revenue decreases are outrunning the reductions in social expenditures. The surge in economic growth, and hence in tax revenues, promised by the radical supply-siders have yet to materialize, and probably never will. The deficit situation has been exacerbated greatly by the monetary policy-induced rise in unemployment.

30. In March 1982 the CPI actually declined for the first time since August 1965. The main sources of the CPI's behavior have been the decline in housing prices and stable and falling food and energy prices. Only the former has much to do with the Reagan administration's policies. Monetary policy in particular has crippled the housing industry, and housing has an exaggerated weight in the CPI.

43 percent in the April 23–26, 1982, survey (the most recent poll available to me). Of all presidents from Eisenhower to Reagan, only President Carter experienced a decline this large—about 25 percentage points—in Gallup poll approval ratings during the first five to six quarters in office.

Voter support for Republicans in the House of Representatives also has fallen to a perilously low level. In the April 2–5, 1982, Gallup poll only 34 percent of registered voters said they would vote Republican "if the elections were held today."[31] Statistical models also indicate that the Republicans are likely to suffer a large decline in their popular vote share and a correspondingly large loss of seats in the 1982 midterm congressional elections.[32] Forecasts based on two models are reported in Table 6.6.

The predictions from my model in the top half of Table 6.6 are based on an equation estimated for midterm congressional outcomes from 1946 to 1978 in which the best fit for the standardized vote loss (SVL) of the president's party in the House was generated by a geometrically weighted average of annualized, quarter-on-quarter growth rates of real personal disposable income per capita (OPEC adjusted) from the first to the sixth quarter of each presidential term:

$$SVL_t = -3.15 + 0.93 \left[\sum_{i=0}^{5} 0.34^i R_{t-i-2} \left(1 \bigg/ \sum_{i=0}^{5} 0.34^i \right) \right], \quad (6.4)$$
$$\quad\;\;(0.55)\quad(0.21)\quad\;\;(0.11)$$

$$R^2 = 0.76, \qquad SER = 1.53 \text{ (standard errors in parentheses)}.$$

To predict the 1982 Republican (two-party) House vote share from Equation (6.4), I set the 1982: 2 real income growth rate (not available at this writing) equal to the latest available Data Resources, Inc. forecast (+0.6 percent). Under this assumption the predicted Republican vote share is 43.6 percent,[33] which implies a vote share loss of 5.0

31. Fifty-four percent indicated an intent to vote Democratic. The two-party split (excluding undecided voters and third-party supporters) was 39 percent Republican, 61 percent Democratic. See A. Clymer, "Democrats Favored in House, Poll Shows," *New York Times*, April 25, 1982, p. 36.

32. The Republicans will probably fare better in the Senate because 19 of the 33 seats up for election in 1982 are held by Democrats. (One seat is held by Henry F. Byrd, Jr., of Virginia, an independent who votes with the Democrats.) However, 1984 is a different matter: 19 of the 33 seats up in that year are currently held by Republicans.

33. The predicted SVL for 1982 from Equation (6.4) is −2.64. Since SVL is equal to the actual vote share less average vote share in eight preceding elections, and because the latter is currently 46.2 percent for the Republicans, the actual vote share prediction for 1980 is (−2.64 + 46.2) = 43.6.

Table 6.6. Forecasts of Republican vote and seat losses in the 1982 House elections.

Model	Vote loss (two-party vote) in percentages	Seat loss (swing ratio)[a]
Hibbs	5.0	39
Tufte		
Gallup approval rating assumed for President Reagan in September–October 1982:		
48%	6.0	34
43%	6.6	37
38%	7.2	41

Note: Predicated vote share losses equal predicted *SVL* plus 46.2 minus 48.6.
a. Swing ratio used for Hibbs model: Eq. (6.5); for Tufte model: 1.3.

percent from the 48.6 percent the Republicans received in the 1980 House elections.

The seat loss projection from Equation (6.4) is based on the "swing ratio" equation (estimated for midyear elections 1946–1978):

$$\Delta S_t = 2.82 + 2.34 \ \Delta V_t, \tag{6.5}$$
$$(1.57) \quad (0.35)$$

$$R^2 = 0.84, \qquad SER = 1.73 \ \text{(standard errors in parentheses)},$$

where ΔS is the change (from the preceding on-year election) in the percentage of House seats held by the president's party after midterm elections, and ΔV is the change in the (two-party) percentage of the popular vote in House contests (from the preceding on-year election) received by the president's party after midterm elections. If Equation (6.5) yields an accurate guide to the shift in the seat share accompanying a given shift in the vote share in 1982, then for a Republican vote loss of 5.0 percent (from Eq. 6.4) we have a projected Republican seat loss of about 39 $[39 \simeq (-5.0 \times 0.0234 + 0.0282) \times 435]$.

The remaining forecasts in Table 6.6 are based on Tufte's well-known model for the expected *SVL* of the president's party in midterm congressional elections.[34] In Tufte's model *SVL* is a linear func-

34. Tufte, *Political Control of the Economy*, chap. 5.

tion of the election-year percentage change in per capita real personal disposable income (R^A) and the president's average September–October Gallup approval rating (*Approve*) in the election year. The most recently available ordinary least-squares estimates of Tufte's equation for midterm elections from 1946 to 1978 (supplied to me by Tufte) are:[35]

$$SVL_t = -10.3 + 0.124 \text{ } Approve + 0.71 \text{ } R_t^A, \qquad (6.6)$$
$$ (2.48) \quad (0.046) \qquad\qquad (0.17)$$

$R^2 = 0.80,$ $SER = 1.42$ (standard errors in parentheses).

Forecasts from Tufte's model depend on the assumption made about the 1981–1982 growth rate of per capita real personal disposable income and on President Reagan's Gallup approval rating in September–October 1982. Concerning the former, all forecasts based on this model in Table 6.6 incorporate the Data Resources, Inc. forecast of the 1981–1982 growth rate of R^A: +1.07 percent.

Three alternative assumptions are made about President Reagan's September–October Gallup approval rating. One is that the president's approval rating will remain at its current (April 23–26, 1982) level—43 percent. In conjunction with the real income growth rate assumption described above, this yields a predicted vote loss of 6.6 percentage points and an associated seat loss projection, based on Tufte's estimate of the 1982 swing ratio of 1.3 (conveyed to me privately), of 37. If the president's approval rating increases from the April level by, say, 5 points to 48 percent, the vote loss predicted by Tufte's model is about 6.0 percent, and this implies a seat loss (given a swing ratio assumption of 1.3) of 34. If, as is more likely, the president's approval rating declines from its April level, for example, by 5 points to 38 percent, Tufte's model predicts a Republican vote loss of 7.2 percentage points, which yields a corresponding seat loss projection of 41.

---

35. Because of data revisions and the inclusion of the 1978 outcomes, the coefficient estimates in Equation (6.6) differ from those reported by Tufte, *Political Control of the Economy*, tab. 5-2, p. 112. Also note that Tufte uses annual real disposable personal income per capita data as published in the annual Economic Report of the President, where the implicit deflator of personal consumption expenditures is used to deflate nominal income data. My equations use the CPI to deflate income data (adjusted for OPEC as noted).

Naturally, if the growth rate of per capita real personal disposable income is more favorable than the values I have assumed, or if the swing ratios are lower than those used here, or, in the case of the Tufte model predictions, if the president's approval rating rises dramatically, the vote (and seat) loss forecasts shown in Table 6.6 would be commensurately smaller. (The reverse, of course, would be true if the assumptions underlying the forecasts in Table 6.6 were too optimistic from the Republicans' point of view.) Yet past experience (as summarized by simple statistical models) indicates that the Republicans will absorb a decline in their House strength in 1982 rivaling their 1974 losses.[36]

The prospects for President Reagan (or, if he does not seek reelection, an alternative Republican nominee) in the 1984 presidential election are altogether a different matter. Because voters appear to weight current performance much more heavily than past performance when making contemporaneous political judgments, the 1984 presidential (and congressional) election result(s) will depend greatly on the administration's performance in periods after the midterm elections. For example, if the lag parameter g, which defines the relative weight given current and past performance outcomes, is on the order of 0.8 as Equation (6.2) indicates, then election-year performance outcomes will receive about 50 percent of the lag weight total, and outcomes during 1983 and 1984 will receive about 80 percent of the total weight.[37]

Nonetheless, the electoral success of President Reagan and the Republicans in 1984 does hinge on an improvement—in fact a very sharp improvement—in current economic conditions. Although the likely Republican losses in the upcoming congressional races may well stimulate a pronounced shift toward an expansionary macroeconomic policy (especially monetary policy), thus far the administra-

36. For a contrary view, see T. Mann and N. Ornstein, "The 1982 Election: What Will It Mean?" *Public Opinion*, June–July 1981, pp. 48–50: "we believe that the Republicans will pick up seats in the 1982 election, but probably not enough to take control of the House of Representatives." These authors see the Republicans gaining the advantage in 1982 because of three major factors: the decennial reapportionment has favored the Republicans, they are expected to raise much more money than the Democrats, and a vigorous candidate recruitment program is likely to yield attractive Republican candidates. A similar view is held by other congressional election specialists, including Gary Jacobson of the University of California at San Diego.

37. For a backward-looking evaluation time horizon of 15 quarters, the proportion of the (geometric) lag weight total realized by the ith quarter is $(1 - g^{i+1})/(1 - g^{15})$.

tion's response to the dismal macroeconomic situation is perhaps best described as "stonewalling it."[38] Yet if the economy does not register dramatic improvement over the next two years, Reaganism and Reaganomics will no doubt be interpreted, in hindsight, not as a reflection of a fundamental "shift to the right" but as a one-term political aberration.

38. Indeed the president's reaction so far to the economic situation bears a marked resemblance to Herbert Hoover's optimistic response to the Great Depression. In June 1930, about a month into the depression, Hoover reportedly told a delegation from the National Catholic Welfare Council: "Gentlemen, you have come 60 days too late. The Depression is over." A year later President Hoover announced a new program of relief: a call for increased private charity. The anecdote comes from L. Silk, "Will the Slump Be Over Soon?" *New York Times*, January 22, 1982, p. D2.

III

Comparative and European Politics and Economics

7

On the Demand for Economic Outcomes: Macroeconomic Performance and Mass Political Support in the United States, Great Britain, and Germany

Many empirical studies show that economic performance has a strong influence on public support for incumbent political parties and chief executives.[1] The response of mass political support to economic fluctuations implicitly reveals information about the public's relative economic priorities and preferences, which in principle constitute the voters' "demand" for economic outcomes.

I assume that democratic governments attempt to maintain a comfortable level of mass political support and perhaps also pursue ideological goals, which might usefully be conceived in terms of the distinctive priorities of their core political constituencies. The way in which political authorities react to voters' economic priorities or demands, subject of course to other constraints, defines the "supply" of economic outcomes. Confronted with shifts in market demand, shocks in market supply, trade union cost-push, and other inflationary pressures, policy authorities are continually forced to make short-

Reprinted from *Journal of Politics*, 44 (May 1982), 426-462. The original article was written with the assistance of R. Douglas Rivers and Nicholas Vasilatos. It is one in a series from a project supported by National Science Foundation Grant SOC-7827022 and by the Center for International Affairs at Harvard University. For comments on earlier drafts of the article I am grateful to Christopher Pissarides, Robert J. Gordon, Alan Blinder, to participants in the labor economics and political behavior seminars at Harvard University and the Social Choice seminar at Washington University, and to members of the National Bureau of Economic Research macroeconomics seminar.

1. The literature is voluminous; selective references are given below. Recent works by Bruno Frey, *Modern Political Economy* (New York: Wiley, 1980); Douglas A. Hibbs, Jr., and Heino Fassbender, eds., *Contemporary Political Economy* (Amsterdam: North-Holland, 1981); and Paul Whiteley, ed., *Models of Political Economy* (Beverly Hills: Sage Publications, 1980) contain extensive discussions of the literature.

run choices between (1) accommodating such pressures by expanding government expenditure and the supply of money and credit, thereby relinquishing control over the price level in order to preserve effective demand and employment; and (2) leaning against such pressures by tightening spending and the money supply, reducing effective demand and employment, but stabilizing the inflation rate.[2]

One interesting political question, then, is why some governments exhibit less "discipline" than others, especially during major episodes of inflationary pressure. Put another way, why are some governments more inclined to "supply" inflation and less inclined to "supply" unemployment than other governments? This chapter treats the demand side of this issue by investigating comparatively the aggregate responses of mass political support for governments to movements in macroeconomic performance variables.

The first section of the chapter develops the basic political support model, which is expressed in terms of a continuously valued, unobserved index of a government's mass support. The model is designed to test the idea that people evaluate an administration's performance relatively rather than absolutely. Moreover, recent performance contributes more heavily than past performance to the formulation of contemporaneous political judgments, because the relevance of information conveyed by past outcomes decreases over time. The first section also reviews a scheme for qualitative responses that maps the qualitative choices revealed by the political survey data onto the unobserved, continuously valued support index motivating the basic theoretical model. The estimation strategy is described at the end of the section.

The second and third sections form the substantive core of the chapter. Section two describes the variables and reports the estimation results. Some of the more important issues addressed there are: (1) the weights that voters appear to attach to the accumulated record of political parties as opposed to the discrete performance of particular administrations, (2) the rate at which the public discounts past performance in making current political judgments, and (3) whether or not voters penalized incumbents for the direct income and price

2. For this way of looking at the problem I am indebted to the seminal paper by Melvin Reder, "Theoretical Problems of National Wage-Price Policy," *Canadian Journal of Economics and Political Science*, 14 (1948), 46–61; and the remarkable paper on the political economy of inflation by Robert Gordon, "The Demand for and Supply of Inflation," *Journal of Law and Economics*, 18 (1975), 807–836.

effects of the OPEC oil supply shock, which presumably were beyond the control of domestic authorities.

Because the dependent variables used in the empirical analysis are a nonlinear function of the observed survey data, and because the macroeconomic performance variables do not share a common metric, the relative and comparative implications of the estimation results are not obvious from the regression coefficients. Therefore, the third section examines the elasticities of the observed political support levels with respect to the macroeconomic variables. The elasticities reveal the public's marginal proportional aversion to, or relative "demand" for, various economic outcomes. Special attention is given to voters' demand for real outcomes (the rate of employment and the rate of growth of real personal disposable income) in relation to the implied demand for nominal outcomes (the rate of inflation and the rate of price acceleration).

The Political Support Model

As was discussed in Chapter 5, in principle a voter's support for an incumbent is not a discrete "yes or no" phenomenon, but instead falls along a continuum. Accordingly, the model developed here is expressed in terms of a continuously valued, *unobserved* index of a government's aggregate mass political support, Y^*. Y^* consists of a weighted sum of interparty performance comparisons, LR, and interadministration performance comparisons, SR, as well as a sequence of constants, a_q, representing the unique popularity of the qth chief executive and unmeasured factors favoring one party or bloc:[3]

$$Y_t^* = wLR_t + (1 - w)SR_t + a_q + u_t, \tag{7.1}$$

where $0 \leq w \leq 1$, and u_t is an independently distributed random disturbance.

LR represents the incumbent party's accumulated stock of mass support; in other words, it is the political capital of a party or bloc. As the subsequent discussion should make clear, my notion of political stock is somewhat similar to the concept of "party identification" in

3. It is not generally possible to distinguish the unique popularity of a particular administration or chief executive from unobserved factors working to the advantage of a party or bloc. All such effects are embedded in the administration-specific constants.

the political science voting literature, but it gives less emphasis to affective content and more weight to objective performance than one usually associates with the concept of party identification.[4]

With the motivation of the model confined to two-party or two-bloc systems, LR depends upon the *difference* between the cumulated, exponentially discounted performance of the incumbent party (bloc) and the cumulated, exponentially discounted earlier performance of the current opposition party (bloc):

$$LR_t = b \cdot D_t \sum_{k=0}^{\infty} g^k Z_{t-k} D_{t-k}, \tag{7.2a}$$

where Z = a vector of performance variables (specified ahead) with associated coefficients b,

g = the rate of decay of the lag weights, $0 \le g < 1$,

$D_t = \begin{cases} +1 \text{ if party/bloc A is in power at time } t, \\ -1 \text{ if party/bloc B is in power at time } t. \end{cases}$

As in Chapter 5, the product of the binary terms $D_t D_{t-k}$ ensures that LR, the incumbent party's or bloc's political capital, is generated by its performance record with respect to Z during periods when it was in power in relation to the competing opposition party's or bloc's performance when it was in power. The weights people give to performance outcomes decay exponentially at rate g^k. In other words, it is assumed that in making contemporaneous political judgments people give more weight to current performance than to past performance. Small values of g (approaching 0) imply that the past is discounted heavily (only an administration's recent performance really matters), whereas large values of g (approaching 1.0) imply that earlier outcomes contribute significantly to voters' current support for an administration. Thus if party/bloc A was in power during the most recent two periods, party/bloc B during the previous two periods, and party/bloc A for the two periods before that, Equation (7.2a) implies:

$$LR_t = b \cdot (Z_t + g Z_{t-1} - g^2 Z_{t-2} - g^3 Z_{t-3} + g^4 Z_{t-4} + \ldots). \tag{7.2b}$$

4. For a comparable conceptualization see Morris Fiorina, "An Outline for a Model of Party Choice," *American Journal of Political Science*, 21 (1977), 601–628.

If one party or bloc has been continuously in power during the observation period, $D_t D_{t-k}$ equals $+1$ for all t and $t - k$ and Equations (7.2a) and (7.2b) yield a conventional distributed lag in Z.[5] The summation index k runs from zero to infinity; the upper bound of the index k is merely a convenient fiction that should be taken to mean that Z_t is evaluated back to the beginning of the relevant political era. It is assumed implicitly that knowledge of past performance is transmitted from generation to generation via political socialization.

Standard manipulations show that the component of political support in (7.2a) can be simplified to a form suitable for estimation:

$$LR_t = g^{t-1} LR_1 \left(\frac{D_t}{D_1} \right) + b \cdot D_t \sum_{k=0}^{t-2} g^k Z_{t-k} D_{t-k}. \tag{7.3}$$

The interadministration component of a government's mass support, SR, is determined by the *difference* between the cumulated, exponentially discounted performance of the current administration and the cumulated, exponentially discounted performance of *all* previous administrations (regardless of partisan composition):

$$SR_t = \sum_{q=1}^{Q} A_{qt} b \cdot \sum_{k=0}^{\infty} g^k Z_{t-k} D^*_{q,t-k}, \tag{7.4a}$$

where $A_{qt} = +1$ during the qth political administration and 0 otherwise,

$D^*_{qt} = +1$ during the tenure of the qth political administration and -1 otherwise.

The dummy variables A_{qt} and $D_{q,t-k}$ ensure that SR is based on discounted interadministration performance comparisons. For example, if the qth administration has been in office for two periods, the SR component of its mass political support is given by:

$$SR_t = b \cdot (Z_t + g Z_{t-1} - g^2 Z_{t-2} - g^3 Z_{t-3} + g^4 Z_{t-4} - \dots). \tag{7.4b}$$

5. In presidential systems, "in power" means controlling the executive; hence no distinction is made here between administrations in which the president's party controls Congress and those in which the opposition party has a congressional majority. Similarly, in parliamentary systems no distinction is made between minority and majority governments.

The SR function is notationally a bit more complex than the LR function and therefore somewhat more tedious to simplify. However, working through the problem shows that Equation (7.4a) may be expressed in a form that involves a finite, observable lag sequence:

$$SR_t = \sum_{q=1}^{Q} A_{qt}b \cdot \sum_{k=0}^{t-2} g^k Z_{t-k}D^*_{q,t-k} + g^{t-1}(SR_1 - 2b \cdot Z_1). \qquad (7.5)$$

Equations (7.2) and (7.4) show that a new administration or party government's initial support depends largely on the situation inherited from its predecessors, but that as time elapses, earlier performance outcomes are discounted by the electorate (g^k becomes small as k becomes large) and the government's political support depends entirely on its own cumulative performance record. This specification differs substantially, then, from earlier work on economic conditions and political support that has assumed a priori that only contemporaneous performance, evaluated absolutely, influences current political support. The tendency of a new government's support to decline from early "honeymoon" levels is an endogenous feature of the theoretical model of Equations (7.1) through (7.5). Substituting (7.3) and (7.5) into Equation (7.1) yields the model:

$$Y^*_t = w \left(b \cdot D_t \sum_{k=0}^{t-2} g^k Z_{t-k}D_{t-k} + R^{LR} \right)$$

$$+ (1 - w) \left(\sum_{q=1}^{Q} A_{qt}b \cdot \sum_{k=0}^{t-2} g^k Z_{t-k}D^*_{q,t-k} + R^{SR} \right)$$

$$+ a_q + u_t, \qquad (7.6)$$

$$\text{where} \quad R^{LR} = g^{t-1}LR_1(D_t/D_1),$$

$$R^{SR} = g^{t-1}(SR_1 - 2b \cdot Z_1).$$

Equation (7.6) represents the reduced form of the political support model, which was derived from the idea that incumbents' mass support is based on a weighted combination of interparty (interbloc) and interadministration discounted, retrospective performance comparisons.[6] Since observations on the performance vector Z are available

6. If expected future performance is based on past performance, then the model is consistent with the idea that support depends on people's predictions of comparative future performance.

for at least thirty-two periods prior to the first observation on the political support indices, the lag function truncation remainders R^{LR} and R^{SR} may safely be dropped for estimation purposes.[7]

However, the continuously valued political support index, Y^*, is *unobserved*; the survey data reveal only whether or not respondents support the current government.[8] Hence we need a model that maps the observed binary choices available in the survey data onto the model developed above for the unobserved support index.

Let the observed survey responses revealing political support for the government be designated by the binary variable Y_{it}: $Y_{it} = 1$ for respondents supporting the government, 0 for respondents not supporting the government (preferring the opposition party/bloc or abstaining).

Since we are investigating movements through time in aggregated survey responses, it will be assumed for the present that individuals react homogeneously to performance with respect to Z. Therefore the Y_{it} are assumed to reflect crudely the underlying continuously valued political support index Y^* such that $Y_{it} = 1$ if $Y_t^* > c$,   0 if $Y_t^* \leq c$, where c is a "critical threshold." Letting $f(Z)$ denote the substantive terms on the righthand side of Equation (7.6) it follows that the probability (P) of observing a "support" response for individuals at time t is:

$$P_t = P(Y_{it} = 1) = P[f(Z) + u_t > c] = P[u_t > c - f(Z)], \quad (7.7)$$

and $(1 - P_t)$ gives the probability of a "nonsupport" response. In other words, people support the government $(Y = 1)$ when Y^* exceeds some critical threshold c. The probability of support therefore hinges on the value of $c - f(Z)$ and the distribution of the random variable u. This means that P_t may be regarded as a cumulative distribution function. Any appropriate distribution for u will yield a well-behaved probability function. It is convenient, however, to assume u logistic (which differs trivially from the normal distribution) with mean zero and scale parameter s, which implies the probability function:

---

7. In other words, for g in the range $0 \leq g < 0.9 g^{32}$ will generally be a negligible quantity and R^{LR} and R^{SR} may therefore be ignored.

8. In some countries the surveys are richer than this, but I treat the problem as one of binary choice. Little is lost by the simplification. See the later discussion of the empirical data.

$$P_t = P[u_t > c - f(Z)] = 1 - \frac{e^{[c-f(Z)]/s}}{1 + e^{[c-f(Z)]/s}}$$

$$= \frac{e^{[f(Z)-c]/s}}{1 + e^{[f(Z)-c]/s}} = L^*\{[f(Z) - c]/s\}, \tag{7.8}$$

where L^* is the logistic operator, $L^*(z) = \exp(z)/[1 + \exp(z)]$. It is obvious from (7.8) that the response probabilities monotonically approach 1 as $f(Z)$ gets large and monotonically approach 0 as $f(Z)$ gets small.

Finally, Equation (7.8) may be manipulated to yield:

$$L^{*-1}P_t = \ln[P_t/(1 - P_t)] = [f(Z)]/s, \tag{7.9}$$

which expresses the natural logarithm of the probability P_t divided by $1 - P_t$ (the logit) as a linear function of the model parameters. Replacing the notational simplification introduced in Equation (7.7) with the terms of the original political support model developed in Equations (7.1) through (7.6) yields the model used in the regression experiments:[9]

$$\ln \frac{P_t'}{(1 - P_t')} = (1/s)[wb \cdot D_t \sum_{k=0}^{t-2} g^k Z_{t-k} D_{t-k}$$

$$+ (1 - w) \sum_{q=1}^{Q} A_{qt}b \cdot \sum_{k=0}^{t-2} g^k Z_{t-k} D_{q,t-k}^*$$

$$+ a_q] + e_t, \tag{7.10}$$

where $P_t' = $ the observed survey proportions (P_t being the unobserved population proportions),
$e_t = \ln[P_t'/(1 - P_t')] - \ln[P_t/(1 - P_t)]$.

All parameters of the support model are identified up the scale factor $(1/s)$ and the threshold c is necessarily embedded within the administration-specific constants a_q; that is, these parameters are not identified. In view of the dynamic nonlinear lag functions in Equation

---

9. It can be shown that the error term e in Equation (7.10) has mean zero and variance $[N_tP_t(1 - P_t)]^{-1}$, where N_t is the number of survey observations used to form P_t'. This means that efficient least-squares estimates are obtained by weighting each term in (7.10) by $[N_tP_t'(1 - P_t')]^{1/2}$. These weights were applied in the regressions reported later. For an alternative approach to the variance-weight issue, see Chapter 9.

(7.10), the weighted logit regressions were undertaken using a standard nonlinear least-squares algorithm.

Empirical Results

This section describes the variables in the performance vector Z and reports the empirical results.

Variables

The regression experiments reported later are based on quarterly observations from the late 1950s or early 1960s through the late 1970s.[10] The variables used to measure political support in each country are as follows:

> United States: The proportion of the public responding "approve" to the well-known Gallup survey question, "Do you approve or disapprove of the way (the incumbent) is handling his job as President?"
>
> United Kingdom: The proportion of the public supporting the principal incumbent party (Labour or Conservative) when asked the question, "If there were a General Election tomorrow, which party would you support?
>
> Germany: The proportion of the public supporting the principal incumbent party (SPD or CDU/CSU)[11] when asked the question, "If there was an election next Sunday, could you please tell me which party you would vote for?"

The political support survey question for the United States (approval of the president) is not strictly comparable to the questions for the United Kingdom and Germany (party vote intention). However, these survey questions are the ones that politicians and others watch most closely in the respective political systems; therefore, they provide the most revelant time-series data on mass political support.

The performance vector, Z, for each country includes the rate of unemployment, U, the rate of inflation of consumer prices, P, and

10. The quarterly observations of political support were formed by aggregating the available monthly survey data.

11. See the later discussion on how the Grand Coalition government of 1966–1969 was treated. The question wording was somewhat different before 1964.

the rate of change of per capita real personal disposable income, R. As in Chapter 5, in the American analyses three additional variables peculiar to that country's recent political life were included in the performance vector: a term for the number (in thousands) of Americans killed in action in Vietnam, a special Watergate variable to capture the decline in Nixon's approval rating associated with that scandal (the number of Watergate "events" were summed in each quarter and weighted on a scale of 1 to 3), and a "rally" variable taken from Mueller's work and extended through the Carter administration.[12] The rally variable is simply the number of such events in each quarter. (For further discussion see Chapter 5, p. 148).

Finally, since British governments of all stripes have been preoccupied for most of the postwar period with defending the international role of sterling,[13] and as a result the external strength of the pound has received great attention in the press, the equations for Britain include a term for changes in the exchange rate, ΔEXR. The pound's performance relative to the dollar (which is the principal international reserve currency) is the quantity watched (and reported) most closely; therefore, ΔEXR is the change in the dollars-per-pound rate of exchange. Over the long run ΔEXR of course reflects in part Britain's relative inflation performance, but in Britain's domestic political life it has been viewed as an index of the nation's international prestige.

The following list summarizes the terms used in the regression analyses.

U	Unemployment rate
$\Delta \ln U$	Percentage rate of change of the unemployment rate (annualized, quarter-on-quarter rate; $\ln(U_t/U_{t-1}) \cdot 400$
U adult	Unemployment rate excluding teenagers in the labor force

---

12. John Mueller, "Presidential Popularity from Truman to Johnson," *American Political Science Review*, 64 (March 1970), 18–34, scored the first period of each administration as a rally point. This was not done here.

13. See, for example, Samuel Brittain, *Steering the Economy* (London: Secker and Warburg, 1969); Susan Strange, *Sterling and British Policy: A Study of an International Currency in Decline* (New York: Oxford University Press, 1971); and especially Stephen Blank, "Britain: The Politics of Foreign Economic Policy, the Domestic Economy, and the Problem of Pluralistic Stagnation," *International Organization*, 31 (1977), 673–721. Perhaps the most dramatic illustration of this point is the resistance of Wilson's first Labour government to devaluation of the pound, which ultimately came in late 1967. Before the demise of pegged exchange rates in 1971, this was the only sizable postwar movement of the dollars-per-pound rate.

P	Inflation rate (annualized, quarter-on-quarter percentage rate of change of consumer prices)
ΔP	Change in inflation rate ($P_t - P_{t-1}$)
P adjusted	Inflation rate adjusted downward for direct adverse price shocks following OPEC, 1973:4–1976:4 (see text)
R	Percentage rate of change of real personal disposable income per capita (nominal income deflated by consumer prices, annualized, quarter-on-quarter rate of change)
R adjusted	Real income growth rate adjusted upward for adverse international redistributions following OPEC, 1973:4–1976:4
ΔEXR	Quarter-on-quarter change in dollar-to-pound exchange rate ($EXR_t - EXR_{t-1}$)
Vietnam	U.S. troops killed in action in Vietnam (in thousands)
Watergate	Press-weighted Watergate events (see text)
Rally	International events, "rally events" (number in quarter—see text)
Dependent variable	The logit: $\ln[P'_t/(1 - P'_t)]$, where P'_t is the proportion of the survey respondents supporting the incumbent party or president

Results for the United States

The American regression experiments for models based on Equation (7.10) are reported in Table 7.1. The most straightforward equation is model (1), which includes *U, P, R, Vietnam, Watergate,* and *rally.* All substantive terms are properly signed and significant by the usual statistical tests. As previous work has indicated, the Vietnam and Watergate catastrophes clearly contributed to the decline of presidential support ratings, as did high rates of inflation and unemployment.[14] Rally events and positive rates of growth in per capita real

14. See Bruno Frey and Friedrich Schneider, "An Empirical Study of Politico-Economic Interaction in the U.S.," *Review of Economics and Statistics,* 60 (1978), 174–183; and Samuel Kernell, "Explaining Presidential Popularity," *American Political Science Review,* 72 (June 1978), 506–522.

Table 7.1. United States: Weighted nonlinear least-squares logit coefficient estimates, 1961:1–1979:1, $T = 73$[a].

	Regression model				Means
	(1)	(2)	(3)	(4)	Means of political support proportions
Constants (a_q)					
Kennedy	0.424	0.483	0.411	0.428	0.702
(1961:1–1963:4)	(0.020)	(0.020)	(0.020)	(0.019)	
Johnson	0.380	0.419	0.365	0.352	0.540
(1964:1–1968:4)	(0.017)	(0.018)	(0.018)	(0.017)	
Nixon	0.617	0.506	0.605	0.633	0.497
(1969:1–1974:3)	(0.012)	(0.017)	(0.012)	(0.012)	
Ford	0.850	0.919	0.891	0.841	0.460
(1974:4–1976:4)	(0.037)	(0.041)	(0.040)	(0.035)	
Carter	0.065	0.183	0.039	0.136	0.489
(1977:1–1980:1)	(0.039)	(0.040)	(0.041)	(0.037)	
Lag weight rate of decay (g)	0.846	0.838	0.851	0.836	—
	(0.006)	(0.007)	(0.006)	(0.006)	
LR weight (w)	0.770	0.855	0.786	0.755	—
	(0.015)	(0.018)	(0.016)	(0.015)	
					Means of variables
Economy[b]					
Unemployment U	−0.017	−0.015	—	−0.017	5.458
	(0.0009)	(0.001)		(0.0009)	

	(1)	(2)	(3)	(4)	(5)
ΔlnU	—	0.002 (0.0001)	—	—	−0.136
U adult	—	—	−0.020 (0.001)	—	4.375
Inflation					
P	−0.017 (0.001)	−0.021 (0.001)	−0.017 (0.001)	—	5.162
ΔP	—	0.024 (0.004)	—	—	0.138
P adjusted	—	—	—	−0.020 (0.001)	5.054
Real income growth					
R	0.015 (0.0008)	0.019 (0.0009)	0.014 (0.0009)	—	2.182
R adjusted	—	—	—	0.018 (0.0008)	2.289
Noneconomic variables					
Vietnam killed-in-action	−0.063 (0.009)	−0.068 (0.002)	−0.064 (0.001)	−0.062 (0.001)	0.626
Watergate scandal	−0.016 (0.0004)	−0.014 (0.0006)	−0.016 (0.0004)	−0.017 (0.0004)	1.205
Rally events	0.276 (0.005)	0.275 (0.005)	0.277 (0.005)	0.269 (0.005)	0.356
x^2/df	47.0	45.8	47.3	45.7	—

Note: Asymptotic coefficient standard errors are given in parentheses.

a. The presidential approval question is not asked in the third quarter of election years; therefore, these quarters are missing from the regression estimation range. Data for 1971:3 are also missing. Data for the lag functions of the performance variables extend back to 1953:1 (see text discussion). Variable means are computed for the regression estimation range.

b. All percentage rates of change are computed $\ln(Z_t/Z_{t-1}) \cdot 400$.

personal disposable income were sources of upward movements in mass political support for the president. Since the real income growth rate appears in all equations, the significant negative estimates for the rate of inflation might be interpreted on purely economic grounds as evidence of an "irrational" popular aversion to inflation. Elsewhere I have reviewed other reasons why people might find rising prices distasteful even when real income is not affected adversely.[15]

The estimate of the lag weight decay-rate parameter, g, is about 0.84 in all models, which means that the experiences of many past periods influence people's current political judgments. If a performance variable Z is held at some equilibrium value Z^* indefinitely, then the ultimate impact on the political support index is $b(z)/(1 - 0.84)$, where $b(z)$ is the regression coefficient of the relevant Z variable reported in the table. The proportion of the ultimate impact of Z felt by the kth lag is given by $1 - 0.84^{k+1}$.[16] Therefore, in the United States about 50 percent of the total impact of a sustained movement in Z is felt after 4 quarters, 75 percent after 8 quarters, and about 94 percent after 16 quarters. Assuming that only conditions in the current period influence the president's political support (as most of the existing literature implicitly does) yields inferior predictions of fluctuations in the support data.

The estimate of the w coefficient in regression model (1) (and in models 3 and 4) suggests that about three-quarters of the systematic part of the mass public's support for a given president is based on the accumulated political capital of the incumbent's party, that is, on comparisons of the incumbent party's performance with the opposition party's performance, rather than on interadministration relative performance evaluations. However, after 24 periods or so have elapsed the lag function weights 0.84^k become negligible in magnitude; hence LR is approximately equal to SR for presidential administrations surviving well into a second term. In other words, *aside* from the component of a party's capital that is embedded in the a_q constants, toward the end of the second term of a given administration, a president's political capital LR consists primarily of his own relative performance record SR. Moreover, after six years or so, the perfor-

15. Chapter 4 and Hibbs, "Public Concern about Inflation and Unemployment in the United States: Trends, Correlates, and Political Implications," *Inflation*, ed. R. E. Hall (Chicago: University of Chicago Press, 1982).

16. The infinite sum of the infinite geometric series $b\sum_{k=0}^{\infty} g^k$ is $b/(1 - g)$, for $0 \leq g < 1$, and the partial sum to lag k of the series is $b[(1 - g^{k+1})/(1 - g)]$. Therefore, the partial sum as a proportion of the infinite sum is $1 - g^{k+1}$.

mance of previous administrations makes almost no contribution to *SR;* therefore, a president's mass approval rating is based almost entirely on a distributed lag of his own record. Remember, though, that until Reagan no president served two full terms since Eisenhower.

Regression models (2)–(4) of Table 7.1 test variations of model (1). One important study of presidential approval in the United States indicates that the public is sensitive to proportional changes in the rate of unemployment rather than to the unemployment level per se.[17] This, of course, means that political costs (benefits) are imposed only by rising (falling) unemployment: if unemployment settles down to any stable rate, no matter how high, political support will not be affected. Obviously, this result, has profound implications for politically feasible macroeconomic policies. Moreover, neoclassical economic thinking suggests that the major costs of rising prices are associated with sudden (unanticipated) accelerations and decelerations of prices (changes in the inflation rate) rather than with the magnitude of the simple rate of change. Model (2) therefore includes terms for the proportional change in unemployment ($\Delta \ln U$) and the rate of price acceleration (ΔP). However, the parameter estimates of both variables have incorrect signs (positive), although estimates of the remaining coefficients are quite robust. In the United States, therefore, changes in the rate of unemployment and inflation apparently do not produce declines in political support beyond what would be predicted from the levels of these quantities alone.

These results contrast sharply with those of Kernell, who reported that the only unemployment variable that matters is the rate of change of U (and even its effects are small and sporadic), and that the most consistent and sizable economic influence on presidential approval ratings is the inflation rate. However, Kernell omitted the real income growth rate from his equations. Since R and P are correlated negatively in the sample, and R and changes in U are correlated negatively structurally in the macroeconomy (Okun's law), it is likely that Kernell's equations exaggerate the impact of inflation and incorrectly identify changes in the rate of unemployment as the more important labor market variable. These inferences follow directly from standard specification error analysis, unless one maintains a priori the implausible assumption that in forming political judgments people are indifferent to the real income growth stream. Such an

17. Kernell, "Explaining Presidential Popularity."

assumption is at odds with the empirical results reported here as well as with the findings of many analyses of economic influences on actual voting outcomes over the long run.[18]

In recent years many macroeconomists have emphasized that the rise in unemployment during the 1970s is explained in part by the changing composition of the labor force, as opposed, say, to contractionary macroeconomic policies and deficiencies in aggregate demand. Particular attention has been given to the increase in the fraction of the labor force consisting of teenagers, since historically teenagers have experienced high unemployment rates because of low job commitment, the lack of work experience, and so on. If on political as well as economic grounds teenage unemployment is heavily discounted, then the politically relevant quantity is the adult unemployment rate. Model (3) of Table 7.1 tests this idea by replacing the conventional unemployment rate (U) with the rate for the non-teenage part of the labor force (U adult). However, model (3) is inferior to model (1), which implies that people do not discount unemployment among the young when evaluating the president's performance.[19]

Model (4) of Table 7.1 evaluates the hypothesis that the public did not hold political authorities responsible for the acceleration of prices and the decline in the real income growth rate caused *directly* by the deterioration in the terms of trade associated with the OPEC oil supply shock, and hence, presumably beyond the control of domestic officials. The idea is tested by forming the adjusted variables: P_t *adjusted* $= (P_t - \phi_t)$, R_t *adjusted* $= (R_t + \phi_t)$, where the adjustment factor, ϕ_t, denotes unfavorable international shifts in relative prices following the OPEC shocks of 1973:4–1976:4 and 1979:1–1980. (Oil prices were stable during 1977–78.) The estimates of the inflation and

18. For example, Gerald Kramer, "Short-Term Fluctuations in U.S. Voting Behavior, 1896–1964," *American Political Science Review*, 65 (March 1971), 131–143; Ray Fair, "The Effect of Economic Events on Votes for the President," *Review of Economics and Statistics*, 60 (1978), 159–173; and Edward Tufte, *Political Control of the Economy* (Princeton: Princeton University Press, 1978), chap. 5.

19. I also estimated equations with the adult male unemployment rate and the head-of-household unemployment rate, but these variables did not perform better than the conventional rate. The appropriate goodness-of-fit test for the validity of the logit specification is the chi square statistic (standardized for degrees of freedom) obtained from the differences between the observed relative frequencies and the estimated probabilities. The smaller the chi square statistic, the better the fit of the model. In the present case, chi square is the sum of squares of the weighted residuals.

real income international shocks (which admittedly are crude) were derived from:

$$\phi_t = \left[\ln \left(\frac{P_t^I}{P_{t-1}^I} \cdot \left(\frac{\text{Imports}_t + \text{Imports}_{t-1}}{\text{GNP}_t + \text{GNP}_{t-1}} \right) \right) \right.$$
$$\left. - \ln \left(\frac{P_t^E}{P_{t-1}^E} \cdot \left(\frac{\text{Exports}_t + \text{Exports}_{t-1}}{\text{GNP}_t + \text{GNP}_{t-1}} \right) \right) \right] \cdot 400, \qquad (7.11)$$

where P^I is the import price index, and P^E is the export price index.[20]

Although the improvement is not dramatic, regression model (4) specified with the OPEC-adjusted inflation and real income growth rate variables yields a fit superior to model (1), which includes the unadjusted variables. This evidence suggests that the performance evaluation standards used by the public may be quite sophisticated in the sense that political leaders are not punished for unfavorable economic disturbances clearly outside their control. However, most of the inflationary surges following the OPEC supply shocks were generated by domestic feedback processes rather than by the direct consequences of the cartel's petroleum pricing.

Since practical interest centers on the survey proportions rather than on the logits, Figure 7.1 shows the actual and fitted proportions approving the president's performance. The fitted values are derived from model (4), Table 7.1, and were generated by $\exp[f(Z)/1 + \exp[f(Z)]$, where $f(Z)$ is the righthand side of the estimated nonlinear logit equation. The fitted values track the actuals quite well and reveal no obvious important errors in functional form, although of course the high support ratings received by Johnson just after Kennedy's assassination are not picked up.

Results for Great Britain

Table 7.2 reports the regression results for Great Britain. Attempts to estimate the LR weight parameter w using a nonlinear algorithm were unsuccessful; therefore, it was necessary to search manually over the parameter space.[21] (A 0.01 grid was used.) Across all models tested

20. Incidentally, the estimated direct unfavorable effects are not large: in 1974, the peak year, they average 1 percent per quarter in the United States, 0.3 percent per quarter in West Germany, and a more sizable 4.9 percent per quarter in Great Britain. I am grateful to Jeffrey Sachs and Dale Jorgenson for suggesting the approximation method.

21. Given the estimated values of g (which were in the vicinity of 0.88) and the partisan sequence of British governments, it is very difficult to distinguish LR from SR.

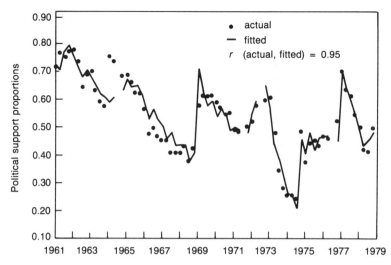

Figure 7.1. United States: Actual and fitted political support proportions, 1961:1–1979:1.

Table 7.2. Great Britain: Weighted nonlinear least-squares logit coefficient estimates, 1959:4–1978:4,[a] $T = 76$.

	Regression model			Means
	(1)	(2)	(3)	Means of political support proportions
Constants (a_q)				
Macmillan	−0.629	−0.624	−0.584	0.342
(1959:4–1963:3)	(0.016)	(0.016)	(0.014)	
Home	−0.592	−0.523	−0.500	0.355
(1963:4–1964:3)	(0.023)	(0.023)	(0.022)	
Wilson I	−0.369	−0.364	−0.349	0.367
(1964:4–1970:2)	(0.009)	(0.009)	(0.010)	
Heath	−0.623	−0.607	−0.579	0.354
(1970:3–1974:1)	(0.019)	(0.019)	(0.023)	
Wilson II	−0.579	−0.519	−0.097	0.384
(1974:2–1976:1)	(0.019)	(0.022)	(0.028)	
Callaghan	−0.044	0.012	0.097	0.356
(1976:2–1978:4)	(0.024)	(0.026)	(0.028)	
Lag weight rate				
of decay (g)	0.878	0.873	0.891	—
	(0.010)	(0.011)	(0.012)	
LR weight[b] (w)	1.000	1.000	1.000	—

Table 7.2 (cont.).

	Regression model			
	(1)	(2)	(3)	Means
				Means of variables
Economy[c]				
Unemployment				
U	−0.021	−0.022	−0.014	2.981
	(0.002)	(0.002)	(0.002)	
$\Delta \ln U$	—	—	−0.00058	6.042
			(0.0001)	
Inflation				
P	0.0038	—	—	7.489
	(0.0006)			
P adjusted	—	0.0032	—	7.136
		(0.0006)		
ΔP adjusted	—	—	−0.016	0.104
			(0.001)	
Real income growth				
R	0.0081	—	—	2.251
	(0.0005)			
R adjusted	—	0.0086	0.0058	2.605
		(0.0005)	(0.0006)	
ΔEXR	0.979	0.926	0.576	−0.011
	(0.041)	(0.041)	(0.034)	
x^2/df	22.6	21.9	18.7	—

Note: Asymptotic coefficient standard errors are given in parentheses.
a. 1964:4 is missing from the regression range. Data for the lag functions of the performance variables extend back to 1951:4. Variable means are computed for the regression estimation range.
b. $w = 1.0$ imposed after manual search.
c. All percentage rates of change are computed $\ln(Z_t/Z_{t-1}) \cdot 400$.

and for all admissible values of g the estimate of w minimizing the error sum of squares was 1.0. Aside from unobserved administration-specific effects picked up by the a_q constants, this, of course, implies that in Britain a government's mass political support is based entirely on discounted, retrospective *inter-party* performance comparisons, that is, on the parties' accumulated political capital as opposed to the relative performance record of discrete administrations. Since the results reported in the next section indicate that w also is 1.0 in West

Germany, as opposed to a value of about 0.76 in the United States, I am tempted to conclude that these *LR* weight estimates reflect the relative importance of political parties in European and American national politics. Indeed, looked at from this point of view, the *LR* weights in the U.S. regressions are surprisingly large. In Britain and Germany (and in most of the rest of Europe) political parties can be viewed realistically as responsible political teams, a fact that facilitates judgments based on interparty performance records. In American national politics parties are not much more than ad hoc, shifting coalitions mobilized by presidents and presidential contenders who frequently have little commitment to the parties *qua* political organizations. However, this interpretation of international variation in the *w* parameters should not be pushed too hard, since the political support question in the United States asks respondents to approve/disapprove of the record of individual presidents, whereas in Britain and Germany the questions ascertain the respondents' party voting intention.

The first regression model for Britain in Table 7.2 includes the rate of unemployment, the rate of inflation, the growth rate of per capita real personal disposable income and the change in the dollars-per-pound exchange rate, along with the administration intercepts. *U*, *R*, and ΔEXR are all properly signed and significant, but *P* enters with a perversely signed (positive) coefficient that is negligible in magnitude.

Model (2) includes the OPEC-adjusted inflation and real income variables defined earlier. It tests the idea introduced in the previous section that political authorities were not held accountable for the direct price and income effects of the OPEC-induced international redistribution. Although the parameter estimates for the equation are generally sharper and the standardized chi square statistic is a bit smaller than in model (1), the *P adjusted* coefficient is still improperly signed, albeit substantively insignificant.

In model (3) the rate-of-inflation term therefore is dropped and terms for the rate of price acceleration and the proportional rate of change of unemployment are added to the regressors in model (2). This specification improves the regression fit substantially. All of the performance variables—*U*, $\Delta \ln U$, ΔP *adjusted*, *R* *adjusted*, and ΔEXR—now have statistically significant, correctly signed coefficients. In contrast to the American results, where the inflation rate coefficient was negative and sizable, the estimates in model (3) suggest that in Britain political support responds instead to price accelerations and decelerations, and to changes in the external strength of the pound. Net of exchange rate movements, the political costs associated with any steady rate of inflation are, therefore, negligible.[22]

Finally, the lag weight rate-of-decay parameter g is about 0.89 for Britain, which implies that people weigh past performance rather heavily in making current political judgments—somewhat more heavily than in the United States, where g was about 0.84. In other words, there appears to be a somewhat larger retrospective element in the British public's performance evaluations (and in the German public's evaluations as well; g is about 0.88 for Germany) than in the American public's evaluations. This is consistent with the finding discussed earlier that, in contrast to the American data, the British (and German) data satisfy a pure interparty comparison model ($w = 1$), since interparty comparisons seem naturally to imply slower discounting (longer political memories) of past outcomes.[23] Hence, in Britain (and Germany) about 37 percent of the ultimate impact of a movement in Z is felt after 4 quarters, about 61 percent is felt after 8 quarters, and about 85 percent is felt after 16 quarters. The comparable numbers for the United States are 50, 75 and 94 percent.

Model (3) is the most satisfactory equation and therefore was used to generate predictions of the proportion of the British public supporting the principal incumbent party, which are plotted along with the actual observations in Figure 7.2. Clearly, the main shortcoming of the model is its failure to track fully the great surge and then dramatic decline in support for Wilson's Labour governments during 1964–1969. Since British electoral specialists have not supplied a systematic explanation for this pattern,[24] it is unlikely that an identifiable variable has been omitted from the model.

Results for West Germany

An important feature of recent German political life—the existence of the "Grand Coalition" SPD and CDU/CSU government of 1966:4–1969:3—is not accommodated by the basic political support model

22. Christopher Pissarides, "British Government Popularity and Economic Performance," *Economic Journal*, 90 (September 1980), 569-581, draws the same conclusion from analyses based on a quite different model applied to similar data.

23. Ideally, the lag weight decay parameter (g) should be permitted to vary across the *LR* and *SR* components of the model. However, this additional nonlinearity would further complicate estimation and is simply not feasible in practice.

24. See, for example, James Alt, *The Politics of Economic Decline* (New York: Cambridge University Press, 1979), chaps. 6 and 7.

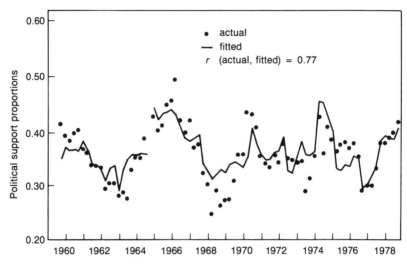

Figure 7.2. Great Britain: Actual and fitted political support proportions, 1959:4–1978:4.

developed in the first section. Since the Grand Coalition included both major parties in the German system, the *LR* component of the political support model, which is determined by interparty performance comparisons, obviously breaks down.

Therefore, in the German regressions the basic model was modified slightly:

$$Y_t^* = w\, \delta_t\, LR_t + (1 - \delta_t w)SR_t + a_q + u_t, \tag{7.12}$$

where $\delta_t = 0$ during the Grand Coalition, 1 otherwise.

Equation (7.12) essentially means that government performance during the Grand Coalition made no contribution to the political stock (*LR*) of either the SPD or the CDU/CSU, and that political support in this period was based entirely on interadministration performance comparisons (*SR*), no matter what the magnitude of the *LR* weight (*w*). Since the major parties presumably shared responsibility more or less equally for the performance record of the Grand Coalition years, Equation (7.12) is fully consistent with the ideas outlined in the first section.

Table 7.3 reports the regression results. As in the case of Britain, attempts to estimate w with a nonlinear algorithm were not successful, but manual searches using a 0.01 grid indicated that $w = 1$ was the optimal value for all models.

The sequence of regressions parallels that in the previous tables. In all equations g is about 0.88; equivalent to the lag weight rate-of-decay parameter estimate in the models for Britain. Across all specifications the coefficients of unemployment, inflation, and the real income growth rate are robust and properly signed. Model (2) indicates that in the presence of U and P neither the rate of change of unemployment nor the rate of acceleration of prices has any impact on political support. In contrast to the results for Britain and the United States, model (3) shows that OPEC-adjusted inflation and real income variables perform no better than the unadjusted variables in model (1). However, the estimated adjustment factors were very small for Ger-

Table 7.3. West Germany: Weighted nonlinear least-squares logit coefficient estimates, 1957:4–1978:4, $T = 85$[a].

	Regression model			Means
	(1)	(2)	(3)	
				Means of political support proportions
Constants (a_q)				
Adenauer	−0.813	−0.807	−0.813	0.314
(1957:4–1963:3)	(0.019)	(0.020)	(0.020)	
Erhard	−0.760	−0.755	−0.758	0.331
(1963:4–1966:4)	(0.017)	(0.015)	(0.017)	
Kiesinger	0.576	0.572	0.576	0.644
(1967:1–1969:3)	(0.008)	(0.009)	(0.009)	
Brandt	−0.587	−0.586	−0.586	0.358
(1969:4–1974:1)	(0.013)	(0.014)	(0.013)	
Schmidt	−0.457	−0.451	−0.465	0.335
(1972:2–1979:4)	(0.031)	(0.038)	(0.029)	
Lag weight rate of decay (g)	0.882	0.877	0.884	—
	(0.021)	(0.029)	(0.021)	
LR weight[b] (w)	1.000	1.000	1.000	—

Table 7.3 (cont.).

	Regression model			Means
	(1)	(2)	(3)	
				Means of variables
Economy[c]				
Unemployment				
U	−0.0060	−0.0061	−0.0058	1.968
	(0.0008)	(0.001)	(0.0009)	
$\Delta \ln U$	—	0.000031	—	0.421
		(0.00004)		
Inflation				
P	−0.0044	−0.0048	—	3.311
	(0.0004)	(0.0004)		
ΔP	—	0.0027	—	−0.023
		(0.0012)		
P adjusted	—	—	−0.0045	3.282
			(0.0004)	
Real income growth				
R	0.0051	0.0054	—	4.115
	(0.0004)	(0.0006)		
R adjusted	—	—	0.0050	4.145
			(0.0004)	
x^2/df	10.8	11.0	11.0	—

Note: Asymptotic coefficient standard errors are given in parentheses.
a. Data for the lag functions of the performance variables extend back to 1951:3. Variable means are computed for the regression estimation range.
b. $w = 1.0$ imposed after manual search.
c. All percentage rates of change are computed $\ln(Z_t/Z_{t-1}) \cdot 400$.

many (see note 20), so this result conveys much less information than the equivalent analyses for the other countries.

Model (1) produced the best fit and therefore was used to generate predictions of the proportion of the public supporting the government, which are plotted in Figure 7.3. Although the Grand Coalition clearly accounts for a large fraction of the variation in the series, the correlation between the actual and fitted observations excluding the Grand Coalition periods is respectable.

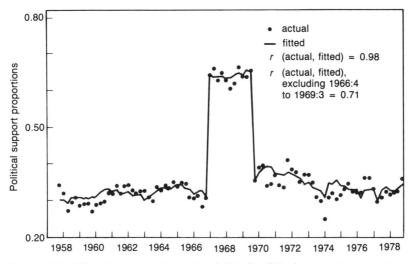

Figure 7.3.   West Germany: Actual and fitted political support proportions, 1957:4–1978:4.

The Relative Impact of Macroeconomic Quantities and the Demand for Expansion and Deflation

Just how much have unemployment, inflation, and real income growth affected popular support for political authorities? This question is difficult to answer in comparative terms by direct inspection of the coefficient estimates because not all of the macroeconomic variables share a common metric, and also because the dependent variables in the regressions were the logits, $\ln[P_t'/(1 - P_t')]$, rather than the actual survey proportions, P_t'.

One useful way of assessing the relative responsiveness of observed political support levels to macroeconomic performance, both within and across countries, is to compute the partial elasticities implied by the parameter estimates. Since elasticities are scale free, giving the proportional response of P' to proportional changes in the performance variables, it is possible to make sensible statements about the relative impact of the macroeconomic variables on mass political support. The elasticities implicitly reveal the public's marginal proportional aversion to, or demand for, various macroeconomic outcomes.

Figures 7.4 through 7.6 graph the implied long-run political support elasticities at each period in the regression range.[25] Since unemployment and inflation are frequently the foci of public discussion and policy debates, these elasticities appear separately in the lower frames of the figures. However, interest also centers on the public's relative sensitivity to real macroeconomic outcomes in relation to nominal, inflation outcomes. Therefore, the upper frames of the figures show the sum of the absolute values of the unemployment and real income elasticities in relation to the absolute value of the inflation (and exchange rate) elasticities. The figures facilitate comparisons of the mass public's relative sensitivity to real and nominal macroeconomic performance without regard for the sign or direction of the effects.

So that persistent developments are not obscured by very short-run realizations of the variables, all plots are based on four-quarter moving averages of the long-run elasticities implied at each period.

Several patterns are apparent from the data in the figures. First, viewed in terms of proportional responses to proportional changes, mass support for elected political officials appears to be more sensitive to economic performance in the United States and the United Kingdom than in West Germany. In large part this simply reflects the fact that macroeconomic performance (particularly unemployment and inflation performance) has been considerably better in Germany than in the other countries.

Second, in all countries the elasticities increase, typically quite dramatically, from the 1960s to the 1970s. For example, in the United Kingdom if all real economic variables (U, $\Delta \ln U$, and R *adjusted*) had changed simultaneously in a perverse direction by a proportional factor of 1 percent during the 1970s, on average the expected long-run proportional decline in political support would be on the order of 0.58 percent.[26] During the 1960s the expected long-run proportional de-

25. The elasticities shown in the figures are estimates of the ultimate proportional response of P' to sustained proportional changes in the Zs. They are based on the instantaneous derivatives: $(1 - P'_t)[b_j/(1 - g)]Z_{jt}$, where b_j is the regression coefficient of Z_j. This gives a very close approximation to exact estimates of the long-run responses, which would require calculating: $(L^{*-1}\{L^*(P'_t) + [b_j/(1 - g)]\Delta Z_{jt}\} - P'_t)Z_{jt}/P'_t\Delta Z_{jt}$, where $L^*(P'_t)$ is the logit of P'_t.

26. Since it is not possible to have a sustained increase in the level *and* rate of change of a variable simultaneously, in the upper frame of Figure 7.5 only the instantaneous effects of the rate of change of unemployment contribute to the magnitudes of the real elasticities. Also, it is unrealistic to imagine the inflation rate accelerating or decelerating "forever" or the exchange rate appreciating or depreciating "forever." The values of the nominal elasticities in the figure for Britain must be interpreted accordingly.

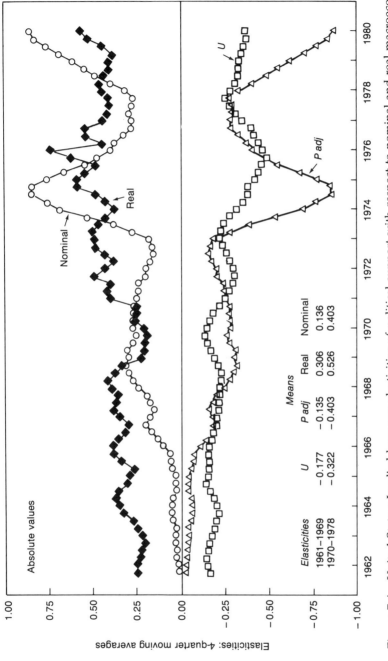

Figure 7.4. United States: Implied long-run elasticities of political support with respect to nominal and real macroeconomic outcomes, 1961:4–1980:1.

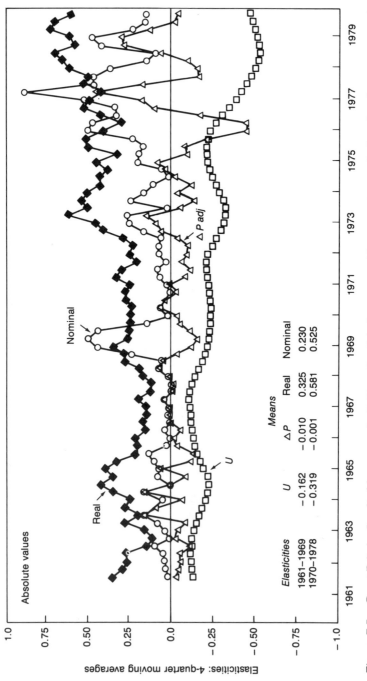

Figure 7.5.   Great Britain: Implied long-run elasticities of political support with respect to nominal and real macroeconomic outcomes, 1960–1978.

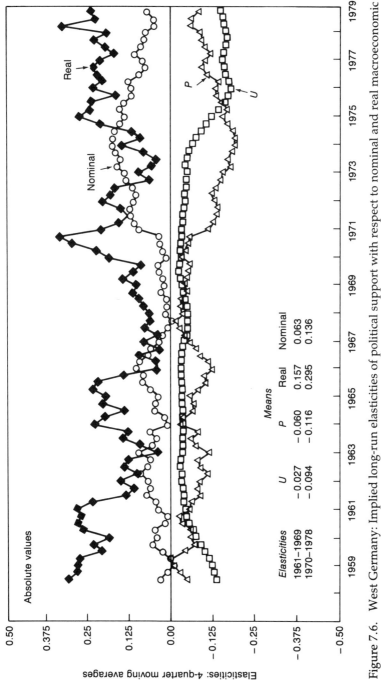

Figure 7.6.   West Germany: Implied long-run elasticities of political support with respect to nominal and real macroeconomic outcomes, 1958–1978.

cline in support from the same sustained movement in the real macroeconomy would have been on the order of 0.33 percent. A simultaneous, sustained 1 percent increase in the nominal variables (ΔP and ΔEXR) in Britain would on average have produced a decline in support of about 0.23 percent in the 1960s. In the 1970s, the expected long-run political cost of such a sustained adverse change in the British nominal macroeconomy would have been a bit more than 0.5 percent. Although the magnitudes are smaller, the same pattern is evident in the United States and West Germany. These results are hardly surprising in view of the favorable economic conditions in the 1960s—virtually a "golden age" of economic performance—and the economic stagnation (or stagflation) characteristic of more recent years.

Third, in all countries the elasticities of the real variables in both decades are larger on average in absolute value than the average elasticities of the nominal terms. In other words, on the margin a government's political support typically depended more on its real income growth and employment record than on the economy's nominal, inflation performance. This point should be underscored, since recent popular political-economic discussions often give the impression that the political fortunes of governments in the industrial democracies are dominated by their inflation performance records. As a general observation this simply is not true, as the elasticity estimates in Figures 7.4–7.6 indicate. (The same conclusion holds for France and Sweden; see Chapters 8 and 9.) The relative impact of the nominal inflation variables did increase substantially in the late 1960s and 1970s in Britain and the United States. Aside from the short-lived impact on political support of the pound's devaluation in late 1967 and 1968, this pattern is not evident in Great Britain until the OPEC-induced acceleration of prices of 1974 and thereafter. In the United States (and to a lesser extent in West Germany) it begins somewhat earlier with the acceleration of inflation brought on by the tight labor markets and policy of (hidden) deficit finance associated with the United States' pursuit of the Vietnam war.

Everywhere the terrible recession of 1975–76 sharply reduced inflation's relative political impact as public attention shifted away from the problem of rising prices to the problem of economic contraction. In Great Britain, however, and only in Great Britain, sustained high rates of inflation did not necessarily have substantial marginal political costs. The earlier empirical analyses that showed that political support there was influenced by the rate of price acceleration and exchange rate changes rather than by the inflation rate per se. Possible explanations of this phenomenon may reside in the differential sensitivity of the real wage to price fluctuations in the three countries as well as in their distinctive historical political-economic experiences. Because of differences in labor market and wage bargaining institutions, the real wage in Britain has been effectively indexed to expected price changes, whereas price fluctuations in the United States often adversely affect the real wage growth rate.[27]

Since inflation is associated more frequently with real pain in the United States, people may exhibit psychological distaste for rising prices even in periods when, objectively, real wages are *not* affected. This sort of aversion to price increases, of course, would be registered in the inflation rate parameter even though the models include a real income growth rate term. As Sachs's work shows, the real wage in Germany, as in Britain, also is virtually indexed to expected price movements. However, in contrast to its British counterpart, there is a strong consensus in the German polity on the importance of stable prices, which generally is attributed to the social memory of the traumatic Weimar hyperinflation but probably also reflects the fact that recent unemployment in Germany has fallen more heavily on foreign guest workers than on the domestic electorate.

What is clear from the evidence presented above is that neither stylized models of the "political business cycle," which assume that the vote-maximizing strategy is an election-year expansion,[28] nor the recent journalistic emphasis on the political pressures for deflation, are reliable *general* guides to politically optimal macroeconomic policies. Rather, the electorate's implicit marginal proportional demand for expansion and deflation varies over time and depends in a complicated way on the existing stock of political support and trajectory of the macroeconomy. Before we can make strong statements about politically optimal economic policy strategies, we need information about the structural relations among macroeconomic quantities and the relations between policy instruments and economic outcomes, as well as knowledge of voters' demands.

27. See Chapter 3 and Jeffrey Sachs, "Wages, Profits, and Macroeconomic Adjustment: A Comparative Study," *Brookings Papers on Economic Activity* (1979:2), 269–319.

28. See William Nordhaus, "The Political Business Cycle," *Review of Economic Studies*, 42 (1975); 169–190; and Tufte, *Political Control of the Economy*.

8

Economics and Politics in France: Economic Performance and Mass Political Support for Presidents Pompidou and Giscard d'Estaing

During recent years the state of the economy has been a very salient issue for the mass publics of the industrial democracies.[1] France is no exception, as the public opinion data in Figure 8.1 indicate. Once the Algerian question was finally resolved in 1962, public concern about the economy increased. By the late 1960s, as the long postwar economic expansion was coming to an end, about four of every ten French voters considered one or more economic issues to be the most important problem facing the country. Although the income tax scandal involving Premier Chaban-Delmas diverted public attention from the economy in 1972, economic performance soon recaptured popular attention: following the OPEC supply shock of late 1973, which simultaneously produced inflation and stagnation, more than two-thirds of the French electorate designated an economic issue as the most important national problem.

Reprinted from *European Journal of Political Research*, 9 (1981), 133–145. The original article was written with the assistance of Nicholas Vasilatos. It also appeared in translation in *Revue d'Economie Politique*, 93 (1983), 44–61. The research reported here was supported by National Science Foundation Grant SOC78-27022. I am grateful to David Cameron, Michael Lewis-Beck, Christopher Pissarides, and participants in the conference on political-economic models organized by J. D. Lafay at Poitiers University, January 1981, for comments on an earlier draft.

1. See, for example, the survey data assembled in 1980 by D. A. Hibbs, Jr., "Inflation, Political Support, and Macroeconomic Policy," a report prepared for the Brooking Project on the Politics and Sociology of Global Inflation, and published in *The Politics of Inflation and Economic Stagnation*, ed. Leon Linberg and Charles Maier (Washington, D.C.: Brookings Institution, 1985), showing public concern about economic issues as opposed to international and domestic political and social questions in the United States, Great Britain, and Germany.

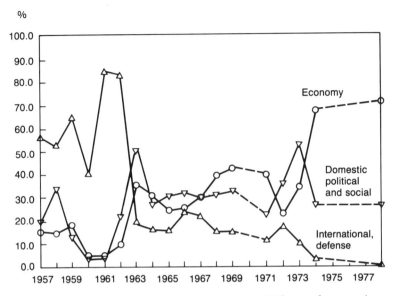

%

Figure 8.1. Aggregate responses to the question "What is the most impor-
tant problem for France at the present time?" (wording varies). (From G. H.
Gallup, *The Gallup International Public Opinion Polls: France 1939, 1944–1975*
(New York, 1976), and J. D. Lafay, "The Impact of Economic Variables on
Political Behavior in France," in *Contemporary Political Economy*, ed. Douglas
Hibbs and Heino Fassbender [Amsterdam: North-Holland, 1981].)

In view of the importance of economic conditions to the public, it is
not surprising that many empirical studies have concluded that mass
political support for incumbent political parties and chief executives
systematically responds to macroeconomic performance.[2] However,
aside from the pioneering work of Rosa and Amson on parliamentary
and constituent electoral outcomes, Lafay's important studies, and
Lewis-Beck's article on political support for French executives, we
have comparatively little evidence about the impact of economic outcomes on mass support for political officials in France.[3]

2. The literature is too voluminous to cite here. See, however, the citations in D. A.
Hibbs, Jr., and H. Fassbender, eds. *Contemporary Political Economy* (Amsterdam: North-
Holland, 1981).
3. M. Lewis-Beck, "Economic Conditions and Executive Popularity: The French Ex-
perience," *American Journal of Political Science*, 24 (1980), 306–323; J. D. Lafay, "Les
Conséquences électorales de la conjoncture economique: essais de prévision chiffrée
pour Mars 1978," *Vie et Sciences économiques*, 75 (1977), 1–7; J. D. Lafay, "The Impact of
Economic Variables on Political Behavior in France," in *Contemporary Political Economy*,

This chapter analyzes how popular satisfaction with Presidents Pompidou and Giscard d'Estaing was influenced by economic performance. The empirical analyses are based on a model of qualitative political responses, which is described in the first section and, more technically, in the appendix to the chapter. The most important features of the model are that people evaluate economic conditions relatively rather than absolutely in judging a president's performance, and that the weights people place on current and past economic outcomes decline geometrically, so that current performance contributes more heavily than past performance to the formation of contemporaneous political judgments.

The second section presents empirical results for variations of the model that include as measures of economic performance the rate of inflation, the rate of unemployment, and the growth rate of per capita real personal disposable income. The results indicate that the real income growth rate was the most systematic economic determinant of Pompidou's and Giscard d'Estaing's standing with the French public. Estimates of the response of the presidents' poll rating to typical movements in the real income growth rate are presented. The final section reviews the political implications of the analysis.

The Political Support Model

Opinion surveys typically force people to make discrete, qualitative responses. In the present case, the survey measure of popular satisfaction with Presidents Pompidou and Giscard d'Estaing is based on the Institut Français de l'Opinion Publique (IFOP) poll question "Are you satisfied or dissatisfied with _____ as president of the Republic? ("Etes-vous satisfait ou mécontent de _____ comme Président de la République?"). However, in principle a person's satisfaction with the president is not a purely qualitative phenomenon, but rather a matter of degree, ranging from strongly positive to strongly negative. A reasonable approximation to such a continuously valued satisfaction index is the natural logarithm of the proportion of the survey sample at each time period expressing satisfaction

---

ed. Douglas Hibbs and Heino Fassbender (Amsterdam: North-Holland, 1981); and J. J. Rosa and D. Amson, "Conditions économiques et elections," *Review Française de Science Politique*, 26 (1976), 1101–24.

with the president (P'_t) divided by one minus this proportion ($1 - P'_t$); that is: $\ln[P'_t/(1 - P'_t)]$. $P'_t/(1 - P'_t)$ gives the satisfaction odds ratio, and the natural logarithm of this odds ratio, known as the logit, ranges from $-\infty$ to $+\infty$.[4] The logits compose the continuously valued satisfaction index used in the regression analyses discussed in the next section. The analyses are based on quarterly observations over the period 1969:4–1978:4. The weighted averages of all poll results available in each quarter were used to form the quarterly proportions P'_t.

Earlier analyses of economic conditions and popular support for French political officials have assumed that people evaluate economic performance absolutely, and that current political support is influenced only by very recent conditions. These assumptions are overly restrictive. It is unlikely that a president's past record is discounted completely by the electorate, or that conditions during a particular presidential administrature are judged by voters absolutely, that is, without regard to the situation existing when the president assumed office. For example, a president coming to power during the trough of a recession who achieves a modest economic growth rate is likely to be evaluated more favorably than a president with the same economic record who assumed office during a sustained economic boom.

Therefore, the analyses reported ahead are based on equations in which a president's satisfaction rating at each time period is influenced by the *difference between* the cumulated economic performance record of his administration and the economic performance record of previous administrations. However, since the present relevance of the information conveyed by past experiences decays over time, the weights people place on current versus past performance outcomes decline geometrically at the rate g^k; g is a decay-rate parameter lying between zero and one. If Z_{t-k} is a performance outcome experienced k periods ago ($k = 0, 1, 2, 3, \ldots$), current and past experiences with respect to Z are weighted $Z_t, gZ_{t-1}, g^2Z_{t-2}, g^3Z_{t-3}$, and so on.

For example, if the current president has been in office for two periods, then his political satisfaction rating depends (in part) on the cumulated, discounted performance difference:

$$Z_t + gZ_{t-1} - g^2Z_{t-2} - g^3Z_{t-3} - \cdots\cdots$$

4. For further discussion see E. Muller, P. Pesonen, and T. Jukam, "Support for the Freedom of Assembly in Western Democracies," *European Journal of Political Research*, 8 (1980), 265–288.

Of course, voters do not necessarily discount past performance outcomes (Z_{t-k}) in exactly this way. As long as people weight past outcomes less heavily than more recent outcomes in making current political evaluations, the geometric weight sequence g^k will yield a close approximation. Large values of g (approaching 1.0) imply that past outcomes play an important role in current political judgments. Small values of g (approaching 0) imply that voters discount (disregard) the past heavily; only a president's own recent performance matters. If in the regression analyses reported later g was estimated to be actually zero, this would mean that, on average, voters have no effective memory of a president's past performance, and that only the current situation, Z_t, viewed absolutely, has any influence on a president's standing with the public. Clearly, then, g is an interesting political quantity. It defines whether performance outcomes are typically judged relatively or absolutely, and whether past experiences contribute to current political support.

The political support equations include four measures of economic performance. The first is the percentage rate of unemployment (U), that is, the number of unemployed (as adjusted from French sources by the U.S. Department of Labor) divided by the size of the labor force.[5] The second is the rate of inflation (I), that is, the annualized quarter-on-quarter percentage rate of change of retail prices. The third is the rate of change of the inflation rate ($I_t - I_{t-1}$), that is, the rate of acceleration or deceleration of retail prices. The fourth is the percentage rate of change of real household disposable income per capita (R). This variable is formed by taking the annualized quarter-on-quarter percentage rate of change of nominal household disposable income per capita deflated by the retail price index.

The regression analyses also include two binary variables representing discrete political events that were expected to influence (negatively) presidential support in the mass public. The first binary variable, scandal (= 1, 1972:2 and 1972:3), is designed to estimate the loss of support suffered by President Pompidou when it was revealed in early 1972 that his appointee as premier, Jacques Chaban-Delmas, had exploited tax loopholes to personal advantage. The ensuing scandal was a source of considerable embarrassment to Pompidou's administration and led to Chaban-Delmas's resignation and replacement by Pierre Messmer in July.

5. U.S. Department of Labor, Bureau of Labor Statistics, *International Comparison of Unemployment* (Washington, D.C., 1979). All percentage rates of change are annualized quarter-on-quarter changes formed as follows: (Z_t/Z_{t-1}) 400.

The second binary variable, *disorganization* (= 1, 1976:3 and 1976:4), is designed to pick up the loss of public support for Giscard d'Estaing associated with the split between the president and his Gaullist political ally and appointee as premier, Jacques Chirac. During mid-1976 Chirac became seriously disaffected by President Giscard d'Estaing's efforts to restrict his scope for independent action, which were prompted by Giscard's attempt to create a more "presidential" style of government. Although Chirac had played an important role in Giscard's election in 1974, by the summer of 1976 the feud became public and Chirac resigned, complaining that he was unable to confront the nation's problems effectively. Giscard replied in a national broadcast that he ruled out "transferring more power from the presidency to the premier's office, because . . . this is against the institutions of the Fifth Republic."[6] The open feud between the head of state and his prime minister antagonized Gaullist partisans in the electorate and made it obvious to the public that Giscard's administration was severely disorganized. The president's standing in the polls declined during this period as a result.

Empirical Results

Empirical results from the regression analyses of the models described above are reported in Table 8.1. The regression models are of course nonlinear by virtue of the lag weight decay parameter g. Therefore, the models were estimated by searching the parameter space manually and choosing the least-squares estimate of the nonlinear parameter g that minimized the sum of squared residuals. (A 0.01 grid search for g was used.) Model (1) of Table 8.1 includes all the performance variables described previously. However, since the rate of unemployment is highly correlated with president-specific intercept constants (the correlation of the Giscard constant and the unemployment rate is +0.88), model (1) is specified with a general intercept constant. As anticipated, the Chaban-Delmas tax scandal and the Chirac affair (disorganization) appear to have produced transitory downward movements in the satisfaction ratings of Pompidou and Giscard respectively. More important for our purposes are the estimates for the economic performance variables. The signs of the coefficients of R and U are consistent with expectations: increases in the per

6. *Kessing's Contemporary Archives,* October 1, 1976, p. 27965.

Table 8.1.   Least-squares coefficient estimates, weighted logit regression models, 1969:4–1978:4.

	Regression model				Means (unweighted) of independent variables
	(1)	(2)	(3)	(4)	
Constants (a_q)					
Pompidou	—	0.216 (0.0105)	0.219 (0.0105)	0.219 (0.0105)	0.514
Giscard	—	0.031 (0.109)	0.043 (0.0111)	0.043 (0.0097)	0.486
General	0.130 (0.008)	—	—	—	1.000
Lag weight					
decay rate (g)	0.8	0.8	0.8	0.8	—
Economy					
Unemployment rate (U)	−0.010 (0.0029)	—	—	—	3.630
Inflation rate (I)	0.004 (0.0010)	0.0013 (0.0004)	—	—	8.689
Change of inflation rate ($I_t - I_{t-1}$)	—	—	−0.0001 (0.0015)	—	0.311
Real personal disposable income growth rate (R)	0.017 (0.0008)	0.014 (0.0007)	0.015 (0.0006)	0.015 (0.0006)	3.261
Noneconomic variables					
Scandal (Chaban-Delmas tax scandal)	−0.134 (0.0129)	−0.195 (0.0515)	−0.184 (0.013)	−0.184 (0.013)	0.054
Disorganization (Chirac affair)	−0.365 (0.014)	−0.331 (0.013)	−0.310 (0.012)	−0.310 (0.0115)	0.054
x^2/df	21.4	15.1	15.5	15.0	—

Note: Data on the dependent variable were unavailable for 1970:3 and 1974:2; therefore, the regressions are based on 35 observations. Data for the lag functions for the independent performance variables extend back to 1951:2. Variable means are for the regression estimation range. The dependent variable is $\ln[P_t'/(1 - P_t')]$; the natural logarithm of the odds ratio. Standard errors are given in parentheses.

capita real income growth rate yield upward movements in the public's satisfaction with the president, and increases in the rate of unemployment are associated with downward movements in the president's political support.

The rate of inflation enters regression model (1) with a positive coefficient, which of course is a perverse result. However, the parameter estimate for the inflation rate is negligible in magnitude; for practical purposes it may be taken to be zero.[7] This implies that the French public is not averse to rising prices per se. As long as money incomes keep pace with the rate of growth of retail prices, there is no political penalty associated with inflation.[8]

Regression model (2) in Table 8.1 drops the unemployment term and is specified with individual intercept constants for the Giscard and Pompidou periods. This model clearly outperforms model (1),[9] which implies that the negative impact of unemployment on public satisfaction with the president is embodied in the difference between the Giscard and Pompidou constants (approximately 0.031 − 0.215 = −0.18). This result is not surprising. We know that unemployment rose sharply in France between the Giscard and Pompidou administrations, but the methods used to estimate movements in unemployment by the French Ministry of Labor and the French National Institute of Statistics and Economic Studies (INSEE) were modified several times during the late 1960s and 1970s, and construction of an accurate unemployment time series is therefore problematic.[10] Consequently,

7. Since the dependent variable is the natural logarithm of $[P'_t/(1 - P'_t)]$, the coefficient magnitudes are difficult to interpret by inspection. I pursue this issue later.

8. This result contrasts with the findings of Lewis-Beck, "Economic Conditions and Executive Popularity," who analyzed economic conditions and popular satisfaction with French presidents for the period 1960–1980. Lewis-Beck concluded that inflation is the most important economic influence on support for the president in the French electorate. However, his model is dramatically different from the one proposed here: among other things, it assumes that voters respond absolutely to recent economic conditions alone; it includes an arbitrary trend term; and it excludes the rate of growth of income. Furthermore, Lewis-Beck's calculations of elasticities to compare the relative effects of inflation and unemployment are incorrect.

9. The appropriate goodness-of-fit test for the validity of the logit specification is the chi square statistic (adjusted for degrees of freedom) obtained from the differences between the observed relative frequencies and estimated probabilities. The smaller the adjusted chi square statistic, the better the fit of the model. In the present case, the adjusted chi square is simply the sum of the squared weighted residuals divided by the degrees of freedom (X^2/df).

10. See the discussion in U.S. Department of Labor, *International Comparison of Unemployment*, which gives an excellent account of the methods used to compile unemployment estimates in France in comparison to the procedures employed elsewhere.

a model with president-specific constants, which permits the satisfaction index to shift (downward) between the Pompidou and Giscard periods, more satisfactorily picks up the political consequences of increased unemployment.

Because the parameter estimate for the inflation rate remains incorrectly signed (positive) and of negligible magnitude in regression model (2), it is replaced by the rate of acceleration of retail prices, $(I_t - I_{t-1})$, in model (3). Since the inflation rate in the recent past is among the best predictors of the inflation rate today, $(I_t - I_{t-1})$ is a sensible measure of *unanticipated* movements in prices, which economic theory suggests are the main cause of arbitrary redistributions of income and wealth. However, the results for model (3) show that although $(I_t - I_{t-1})$ enters with a negative coefficient, it is indistinguishable from zero. In other words, neither the rate of acceleration nor the rate of change of retail prices appears to have led to significant decreases in the satisfaction rating obtained by French presidents. The domestic political consequences of inflation appear, then, to be transmitted entirely through the impact of rising prices on the per capita real personal income growth stream.

Because I and $(I_t - I_{t-1})$ have little or no impact on presidential support net of movements in R, and because the decline in support attributable to rising unemployment is best captured by specifying president-specific intercepts, the most satisfactory equation in Table 8.1 is regression model (4), which includes only the growth rate of per capita real personal income as an explicit measure of politically relevant economic conditions. The success of model (4) in fitting the data is illustrated by Figure 8.2. Practical interest centers on the survey percentages rather than on the logits $[\ln(P_t'/1 - P_t')]$, therefore, Figure 8.2 shows the actual and fitted percentages of the French public satisfied with Pompidou and Giscard at each period. The fitted values track the actuals quite well (the correlation is 0.91), and no serious autocorrelation or other obvious errors in the functional form are revealed by the data.[11]

In Table 8.1 the optimal estimate of the lag weight rate-of-decay parameter g is about 0.8 in all models. This means that the performance outcomes of many past periods influence voters' current political evaluations of the president. The impact of current and past real

11. Lewis-Beck's equation applied to these data yields an inferior fit ($r = 0.61$) and substantial residual autocorrelation, which indicates there are problems with his specification. The fitted proportions in Figure 8.2 were generated by $\exp[f(Z_t)]/\{1 + \exp[f(Z_t)]\}$. Since the equation estimated is of the form $\ln[P_t'/(1 - P_t')] = f(Z_t) + e_t$, the former expression gives the fitted proportions implied by the logit model estimates.

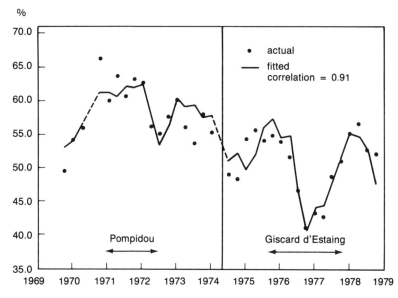

Figure 8.2. Actual and fitted percentages of the public satisfied with the president. (Fitted values are derived from model 4, Table 8.1.)

income-growth rates (R_{t-k}) on the president's popular satisfaction rating in the current quarter is therefore given by the geometric lag sequence:

$$0.015 \sum_{k} 0.8^k\, R_{t-k} \cdot D_{q,t-k} = 0.015(1.0\, R_t \cdot D_{qt}$$
$$+ 0.8\, R_{t-1} \cdot D_{q,t-1}$$
$$+ 0.64\, R_{t-2} \cdot D_{q,t-2}$$
$$+ 0.51\, R_{t-3} \cdot D_{q,t-3} + \ldots),$$

where 0.15 is the contemporaneous impact of R estimated by the regression coefficient in model (4) of Table 8.1 and $D_{q,t}$ is a "switching" variable equal to $+1$ during the current (qth) presidency and -1 otherwise. If the per capita real income growth rate were held at some equilibrium value R^* indefinitely, the above implies that the ultimate impact on political support would be:

$$\frac{0.015}{(1 - 0.8)}\, R^* = 0.075\, R^*.\text{[12]}$$

12. Recall that the sum of the geometric series $b(1 + g + g^2 + g^3 + \cdots +)$ is $b/(1 - g)$, for $0 < g < 1$.

The percentage of the ultimate impact felt by the kth lag is given by $1 - 0.8^{k+1}$.[13] Therefore, about 20 percent of the total political effect of a sustained change in the real income growth rate is felt immediately, about 60 percent is felt after one year (4 quarters), 84 percent after two years (8 quarters), and about 97 percent after four years (16 quarters). Politically, this means that after three to four years in office the systematic part of a president's popular satisfaction rating is based almost entirely on his own absolute performance record. Before that time his record in relation to that of his predecessor(s) is an important factor in determining his support by the mass public. This result contrasts sharply with the assumptions of earlier studies that only current performance, viewed absolutely, influences a president's contemporaneous political support.

The coefficients in Table 8.1 pertain to the impacts of movements in the independent variables on the dependent variable in the regression experiments, that is, on the logit $\ln[P'_t/(1 - P'_t)]$. But of course practical interest again centers on the implications of changes in economic performance on the percentage of the electorate satisfied with the president. Since the survey proportions, P'_t, are a nonlinear function of the logits, $\ln[P'_t/(1 - P'_t)]$, the effects of practical interest are difficult to judge by direct inspection of the regression coefficients, and they need not, in general, be homogeneous through time.[14] Therefore, to give an idea of the practical political consequences of fluctuations in the per capita real income growth rate, I have computed the long-run change in the percentage of the French public reporting satisfaction with the president expected at each period from sustained changes in R of one-half and one standard deviation.[15]

Figure 8.3 displays the time series of these impact measures computed at each period in the regression range. Although the expected changes in the support percentage associated with movements in the

13. The partial sum of the series $\Sigma^x_{k=0}g^k$ is $(1 - g^{k+1})/(1 - g)$. Therefore, the partial sum as a proportion of the infinite sum is $[(1 - g^{k+1})/(1 - g)]/[1/(1 - g)] = (1 - g^{k+1})$.

14. Note that the derivative of P'_t with respect to $f(Z)$ is: $P'_t(1 - P'_t) \cdot d\ln[P'_t/(1 - P'_t)]/df(Z)$, which varies through time and takes its maximum value at $P'_t = 0.5$.

15. Given the model, the change in the proportion of the electorate satisfied with the president at time t, expected from a sustained increase of one standard deviation in the per capita real income growth rate, is:

$$(P_{t+1} - P'_t) = L^*\{\ln[P'_t/(1 - P'_t)] + 0.15/(1 - 0.8) \cdot 1SD\} - P'_t,$$

where SD = the standard deviation of R, and L^* = the logistic distribution, $L^*(Z) = \exp(Z)/[1 + \exp(Z)]$. The expected long-run political impact of other sustained changes in R are computed in the same way.

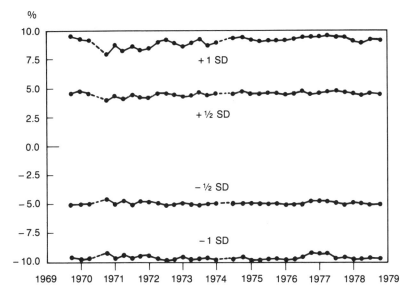

Figure 8.3.   Changes in the percentage of the public satisfied with the president, expected from changes of one-half and one standard deviations in the per capita real income growth rate (R).

per capita real income growth rate may vary over time and across positive and negative changes in R, the data in Figure 8.3 show that such variations are small. Giscard's average satisfaction rating lies close to 0.50 ($\bar{P}' = 0.51$); thus the effects of positive and negative movements in R were, on average, symmetrical during his presidency. Pompidou's mean satisfaction rating was somewhat higher ($\bar{P}' = 0.585$); therefore, decreases in R during his presidency had slightly greater effects than positive movements in R, and, on average, these effects were somewhat smaller than the corresponding effects of changes in R during the Giscard years.[16]

However, these differences are on the whole negligible. The main message of Figure 8.3 is that a movement of plus or minus one-half standard deviation in the per capita real income growth rate sustained for four years or more yields changes in presidential satisfaction ratings of just under plus or minus 5 percentage points. A sustained change of plus or minus one full standard deviation in R

16. Again, this simply follows from the fact that the impact of a change in R on P' is greatest at $P' = 0.50$. See notes 14 and 15.

produces in the long run a movement in the public's satisfaction with the president just less than twice the former magnitude—between 9 and 9.5 percentage points. If movements in the real income growth rate are accompanied by opposite changes in the rate of unemployment (we know from Okun's law in economics that declines in the real growth rate are accompanied by increases in the unemployment rate), then the political consequences would of course be even more pronounced.

As I pointed out earlier, Giscard's average satisfaction rating (51 percent) was about 7.5 points below Pompidou's (58.5 percent). Of course there were dramatic oscillations about these averages, but it is useful to identify the sources of change in the mean or equilibrium support levels experienced by these presidents. Approximate calculations indicate that about 3 percentage points (or two-fifths) of the decline in presidential support from Pompidou to Giscard was due to the decline in the real income growth rate, which averaged 4.3 percent per year during Pompidou's administration and only 2.2 percent per year during the first three years of Giscard's presidency. The effect of the rise in unemployment from the Pompidou to the Giscard years is embedded in the difference between the president-specific intercepts for the reasons discussed previously. Therefore, all we can estimate is the upper limit of the contribution of unemployment to the difference between the mean support levels: it is about 4 percentage points. The remaining 0.5 percentage point difference is attributable to the difference in the impact of the binary, noneconomic terms. The Chirac affair was slightly more costly for Giscard d'Estaing than the Chaban-Delmas tax scandal was for Pompidou.

The economic effects described above are sizable but not overwhelming. There is a considerable stability or inertia in the presidential support data stemming from long-standing popular political loyalties anchoring classes of voters to political parties and blocs that is not based on comparative economic performance. A discussion of these factors, however, is beyond the scope of this chapter.

Summary and Conclusions

Since the late 1960s the state of the economy has been quite salient to the French mass public; therefore, it is natural to expect that political support for Presidents Pompidou and Giscard d'Estaing was influenced significantly by macroeconomic conditions. The model presented in this chapter incorporates the idea that people evaluate economic performance in relative rather than absolute terms by implicitly comparing a president's cumulative record with that of his predecessors. However, the weights attached to current and past economic outcomes ($\Sigma_k Z_{t-k}$) were estimated to decline geometrically at rate 0.8^k, which means that after three years (12 quarters) or so a president is judged largely on his own current and past performance record.

The empirical results in Table 8.1 showed that the per capita real income growth rate was the principal systematic economic influence on movements in Pompidou's and Giscard's popular satisfaction rating in the IFOP polls. Since the real income growth rate is simply the nominal income growth rate less the inflation rate, price rises lead to declines in political support only to the extent that money incomes lag behind, either relatively or absolutely. This of course has been a persistent tendency in France and elsewhere since the first great OPEC supply shock of late 1973 and 1974, which represented an enormous transfer of real resources from the petroleum-consuming nations to the petroleum producers. Before the OPEC shock (over the period 1969:4–1973:3) per capita real income in France increased on average at a rate of nearly 5 percent per annum; afterward (over the period 1973:4–1978:4) the real growth rate declined to barely 2 percent per year.

The mechanism of the shift in the terms of trade induced by the cartel's actions was of course an inflation, but the economic pain was caused by the real loss, not by the price rises it produced. Deflationary macroeconomic policies sacrificing employment, real output, and real personal income in order to achieve price deceleration are therefore not likely to enhance a president's support among the French mass public. Indeed, the estimates graphed in Figure 8.3 indicate that a sustained standard deviation reduction in the growth rate of per capita real disposable income alone would, on average, yield a decline of 9–9.5 percentage points in the president's satisfaction rating in the polls.

Appendix: The Formal Political Support Model

The political support model described in the main body of the chapter is expressed theoretically in terms of an *unobserved*, continuously valued index of the president's popular satisfaction rating, Y^*. Y^* is determined by the cumulated, exponentially discounted performance of the current president's administration *in relation to* the cumulated, exponentially discounted performance of all previous presidential administrations, as well as by a sequence of constants, a_q, representing the unique popularity of the qth chief executive:

$$Y_t^* = \sum_{q=1}^{2} A_{qt}(b \cdot \sum_{k=0}^{\infty} g^k Z_{t-k} D_{q,t-k}) + a_q + u_t \qquad (8A.1)$$

where Z = a vector of performance variables with associated coefficients b,

g = the rate of decay of the lag function weights, $0 < g < 1$,

a_q and A_{qt} = +1 during the qth presidential administration, 0 otherwise,

D_{qt} = +1 during the qth presidential administration, −1 otherwise,

t = 41, 42, . . . , T,

and u_t is an independently distributed random disturbance.

As described in more detail in the main text, Equation (8A.1) says that the qth president's satisfaction rating at any time t depends upon the difference between the accumulated performance record of his administration with respect to Z and the performance record of previous administrations. The weights people give to performance outcomes decay exponentially at rate g^k; in other words, it is assumed that in making contemporaneous political judgments people give more weight to current performance than to past performance.

The binary "switching" variable D_{qt} ensures that Y_t^* is indeed based on interadministration performance comparisons. For example, if the qth president has been in office for two periods, Equation (8A.1) yields:

$$Y_t^* = b \cdot (Z_t + g Z_{t-1} - g^2 Z_{t-2} - g^3 Z_{t-3}$$
$$- g^4 Z_{t-4} - . . .) + a_q + u_t. \qquad (8A.2)$$

Although the lag functions and hence the performance comparisons represented by (8A.1) and (8A.2) imply that the Zs extend back to the infinite past, this is merely a convenient fiction that should be taken to mean that evaluations go back to the beginning of the relevant political era. It is implicitly assumed that knowledge of past performance is transmitted from generation to generation via political socialization.

The model may be expressed in a form suitable for estimation if (8.A1) is written:

$$Y_t^* = \sum_{q=1}^{2} A_{qt}\left[b \cdot \sum_{k=0}^{t-2} g^k Z_{t-k} D_{q,t-k} + g^{t-1} E(Y_1)\right]$$
$$+ a_q(1 - g^{t-1}) + u_t, \qquad\qquad (8A.3)$$

which involves a finite observable lag sequence in the Z_{t-k}. Moreover, because data on the performance variables are available for more than 40 quarters before the first observation on Y^* (that is, before Pompidou's first satisfaction rating), g^{t-1} is never larger than g^{40}. Since $g < 1$, the terms $g^{t-1}E(Y_1)$ and $-g^{t-1}a_q$ are negligible quantities and therefore may be dropped safely from Equation (8A.3) for estimation purposes.

Remember, however, that the continuously valued satisfaction index, Y^*, is unobserved; the survey data reveal only whether respondents are satisfied or dissatisfied with the president of the French Republic. Hence, we need a model that maps the observed individual binary choices in the surveys onto the unobserved satisfaction index.

Let the observed survey responses in the IFOP surveys be designated by the binary variable Y_{it}; $Y_{it} = 1$ for respondents satisfied with the president and 0 for respondents dissatisfied with the president. Since this chapter investigates movements through time in aggregated survey responses, it will be assumed here that individuals react homogeneously to presidential performance with respect to Z. Therefore, the Y_{it} are assumed to reflect crudely the underlying continuously valued popular satisfaction index Y^* such that $Y_{it} = 1$ if $Y_t^* > c$, 0 if $Y_t^* \le c$, where c is a "critical threshold." Letting $f(Z)$ denote the substantive terms on the righthand side of Equation (8A.3), it follows that the probability (P) of observing a "satisfied" response for individuals at time t is:

$$P_t = P(Y_{it} = 1) = P[f(Z) + u_t > c] = P[u_t > c - f(Z)] \quad (8A.4)$$

and $(1 - P_t)$ gives the probability of a "dissatisfied" response.

In other words people are satisfied with the president $(Y = 1)$ when Y^* exceeds some critical threshold c. The probability of being satisfied therefore hinges on the value of $c - f(Z)$ and the distribution of the random variable u.

The above implies that P_t may be regarded as a cumulative distribution function. Any appropriate distribution for u will yield a well-behaved probability function. It is convenient, however, to assume u logistic (which differs trivially from the normal distribution) with mean zero and scale parameters, which implies the probability function:

$$P_t = P[u_t > c - f(Z)] = 1 - \frac{e^{[c-f(Z)]/s}}{1 + e^{[c-f(Z)]/s}}$$

$$= \frac{e^{[f(Z)-c]/s}}{1 + e^{[f(Z)-c]/s}} = L^*\{(f(Z) - c]/s\}, \tag{8A.5}$$

where L^* is the logistic operator, and $L^*(Z) = \exp(Z)/[1 + \exp(Z)]$.

Equation (8A.5) means that the response probabilities monotonically approach 1 as $f(Z)$ goes to $+\infty$ (gets large) and monotonically approach 0 as $f(Z)$ goes to $-\infty$ (gets small).

Finally, notice that Equation (8A.5) may be manipulated to yield:

$$L^{*-1}P_t = \ln[P_t / (1 - P_t)] = [f(Z) = c]/s. \tag{8A.6}$$

which expresses the natural logarithm of the probability odds ratio (the "logit") as a linear function of the logistic model parameters. Replacing the notation simplification introduced in Equation (8A.4) with the terms of the original political support model in Equations (8A.1)–(8A.3) yields the model used in the regression experiments:

$$\ln[P_t'/(1 - P_t')] = \sum_{q=1}^{2} A_{qt}[(1/s)b\sum_{k=0}^{t-2} g^k Z_{t-k} D_{q,t-k}]$$

$$+ a_q + e_t, \tag{8A.7}$$

where P_t' = the observed survey proportion expressing "satisfaction" with the president (P_t being the unobserved population proportion),

$e_t = \ln[P_t'/(1 - P_t')] - \ln[P_t/(1 - P_t)]$.

It can be shown that the error term e has mean zero and variance $[N_t P_t(1 - P_t)]^{1/2}$, where N_t is the number of survey observations used to form P_t'. This means that efficient least-squares estimates are obtained by weighting each term in Equation (8A.7) by $[N_t P_t'(1 - P_t')]^{1/2}$. These weights were applied in the regressions reported in the main body of the chapter.

9

The Impact of Economic Performance on Electoral Support in Sweden, 1967–1978

Written with Henrik Jess Madsen

Introduction

Although economic issues probably were less important in Swedish political life in the 1960s than during the immediate postwar period (or during the 1930s), public concern about employment, inflation, and taxation had by no means expired. Table 9.1, reporting survey data on policy priorities of the Swedish electorate in 1960, 1973, and 1976, illustrates the persistent salience of these macroeconomic issues. During the 1970s, when there was a steady expansion of social programs and public expenditures, questions of social reform commanded the electorate's foremost attention. Of those responding to the policy priorities questions in the 1973 and 1976 surveys, 61 and 47 percent, respectively, identified explicitly economic policy and taxation as salient political issues. Because social reform issues have important implications for state spending, and hence touch directly upon general economic concerns, these numbers may well understate the extent to which economic factors influenced voters' evaluation of the government.

Indeed, more detailed survey evidence supports this conjecture. Table 9.2 presents the electorate's view of the importance of employment, inflation, taxes, and energy for their vote in the 1976 election.

Reprinted from *Scandinavian Political Studies*, 4 (1981), 33–50. The original article was written with Henrik Jess Madsen. The research was supported by National Science Foundation Grant SOC 78-27022 (to Douglas A. Hibbs, Jr.) and by a Danish Social Science Research Council grant (to Henrik Jess Madsen). I am grateful to Nicholas Vasilatos for computational assistance and to Christine Aquilino for typing the manuscript.

Table 9.1. Policy priorities of the Swedish electorate, 1960, 1973, and 1976, in percentages.

Policy item	1960[a]	1973[b]	1976[b] (pre-election)	1976[b] (post-election)
Economic policy	19	25	21	17
General social policy, social reforms	10	47	41	9
Pensions[c]	22	41	37	5
Specific areas of social policy (health care, regulation of working hours, holiday legislation, etc.)	12	30	26	5
State control, socialism[d]		19	37	2
Taxes, public expenditure[e]	27	36	26	28
Energy policy	n.a.	n.a.	15	60
Total percentage naming at least one policy item	83	73	73	58

Sources: For 1960, B. Särlvik, "Recent Electoral Trends in Sweden," in *Scandinavia at the Polls,* ed. K. H. Cerny (Washington, D.C.: American Enterprise Institute, 1977); for 1973 and 1976, O. Petersson, *Väljarna och valet 1976* (Stockholm: Liber-Förlag/Allmänna Förlaget), table 5.1.

Note: The percentages in the table are based on the number of respondents naming the policy item, divided by the total number of respondents naming at least one item. Multiple responses were possible.

a. Question: "What do you think the party which you like best/for which you voted/ for which you could think of voting/the Government or the Riksdag should mainly work for during the next few years?"

b. Question: "Which policies of the present government do you particularly like? . . . particularly dislike?"

c. In 1973 and 1976 includes "care for elderly."

d. In 1976 includes "economic democracy."

e. In 1973 and 1976, only "taxes."

The data show rather convincingly that these policy areas were of crucial importance. Fully 82 percent of the respondents saw the taxation issue as either one of the "most important" influences or as a "rather important" influence on their vote, whereas about 52 percent attached equivalent importance to the energy question. Despite the decisive role played by *energi frågan* ("the energy question") for the outcome of the 1976 election (a point that has been emphasized by

Table 9.2. Voters' evaluation of the importance of issues for their vote in 1976 (preelection and postelection surveys combined), in percentages.

Evaluation of issues	Employment		Prices		Taxes		Energy	
1. One of the most important	30	\} 70	24	\} 77	33	\} 82	16	\} 52
2. Rather important	40		53		49		36	
3. Not particularly important	21		17		13		34	
4. Not important	6		3		3		11	
5. Don't know	2		3		3		3	
Total	99		100		101		100	

Source: O. Petersson, *Valundersökning 1976: Teknisk Report* (Stockholm: Liber-Förlag/ Allmänna Förlaget, 1978), variables 27, 28, 29, 77.

Swedish election specialists),[1] the data in Table 9.2, as well as other evidence,[2] serve as a warning against minimizing the electoral impact of economic concerns.

The 1976 election aside, have macroeconomic conditions contributed in a systematic way to the electorate's support for Swedish governments? Since 1967 SIFO (the Swedish Institute of Public Opinion) has regularly probed the vote intention of a representative sample of the Swedish electorate,[3] and this time series (monthly surveys aggregated to quarterly observations) is used to analyze the influence of macroeconomic performance on fluctuations in mass political support for Swedish governments. The next section presents a statistical model of qualitative political choices that formalizes the idea that the discrete support/nonsupport responses elicited by surveys are reflections of underlying, *continuously valued* voter sentiments about the incumbent political party or bloc ranging from strongly positive to strongly negative.

1. See, for example, O. Petersson, "The 1976 Election: New Trends in the Swedish Electorate," *Scandinavian Political Studies*, 1 (1978), 109–121; and H. Zetterberg, "The Swedish Election of 1976" (Paper presented to the World Association of Public Opinion Research, Uppsala, August 14–19, 1977).

2. For example, in the postelection sample of the 1976 election survey, 33 percent of the respondents who reported changing party between the 1973 and 1976 election rated taxation as one of the absolutely most important issues for their vote in 1976; 31 percent identified the nuclear power problem as the most important; 20 percent thought of inflation in that way; 15 percent emphasized the employment issue.

3. Until 1969 the question asked was "Which party do you prefer today?" Since 1970 the phrasing has focused more explicitly on vote intention: "Which party do you consider voting for at the next election?" A similar survey was initiated by Statistiska Centralbyrån in 1972 but is conducted less frequently.

The third section develops several specifications for the way in which voters evaluate governments' economic performance and reports the empirical results. Four measures of economic performance appear in the political support equations: the rate of inflation; the rate of unemployment; the growth rate of per capita real disposable income; and the difference, or gap, between the growth rate of post-tax, post-transfer per capita disposable income and pretax, pretransfer per capita earnings. The latter variable, designated *tax gap*, essentially measures the wedge between the growth streams of final disposable income and original market income opened up by state tax and transfer policies.

The specification for voters' evaluations favored by the evidence incorporates the idea that people evaluate economic performance relatively rather than absolutely, by comparing current economic conditions with those "expected" from recent experience. This specification also embodies the notion that a government's current support is based on its *cumulative* relative performance record; however, since the present relevance of information conveyed by past performance decays over time, it is assumed that voters discount backward in time the retrospective relative performance streams.

The regression coefficient estimates for this model indicate that deviations of the unemployment rate from its expected level exert the strongest influence on variations over time in support for the governing party or bloc. Inflationary bursts also have important political consequences, whereas the estimated impact of tax gap is small and that of the real disposable income growth rate is negligible.

The final section reviews the results and develops their larger implications.

A Model for Qualitative Political Choices

Although public opinion polls typically force people to make discrete, qualitative responses—in this case whether the respondent intends to vote for (or prefers) the incumbent party or bloc—in principle a voter's preference is not a discrete "for or against" phenomenon, but instead ranges from strong positive to strong negative feelings about the governing party or bloc. Therefore, the dependent variable in the model is a continuously valued, unobserved index of support for the governing party/bloc at time t, Y_t^*. Y^* is determined by:

$$Y_t^* = f(Z) + u_t, \tag{9.1}$$

where $f(Z)$ represents an evaluation function for the vector of economic performance variables, Z, described ahead; and u_t is an independently distributed random disturbance.

Y^* is unobserved; the SIFO survey data reveal only voters' discrete party preferences or vote intentions. Hence we need a model that maps the discrete choices in the SIFO surveys onto the unobserved, continuously valued support index. Let the observed survey responses be designated by the binary variable Y_{it}: $Y_{it} = 1$ for respondents who intend to vote for (or who prefer) the incumbent party or bloc, 0 for respondents who intend to vote for (or who prefer) opposition parties (or who abstain). Since our focus is on movements through time in aggregate political support, we shall assume that individuals react homogenously to government performance, $f(Z)$, and, therefore, that Y_{it} reflects the underlying continuously valued support index such that $Y_{it} = 1$ if $Y_t^* > c$, 0 if $Y_t^* \leq c$, where c is a critical threshold.

It follows that the probability (P) of survey responses supporting the government at time t is:

$$P_t = P(Y_{it} = 1) = P[f(Z) + u_t < c] = P[u_t > c - f(Z)], \tag{9.2}$$

and $(1 - P)$ gives the probability of support for nonincumbent parties (or of abstention). The probability of supporting the incumbent party therefore hinges on the value of $c - f(Z)$ and the distribution of the random variable u. The point is illustrated by Figure 9.1.

Equation (9.2) implies that P_t may be regarded as a cumulative distribution function. Any appropriate distribution for u will yield a well-behaved probability function. It is convenient, however, to assume u logistic (which differs trivially from the normal distribution) with mean zero and unit scale parameter, which implies the probability function:

$$P_t = \frac{\exp[f(Z) + v_t - c]}{1 + \exp[f(Z) + v_t - c]}, \tag{9.3}$$

where the conventional Berkson logistic function model has been modified along the lines proposed by Amemiya and Nold to include the random variable v_t to take account of omitted independent vari-

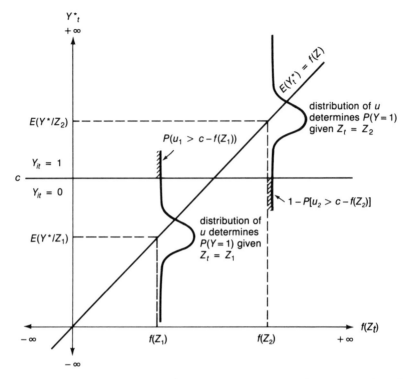

Figure 9.1. Observed binary responses and unobserved continuously valued support ratings.

ables.[4] v_t is assumed to have constant variance σ^2. As illustrated by Figure 9.2, Equation (9.2) means that the response probabilities monotonically approach one as $f(Z) + v_t$ goes to $+\infty$ and monotonically approaches zero as $f(Z) + v_t$ goes to $-\infty$.

Replacing the true probabilities (P_t) with the aggregate proportions observed in the survey data ($P'_t = \Sigma_{i=1}^{N} Y_{it}/N_t$) and manipulating (9.3) gives the logit estimating equation:

$$\ln[P'_t/(1 - P'_t)] = f(Z) + v_t + e_t, \tag{9.4}$$

4. J. Berkson, "Maximum Likelihood and Minimum X^2 Estimates for the Logistic Function," *Journal of the American Statistical Association*, 50 (1955), 130–162; and T. Amemiya and F. Nold, "A Modified Logit Model," *Review of Economics and Statistics*, 57 (1975), 255–257.

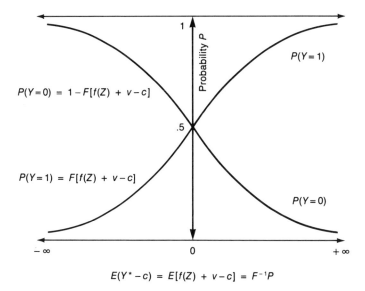

$$E(Y^* - c) = E[f(Z) + v - c] = F^{-1}P$$

Figure 9.2. Response probabilities, $P(Y)$, as a logistic function of observed data and model, $f(Z) + v$, and unobserved support index, Y^*.

where $e_t = \ln[P'_t/(1 - P'_t)] - \ln[P_t/(1 - P_t)]$, and without loss of generality c is arbitrarily set equal to zero.[5] It can be shown that (9.4) implies a regression equation with heteroscedastic residuals: the variance of the tth residual is $\sigma^2 + [N_t P_t(1 - P_t)]^{-1}$; therefore, we employed the two-step, weighted least-squares estimator developed by Amemiya and Nold.

The next section describes alternative specifications of the performance evaluation function, $f(Z)$, and reports the empirical results.

Performance Equations and Empirical Results

The regression analyses are based on quarterly observations over the period 1967:1–1978:3, which includes part of the Erlander govern-

5. Since c is necessarily embedded within the intercept constants of the performance evaluation equation $f(Z)$, nothing is lost by setting it to zero here.

The proof that Eq. (9.3) implies Eq. (9.4) is as follows. For simplicity let $P' = \exp(Z)/[1 + \exp(Z)]$, which is the form of Eq. (9.3). Then, $1 - P' = 1 - \{\exp(Z)/[1 + \exp(Z)]\}$; hence $(1 - P')/P' = \exp(Z)^{-1}$, and $P'/(1 - P') = \exp(Z)$, from which it follows that $\ln[P'/(1 - P')] = Z$, which is the form of Eq. (9.4).

ment and all periods of the Palme and Fälldin governments. For the reasons reviewed in the preceding section, the dependent variable in the regression equations is $\ln[P_t'/(1 - P_t')]$ (the logit of P_t'), where P_t' is the proportion of the SIFO sample indicating a preference or willingness to vote for the governing party(ies) in quarter t.[6] The economic performance variables are the unemployment rate, the inflation rate, the per capita real disposable income growth rate, and the gap, or difference, between the per capita growth rates of final disposable income and original market income, which is induced by the tax-transfer system (*tax gap*).[7] Each regression also includes a separate intercept constant for Social Democratic and bourgeois governments. These constants are essentially ignorance terms that pick up factors unrelated to economic performance that conferred an advantage on one or the other party or bloc.

Three specifications of the performance evaluation function, $f(Z)$, were entertained. The first is a rather naive model that assumes that voters' political support for governing parties responds only to contemporaneous macroeconomic performance:

$$\ln[P_t'/(1 - P_t')] = a_1 \text{ Soc. Dem. } + a_2 \text{ bourgeois } + bZ_t, \qquad (9.5)$$

where a_1, a_2 denote party/bloc intercept constants; Z is a vector representing the economic performance variables with associated coefficients b; and heteroscadiscity weights have been omitted for convenience.

Equation (9.5) is essentially the same as the model applied by Jonung and Wadensjö to monthly data on untransformed support proportions and, not surprisingly, yields results not too dissimilar to the findings of their study.[8] The coefficient estimates for this model, reported in Table 9.3, show that the unemployment, inflation, and

6. During the Erlander and Palme governments P_t' is the proportion supporting the Social Democrats; during the Fälldin government it is the sum of the proportions supporting each of the bourgeois parties in the government.

7. Hence *tax gap*$_t = (Z_{1t} - Z_{2t})$, where Z_{1t} is the growth rate of per capita personal disposable income, and Z_{2t} is the growth rate of per capita market earnings. All rates of change are formed $[\ln(Z_t/Z_{t-1})] \cdot 400$, that is, quarter-on-quarter differences of the logs expressed at annual rates.

8. L. Jonung and E. Wadensjö, "The Effects of Unemployment, Inflation, and Real Income Growth on Government Popularity in Sweden," *Scandinavian Journal of Economics*, 81 (1979), 343–353, also estimate models with a lagged endogenous variable to pick up (via the Koyck transformation) distributed lag effect. However, the Durbin's *h*-statistics they report are significant, indicating that the disturbances are autocorrelated and therefore that the regression coefficient estimates are biased and inconsistent.

Table 9.3. Weighted least-squares logit coefficient estimates, quarterly
1967:1–1978:3.

Coefficient of:	(1) Eq. 9.5	(2) Eq. 9.6	(3) Eq. 9.7
Social Democratic governments	0.19	0.26	0.13
(Erlander, Palme)	(0.11)	(0.12)	(0.03)
Bourgeois government	0.33	0.41	0.10
(Fälldin)	(0.12)	(0.14)	(0.06)
Inflation rate	−0.0061	−0.010	—
	(0.005)	(0.006)	
Deviations from expected	—	—	−0.047
inflation rate			(0.01)
Unemployment rate	−0.21	−0.23	—
	(0.04)	(0.05)	
Deviations from expected	—	—	−1.09
unemployment rate			(0.18)
Real disposable income	−0.00034	−0.00054	—
growth rate	(0.001)	(0.002)	
Deviations from expected real	—	—	0.0021
disposable income growth rate			(0.005)
Tax gap	0.0012	0.0061	—
	(0.004)	(0.005)	
Deviations from expected tax gap	—	—	0.013
			(0.006)
Lag weight rate of decay (g)	0	0.4	0.8
Fit: Correlation of actual and fitted			
proportions (P'_t)	.615	.63	.701

Note: Dependent variable in regressions: $\ln[P'_i/(1 - P'_i)]$. Standard errors are given in parentheses.

tax gap variables are correctly signed, but only the unemployment estimate is statistically significant. Hence there is little doubt from these results that political support for governing parties is quite sensitive to movements in unemployment. Notice that the real income growth rate enters the regression with a perverse (negative) sign; however, the magnitude of its coefficient is negligible and statistically insignificant.

Column 2 of Table 9.3 gives estimates for a more plausible model in which current political support is based on an exponentially weighted moving average of economic outcomes during the entire course of a government. A government's contemporaneous standing with the electorate therefore depends on its cumulative economic record, rather than solely on economic conditions in the current period. The estimates for this model are derived from:

$$\ln[P'_t/(1 - P'_t)] = a_1 \text{ Soc. Dem.} + a_2 \text{ bourgeois}$$

$$+ A_q \cdot b \left(\frac{1 - g}{1 - g^{qt}}\right) \sum_{k=0}^{q_t-1} g^k Z_{t-k}, \quad (9.6)$$

where q = an index of each government (1 = Erlander, 2 = Palme, and 3 = Fälldin),

   g = the rate of decay of the distributed lag weights, $0 \leq g < 1$,

   A_q = +1 during the qth government and zero otherwise,

   q_t = the number of quarters that the qth government has been in power,

   Z = the economic performance variables with associated coefficients b.

As Equation (9.6) implies, the regression coefficient b gives the total impact of a movement in Z on the political support index $\ln[P'_t/(1 - P'_t)]$. The total impact of a sustained change in Z is distributed over the life of a government according to the geometric lag sequence[9]

$$b \left(\frac{1 - g}{1 - g^{qt}}\right) (Z_t + g Z_{t-1} + g^2 Z_{t-2} + \ldots + g^{qt-1} Z_{t-qt-1}).$$

The estimate of the nonlinear coefficient g was obtained manually by searching over the parameter space and choosing the value minimizing the error sum of squares.

The estimates for Equation (9.6) in Table 9.3 show that it explains variations in the underlying political support proportions slightly better than Equation (9.5); the correlation of the actual proportions and the fitted proportions implied by the logit model is 0.63 as opposed to 0.615 for the previous equation. However, the substantive implica-

---

9. Since the sum of the geometric lag weight sequence $\sum_{k=0}^{q_t-1} g^k$ is $(1 - g^{qt})/(1 - g)$, premultiplying the lag distribution by $(1 - g)/(1 - g^{qt})$ simply acts as a normalizing constant that ensures that the lag weights sum to 1.0 at every period during the life of a government. This is why b gives the total impact of a sustained movement in Z and the lag weights define its distribution backward through time.

tions are basically the same: only unemployment has a sizable and statistically significant impact on political support. The persistent political impact of unemployment fluctuations revealed by the results for Equations (9.5) and (9.6) causes little surprise. Although unemployment compensation and other transfer payments cushion many of the unemployed against significant income losses,[10] only about half the unemployed are members of an insurance fund. For at least a small fraction of the electorate, then, unemployment means real hardship.[11] However, regardless of financial compensation, unemployment imposes psychological costs that, though difficult to measure quantitatively, are nonetheless likely to be sharply felt. Also, in addition to households touched directly by some form of unemployment or underemployment, an even larger number will be aware of unemployment among relatives, friends, neighbors, and workmates. Moreover, since unemployment represents forgone real output and underutilized human resources, it confers costs on society as a whole as well as on the individuals affected directly.

The discomfort associated with inflation, on the other hand, arises primarily from unanticipated movements in prices rather than from the inflation rate per se. Anticipated inflation presumably is reflected in wage claims and settlements and in other nominally priced contracts that are not explicitly indexed and, therefore, does not generate great dissatisfaction in the electorate. Voters probably also give governing parties little credit for rates of growth in real disposable income, or for growth in disposable income relative to market income, that simply reinforce customary experience or prior trends. Therefore, the small, statistically insignificant coefficients for the inflation and income variables reported in Table 9.3 for Equations (9.5) and (9.6) have a sensible interpretation.

The third performance evaluation function investigated takes explicit account of actual economic performance *in relation to* customary or expected performance. This model formalizes the idea that voters react to sharp deviations of actual economic outcomes from their customary or expected levels, rather than to economic outcomes per

10. For example, the annual disposable income of a male metalworker unemployed for one month in 1978 amounted to 97 percent of his full employment annual income. If unemployed for six months, he would have 90 percent of his full employment annual disposable income. (See J. I. Persson-Tanimura, "Vad kostar arbetslösheten?" *Ekonomisk debatt*, 8 [1980], 107–115, tab. 1).

11. The Swedish Low Income Commission identified unemployment as accounting for about 50 percent of the poverty gap.

se. If, for example, the contemporaneous inflation or unemployment rates exceed what people are accustomed to, political support will decline. Conversely, support is enhanced when unemployment declines briskly to historically low levels or inflation decelerates sharply. The same holds for the difference between the customary and actual tax gap or real income growth rate, but with opposite effects on political support. This reasoning implies:

$$\ln[P_t'/(1 - P_t')] = a_1 \text{ Soc. Dem.} + a_2 \text{ bourgeois}$$
$$+ \sum_{g=1}^{3}\left(\frac{1 - g}{1 - g^{qt}}\right) \sum_{k=0}^{q_t-1} g^k(Z - Z^*)_{t-k}, \qquad (9.7)$$

where $Z_i^* = c_0 + \sum_{j=1}^{l} c_j Z_{t-j}$, and other terms are as defined earlier.

As in Equation (9.6), the relative performance deviations in Equation (9.7), $Z - Z^*$, are cumulated over the life of each government, with past deviations weighted g_k. Customary or expected performance outcomes, Z^*, which serve as the benchmarks for voters' reactions to actual outcomes, Z, are generated autoregressively. In other words, the Z_t^* are formed from linear combinations of previous outcomes with coefficients c_j obtained by regressing Z_t on Z_{t-1}, Z_{t-2}, . . . , Z_{t-j}. Notice that customary performance, Z^*, is not fixed:[12] the equation for Z^* in (9.7) means that performance standards are relative rather than absolute and adjust dynamically over time. Hence any sustained rate of inflation, unemployment, real income growth, or tax gap will eventually become "customary" to the electorate, satisfying $(Z_t - Z_t^*) = 0$. Political rewards and penalties are conferred only by fluctuations in economic conditions producing nonzero deviations of Z from Z^*, that is, deviations of current conditions from a linear combination of conditions in the recent past.

The parameter estimates for Equation (9.7) are shown in column 3 of Table 9.3. The correlation of the predicted and actual SIFO proportions shown at the bottom of the table ($r = 0.7$) indicates that this equation does a better job of explaining the underlying empirical data on political support than do Equations (9.5) and (9.6). All parameters have the anticipated sign and, with the exception of the real income growth rate coefficient, are statistically significant. It is clear from

12. Since the c_j coefficients in the autoregressive equations generating Z^* are likely to evolve through time, these equations were reestimated for each government using observations up to the beginning of that government.

these results, then, that sharp upward movements in the rates of unemployment and inflation (positive deviations of Z from Z^*) yield losses of support for the governing party or political bloc, and that unexpected upward movements in disposable income growth rates relative to market income growth rates (*tax gap*) produce increases in the government's support in the electorate. It should be noted that large gaps between disposable and market income growth rates generally imply expansions (if the gap is positive) or contractions (if the gap is negative) of cash transfers relative to collective consumption. Nonzero values of this term may also stem from reductions (if $Z - Z^*$ is positive) or increases (if $Z - Z^*$ is negative) of direct rates of personal taxation that are not accompanied by changes in transfers. The significant positive coefficient for the tax gap variable in Equation (9.7) means, therefore, that voters reward governments for unexpected increases in transfers relative to collective consumption expenditures or, alternatively, react favorably to sharp reductions in direct taxation that do not adversely affect the flow of transfer spending.[13] Finally, the empirical results indicate that in the presence of the unemployment, inflation, and tax gap variables, the real disposable income growth rate alone does not have a sizable impact on the government's standing in the SIFO polls.

The estimate of the lag weight decay parameter g in (9.7), which defines the distribution over time of the ultimate impact of a sustained value of $(Z - Z^*)$, is about 0.8. This implies that the electorate's current vote intentions are influenced by relative performance outcomes extending many periods back through time. As the normal electoral period is three years (12 quarters), we have at the election quarter:

$$\frac{1 - 0.8}{1 - 0.8^{12}} \sum_{k=0}^{11} g^k (Z - Z^*)_{t-k};$$

therefore, the percentage of the election-quarter impact of a persistent unit deviation of Z from Z^* that is felt by the kth lag is given by $(1 - 0.8^{k+1})/(1 - 0.8^{12})$.[14] Hence, at the typical election period contempora-

---

13. See D. A. Hibbs, Jr., and H. J. Madsen, "Public Reactions to the Growth of Taxation and Government Expenditure," *World Politics*, 33 (1981), 413–435, for some comparative evidence on this point.

14. The sum of the finite geometric series $(1 - 0.8)/(1 - 0.8^{12}) \sum_{k=0}^{11} g^k$ is $(1 - 0.8)/(1 - 0.8^{12}) (1 - 0.8^{k+1})/(1 - 0.8) = (1 - 0.8^{k+1})/(1 - 0.8^{12})$. Since by construction the lag weights sum to 1.0 at every period, this gives immediately the percentage of the ultimate impact felt by the kth lag.

neous relative economic performance ($k = 0$) accounts for about 21 percent of the economy's impact on voting preferences, relative performance over the previous year ($k = 0, 1, 2, 3$) picks up about 63 percent of the economy's election-quarter impact, and relative performance over the preceding two years ($k = 0, 1, . . . , 7$) represents about 89 percent of the economy's effect on the governing parties' electoral support.

Implications for Observed Political Support

The empirical results discussed above indicated that Equation (9.7) is the most satisfactory specification of the impact of economic performance on electoral support. However, the regression coefficient estimates pertain to the logits, $\ln[P'_t/(1 - P'_t)]$, whereas practical interest centers on the consequences of relative economic performance for the *percentages* (or proportions) of the electorate supporting governing parties. Since the survey proportions, P'_t, are a nonlinear function of the corresponding logits, $\ln[P'_t/(1 - P'_t)]$, the precise effects of practical interest are not immediately obvious from direct inspection of the parameter estimates. Therefore, to illustrate the practical political consequences of fluctuations in the significant economic variables, I computed the changes in the percentage of the electorate supporting the governing parties following unfavorable movements of Z relative to Z^* and sustained for 1 and 4 quarters before the end of the Erlander, Palme, and Fälldin regimes. To facilitate comparisons of the estimated effects of movements in the economic variables, changes of one standard deviation in the $(Z - Z^*)$ terms are considered. Table 9.4 summarizes the results.[15]

15. The losses are inferred by comparing the support percentages predicted by Eq. (9.7) from the actual, historical economic data with the predictions generated by the equation, holding the $(Z - Z^*)$ variables one standard deviation above or below their historical values.

The end of the Erlander and the Fälldin governments of course did not follow election defeats. Nevertheless, for illustrative purposes the impact calculations in Table 9.4 might be interpreted as the implied losses of support on "election days." The Erlander government was considered to have been in office since 1964:3; thus the standard deviations were calculated for a period starting at this date and ending in 1978:3. Since the economic variables are expressed as deviations from autoregressively formed expectations, a 4-quarter sustained change implies accelerating rates of inflation, unemployment, and tax gap. The mean and standard deviations of the three $(Z - Z^*)$ performance variables are: for inflation, 1.85 and 3.81; for unemployment, 0.05 and 0.23; for the tax gap, −0.05 and 6.35, respectively.

Table 9.4. Simulated losses of aggregate political support resulting from unexpected, unfavorable changes of one standard deviation in the macroeconomy $(Z - Z^*)$, in percentage points.

Government	Losses of support sustained for:	
	1 quarter	4 quarters
Erlander (1967:1–1969:3)		
Inflation	0.88	2.58
Unemployment	1.22	3.58
Tax gap	0.42	1.23
Palme (1969:4–1976:2)		
Inflation	0.87	2.54
Unemployment	1.20	3.52
Tax gap	0.41	1.21
Fälldin (1976:3–1978:3)		
Inflation	1.06	3.11
Unemployment	1.47	4.31
Tax gap	0.50	1.48
Average loss of political support		
Inflation	0.94	2.74
Unemployment	1.30	3.08
Tax gap	0.44	1.31

Adverse fluctuations in unemployment relative to expectations based on recent experience clearly exhibit stronger influence on electoral preferences during the Erlander, Palme, and Fälldin governments than do unfavorable shifts in the inflation or tax gap variables. Averaged over all governments, a standard deviation increase of unemployment beyond the expected level and lasting only 1 quarter produces a decline of about 1.3 percentage points in the governing parties' mass political support. Sustained a full year (4 quarters), the same adverse increase (acceleration) of unemployment relative to expectations on average generates losses of 3 percentage points in governments' electoral support.

The political consequences of unfavorable relative changes in the inflation and tax gap variables are smaller, with the former variable being about twice as important as the latter. Sustained just 1 quarter, adverse movements in inflation and the tax gap relative to voters' recent experience decrease political support on average by 0.9 and 0.4 percentage points, respectively. The political penalties are larger if the same unfavorable relative changes in these variables are sustained over 4 quarters: the loss associated with inflation averages 2.7 percentage points, with the tax gap 1.31 percentage points.[16]

In view of the extremely competitive electoral politics of the postwar Swedish party system, the losses of political support attributed to reasonable movements in the macroeconomy in Table 9.4 are hardly trivial. Although the "Socialist bloc" (Social Democrats and Communists) commanded a comfortable lead during the 1960s, subsequent electoral margins were much narrower. As Table 9.5 shows, averaged over all elections beginning in 1952, the margin of victory separating the Socialist and bourgeois blocs has been only 1.6 percent of the vote.[17] Even though partisan preferences are obviously also based on more enduring characteristics of political life than those incorporated explicitly in the model, here, the results indicate that macroeconomic management can play a pivotal role in electoral shifts.

The comparatively strong electoral effects arising from movements in the unemployment rate illustrated in Tables 9.3 and 9.4 obviously reflect the salience of the employment issue in postwar Swedish politics. While the anticyclical policies pursued by the Social Democrats in the 1930s provided only marginal relief from the severe recession, they skillfully exploited its symbolic significance and became identified with full employment and prosperity. The specter of a repetition of the mass unemployment of the 1930s under a bourgeois government became the underlying theme in the Social Democrats' electoral strategy, and it proved to be an advantageous mobilizing device. However, it gradually receded in importance as postwar cohorts en-

---

16. The difference in the simulated losses of political support between the three administrations partly reflect differences in the lengths of time in office. As the Fälldin government ruled for only 8 quarters (compared to 72 for Erlander's and 28 for Palme's), the economic effects tend to be larger, due to the g lag weight scheme, for the bourgeois coalition.

The estimated electoral losses based on Eq. (9.6) (for appropriately calculated standard deviations of the original variables) are similar to those presented in Table 9.4. The implied electoral losses in percentage points, averaged over all three governments for 1 and 4 quarters, are: for inflation, -0.54 and -0.86; for unemployment, -1.36 and -2.22; for the tax gap, -0.57 and -1.09, respectively. Notice that movements in the rate of unemployment and in tax gap variable are relatively more important here.

17. When evaluating Table 9.5 in conjunction with Table 9.4, it should be remembered that the dependent variable in the regressions for Socialist governments was based on the survey proportions supporting the Social Democrats only.

Table 9.5. The margin of victory separating the Socialist and bourgeois blocs in parliamentary elections, 1952–1976.

Year	Percentage points
1952	0.4
1956	0.35
1958	0.4
1960	2.35
1964	4.15
1968	4.0
1970	1.25
1973	0.05
1976	1.65
Average	1.6

Note: The margin of victory is defined as the minimum share of those voting that was necessary to give the losing bloc a majority, that is, the absolute value of (% voting for the Socialist bloc −% voting for the bourgeois bloc)/2.

tered the electorate and as bourgeois parties succeeded in convincing the electorate that they also were committed to full employment.[18] As a result, by the late 1960s the relative tightness of labor markets was the preeminent measure of governments' economic performance, which is what our estimates suggest.

18. See, for example, B. Särlvik, "Recent Electoral Trends in Sweden," in *Scandinavia at the Polls,* ed. K. H. Cerny (Washington, D.C.: American Enterprise Institute, 1977).

10

Economic Outcomes and Political Support for British Governments among the Occupational Classes: A Dynamic Analysis

In March 1968, Prime Minister Harold Wilson reportedly declared to the Parliamentary Labour Party: "All political history shows that the standing of a Government and its ability to hold the confidence of the electorate at a General election depend on the success of its economic policy."[1] Though perhaps overstated, Wilson's declaration is consistent with the conclusions of several time-series studies of the impact of macroeconomic performance on aggregate mass political support for governing British parties.[2]

Reprinted from *American Political Science Review*, 76 (June 1982), 259–279. The original article was written with the assistance of Nicholas Vasilatos. The research was supported by National Science Foundation Grant SOC78-27022 and by the Center for International Affairs at Harvard University. All computations and graphical displays were done by Nicholas Vasilatos. Douglas Rivers assisted during earlier phases of the research. Christine Aquilino and Elizabeth Welch typed the manuscript. James Alt, Samuel Beer, Bruce Cain, Alan Zuckerman, and anonymous reviewers gave very helpful comments on an earlier draft. I am particularly grateful to William Keech for pushing me to extend the discussion of the behavioral implications of the political support model.

1. Reported by David Watt in the *Financial Times*, March 8, 1968.
2. See James E. Alt, *The Politics of Economic Decline: Economic Management and Political Behavior in Britain since 1964* (Cambridge: Cambridge University Press, 1979), chap. 6; Bruno S. Frey and Friedrich Schneider, "A Politico-Economic Model of the United Kingdom," *Economic Journal*, 88 (1978), 243–253; Douglas A. Hibbs, Jr., and Nicholas Vasilatos, "Macroeconomic Performance and Mass Political Support in the United States and Great Britain," in *Contemporary Political Economy*, ed. D. A. Hibbs, Jr., and H. Fassbender (Amsterdam: North-Holland, 1981); Samuel Kernell, "Unemployment, Inflation, and Party Democracy: A Study of the Strategic Bases of Economic Policy in Advanced Industrial Democracies" (Mimeograph, University of California at San Diego, 1980); Christopher Pissarides, "British Government Popularity and Economic Performance," *Economic Journal*, 90 (1980), 569–581.

The conclusions of the earlier, aggregate time-series studies come as no surprise in view of macroeconomic developments since the mid-1960s, which made economic issues much more salient to the British electorate. The Gallup poll data in Figure 10.1, for example, show that the economy has loomed large among the concerns of the British public for fifteen years. Indeed, during the 1970s on average two-thirds of the public designated one or more economic issues as "the most urgent problem facing the country."

For aggregate analyses of political behavior to be consistent with an underlying micromodel of individuals making discrete political choices, it must be assumed that voters respond more or less homogeneously to macroeconomic (and noneconomic) outcomes. However, voters' responses to economic conditions (as well as to other salient social and political issues) are likely to vary considerably because of differences in the objective, concrete interests at stake, and perhaps also because group loyalties and contextual influences affect voters' perceptions and interpretations of politically relevant information. In particular, movements in the macroeconomy are not likely to have the same effect on the government's political support among

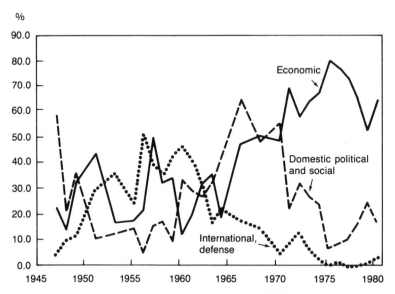

Figure 10.1. Aggregate responses to the question "What is the most urgent (most important) problem facing the country today?" (wording varies). (From Gallup Political Index, *Gallup Poll Limited*, monthly, various issues.)

different electoral groups because the burdens and rewards associated with economic fluctuations are distributed unevenly within the electorate.

We know, for example, that unemployment is heavily concentrated among manual-grade workers in the British electorate. Data from both the General Household Survey (GHS) of 1971 and the Department of Employment (DOE) survey of the registered unemployed in 1973 show that the incidence of unemployment among skilled and supervisory manual (blue-collar) workers was nearly twice that among nonmanual employees, and the unemployment rates among unskilled and semiskilled workers ranged from three to four times the rate prevailing among nonmanual (white-collar) employees.[3] Although transfer payments provide a significant cushion against income losses from unemployment, the experience imposes real economic pain on those affected. The DOE data indicate that only a small fraction of the unemployed received benefits exceeding their likely wage in employment. The GHS data show that the shortfall of unemployment-related benefits to previous employment earnings ranged from 22 to 78 percent, with the median shortfall in the range of 32 to 37 percent.[4] These data are consistent with Nickell's more sophisticated analysis of the ratio of actual post-tax income to potential post-tax income for households in which the male was out of work.[5] Nickell found that, with all benefits and tax refunds taken into account, the average shortfall of household income was 28 percent for a 1972 sample of the unemployed.

The alleged disincentives to job seeking provided by earnings-related supplementary unemployment benefits notwithstanding,[6] it is not surprising that in the GHS survey, 71 percent of all respondents seeking work considered unemployment a "very bad" or "quite bad"

3. I have computed the unemployment ratios from the data in William W. Daniel, *A National Survey of the Unemployed* (London: National Economic Research Council, 1974), tab. II 5, p. 11. The relative unemployment incidence among occupational groups in Britain is quite similar to that in the United States; see Chapter 5 of this volume.

4. See Daniel, *National Survey of the Unemployed*, tab. XI 1, p. 114, and "Characteristics of the Unemployed: Sample Survey June 1972," *Department of Employment Gazette*, 82 (March 1974), tab. 8, p. 220.

5. S. J. Nickell and D. Metcalf, *The Plain Man's Guide to the Out-of-Work* (London: London School of Economics, 1977).

6. See, for example, the discussion in Martin Feldstein, "The Economics of the New Unemployment," *Public Interest*, 33 (Fall 1973), 3–42, and the analysis of D. I. MacKay and G. Reid, "Redundance, Unemployment, and Manpower Policy," *Economic Journal*, 82 (1972), 1256–72.

experience; the most important reasons were economic hardship ("lack of money") or psychological distress ("depression" and "boredom") or both.[7] Given the social incidence and economic impact of joblessness, it follows that rising unemployment accentuates inequality.

The shortcomings of the available data make it more difficult to draw firm conclusions about the impact of inflation on the economic well-being of various groups in Britain. It is clear from data on the cyclical behavior of factor shares (that is, shares of national income going to labor versus capital over the business cycle) that the wage and salary share of national income is not eroded by inflation. Indeed, gross corporate profits appear to suffer relative declines during periods of rising prices. Similarly, as Piachaud has shown, the general failure of investment yields to keep pace with inflation has worked to the disadvantage of the rich and others dependent on unearned income in Britain.[8] Piachaud's data also indicate that the heaviest burden of inflation-induced increases in direct taxation rates, which until 1978 were not formally indexed and are based on progressive nominal schedules, has fallen on higher (and to a lesser degree lower) income groups.

Studies of wage formation in the manufacturing sector show that, contrary to the situation in the United States, bursts of inflation have not in general affected adversely the real wage of British manufacturing workers. The power of British trade unions and of other institutional arrangements in the labor market has effectively insulated the real wage from inflation shocks. Apparently inflation also has not been painful for state pensioners, that is, for the lower-income aged. Since 1975 national retirement pensions in Britain have been formally indexed, and data for prior years indicate that over the entire postwar period, the real value of pensions was maintained, or actually increased, during years of high inflation. On the other hand, the evidence suggests that once differences in expenditure patterns are taken into account, the price-level increases experienced since the

7. See Daniel, *National Survey of the Unemployed*, tabs. V 1 and V 2, pp. 43 and 44. For comparable data on the United States, see Kay L. Schlozman and Sidney Verba, *Injury to Insult: Unemployment, Class, and Political Response* (Cambridge, Mass.: Harvard University Press, 1979).

8. David Piachaud, "Inflation and the Income Distribution," in *The Political Economy of Inflation*, ed. J. H. Goldthorpe and Fred Hirsch (Cambridge, Mass.: Harvard University Press, 1978), and Douglas Hibbs, *Economic Interest and the Politics of Macroeconomic Policy* (Cambridge, Mass.: Center for International Studies, MIT, 1976).

1950s by lower-income groups as a whole typically were greater than those experienced by higher-income groups.[9]

Although it is difficult to reach unambiguous conclusions about the singular impact of inflation on social groups, all the available evidence on the incidence and distributional consequences of inflation and unemployment implies strongly that lower-status groups are likely to exhibit greater aversion to unemployment and less concern about inflation than are higher-status groups. The survey data presented in Figure 10.2 on sensitivity to unemployment among occupational groups (social grades) provide some evidence favoring this expectation, although only the May 1975 survey question pertains to concern about unemployment relative to inflation.[10] Skilled workers typically express somewhat greater concern about unemployment than do semiskilled and unskilled workers. Although the evidence reviewed earlier shows that semiskilled and unskilled workers experience considerably higher unemployment rates than all other occupational groups, the lowest social-grade category in the published survey reports also includes widows and state pensioners who are outside the labor force and therefore presumably not affected directly by unemployment.

The electorate's preferences and objective economic interests in macroeconomic issues and outcomes appear to be class related. Nonetheless, most earlier time-series studies of economic influences on political support have been based solely on aggregate survey data. (See note 2.) Therefore, in order to investigate the sources and magnitudes of differences in group responses to economic events within the framework of a dynamic model of a government's political support, time-series analyses were undertaken in which the relative importance (regression weights) attached to the economic performance variables are allowed to vary across occupational classes. Occupation of the household's primary wage earner was selected as the dimension of disaggregation because of its relevance to the distributional issues reviewed earlier and, more important, because even though class voting is believed by many specialists to have declined some-

9. See Chapter 3 of this volume; J. Muellbauer, "Prices and Inequality: The United Kingdom Experience," *Economic Journal*, 84 (1974); and Jeffrey Sachs, "Wages, Profits, and Macroeconomic Adjustment: A Comparative Study," *Brookings Papers on Economic Activity* (1979:2), 269–319.

10. Unfortunately, because opinion polls chronically confuse the "cost of living" (the price level and standards of living) with "rising prices" (the inflation rate), data from many surveys cannot be used to assess the public's relative concern about inflation.

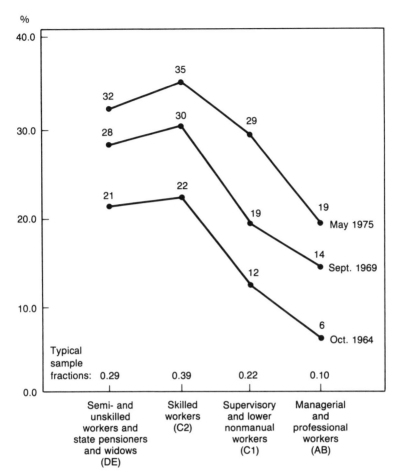

Figure 10.2. Sensitivity to unemployment among occupational class groups in selected surveys. (wording approximate). October 1964: "Which issue will be particularly important to you at the coming General Election?" September 1969: "Pick the most important problems facing the government." May 1975: "Do you prefer the government to control rising prices or to prevent unemployment?" (From *National Opinion Poll Bulletin*, January 1965 and September 1969; Opinion Research Centre, *The State of Britain*, May 1975.)

what in Britain, occupational position remains the preeminent source of persistent partisan voting cleavages.

The second section of this chapter describes a theory of how people make qualitative political choices, which formalizes the idea that survey responses concerning voters' party preferences are discrete reflections of underlying, continuously valued sentiments that range from strongly positive to strongly negative. As in earlier chapters, the two most important substantive features of the theoretical model are: (1) voters evaluate the cumulative performance of the governing party in relation to the prior performance of the current opposition, and (2) the weights that voters place on current and past economic outcomes decline geometrically, so that current performance contributes more heavily than past performance to the formation of contemporaneous political judgments.

The third section presents the empirical results. The political support equations include measures of nominal economic performance (inflation and exchange rate movements) and real economic performance (unemployment and real income fluctuations). The regression analyses indicate that variations in the relative sensitivity of occupational classes to macroeconomic configurations are sizable and are broadly consistent with patterns in survey preferences and objective costs reviewed earlier.

The fourth section develops the electoral implications of the results of the estimation by computing the changes in support for the governing party to be expected from reasonable movements in the macroeconomic performance variables. This section also develops a novel interpretation of trends in class-based political support for the parties, which challenges the argument that there has been a persistent pattern of class dealignment in the 1960s and 1970s.

The Political Support Model

The theoretical model of mass political support enjoyed by the principal governing party is represented by:

$$Y_{jt}^* = a_{qj} + b_j \cdot D_t \sum_{k=0}^{\infty} g^k Z_{t-k} D_{t-k} + u_{jt}, \tag{10.1}$$

where Y_{jt}^* = a latent, continuously valued index of support for the incumbent party in group j at time t,
a_q = government-specific constants,
Z = a vector of performance variables (specified later) with associated coefficients b,
g = the rate of decay of the lag weights, $0 < g < 1$,

D_t = +1 if Labour is in power at time t, −1 if the Conservatives are in power at time t,

j = group indices,

q = government indices.

Political opinion surveys typically force people to make discrete, qualitative responses. In the present case, the survey measure of popular support for the principal governing party (Labour or Conservative) is based on the Gallup poll question for Great Britain "If there were a General Election tomorrow, how would you vote?" In principle, however, support for the governing party is not a strictly discrete phenomenon but a matter of degree. As I showed in Chapter 7, a reasonable approximation to such a continuously valued support index (Y^*_{jt}) is the natural logarithm of the proportion (of the jth group) of the survey sample at each period expressing support for the governing party (P'_{jt}) divided by one minus this proportion ($1 - P'_{jt}$). That is, $\ln[P'_{jt}/(1 - P'_{jt})]$. $P'_{jt}/(1 - P'_{jt})$ gives the support odds ratio, and the natural logarithm of this odds ratio, known as the logit, ranges from $-\infty$ to $+\infty$. The logits constitute the continuously valued support index used in the regression analyses discussed in the next section.

Several features of the political support model in Equation (10.1) warrant explanation. First, the governing party's political support depends on its cumulative performance record with respect to the variables Z. However, since the present relevance of the information conveyed by past performance decays over time, the weights given to past performance outcomes (Z_{t-k}) in the model decline at rate g^k, where g is a decay-rate parameter lying between zero and one. Z_{t-k} is a vector of economic performance outcomes experienced k periods ago ($k = 0, 1, 2, 3, \ldots$); therefore, current and past experiences with respect to Z are weighted $g^0 Z_t = Z_t, g Z_{t-1}, g^2 Z_{t-2}, g^3 Z_{t-3}, \ldots$. Of course the electorate need not discount past performance outcomes in exactly this way. As long as voters weight recent performance outcomes more heavily than prior outcomes when making current political evaluations, the geometric weight sequence g^k will yield a good approximation of the actual behavioral process.

Moreover, this feature of the model can be tested. If, on average, voters in a particular group discount past performance completely and consider only the current situation when evaluating the government, then the estimate of g will approximate zero. Small, nonzero values of g mean that voters discount the past record heavily but not completely. Large values of g (approaching 1.0) imply that past performance outcomes play an important role in explaining a government's current political support. Clearly, then, g is an interesting parameter from a political point of view; it summarizes how much the past performance record contributes to current support for the governing party and it defines in the way described below whether, typically, the government's economic record is judged absolutely or relatively.

The second feature of the model that should be described is the way in which support for the governing party depends on that party's relative performance record. The product of the binary switching terms $D_t D_{t-k}$ in Equation (10.1) ensures that Y^* is generated by the difference between the cumulative discounted performance of the governing party with respect to Z and the cumulative discounted performance record of the current opposition party during the preceding periods when it controlled the government. For example, for a sequence of observations in which the Conservatives became the principal governing party in the most recent period and Labour was the principal governing party for all previous periods, then Equation (10.1) implies that political support (Y^*_{jt}) will depend on:

$$Y^*_{jt} = a_{qj} + b_j(Z_t - gZ_{t-1} - g^2 Z_{t-2} - g^3 Z_{t-3} - g^4 Z_{t-4} - \ldots).$$

(10.2)

Equation (10.2) shows explicitly how political support depends on cumulated discounted relative performance. First, the worse (better) the performance of the previous government, the higher (lower) will be the initial support of the new government. For example, suppose that Z includes only the rate of unemployment, which has been constant at 10 percent under both the old and new governments, and that the coefficient $b_j = -0.02$. If $g = 0.8$ and $a_{qj} = 0$, then Equation (10.2) implies that Y^*_{jt} will equal $+0.60$, which in terms of percentage points in the polls corresponds to 65 percent support.[11] By contrast, had the new Conservative government inherited a 5 percent unem-

11. For Z held at some constant value Z^* and for $0 \leq g < 1$, the partial sum through lag k of the infinite series $b\Sigma_{k=0}^{\infty}(g^k Z^*$ is $bZ(1 - g^{k+1})/(1 - g)$. The partial sum from lag k is $bZ^* g^{k+1}/(1 - g)$. Hence, the Y^* value corresponding to Eq. (10.2) for the example discussed in the text is $+0.6 = -0.02 \cdot 10[(1 - 0.8)/(1 - 0.8) - 0.8/(1 - 0.8)]$.

Since Y^* is the logit $\ln[P'_{jt}/(1 - P'_{jt})]$, the corresponding proportion (percentage support in the polls) is $e^{Y^*}/(1 + e^{Y^*})$, that is, $0.65 = (e^{0.6}/(1 + e^{0.6})$, or 65 percent.

ployment record from the preceding Labour governments, its initial support would have been lower—on the order of $Y^*_{jt} = +0.30$, which corresponds to a 57 percent poll rating. A new government's support, then, is proportional to the (mal)performance of previous opposition-party governments. In other words, governments following "bad acts" by the opposition are likely to enjoy greater initial support than governments following "good acts."

Depending on the rate at which voters discount previous performance—that is, on voters' effective political memory represented by the decay parameter g—the new government's support, however, will eventually depend entirely on its own performance record. For example, if the new Conservative government inheriting a 10 percent unemployment rate from Labour remains in office and does nothing to change matters, its support will ultimately decline from $Y^*_{jt} = +0.60$ (65 percent) to $Y^*_{jt} = -0.02 \, (\Sigma_k \, 0.8^k) \, 10 = -1.0$, which implies a poll rating of 27 percent.[12]

Of course if the current government's performance is more favorable than that of earlier opposition-party governments, this trend will be reversed. Conversely, the trend of declining support will be accelerated if the government's performance is less favorable than the situation inherited from the opposition. Support will eventually converge to the equilibrium level implied by any sustained performance record. The important point is that the model of Equation (10.1) provides an explicit theory for the tendency of a government's political support to decline from early honeymoon levels, which in earlier time-series analyses of government support (including some work of my own) had been picked up via ad hoc dummy variables and time-trend terms.[13]

12. The infinite sum of the geometric series $b\Sigma^\infty_{k=0}(g^k Z^*$ is $bZ^*/(1 - g)$, which for $b = -0.2$ and $g = 0.8$ yields -1.0. This implies the poll rating (as indicated in n. 11) 0.27 $= e^{-1.0}/(1 - e^{-1.0})$, or 27 percent.

13. See, for example, Kernell, "Unemployment, Inflation, and Party Democracy," who uses "early term" trend variables, or Frey and Schneider, "A Politico-Economic Model," and Hibbs and Vasilatos, "Macroeconomic Performance and Mass Political Support," who use time-trend and time-cycle terms, respectively. The model developed in Eqs. (10.1) and (10.2) and discussed in the text represents an extension of the evaluation models presented in the aggregate analysis of Hibbs and Vasilatos. But the present formulation is superior because, for the reasons already given, it makes honeymoon effects and time trends in political support endogenous. The specification of the dependent variable is also superior theoretically to what appears in Hibbs and Vasilatos.

Empirical Results

As Equations (10.1) and (10.2) indicate, the political support model is nonlinear by virtue of the distributed lag decay-rate parameter g; as a result, the regression analyses involved searching the parameter space with a 0.01 grid and choosing the value of g: minimizing chi square or the sum of squared residuals.[14] All regressions are based on quarterly observations over the period 1962:3–1978:4.

For the reasons reviewed earlier, the dependent variable in the regressions is the logit $\ln[P'_{jt}/(1 - P'_{jt})]$, where P'_{jt} is the proportion of the jth group in quarter t supporting the principal incumbent party (Labour or Conservative) in the Gallup polls. The economic performance variables (Z) include two unemployment measures: the level of the unemployment rate (U) and the annualized percentage rate of change of the unemployment rate $[\ln(U_t/U_{t-1})] \cdot 400$. The latter variable appears in order to test the argument that political support is affected less by the unemployment level, even when it is high, than by movements into and out of recessions, which generate widespread feelings of anxiety or reassurance in the electorate. The regression experiments also included the rate of inflation of consumer prices (P) and the rate of acceleration of prices ($P_t - P_{t-1}$). Since a good prediction of this quarter's inflation rate can be made from the inflation rate one quarter ago,[15] the price acceleration term ($P_t - P_{t-1}$) is a simple measure of inflationary surprises, which economic theory suggests are the principal cause of arbitrary inflation-induced income and wealth redistributions. The growth rate of per capita real personal disposable income (R) also appears in the equations. Real personal disposable income measures the income available to households for saving and consumption after direct taxes and income transfers and

---

14. The appropriate goodness-of-fit test for the logit model specification is the chi square statistic obtained from differences between the observed relative frequencies and the fitted probabilities. The smaller the chi square statistic, the better the fit of the model. In the present case, chi square is simply the sum of squared residuals from the weighted least-squares model.

15. Over the period 1962:3–1979:4, the best least-squares equation for predicting the current consumer (retail) price inflation rate from the inflation rate one quarter ago is:

$$P_t = 1.24 + 0.85\ P_{t-1}$$
$$(0.66)\quad (0.07)$$

$R^2 = 0.72,\qquad SER = 3.3,\qquad DW = 1.7$ (standard errors in parentheses),

where $P_t = [\ln(RPI_t/RPI_{t-1})] \cdot 400$, and RPI is the retail price index.

consumer price rises.[16] Finally, since both Labour and Conservative governments have attached great importance to defending the international role of sterling,[17] with the result that the external strength of the pound has received great attention in the press, the equations include a term for changes in the exchange rate ($EXR_t - EXR_{t-1}$). The performance of the pound relative to the dollar is the quantity watched and reported most closely; therefore, $EXR_t - EXR_{t-1}$ is the change in the dollars-per-pound rate of exchange.

Table 10.1 reports the estimation results. As the correlations at the bottom of the table show, the equations generate fitted values that track closely the actual proportions (P'_{jt}) in the survey time series. There is considerable variation across occupational classes in the coefficients, and the differences are consistent with earlier discussion of the incidence and distributional impact of macroeconomic performance.

Government-Specific Intercepts: A Decline in Class-Based Political Support?

Consider first the government-specific intercept constants in Table 10.1. These a_{qj} parameters represent sources of variation among the occupational classes in political support to the advantage of Labour or the Conservatives that are not observed directly and are unrelated to interparty comparisons of the measured economic performance variables. Not surprisingly, the differences across occupational classes in the intercept coefficients are sizable, indicating that fundamental class allegiances to the principal governing parties in Britain are largely unexplained by recent trends in macroeconomic performance. In other words, net of the group variations in responses to economic outcomes, the intercept estimates show that nonmanual, middle-class voters are far more supportive of Conservative governments than of Labour governments, whereas manual, working-class voters, particularly those who are semiskilled and unskilled, are far more supportive of Labour governments.

16. The inflation and the real-income growth rate variables were adjusted downward and upward, respectively, by the magnitude of the unfavorable shifts in relative prices following the OPEC supply shock of 1973:4–1976:4. The idea is tested and described more fully in Chapter 7.

17. See Chapter 7, note 13.

Table 10.1. Economic influences on political support among occupational groups, 1962:3–1978:4, by weighted least-squares estimates ($T = 65$).

	Nonmanual workers, social grades ABC1	Skilled workers, social grade C2	Semi- and unskilled workers, state pensioners, and widows, social grades DE	Means Support proportions
Average sample fraction	0.38	0.32	0.30	—
Constant terms (a_{jq})				
Macmillan–Home	-0.13 (0.025)	-1.03 (0.035)	-1.43 (0.04)	0.32
Wilson I	-1.10 (0.019)	-0.11 (0.019)	0.078 (0.019)	0.37
Heath	0.12 (0.015)	-0.83 (0.017)	-1.10 (0.017)	0.35
Wilson II	-0.92 (0.043)	0.15 (0.042)	0.36 (0.045)	0.38
Callaghan	-0.73 (0.048)	0.39 (0.044)	0.56 (0.048)	0.36
Lag weight rate of decay (g)	0.88	0.85	0.38	—

				Variables
Economic terms (Z)				
Unemployment rate (U)	-0.0095 (0.0015)	-0.023 (0.0015)	-0.016 (0.0014)	3.19
Change in unemployment rate $\ln(U_t/U_{t-1}) \cdot 400$	0.00016 (0.00014)	0.00022 (0.00016)	-0.00061 (0.00016)	6.63
Per capita real income growth rate (R)	0.0032 (0.00094)	0.0085 (0.0009)	0.0055 (0.00090)	2.64
Change in inflation rate $(P_t - P_{t-1})$	-0.016 (0.0051)	-0.017 (0.006)	-0.017 (0.0019)	0.02
Change in exchange rate $(EXR_t - EXR_{t-1})$	0.59 (0.060)	0.71 (0.060)	0.63 (0.062)	-0.03
Fit: χ^2/df	7.04	8.24	7.41	—
Correlation of actual and fitted proportions	0.98	0.93	0.96	—

Note: Data on P'_{jt} for 1966:1 were missing. All percentage rates of change are quarter-on-quarter changes of the logs at annual rates: $\ln(Z_t/Z_{t-1}) \cdot 400$. Dependent variable in the regressions is the logit: $\ln[P_{jt}/(1 - P'_{jt})]$. Inflation and real income variables are adjusted for the OPEC supply shocks (see note 13). Numbers in parentheses are asymptotic standard errors.

Table 10.2. Trends in exogenous occupational class-party loyalties: Group differences in government-specific intercepts.

Governments (regression ranges)	Group intercept differences		
	Nonmanual *minus* semi- and unskilled workers (ABC1 − DE)	Nonmanual *minus* skilled workers (ABC1 − C2)	Skilled workers *minus* semi- and unskilled workers (C2 − DE)
Macmillan-Home (1962:3–1964:3)	1.30	0.90	0.40
Wilson I (1964:4–1970:2)	−1.18	−0.99	−0.19
Heath (1970:3–1974:1)	1.22	0.95	0.27
Wilson II (1974:2–1976:1)	−1.28	−1.06	−0.21
Callaghan (1976:2–1978:4)	−1.29	−0.98	−0.17
Absolute value of time-weighted averages of intercept differences	1.21	0.99	0.22

Source: logit models in Table 10.1.

It is hardly news to students of British electoral politics that class-related political loyalties exhibit considerable inertia and are based on long-standing political judgments unrelated to the comparatively recent economic performance of the governing parties. What perhaps is surprising, however, is that the government-specific intercept constants in Table 10.1 do not register any long-term erosion of class political alignments.

Table 10.2 shows interoccupational differences in the intercept parameters for each government in the regression range (Macmillan–Home through Callaghan). Since the a_{qj} constants represent class-based support for the various governments that is unrelated to and unexplained by Labour and Conservative economic performance, the absolute values of the cross-occupational intercept differences should decline systematically from one government to the next if there has been a persistent secular erosion of fundamental class political allegiances. Contrary to the conclusions of, for example, Butler and

Stokes or Crewe, Sarlvik, and Alt,[18] which were based on election surveys from the 1960s and early 1970s, the computations in Table 10.2 yield no evidence of a decline over time in fundamental class loyalties.

The data most relevant to the class dealignment argument appear in the first two columns of Table 10.2, which show the intercept differences for nonmanual versus semiskilled and unskilled workers and the differences for nonmanual versus skilled workers. The data in the first column (nonmanual versus semiskilled and unskilled workers) indicate that from the Macmillan–Home to the Wilson I and Heath governments, there indeed appears to have been some decline in exogenous class-based political loyalties. The cross-occupational intercept differences decrease from 1.3 to approximately 1.2, but the erosion was small and transitory. This result reinforces the view of Franklin and Mughan and of Zuckerman and Lichbach that earlier studies overestimated the magnitude of the phenomenon.[19] Neither the (absolute values of) intercept differences between nonmanual and unskilled workers nor those between nonmanual and skilled workers exhibit a clear secular trend. Indeed, the only glimmer of a trend in Table 10.2 is the apparent downward movement in the intercept differences between skilled workers and semiskilled and unskilled workers. If the estimates in fact register a systematic pattern in the class-induced political behavior of skilled and unskilled workers over time (third column), the trend implies increasing homogeneity of working-class political loyalties rather than class-party dealignment.

The time-weighted averages (of the absolute values) of the intercept differences are reported at the bottom of Table 10-2. The means of the differences between the nonmanual and manual intercepts are

18. David Butler and Donald Stokes, *Political Change in Britain,* 2d ed. (New York: St. Martin's, 1974); Ivor Crewe, Bo Sarlvik, and James Alt, "Partisan Dealignment in Britain 1964–1974," *British Journal of Political Science,* 7 (1977), 129–190.

19. Mark Franklin and Anthony Mughan, "The Decline of Class Voting in Britain," *American Political Science Review,* 72 (June 1978), 523–534; and Alan Zuckerman and Alan Lichbach, "Stability and Change in European Electorates," *World Politics,* 29 (1977), 523–551. The apparent strengthening of class-based political alignments after the Heath government may partly reflect the changing generational composition of the electorate. Ivor Crewe, Bo Sarlvik, and James Alt, "Partisan Dealignment in Britain 1964–1974," found that during the period 1967–1974 the class-party alignment had weakened most in the interwar generation and had become strongest in the postwar generation. Since that time the postwar generation presumably has increased and the interwar generation decreased in number. The same study also suggested (correctly) that dealignment was due to short-term forces.

1.21 and 0.99. However, these estimates pertain to the political support logits $\ln[P'_{jt}/(1 - P'_{jt})]$, whereas practical interest centers on the underlying support proportions P'_{jt}. Translated into percentage points in the political support surveys, these averages imply that the differences between nonmanual and manual workers in exogenous class-based political loyalties oscillated without secular trend around 26 percentage points (for nonmanual versus unskilled workers) and 22 percentage points (for nonmanual versus skilled workers) over the 1962–1978 period.[20] Thus there is no evidence of a persistent decline in the fundamental occupational class alignment of political support for Labour and Conservative governments.

However, this does not mean that oscillations in class voting have been illusory. The data on class-related political support observed directly in the polls indeed demonstrate fluctuations, as Figure 10.3 shows. Although the figure indicates there has not been a steady erosion of cross-class differences in directly observed support for the governing parties during the 1960s and 1970s, the cross-class cleavages did decline sharply from 1967 to 1971 and declined once again after 1974.[21] But the computations in Table 10.2 suggested that these trends are not accounted for by movements in fundamental class alignments, that is, by class-based loyalties unrelated to the parties' economic performance. Therefore, the explanation for oscillations in class-related political allegiances observed directly in the raw poll data must reside at least partly in the differential responses of occupational groups to trends in the macroeconomy, in particular to the poor economic performance of Britain in recent years. I will return to this important point.

The Lag Weight Rate-of-Decay Parameter

As the earlier discussion of the model indicated, the lag weight parameter g in the equations defines the electorate's effective memory of earlier economic performance outcomes or, equivalently, the rate at which earlier experience is discounted when voters make contempo-

20. The percentage point figures are computed from interoccupational differences in expressions of the form: $[F(F^{-1}\bar{P}'_{j-\bar{a}j}) - \bar{P}'_j] \cdot 100$, where $\bar{a}_i$ are mean intercepts for each occupational class for Labour and Conservative governments, respectively; $\bar{P}_j$ are mean political support proportions in each occupational class for Labour and Conservative governments, respectively; and F is the logistic distribution operator.

21. Alternative measures of the degree of class-related political support exhibit similar behavior. See the appendix to this chapter.

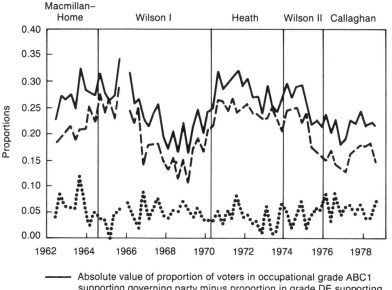

Figure 10.3. Interoccupational class cleavages in political support for the governing party, observed Gallup poll data, 1962:3–1978:4.

raneous political judgments.[22] When g is zero or nearly so, the political support equations collapse to a static model used in much of the existing empirical work, which implies that only current economic outcomes affect the governing party's political support.[23]

22. If the distributed lag equations were written as backward discount functions with weights $1/(1 + r)^k$, as opposed to voter memory functions with weights g^k, estimates of the discount rate r would simply be equal to $(1 - g)/g$.

23. In their study of the governing party's lead in the polls, Frey and Schneider, "A Politico-Economic Model," report estimates for a model that includes a lagged endogenous (dependent) variable among the regressors to capture distributed lag effects. This specification directly implies a distributed lag in which support for the incumbent party is influenced by its own performance and the performance of previous opposition party governments in the *same* way. Since it is implausible, for example, that an acceleration of prices under a Labour government would produce declines in support for a subsequent Conservative government, it is unlikely that such an equation conveys accurate information about the dynamics of political support.

The estimates of g in Table 10.1 range from 0.85 to 0.88, indicating that the politically relevant memory of past economic performance is roughly homogenous across occupational classes and extends many periods back. Hence the assumption in the equations that political support is based on cumulative, relative performance is not merely an appealing theoretical fiction. Assuming g to be less than 0.85 to 0.88 would yield inferior predictions of fluctuations in the political support data.

If an economic performance variable, Z, is held at some equilibrium value Z^* indefinitely, the ultimate impact is $Z^* \cdot b(z)/(1 - g)$, where $b(z)$ is the contemporaneous impact of Z estimated by the relevant regression coefficient in Table 10.1. The proportion of the total impact of a sustained movement in Z felt by the kth lag is given by $1 - g^{k+1}$. Therefore, for an average g of 0.87, only about 13 percent of the ultimate impact of a sustained movement in economic performance is felt contemporaneously, 42 percent is felt after one year (4 quarters), 67 percent after two years (8 quarters) and approximately 94 percent after five years (20 quarters). Hence only at the very end of a full five-year electoral period is a government evaluated almost entirely on its own past performance record. Earlier in the electoral period, the government's record is evaluated relative to that of previous governments in the way indicated by Equations (10.1) and (10.2). It is clear, then, that although voters discount previous economic outcomes, the electorate is not nearly as myopic as strong versions of political business cycle theories imply.[24]

Macroeconomic Performance

As I emphasized earlier, it is natural to expect political responses to macroeconomic performance to vary across occupational classes because the incidence and distributional impact of fluctuations in economic conditions are not distributed uniformly through the class structure. In particular, this is true of the economy's real performance, as the parameter estimates for the unemployment and real income variables show.

The coefficients for the rate of unemployment (U) vary sharply across groups. The political support of nonmanual, white-collar employees exhibits substantially less sensitivity to the unemployment

24. This observation is also true of the American electorate. Chapters 5 and 7 show g to be in the 0.8 to 0.9 range for the United States.

level than does the political support of manual blue-collar workers.[25] Among manual workers, the estimates indicate that the skilled occupational grade is more averse to unemployment than the semiskilled and unskilled group, but this finding undoubtedly reflects the fact that the later category also includes widows and state pensioners, who are outside the labor force and therefore are not affected directly by the tightness of labor markets. Had disaggregated time-series survey data been readily available on the party preferences of semiskilled and unskilled workers alone, the unemployment coefficient for this occupational class probably would have been larger (negative) than that of the skilled workers, because the unskilled typically are more exposed to unemployment.

Nonetheless, the parameter estimate of percentage changes in the rate of unemployment, $[\ln(U_t/U_{t-1})] \cdot 400$, is significant only for social grades DE. Since we know that the incidence of unemployment among the unskilled is affected enormously by cyclical macroeconomic fluctuations, this result is not surprising, even though the DE category includes people outside the labor force. Yet the macropolitical costs and benefits imposed by the rate of change of unemployment are relatively small. By comparison, the unemployment level has important macropolitical effects.[26]

The results of the regression estimation for the growth rate of per capita real personal disposable income parallel the results for the rate of unemployment, which undoubtedly is not coincidental since both variables measure performance of the real macroeconomy. Again, nonmanual white-collar employees exhibit less sensitivity than either of the manual groups to the per capita real income growth rate, and, as in the case of the results for the unemployment rate, the political support of skilled workers is more responsive than the support of the lowest social grade to real income movements. It is unlikely that the economic well-being of semiskilled and unskilled workers is less sensitive than that of skilled workers to aggregate income fluctuations, and so the coefficient estimate for social grade DE probably reflects the fact that the income stream of widows and state pensioners de-

25. To conserve space I have not reported pooled results in which all parameters (except the intercepts) are assumed to be common across groups. However, the null hypothesis that there is no variability in parameters across groups is rejected at virtually any test level.

26. The next section gives precise calculations of the comparative impact of the economic variables in terms of percentage points in the political support polls.

pends on government transfer policies unrelated to movements in other sources of aggregate disposable income.

Over the long run, changes in the exchange rate $EXR_t - EXR_{t-1}$ register Britain's relative international inflation performance, although more recently the demand for sterling associated with the flow of North Sea oil has also been an important factor. However, from a domestic political point of view, the dollars-per-pound rate of exchange appears to have been interpreted by the public as an index of British prestige, which is one of the reasons the first Wilson government resisted for so long the devaluation that ultimately proved necessary in late 1967. Before the demise of pegged exchange rates in 1971, this was the only sizable postwar movement in the pound's rate of exchange, and it was followed by a substantial decline in the government's support in the polls. The parameter estimates in Table 10.1 suggest that manual workers, particularly skilled manual workers, were somewhat more sensitive than other groups to movements in the international status of sterling, but there is no obvious explanation for this.[27]

Inflation, however, is the more enduring index of nominal economic performance, and its impact on political support has a more straightforward interpretation. In most of the regression experiments, estimates for the impact of the inflation rate P_t were negligible; therefore, only the rate of price acceleration, $P_t - P_{t-1}$, appears in Table 10.1. This finding implies that the British electorate is not averse to inflation per se, but that sudden changes in the inflation rate (accelerations and decelerations of prices) have important political consequences. Since the first difference of the inflation rate is a reasonable (though simple) measure of inflationary surprises,[28] the significant coefficients for $P_t - P_{t-1}$ are very small, which is consistent with evidence discussed earlier indicating that the distributional consequences of inflationary bursts are not sharply stratified along class lines. Viewed in relation to the results for the unemployment rate, however, the picture changes dramatically.

Since recent studies by economists suggest that the relevant macroeconomic tradeoff is between the rate of change in the inflation rate

27. Alt, *The Politics of Economic Decline*, chap. 5, reports empirical results showing that the sterling-dollar exchange also affects the British public's perceptions and expectations of the economic state of the country.

28. A more desirable way to measure inflationary surprises would be to deviate observed inflation rates from voters' actual inflationary expectations as demonstrated over time by relevant surveys. Developing the relevant measure would, however, involve a very sizable research project.

and in the unemployment rate, it is economically as well as politically informative to examine the relative magnitude of the associated regression coefficients across occupational classes. The ratios of the U and $P_t - P_{t-1}$ parameter estimates yield the marginal rates of substitution (MRS); that is, the implicit rates at which voters are willing to substitute price acceleration for unemployment. These are: 0.58 for manual workers, 1.36 for skilled manual workers, and 0.97 for semi-skilled and unskilled manual workers, widows, and state pensioners.

The coefficient ratios, or marginal rates of substitution, show that in order to maintain a given level of the political support index among the lowest social grade (DE), a 1 percentage point increase in unemployment would have to be accompanied by a deceleration of inflation of approximately 0.97 point, which indicates that this group is just about indifferent to compensating, equivalent movements in unemployment and inflation acceleration. The implied preference (indifference) curve for skilled workers, however, is steeper. A politically innocuous percentage point increase in unemployment requires price deceleration of about 1.36 points. By contrast, nonmanual white-collar voters appear to have a much flatter, more inflation-averse preference curve. For this group's political support to remain unchanged, a percentage-point increase in unemployment need be accompanied by only 0.58 point of price deceleration.

Equivalently, nonmanual employees, skilled workers, and semi-skilled and unskilled workers would be indifferent to a 1 percent acceleration of prices if the unemployment rate declined by 1.7 (1/ 0.58), 0.74 (1/1.36), and 1.03 (1/0.97) percentage points, respectively. It is clear, then, that the politically acceptable short-run macroeconomic policy tradeoffs in Britain differ considerably across occupational classes, although in the absence of time-series data on class-specific inflation and unemployment experiences, it is not possible to allocate these differences between class-based variations in the incidence and class-based variations in the underlying sensitivities to economic conditions.

Implications for Electoral Change and Class Dealignment

The regression coefficient estimates in Table 10.1 pertain to the logits $\ln[P'_{jt}/(1 - P'_{jt})]$, whereas practical interest centers on the consequences of economic conditions for the percentages (or proportions) of the electorate supporting governing parties. Since the proportions

Table 10.3. Changes in political support for the governing party following sustained changes in the macroeconomy (percentages).

Group	Average political support	Unemployment rate +2 percentage points		
		4 quarters	8 quarters	Indefi-nitely
Nonmanual workers				
Labour governments	22.6	−1.1	−1.7	−2.6
Conservative governments	49.3	−1.6	−2.5	−3.9
Mean	32.5	−1.3	−2.0	−3.1
Skilled workers				
Labour governments	41.5	−3.5	−5.3	−7.2
Conservative governments	26.3	−2.8	−4.1	−5.5
Mean	35.9	−3.2	−4.9	−6.6
Semi- and unskilled workers, widows, and state pensioners				
Labour governments	46.6	−2.7	−4.3	−6.6
Conservative governments	21.3	−1.8	2.8	−4.2
Mean	27.2	−2.3	−3.7	−5.7

observed in the polls, P'_{jt}, are a nonlinear function of the corresponding logits, the effects of practical interest are not obvious from direct inspection of the parameter estimates. Therefore, to illustrate the consequences of macroeconomic fluctuations for the political variable actually observed by politicians in the polls, I have computed the implied changes in the percentage of each occupational class expressing support for the governing party following reasonable movements in the economic performance variables.

The results appear in Table 10.3.[29] Since the effects of transitory movements in the macroeconomy lasting only a quarter or so are

29. The computations are based on the expression

$$F[F^{-1}(\bar{P}'^q_j) + b_j(1 - g^k_j)/(1 - g_j)\Delta Z] - P'^q_j = \Delta \bar{P}'^q_j,$$

where F is the logistic distribution function, $F(Z) = e^Z/(1 + e^Z)$, F^{-1} is the inverse logistic, $F^{-1}(P) = \ln[P'/(1 - P')]$, $\bar{P}'^q_j$ is the mean support proportion for govern-

Adjusted per capita real disposable income growth rate			Change in adjusted inflation rate		Change in unemployment rate		Change in exchange rate (dollars per pound)	
+2 percentage points			+2 percentage points		+33.7% (1σ)		+0.07 (1σ)	
4 quarters	8 quarters	Indefi- nitely	4 quarters	8 quarters	4 quarters	8 quarters	4 quarters	8 quarters
0.4	0.6	0.9	−1.8	−2.9	—	—	2.5	4.1
0.5	0.8	1.3	−2.7	−4.3	—	—	3.4	5.5
0.4	0.7	1.1	−2.2	−3.4	—	—	2.9	4.6
1.3	2.0	2.8	−2.6	−3.9	—	—	3.9	6.0
1.1	1.6	2.3	−2.0	−3.1	—	—	3.2	5.0
1.2	1.9	2.6	−2.4	−3.6	—	—	3.6	5.6
0.9	1.5	2.3	−2.8	−4.4	−1.7	−2.7	3.7	5.9
0.6	1.0	1.6	−1.8	−2.9	−1.1	−1.7	2.6	4.2
0.8	1.3	2.0	−2.4	−3.8	−1.5	−2.3	3.2	5.2

small, the computations are based on increases in the economic variables sustained for 4 quarters, for 8 quarters, and, where it is sensible, for an indefinite period.[30] Increases of one standard deviation were applied to the exchange-rate change and the percentage change in unemployment variables in the experiments. The remaining variables were increased by 2 percentage points.

Across occupational classes, the pattern of political responses induced by these increases in the macroeconomic variables mimics the

ment q in group j, k is the number of periods during which the change in the economy is sustained (4, 8, indefinitely, and ΔZ is the magnitude of the increase in the macroeconomic variables.

30. Given the values of the memory parameter g, "indefinitely" essentially means five to six years. Since it makes no sense to imagine price accelerations, exchange rate appreciations, and percentage unemployment rate increases lasting this long, such computations were not made for those variables.

intergroup pattern of the logit-model regression coefficients, but now the political responses are expressed in terms of percentage-point changes in electoral support for the governing parties. Surprisingly, the responses to movements in the exchange rate are quite large. Sustained for 4 quarters, an appreciation of the pound of seven cents per quarter (one standard deviation) yields mean increases in political support ranging from 2.9 percentage points (among nonmanual employees) to 3.6 percentage points (among skilled workers). Sustained for two years (8 quarters), the same rate of appreciation of the pound enhances electoral support between 4.6 and 5.6 percentage points across social grades. The intergroup differences are not large, but the favorable political responses are. Whether this represents public reaction to the effects on the exchange rate of favorable international inflation performance and the flow of North Sea oil (which I doubt) or positive reactions to the prestige associated with a strengthening pound (which I think is more likely), is ambiguous without more information about how the electorate interprets changes in the international standing of sterling.

By contrast, the political effects of a 2 percentage point increase in the growth rate of per capita real disposable income are quite modest. (The average growth rate during the sample period was only 2.6 percent, so this experiment represents a sizable increase in the real income growth rate stream.) Even when this favorable change in the real growth rate is sustained indefinitely, which practically speaking means five to six years, the mean increases of electoral support for the governing party range only from 1.1 to 2.6 percentage points. The greater relative sensitivity of working-class voters to real economic performance is nonetheless evident; the mean political responses of manual workers are typically between two and two and one-half times greater than the responses of nonmanual employees.

Responses to an increase of 2 percent in the unemployment rate also exhibit sharp class cleavages, and the magnitudes are relatively large. Sustained for only 4 quarters, the mean responses range between -1.3 and -3.2 percentage points for nonmanual employees and skilled workers, respectively. An increase of this magnitude in unemployment for an indefinite period depresses mean political support between 3.1 and 6.6 percentage points, and again, nonmanual white-collar employees show the smallest average response. The mean political support losses following an increase of 2 percentage points in the rate of change of the inflation rate are of comparable magnitude, ranging between -3.4 and -3.8 percentage points when the price acceleration is sustained for 8 quarters. However, as the earlier MRS calculations illustrated, the principal cleavages are between the class responses to inflation acceleration relative to the class responses to increased unemployment.

So far the discussion has focused on the mean political responses of occupational classes to changes in the macroeconomic variables, that is, on the responses averaged over all governments. In Table 10.3, however, gains and losses of political support for Labour and Conservative governments deviate significantly from the corresponding mean political support changes. The cross-party variations depend on the proximity of each occupational group's baseline political support proportion (P'_{jt}) to 0.5. $P'_{jt} = 0.5$ implies that individuals will support the governing party with probability 0.5; in other words, the odds of support are 50/50. Hence, at $P'_{jt} = 0.5$, changes in the macroeconomy yield relatively large shifts in political support because individuals (groups) are pushed across the threshold of opinion change.[31] By contrast, at $P'_{jt} = 0.2$, for example, the shift in political support after the same change in the macroeconomy will be smaller because voters are further from the 0.5 critical threshold.

Since exogenous political loyalties anchor working-class voters close to a political support baseline of 0.5 for Labour governments, and anchor middle-class voters close to a political support baseline of 0.5 for Conservative governments, shifts in the political support of occupational classes after macroeconomic changes are not homogeneous across party governments. Consequently, working-class political support is more sensitive to macroeconomic conditions during Labour than during Conservative administrations. And just the reverse is true for middle-class political support; support for the governing party among nonmanual voters is more responsive to economic outcomes when the Conservatives are in power. Moreover, the

31. Recall that at $P'_{jt} = 0.5$, $\ln[P'_{jt}/(1 - P'_{jt})] = 0 = E(Y^*_{jt})$, and notice that $\text{Prob}(Y_{ijt} = 1)$ = $\text{Prob}(Y^*_{jt} > 0)$, where $Y_{ijt} = 1$ denotes support for the governing party. Hence, $P'_{jt} = 0.5$ is the threshold of opinion change, and movements about this point cause relatively great shifts in the probability of support responses ($Y_{ijt} = 1$) or, equivalently, nonsupport responses ($Y_{ijt} = 0$).

Note also that the instantaneous marginal response of P'_{jt} to a marginal change in Z (the derivative, dP'_{jt}/dZ) is $[P'_{jt}(1 - P'_{jt})] \cdot bj$, which takes its maximum value at $P'_{jt} = 0.5$. For further discussion, see Samuel Kernell and Douglas A. Hibbs, Jr., "A Critical Threshold Model of Presidential Popularity," in *Contemporary Political Economy*, ed. Douglas Hibbs and H. Fassbender (Amsterdam: North-Holland, 1981).

coefficients of unemployment and real income growth are significantly larger in absolute value for manual, working-class voters than for nonmanual, middle-class voters. As a result, during Labour governments, exogenous political loyalties interact with these class-related coefficient differences to produce class dealignment of political support in periods of deteriorating real economic performance.

This finding helps to explain the transitory decline of class alignments observed in the political support data during 1967–1969 (Wilson I) and the more persistent decline observed from 1975 through 1977–1978 (primarily Callaghan), which was discussed earlier and illustrated in Figure 10.3. For example, after 1975:1, real economic performance deteriorated sharply: unemployment rose by more than 2.5 percentage points, and the per capita real income growth rate declined markedly. Since Labour was in power, the government's baseline political support proportion in the working class was in the vicinity of 0.4 to 0.5, whereas its baseline political support among middle-class voters was closer to 0.22. In conjunction with the fact that manual workers are always more sensitive than nonmanual workers to unemployment and the real income growth rate, this situation meant that the post-1975:1 trajectory of the economy produced a much greater decline in the Wilson and Callaghan government's support among working-class voters than among middle-class voters. The cross-class difference in support for these Labour governments observed in the polls therefore declined, but the decline was not based on a weakening of fundamental class loyalties. Instead, it was generated by the interaction of enduring, class-based partisan loyalties and class-differentiated economic sensitivities.

Figures 10.4 and 10.5 illustrate the success of the equations in Table 10.1 in tracking fluctuations in the class alignment of political support observed directly in the polls. In both figures, the 1964–1966 peak and the 1968–69 trough in the actual alignment data are understated by the fitted observations. In other words, some of the surge and decline in interclass political support cleavages are missed by the model, but the fitted observations mimic the broad pattern of fluctuations in the actual class-alignment data in the 1960s and succeed in tracking the trends in the 1970s very closely. It was demonstrated earlier that these trends are, in general, not the results of movements in fundamental class-based political allegiances (Table 10.2). Figures 10.4 and 10.5 support the argument that these oscillations in class alignments were driven primarily by the differentiated responses of occupational classes to economic conditions. Undoubtedly this is why virtually all

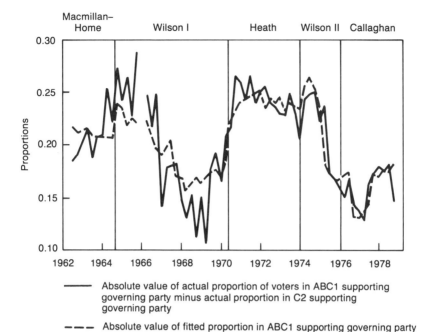

Figure 10.4. Actual and fitted interoccupational class cleavages in political support for the governing party, nonmanual (ABC1) versus skilled manual (C2), 1962:3–1978:4.

measures of class-related party support do not exhibit well-defined secular trends but instead appear to oscillate cyclically over time.[32]

Indeed the responses of political support to the macroeconomic changes shown in Table 10.3 undoubtedly are not larger because of the persistence of fundamental class-based party allegiances, which anchor voters to the parties and thereby create a considerable stability or inertia in the partisan division of electoral support. Of course such fundamental partisan attachments, which are absorbed by the (class-specific) intercepts in the equations, are not immune to variations in

32. See the appendix. This conclusion is consistent with the spirit of Alt's observations about class, economic performance, and party allegiance in *The Politics of Economic Decline*. In view of the collapse of the British economy (the sharp rise in unemployment and decline of real income and output) since Mrs. Thatcher assumed office in June 1979, my argument implies that carrying the analysis forward through more recent periods would demonstrate a substantial upturn in interoccupational class cleavages in support for the new Conservative government.

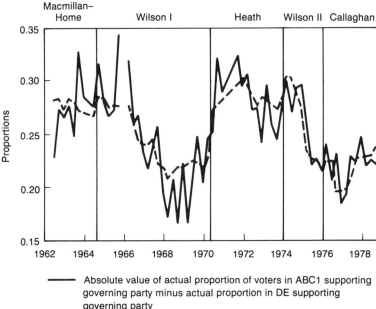

Figure 10.5. Actual and fitted interoccupational class cleavages in political support for the governing party, nonmanual (ABC1) versus unskilled manual (DE), 1962:3–1978:4.

the parties' policy behavior and relative governmental performance. On the contrary, in my view they are primarily determined by very long-run patterns in the priorities and performance of the parties as transmitted from generation to generation by socialization processes that effectively constitute the historical political memories of social classes.[33] Nonetheless, the magnitudes of shifts in political support induced by relatively short-lived changes in macroeconomic performance are hardly trivial. Over all elections from 1959 to 1979, the average difference between the shares of the electorate going to Labour and the Conservatives has been approximately 4.1 percentage points. Hence, on average, a vote-share shift from one major party to the other of only a little more than 2 percentage points was enough to

33. In this connection it is worth noting that the new Social Democratic party, which burst upon the British political scene in 1981 and has done very well both in the polls and in by-elections, is not a "new" political movement at all, but rather constitutes the moderate (and plurality) wing of the Labour party.

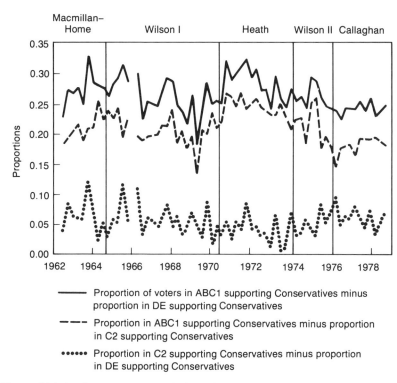

Figure 10A.1.   Interoccupational class cleavages in political support for the Conservative party, 1962:3–1978:4 (Butler-Stokes index).

change the plurality winner.[34] Viewed in this light, it is clear that short-run macroeconomic management can play a critical role in election outcomes.

Appendix: Alternative Measures of Class Dealignment

The data in Figures 10.3 through 10.5 pertain to class differences in political support for the governing party over time. However, alternative measures of class-related political support derived from the Gallup poll vote-intention data series tell essentially the same story. Time-series data on three alternative class-voting indices appear in Figures 10A.1–10A.3.

34. Paul Whiteley, "Electoral Forecasting from Poll Data: The British Case," *British Journal of Political Science*, 9 (1979), 219–236, shows that the Gallup poll vote intervention data yield accurate forecasts of actual voting outcomes. Therefore, the results in Table 10.3 have direct implications for electoral changes.

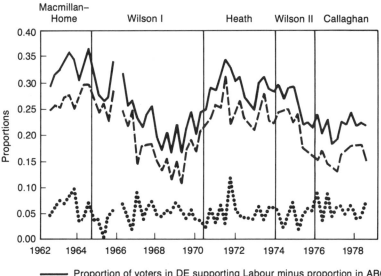

Figure 10A.2.   Interoccupational class cleavages in political support for the Labour party, 1962:3–1978:4 (Alford index).

Figure 10A.1 shows cross-occupational class differences in support for the Conservatives over time. This is the same index used by Butler and Stokes to assess changes in the strength of class alignments, except that "other" parties (notably the Liberals) were not excluded from the denominator in computing the proportions. Figure 10A.2 shows data on what is known as the Alfred index, that is, interclass differences in support for the Labour party. Figure 10A.3 reports time-series data on an intraclass measure of class dealignment suggested to me by Samuel Beer. This index is the difference between Labour and Conservative support within occupational classes. Related measures based on the ratios of the occupational class support data (proposed to me by James Alt) show the same pattern as Figures 10A.1–10A.3.

The data in Figures 10A.1–10A.3 reinforce my previous conclusions about class dealignment: the predominant patterns in the time-series

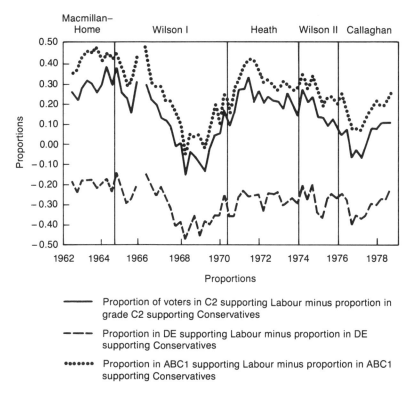

Figure 10A.3. Intraoccupational class cleavages in political support for the parties, 1962:3–1978:4 (Beer's index).

are cyclical rather than secular, and substantial downward movements in class-related political support occur only during Labour governments. Recall from the earlier analyses, however, that these directly observed downward drifts in class alignments can be explained without any recourse to the idea of a secular deterioration of fundamental class loyalties—defined as class-based support for the parties unrelated to macroeconomic performance.

Finally, it should be emphasized that the data and conclusions presented here pertain to the reported vote intentions of occupational classes and not to party identification or other conceptions of partisan attachments.

11

Political Parties and Macroeconomic Policy

The most important problem of macroeconomic policy facing public authorities in industrial societies during the postwar period has been the unfavorable tradeoff that exists between unemployment and inflation—the so-called Phillips curve. Although the unemployment/inflation tradeoff has not exhibited great stability in recent years—for example, the U.S. economy is undoubtedly more vulnerable to inflation at low levels of unemployment now than it was a few years ago—there is widespread agreement among economists that in capitalist economies wage and price stability requires relatively high levels of unemployment, and, conversely, that low rates of unemployment yield relatively high rates of inflation.[1] Put another way, price

Reprinted from *American Political Science Review*, 71 (December 1977), 1467–87. The original article was taken from my monograph "Economic Interest and the Politics of Macroeconomic Policy," Center for International Studies, MIT, Monograph Series, C/75-14, January 1976. Earlier versions were presented as papers to the Econometric Society World Congress, Toronto, Canada, August 1975, and the Annual Meeting of the American Political Science Association, San Francisco, August 1975. The research was supported by National Science Foundation Grants GS 33121 and SOC75-03773. The Computer Research Center of the National Bureau of Economic Research provided computational support. I am indebted to Hayward Alker, Suzanne Berger, Bob Brito, Randy Forsberg, J. David Greenstone, David Held, Mike Intriligator, Robert Jackman, Peter Lemieux, Frank Lerman, Andrew Martin, Benjamin Page, Adam Przeworski, Martin Rein, William Schneider, Robert Solow, and Paolo Sylos-Labini for comments on an earlier draft. I gratefully acknowledge the research assistance of Warren Fishbein, Marilyn Shapleigh and especially Nick Vasilatos.
1. For a detailed review of the theoretical and empirical literature on Philips-curve inflation model, see Hibbs, "Economic Interest."

stability and full employment are incompatible goals in the sense that conventional macroeconomic policy has not been able to achieve both simultaneously. Since political authorities can (and do) influence the rate of unemployment and inflation by manipulating monetary and fiscal policy instruments, macroeconomic policy has been the focus of intense controversy and conflict between key political actors and interest groups.

This chapter examines postwar patterns in macroeconomic policies and outcomes associated with left- and right-wing governments in capitalist democracies. There are three main sections. The first briefly reviews evidence, documented in great detail elsewhere,[2] indicating that different unemployment/inflation outcomes have important, class-linked effects on the distribution of national income. It is argued that the economic interests at stake in various macroeconomic configurations are (implicitly) reflected in public opinion data on the relative aversion of different income and occupational groups to unemployment and inflation. The second section presents a general scheme rank-ordering the preferences of political parties, arrayed along the traditional left-to-right spectrum, for various economic goals and analyzes highly aggregated data on unemployment and inflation outcomes in relation to the political orientation of regimes in twelve West European and North American nations. These international comparisons suggest that the "revealed preference" of leftist governments has been for relatively low unemployment at the expense of high rates of inflation, whereas comparatively low inflation and high unemployment characterize political systems dominated by center and right-wing parties. The third and longest section presents time-series analyses of quarterly postwar data on unemployment in the United States and Great Britain. The estimation results from the time-series models support the conclusion that unemployment has been driven downward during Democratic and Labour administrations and has moved upward during periods of Republican and Conservative dominance.

The general conclusion of the chapter is that the macroeconomic policies pursued by left- and right-wing governments are broadly in accordance with the objective economic interests and subjective preferences of their class-defined core political constituencies.

2. See ibid.

Unemployment and Inflation: Objective Economic Interests and Subjective Preferences

A common rationalization for deflationary macroeconomic policies is that inflation adversely affects the economic position of wage and salary earners and, in particular, erodes the economic well-being of the poor. Empirical studies, however, give little support to this argument. The work of Blinder and Esaki, Hollister and Palmer, Metcalf, Thurow, Schultz, and others strongly indicates that a relatively low unemployment–high inflation macroeconomic configuration is associated with substantial relative and absolute improvements in the economic well-being of the poor and, more generally, exerts powerful equalizing effects on the distribution of personal income.[3]

Although these studies suggest that inflationary periods with tight labor markets are associated with a general equalization of the income distribution—the poor and certain middle-income groups gaining at the expense of the rich—it nevertheless has been argued that the economic position of a substantial fraction of the labor force suffers a net decline during periods of vigorous economic expansion. The usual observation is that price rises tend to outstrip money wage increases during cyclical upswings and real wage rates therefore fall. Moreover, business expansions bring a general inflation of profits that yields increases in the share of the national income going to capital.[4] If the profit-inflation and wage-lag hypotheses are accurate,

3. See, for example, A. Blinder and H. Eskai, "Macroeconomic Activity and Income Distribution in the Postwar U.S." (Mimeo, Princeton University, November 1976); Robinson G. Hollister and John L. Palmer, "The Impact of Inflation on the Poor," in *Redistribution to the Rich and the Poor*, ed. K. E. Boulding and M. Pfaff (Belmont, Calif.: Wadsworth, 1972), pp. 240–270; Charles E. Metcalf, *An Econometric Model of the Income Distribution* (Chicago: Markham, 1972); Lester C. Thurow, "Analyzing the American Income Distribution, *American Economic Review: Papers and Proceedings*, 60 (May 1970), 261–269; and T. Schultz, "Secular Trends and Cyclical Behaviour of Income Distribution in the United States: 1944–1964," in *Six Papers on the Size Distribution of Wealth and Income*, ed. L. Soltow (New York: National Bureau of Economic Research, 1969), pp. 75–100.

4. These hypotheses have received support from many distinguished economists, including Alvin Hansen, "Factors Affecting the Trend of Real Wages," *American Economic Review*, 15 (1925), 27–42; John Maynard Keynes, *The General Theory of Employment, Interest and Money* (New York: Harcourt, 1936); Jacques Rueff, "Nouvelle discussion sur le chomage, les salaires et les pris," *Revue d'Economie Politique*, 61 (1951), 761–91; Earl J. Hamilton, "Prices and Progress," *Journal of Economic History*, 12 (Fall 1952), 325–349; and Sidney Weintraub, *An Approach to the Theory of Income Distribution* (Westport, Conn.: Greenwood Press, 1958). Weintraub, for example, has flatly asserted that "only entrepreneurs and the actual unemployed have an unequivocal stake in maximum employment, while rentiers and the employed find their interest better served at lower levels of activity" (p. 60).

it is possible in principle that the relative and absolute gains enjoyed by lower-income groups during economic booms come at the expense of other wage-earning groups and conceal substantial declines in the national income share of labor as a whole.

However, contemporary empirical work provides little or no evidence in favor of either the profit-inflation or wage-lag hypothesis. Long's examination of historical relationships in the United States (1860–1958) found that real wage movements were not countercyclical, as Keynes and others argued, but on the whole corresponded quite closely to business fluctuations.[5] Bodkin's analysis of postwar quarterly and longer-run annual data on trend-corrected real wage changes in Canada and the United States detected no systematic association one way or the other between real wage movements and unemployment in Canada, whereas inverse associations prevailed in the United States.[6] Finally, studies by Bach and Stephenson, Boddy and Crotty, Burger, Hibbs, Hultgren, Kuhn, and the Organization for Economic Cooperation and Development on the cyclical behavior of factor shares— that is, shares of the national income going to capital and labor over the business cycle—show that in general the ratio of profits to wages increases steadily after a trough in business activity, reaches its highest point about midway through an expansion, and thereafter drops off markedly.[7] Thus the latter halves of business upswings, during which unemployment typically falls and the rate of inflation rises, are associated with a pronounced squeeze on profits and are more accurately described as periods of *wage lead* and *profit deflation*. Although it is difficult to say whether these patterns in the cyclical behavior of wages and profits would persist in prolonged expansions, the evidence does demonstrate that the economic position of wage and salary earners as a group improves substantially, in

5. Clarence D. Long, "The Illusion of Wage Rigidity: Long and Short Cycles in Wages and Labor," *Review of Economics and Statistics*, 42 (May 1969), 140–151.

6. Ronald G. Bodkin, "Real Wages and Cyclical Variations in Employment: A Re-Examination of the Evidence," *Canadian Journal of Economics*, 2 (February–November 1969), 353–374.

7. G. L. Bach and James B. Stephenson, "Inflation and the Redistribution of Wealth," *Review of Economics and Statistics*, 61 (February 1974), 1–13; Ratford Boddy and James Crotty, "Class Conflict and Macro-Policy: The Political Business Cycle," *Review of Radical Political Economics*, 7 (Spring 1975), 1–19; Albert Burger, "Relative Movements in Wages and Profits," *Federal Reserve Bank of St. Louis Review*, 55 (February 1973), 8–16; Hibbs, "Economic Interest"; Thor Hultgren, *Costs, Prices and Profits: Their Cyclical Relations* (New York: National Bureau of Economic Research, 1965); Edwin Kuhn, "Income Distribution and Employment over the Business Cycle," in *Brookings Quarterly Econometric Model of the United States*, ed. J. Dusenberry et al. (Chicago: Rand McNally, 1965), pp. 227–278; and OECD, *Inflation: The Present Problem* (Paris, 1970).

both relative and absolute terms, during periods of relatively low unemployment and high inflation.

If sustained economic expansions confer such obvious benefits on wage and salary earners generally and on low- and middle-income groups in particular, why have macroeconomic policymakers exhibited such keen sensitivity to the inflationary consequences of full employment? One explanation of political authorities' willingness to accept less than full employment is that the mass of wage and salary earners have an irrational aversion to inflation, perhaps because people tend to view rising prices as an arbitrary tax.[8] Deflationary macroeconomic policies may therefore represent a political response to widespread anti-inflation sentiment among the mass public.[9] Sample survey evidence for the United States and Great Britain squarely contradicts this argument. For more than twenty years George Katona and his associates at the University of Michigan's Survey Research Center have polled national samples of American households about their expectations and attitudes toward inflation, unemployment, and other socioeconomic issues. Katona writes that until 1973 more people felt that unemployment was a greater evil than inflation. Moreover, a majority of the respondents in the SRC surveys repeatedly indicated that they were hurt "little" or "not at all" by inflation and that they would not be willing to accept substantial increases in unemployment in order to halt increasing prices.[10]

My own analyses of British and American survey data on public aversion to unemployment and inflation support the inferences of Katona and his associates. The general conclusions of these analyses are as follows.[11] First, the public opinion data clearly show that in the postwar period solid majorities of the British and American mass public typically expressed greater aversion to unemployment than to inflation. Second, popular concern about unemployment and infla-

8. See, for example, William D. Nordhaus, "The Political Business Cycle," *Review of Economic Studies*, 42 (April 1975), 169–190.

9. As one White House economist reportedly put it in April 1975, "One hundred percent of the people have been hit by inflation. Only ten percent really worry about unemployment"; quoted by S. Golden, "High Joblessness Expected to Persist as a Condition of U.S. through Decade," *New York Times*, April 21, 1975, p. 46.

10. George Katona, "Disputing Galbraith," *New York Times*, December 22, 1974, p. D1. and George Katona et al., *Aspirations and Affluence* (New York: McGraw-Hill, 1971). Many of the results from these surveys appear in annual volumes of the *Survey of Consumer Finances* (Ann Arbor: Survey Research Center, 1960–72). Results of surveys taken before 1960 are available as mimeo reports from the SRC.

11. The analyses are presented fully in Hibbs, "Economic Interest," pp. 24–40.

tion is class-related. Low and middle income and occupational status groups are more averse to unemployment than to inflation, whereas upper income and occupational status groups are more concerned about inflation than about unemployment. Although the available survey evidence is by no means definitive, it does appear that the subjective preferences of class or status groups are at least roughly in accordance with their objective economic interests, insofar as these are reflected by the behavior of wages, profits, and the distribution of personal income under various unemployment/inflation macroeconomic configurations.[12]

Given these group or class cleavages regarding the unemployment/ inflation tradeoff, we can now consider to what extent these cleavages are reflected in the economic policies pursued by governments of different political orientations.

Macroeconomic Policies and Outcomes: International Comparisons

The evidence reviewed in the previous section suggests that in terms of the unemployment/inflation tradeoff, the objective economic interests and subjective preferences of lower-income, blue-collar groups differ markedly from those of higher-income, white-collar groups. Although the importance of socioeconomic status as a basis of electoral cleavage varies substantially across party systems, the mass constituencies of political parties in most advanced industrial societies are distinguished to a significant extent by class, income, and related socioeconomic characteristics. Even a casual examination of the historical record makes it clear that differences in the economic interests and preferences of income and occupational groups are reflected in the contrasting positions toward various economic goals associated with left- and right-wing political parties. (This is not to suggest,

12. The class interest at stake in unemployment/inflation outcomes and policies shows up in the policy positions taken by organized labor and capital as well as in the distribution of mass opinion. Throughout the postwar period, trade union spokesmen have invariably placed primary emphasis on the objective of full employment, while business elites have attached far more importance to price stability. A clear statement of labor's position is given by Nat Goldfinger, "Full Employment: The Neglected Policy?" *American Federationist*, 79 (November 1972), 7–8. For data on corporate thinking on the inflation and unemployment issues, see L. Silk and D. Vogel, *Profit and Principles: The Social and Political Thinking of American Businessmen* (New York: Simon and Schuster, 1977).

incidentally, that the influence linkages between mass constituencies and party elites are unidirectional.) Hence, labor-oriented, working-class-based Socialist and Labor parties typically attach far greater importance to full employment than to inflation, whereas business-oriented, upper-middle-class-based Conservative parties generally assign higher priority to price stability than to unemployment. The implied preferences or issue positions of political parties (or *tendances*), arrayed along the traditional left–right spectrum, are outlined more systematically in Table 11.1. The table is adapted from a study by Kirschen et al. and is based on questionnaires administered to experts in eight industrial societies.[13] Significantly, the relative preferences of the parties for various economic goals are reversed as one moves across the political spectrum. In particular, the party preferences concerning unemployment and inflation are consistent with the class-related cleavages surrounding these issues that were identified previously.

Since political authorities in the post-Keynesian age have considerable influence on macroeconomic outcomes, we would expect to observe (*ceteris paribus*, of course) a relatively low unemployment–high inflation macroeconomic configuration under leftist regimes and the reverse under rightist regimes. Highly aggregated, cross-national evidence supporting this proposition appears in Figure 11.1, which shows a Phillips curve–like scatter diagram of the average rates of unemployment and inflation for 1960–1969 in twelve industrial societies. The vertical and horizontal axes in the figure show the median average rates of unemployment and inflation, respectively. Five of the six nations enjoying an average level of unemployment below the West European–North American median (that is, the nations to the left of the vertical axis) are countries with large Socialist or Social Democratic parties (closely linked to organized labor) that have governed for much or most of the time since World War II. Socialist parties have been in power (or have shared power as members of coalition governments) for the entire postwar period in Sweden, for the bulk of the period in Denmark, Finland, and Norway, and for about two-thirds of the period in the Netherlands. As one would

13. E. S. Kirschen et al., *Economic Policy in Our Time*, vol. 1 (Amsterdam: North-Holland, 1964). With the exception of the balance-of-payments issue (the importance of which depends critically on the international economic position of a given nation), the positions attributed to the various *tendances* were homogeneous across countries. For a similar scheme see Bruno Frey and Lawrence J. Lau, "Towards a Mathematical Model of Government Behaviour," *Zeitschrift für Nationalökonomie*, 28 (1968), 355–380.

Table 11.1. Preferences of political parties in advanced industrial societies regarding various economic goals.

	Socialist-Labor	Center	Conservatives
	Full employment		Price stability
	Equalization of income distribution		
		Price stability	
	Economic expansion		
		Economic expansion	Balance-of-payments equilibrium
		Full employment	
		Equalization of income distribution	
	Price stability		Economic expansion
		Balance-of-payments equilibrium	Full employment
	Balance-of-payments equilibrium		
			Equalization of income distribution

Source: Based on E. S. Kirschen et al., *Economic Policy in Our Time,* vol. 1 (Amsterdam: North-Holland, 1964).

anticipate from the Phillips curve (inverse association of unemployment and inflation), the majority of the nations lying below the unemployment median have on the average experienced above-median rates of inflation. The principal exception to these generalizations is West Germany, which has been governed for most of the postwar period by the conservative CDU party and has experienced both low unemployment and low inflation.

With the exception of Belgium and to a lesser extent the United Kingdom, the governments of all nations in Figure 11.1 falling above (that is, to the right of) the average unemployment median have been dominated by center or right-wing political parties. In the United States and Canada, where problems of deficient aggregate demand are chronic, unemployment rates have consistently been the highest in the Western industrial world. Neither of these countries has politi-

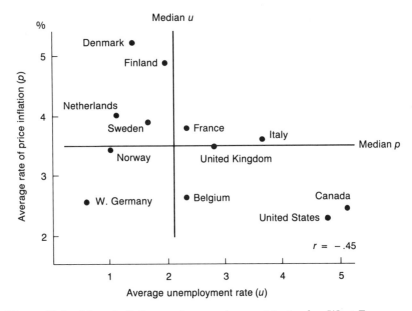

Figure 11.1. Mean inflation and unemployment in twelve West European and North American nations, 1960–1969. (Unemployment data for Canada, France, Italy, Sweden, the United Kingdom, the United States, and West Germany from Constance Sorrentino, "Unemployment in the United States and Seven Foreign Countries," *Monthly Labor Review*, 93 [September 1970], 12–23. All other data from ILO, *Yearbook of Labor Statistics*, various volumes.)

cally important Socialist or Labor parties,[14] and centrist or rightist governments have ruled throughout the postwar era.

The Communist and Socialist political blocs in France and Italy have commanded a sizable share of the vote in all postwar elections, but aside from the governments of national unity in the immediate postwar period and the marginal representation of the French and Italian Socialists in various center coalition governments, they have been largely frozen out of positions of executive power.[15] Belgium

14. Canada's New Democratic party, a genuinely Socialist party with close connections to organized labor, has exhibited increasing political vitality in recent years (capturing several provincial governments) but remains a "minor" party with little influence on national policy.

15. There was one brief period of Socialist-led rule in France after 1951: Guy Mollet's government of February 1956 to May 1957. Analysis of annual data shows that unemployment was lower and inflation higher during Mollet's government (as well as during the subsequent center-left government of Bourgès-Maunoury) than during the right-wing Gaullist governments of the late 1950s and 1960s. The center-left govern-

deviates from the general pattern in that the Socialists have ruled (in coalition with other parties) for just over half of the postwar years, and the average rate of unemployment stands just above the Western European–North American median. However, unemployment has on the average been lower (and the rate of inflation on the average higher) during the tenure of Socialist coalition governments than during periods of center-right rule. Great Britain also constitutes something of an exception. The Labour and Conservative parties have alternated in power (although the Conservatives ruled continuously from 1951 to 1964) and the average unemployment rate is above the median. The mean British unemployment rate, however, is substantially less than the average rates prevailing in the United States, Canada, and Italy.

Taken as a whole, the evidence in Figure 11.1 indicates that the revealed preference of governments of the nations in the upper left-hand quadrant of the figure has been for relatively low unemployment at the expense of high inflation, whereas the opposite appears to be true for governments of the countries in the lower righthand quadrant. This pattern is reinforced by Figures 11.2 and 11.3, which show simple scatter diagrams of the average rates of inflation and unemployment in relation to average government participation (percentage of postwar years in the executive branch) of Socialist and Labor parties. These plots merely provide a slightly different illustration of the earlier argument. Nations in which Social Democratic and Labor parties have governed for most or much of the postwar period have generally experienced high rates of inflation. Conversely, low rates of inflation have prevailed in countries where center and right-wing parties have dominated policymaking (Figure 11.2). The opposite association obtains between average unemployment and average Socialist-Labor executive participation. Compara-

---

ment of the middle 1950s clearly assigned higher priority to full employment and expansion than did the Gaullist regime, which pursued policies geared to disinflation and economic "stabilization." As a result, France's location on the "international Phillip curve" has changed dramatically. (Compare the data shown in Figure 11.1 with a similar display of average rates of inflation and unemployment reported by D. Smyth, "Unemployment and Inflation: A Cross-Country Analysis of the Phillips Curve," *American Economic Review*, 61 [1971], 426–429, for the period 1950–1960.) Of course France's entry into the European Economic Community in 1958 increased the importance of the external balance-of-payments constraint during the Fifth Republic. However, the deflationary policies of the Gaullist governments must be attributed to some extent to the priorities of the regime. See M. Maclennan et al., *Economic Planning and Policies in Britain, France, and Germany* (New York: Praeger, 1968).

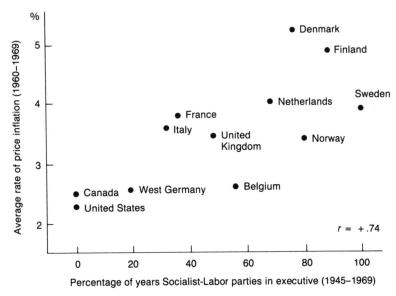

Figure 11.2. Mean inflation and Socialist-Labor executive participation in twelve West European and North American nations.

tively low rates of unemployment characterize systems in which left-wing parties have regularly controlled the executive, and high unemployment rates have been typical in systems governed primarily by center and right-wing parties.[16]

If a common unemployment/inflation tradeoff (or "menu of policy choices") confronted each of the nations appearing in Figures 11.1 through 11.3, the cross-national variation in unemployment/inflation configurations might be attributed primarily to systematic differences in the short-run monetary and fiscal policies pursued by political authorities.[17] The modest but inverse relationship between the average rates of inflation and of unemployment (the correlation is −.45)

16. Since the macroeconomic policies (and outcomes) of the 1960s were to a significant extent influenced by the performance record of the late 1940s and 1950s (especially in countries in which Social Democratic–led governments managed to maintain full employment after the war), the Socialist-Labor participation rate has been calculated over the entire postwar period (1945–1969) rather than for the years 1960–1969 alone.

17. This has been suggested, for example, in reference to the difference in unemployment rates between North America and Western Europe, by Albert Ress, "The Phillips Curve as a Menu for Policy Choice," Economica, 37 (August 1970), 227–238. Monetary policy instruments include interest rates and the supply of credit and money. Fiscal policy instruments include taxation and public spending.

suggests that there is some merit in this interpretation. Rates of un-employment even approaching those typical of Canada and the United States are simply not politically feasible or acceptable in countries with large Socialist-Labor parties that are frequently governed by the left. Prior economic performance and continued emphasis on low unemployment in political discourse has generated widespread public expectations of sustained full employment, which ensures that short-run macroeconomic policy is geared to preserving the low-un-employment, continuous-inflation pattern observed in the upper left-hand quadrant in Figure 11.1.

However, empirical time-series studies have established that un-employment/inflation tradeoffs exhibit considerable cross-national diversity. A comparative investigation by Flanagan, for example, has shown that over the period 1951–1968 the Phillips curve tradeoff

Figure 11.3.   Mean unemployment and Socialist-Labor executive participation in twelve West European and North American nations.

available to political authorities in the United States was less favorable than the tradeoff curves for Great Britain and Sweden.[18] Evidence of this sort indicates that international differences in institutional and structural arrangements underlie, at least to some extent, the cross-national variation in aggregate, equilibrium outcomes depicted in Figures 11.1 through 11.3. In particular, the enormous emphasis placed on full employment in nations with large Socialist-Labor parties has led to the introduction of centralized economic planning and coordination, extensive public-sector investment, and, perhaps most important, a wide range of labor market and manpower policies that are designed to minimize the incidence and duration of unemployment.[19] Hence, the critical historical role of the left in shaping longer-run policies and institutional arrangements must also be considered in order to account adequately for cross-national variation in unemployment/inflation configurations.

Macroeconomic Policies and Outcomes: Time-Series Analyses

Thus far only static, aggregated evidence has been presented in support of the hypothesis that macroeconomic outcomes systematically covary with the political orientation of governments. A dynamic country-by-country analysis of postwar time-series data might provide a more convincing test of this general proposition except for the major constraint that many advanced industrial societies have simply not experienced very much partisan variation (defined in the traditional left–right sense) in their governments.

Time-series analyses of unemployment rates have been undertaken for Great Britain and the United States. Great Britain is an ideal candi-

18. Robert J. Flanagan, "The U.S. Phillips Curve and International Unemployment Rate Differentials," *American Economic Review*, 63 (1973), 114–131. For additional evidence on cross-national variation in Phillips curves see Ronald G. Bodkin et al., *Price Stability and High Employment: The Options for Canadian Economic Policy* (Ottawa: Economic Council of Canada, 1967).

19. Leftist governments have not been equally effective in this regard. For example, British Labour governments have been much less imaginative in developing macroeconomic policy (and have pursued a more centrist political strategy) than Swedish Social Democratic administrations. See the perceptive comparative analysis in Andrew Martin, *The Politics of Economic Policy in the U.S.: A Tentative View from a Comparative Perspective* (Beverly Hills: Sage, 1973). The best treatment in English of the archetypal Swedish model is probably A. Lindbeck, *Swedish Economic Policy* (Berkeley: University of California Press, 1974).

date for dynamic analysis in that national political power has oscillated between the working-class-based Labour party and the middle-
class-based Conservative party. In comparison to the British Labour
and Conservative parties, the two dominant American political parties are less distant ideologically and have more heterogeneous social
bases.[20] Nonetheless, the Democratic party has relatively close connections to organized labor and lower income and occupational status
groups, while the Republican party is generally viewed as being more
responsive to the interests of capital or business and upper income
and occupational status groups.[21] Other things being equal, one
would therefore expect to observe a downward movement in the
unemployment rate during Democratic and Labour governments and
an upward movement in the unemployment rate during Republican
and Conservative rule.

In order to evaluate this proposition rigorously, we need a model
that permits estimation of the hypothesized effects of government
macroeconomic policies on the unemployment rate, net of trends,
cycles, and stochastic fluctuation in the unemployment time-series
observations. In contrast to more conventional approaches, I have
used the "intervention analysis" scheme of Box, Jenkins, and Tiao.[22]
Box-Jenkins or Box-Tiao models represent time-series observations on
the endogenous variable (in this case unemployment) as the realiza-
tion of a linear stochastic process of autoregressive, moving average,
or mixed, autoregressive-moving average form. The autoregressive-
moving average (ARMA) model provides a stochastic benchmark
against which intervention-induced changes in the slope and/or level
of the endogenous time-series are assessed. Intervention occurrences
(in this case partisan changes in government) are represented by binary variables (0, 1) or by related coding schemes (such as +1, −1),

20. See, for example, Robert Alford, *Party and Society* (Chicago: Rand McNally, 1963).
21. For an argument that organized labor and the Democratic party in the United
States are interpenetrated in a way that is at least partially equivalent to Socialist party–
labor union alliances in much of Western Europe, see J. D. Greenstone, *Labor in American Politics* (New York: Alfred A. Knopf, 1969).
22. See G. E. P. Box and G. M. Jenkins, *Time Series Analysis: Forecasting and Control*
(San Francisco: Holden-Day, 1970), part 3; and G. E. P. Box and G. C. Tiao, "Intervention Analysis with Applications to Economic and Environmental Problems," *Journal of
the American Statistical Association*, 70 (March 1975), 70–79. I contrast the scheme of Box,
Jenkins, and Tiao with the conventional structural equation approach in "On Analyzing the Effects of Policy Interventions: Box-Jenkins and Box-Tiao vs. Structural Equation Models," in *Sociological Methodology 1977*, ed. D. Heise (San Francisco: Jossey Bass,
1977), pp. 137–179.

and the effects of interventions are specified by simple "transfer functions."

Regarding the problem at hand, the most plausible hypothesis is that shifts in the political orientation of governments during the postwar period in Great Britain and the United States will be associated with *gradual* changes in the net *levels* of the British and American unemployment rates. The intervention models therefore take the general form:

$$U_t = \frac{\beta}{1 - \delta L} G_{t-1} + \frac{\theta_0 + \theta_q(L)}{\phi_p(L)(1 - L)^d} a_t, \tag{11.1}$$

where U_t = the percentage of the civilian labor force unemployed (quarterly data);

G_t = +1 during Labour or Democratic administrations, -1 during Conservative or Republican administrations;

β, δ = parameters describing the effects of shifts in G_t on U_t;

L = lag operator such that $LU_t = U_{t-1}$, $L^i U_t = U_{t-i}$, etc.;

$(1 - L)^d$ = a lag difference operator such that $(1 - L)U_t = U_t - U_{t-1}$, $(1 - L)^2 = (1 - 2L + L^2)U_t = U_t - 2U_{t-1} + U_{t-2}$, etc.;

$\theta_q(L) = 1 - \theta_1 L - \theta_2 L^2 - \ldots - \theta_l L^q$ and $\phi_p(L) = 1 - \phi_2 L - \phi_2 L^2 - \ldots - \phi_p L^p$ are moving average and autoregressive polynomials in L of order p and q, respectively;

θ_0 = a constant indexing a deterministic time trend of degree d in U_t;

a_t = a sequence of independently distributed random variables with mean zero and variance σ_a^2.

Equation (11.1) simply expresses the proposition that—net of trends, cycles, and stochastic fluctuation in the unemployment time-series, which are captured by the autoregressive-moving average terms in the model[23]—a gradual rise in unemployment levels is anticipated under Conservative and Republican governments and, conversely, a gradual decline in unemployment levels during Labour and Democratic administrations. If a partisan change in government, occurring,

---

23. The cyclical or seasonal component of the model is not represented explicitly by the ARMA terms of Eq. (11.1).

for example, at time n, was sustained indefinitely (that is, $G_t = +1$ for all $t \geq n$), the unemployment rate would eventually fluctuate about the steady state or equilibrium value $\beta/1 - \delta$. The rate of adjustment to the new equilibrium depends on the magnitude of the dynamic parameter δ. Since it is assumed that the macroeconomic policies of a new government are not introduced or implemented instantaneously, the intervention term G_t is specified with a 1-quarter delay or lag.[24]

The British Unemployment Model

The first step in the model-building process is to develop a preliminary specification of the stochastic or ARMA component of Equation (11.1) by analyzing the sample autocorrelation and partial autocorrelation functions of the endogenous variable (unemployment).[25] Figure 11.4 graphs the sample autocorrelation function[26] r_k for seasonally unadjusted quarterly observations on the British unemployment rate for 1948:1–1972:4.[27] The sample autocorrelations decay steadily as the lag k increases, indicating that a low-order autoregressive process is compatible with the British unemployment observations. Since the partial autocorrelations (which are not reported here) are insignificant for $k > 1$, we tentatively entertain a first-order autoregressive specification:

$$U_t = \phi_1 U_{t-1} + e_t, \quad \text{or} \quad (1 - \phi_1 L)U_t = e_t. \tag{11.2}$$

Figure 11.5 presents the sample autocorrelations of the residuals $\hat{e}_t$, that is, the autocorrelations of the transformed data $U_t - \hat{\phi}_1 U_{t-1}$. The

24. The 1-quarter lag on G_t may be too short, especially for the United States. However, since the intervention function allows U to respond gradually to shifts in G, this is not an important problem.

25. The ARMA model-building process is systematically reviewed in Hibbs, "On Analyzing Policy Interventions," and developed in great detail by Box and Jenkins, *Time Series Analysis.*

26. Sample autocorrelations are simply the correlations between observations separated k periods in time and are given by: $r_k = \Sigma(U_t - \bar{U}_t)(U_{t-k} - \bar{U}_t)/\Sigma(U_t - \bar{U}_t)^2$ $k = 1,$ 2, . . . Thus r_1 denotes the correlation between U_t and U_{t-1}; r_2 denotes the correlation between U_t and U_{t-2}; and so on.

27. The British unemployment data (wholly unemployed as a percentage of the civilian labor force) were obtained from the *Ministry of Labour Gazette*, various issues. In view of the unprecedented exogenously imposed economic crisis facing advanced industrial societies since 1973, the time-series analyses are not taken beyond the fourth quarter of 1972.

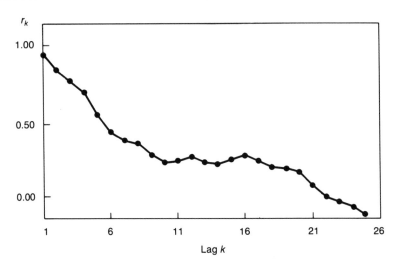

Figure 11.4.   Sample autocorrelation function of the British unemployment rate data, 1948:1–1972:4.

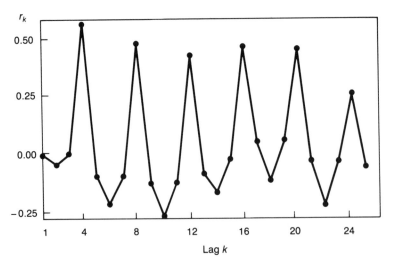

Figure 11.5.   Sample autocorrelation function of the transformed British unemployment data $(1 - \varphi L)U_t$, 1948:1–1972:4.

autocorrelations exhibit distinct peaks every fourth quarter—at $k = 4$, 8, 12, 16 . . .—which suggests a strong seasonal dependence between unemployment rates of the same quarter in different years. This dependence comes as no surprise, since it is well known that unemployment is influenced by seasonal factors and the British data were not available in seasonally adjusted form. The seasonal dependence identified in Figure 11.5 shows no tendency to die out as the lag k increases; therefore, 4-quarter, seasonal differencing is called for. Hence I propose the model:

$$(1 - L^4)e_t = \theta_0 + a_t, \quad \text{or} \quad e_t = \frac{\theta_0 + a_t}{(1 - L^4)}. \tag{11.3}$$

Substituting (11.3) into (11.2) yields the following expression for the stochastic component of the general intervention scheme given in (11.1):

$$(1 - \phi_1 L)U_t = \frac{\theta_0 + a_t}{(1 - L^4)}, \quad \text{or} \quad U_t = \frac{\theta_0 + a_t}{(1 - L^4)(1 - \phi_1 L)}. \tag{11.4}$$

Adjoining (11.4) to the intervention function proposed in (11.1) to represent the hypothesized net impact of partisan changes in government on the unemployment level, we arrive at the equation:

$$U_t = \frac{\beta}{1 - \delta L} G_{t-1} + \frac{\theta_0 + a_t}{(1 - L^4)(1 - \phi_1 L)}, \tag{11.5}$$

where U_t = the percentage of the civilian labor force wholly unemployed in Great Britain quarterly, 1948:1–1972:4,

G_t = +1 during Labour governments and −1 during Conservative governments,

and all other terms are as previously defined.

A second intervention term should be added to the British unemployment model in order to take account of an important change initiated in October 1966 in the British unemployment compensation scheme. Until 1966, the unemployed in Great Britain received a relatively flat-rate benefit that was not tied to previous earnings. The change initiated by the Labour government provided for an "earnings-related supplement" equal to about one-third of the unemployed person's previous average weekly earnings between £9 and £30. This represented a substantial increase in benefits for most wage-earning groups.[28] As a result, unemployed workers were under less financial pressure to accept unattractive jobs and presumably spent more time in searching for new employment. It is therefore widely believed that the new compensation scheme increased the rate and duration of unemployment.[29] Thus we define a new variable, C_t, with a value of 0 before 1966:4 and a value of $+1$ otherwise, and specify the revised model:

$$U_t = \frac{\beta_1}{1 - \delta_1 L} G_{t-1} + \frac{\beta_2}{1 - \delta_2 L} C_t + \frac{\theta_0 + a_t}{(1 - L^4)(1 - \phi_1 L)}. \qquad (11.6)$$

The revised model in (11.6) allows the introduction of the new unemployment compensation system as well as unrelated interparty differences in macroeconomic policy to alter gradually the level of British unemployment.

Table 11.2 reports the estimation results for Equation (11.6).[30] All coefficients (except the constant or trend term θ_0) are substantially larger than their estimated standard errors and therefore are significant by conventional statistical criteria. Before considering the implications of these estimates, let us first evaluate the adequacy of the fitted model. Figure 11.6 shows the actual and predicted levels of the

28. For example, it is estimated that the earnings-related benefits increased the unemployment income of a typical married male worker with two children from about 40 percent to 60 percent of average employment income. See OECD, *Manpower Policy in the United Kingdom* (Paris, 1970).

29. Unfortunately, the picture is complicated by the fact that a number of other macroeconomic policy changes were implemented during the period 1965–1967. These policy changes are reviewed by Bowers et al., "The Change in the Relationship between Unemployment and Earnings Increases: A Review of Some Possible Explanations," *National Institute Economic Review*, November 1970, pp. 44–63. However, the survey-based analysis of D. MacKay and G. Reid, "Redundancy, Unemployment and Manpower Policy," *Economic Journal*, 82 (December 1972), 1256–72, leaves little doubt that the new compensation law had a significant effect on the duration (and thus the rate) of unemployment. Also see the discussion by M. Feldstein, "The Economics of the New Unemployment," *Public Interest*, 33 (Fall 1973), 3–42.

30. The models in this section were estimated with Kent D. Wall's ERSF program, which provides full information maximum likelihood (FIML) estimates of rational distributed lag structural form equations. Details are given in Wall, "FIML Estimation of Rational Distributed Lag Structural Form Models," Working Paper No. 77 (National Bureau of Economic Research, Cambridge, Mass., March 1975).

Table 11.2. Estimation results for the British unemployment rate model (Eq. 11.6).

	Parameter estimates	Standard errors
G_{t-1}	$\hat{\beta}_1 = -0.094$	.035
	$\hat{\delta}_1 = +0.692$	.118
C_t	$\hat{\beta}_2 = +0.511$	.115
	$\hat{\delta}_2 = +0.407$	.228
Trend (4-quarter)	$\hat{\theta}_0 = +0.002$	.023
Autoregressive	$\hat{\phi}_1 = +0.773$	.071
	Residual variance, $\hat{\sigma}_a^2 = .045$	$R^2 = .95$[a]

a. The R^2 reported here pertains to the level data rather than to the 4-quarter difference data. The 4-quarter difference R^2 is .85.

unemployment time series.[31] The predicted unemployment observations track the actual data quite well, which of course is expected in view of the highly significant parameter estimates and small residual variance reported in Table 11.2. Diagnostic checks applied to the residuals provide more convincing evidence of the model's adequacy. Figure 11.7 presents the residual autocorrelations $r_k(\hat{a}_t)$ for lags 1 through 25. The autocorrelations exhibit no systematic patterns and, except for $k = 4$, fall within the approximate ± 2 standard deviation limits.[32] The mean of the residuals is $\bar{a} = 0.0000003$ and the estimated standard error $= 0.023$. Thus the sample evidence strongly suggests that the a_t are independently distributed random variates with zero means.

Of the parameter estimates in Table 11.2, my interest centers on the intervention coefficients $\hat{\beta}$ and $\hat{\delta}$. The coefficients associated with the unemployment compensation dummy variable C_t ($\hat{\beta}_2$, $\hat{\delta}_2$) indicate that the additional unemployment benefits available since October

31. The predicted level data are obtained by summing the predicted 4-quarter differences series, that is: $\hat{U}_t = U_0 + \Sigma_t(1 - L^4)\hat{U}_t$. The summation operator Σ is the inverse of the difference operator $(1 - L)$ in the same way that integration is the inverse of differentiation in continuous-time problems.

32. The lag 4 autocorrelation is significant; therefore, the model might be improved by specifying $a_t = (1 - \theta_4 L^4)v_t$, where the v_t are $N(0, \sigma_v^2)$. Since the $k = 4$ autocorrelation was essentially induced by the seasonal differencing (which overcompensates for the 4-quarter seasonal dependency) and we are primarily interested in predicting the level unemployment series, modification of the model in this way is not advantageous.

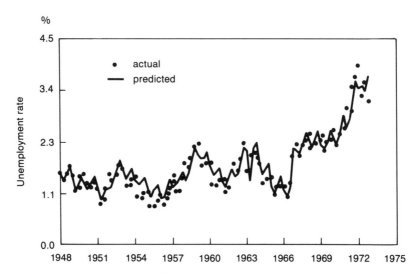

Figure 11.6. Actual and predicted values from the British unemployment rate model (Eq. 11.6), 1948:1–1972:4.

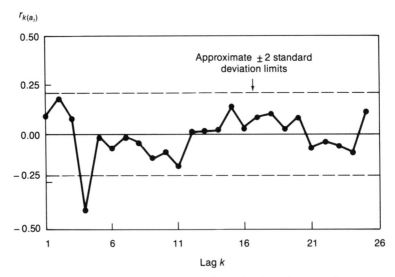

Figure 11.7. Residual autocorrelations from the British unemployment rate model.

1966 produced a net increase of about 0.86 percent in the equilibrium level of unemployment, that is, $+\hat{\beta}_2/(1 - \hat{\delta}_2) = +.511/(1 - .407) = 0.86$. In view of the fact that the dynamic response parameter $\hat{\delta}_2 = 0.407$, the steady-state effect of 0.86 percent was fully realized rather quickly—after only 4 or 5 quarters. However, effects associated with the C_t term, though sizable, are of only incidental interest in this study.

More important for our purposes are the maximum likelihood estimates of β_1 and δ_1, which clearly support the initial proposition concerning the impact of partisan change on the British unemployment rate. Net of the effects attributed to the new unemployment compensation law, and independent of trends, seasonal dependencies, and stochastic fluctuation in the time series, the unemployment rate appears to be driven downward during the tenure of Labour governments and to move upward during that of Conservative governments. The estimated steady-state effects are ± 0.31 percent, that is: $\pm \hat{\beta}_1/(1 - \hat{\delta}_1) = \pm 0.094/(1 - 0.692) = \pm 0.31$, which implies a difference of about 0.62 percent between the equilibrium unemployment levels associated with Labour and Conservative governments. With the C_t variable and the stochastic ARMA terms in the model held fixed, the expression $U_t = [\hat{\beta}_1/(1 - \hat{\delta}_1 L)]G_{t-1}$ implies $U_t = \hat{\delta}_1 U_{t-1} + \hat{\beta}_1 G_{t-1}$, which upon repeated substitution gives:

$$U_t = \hat{\delta}_1^t U_0 + \hat{\beta}_1 \sum_{i=0}^{t-1} \hat{\delta}_1^i G_{t-1-i}. \tag{11.7}$$

Imposing the arbitrary initial condition $U_0 = 0$ and applying the coefficient estimates $\hat{\beta}_1 = -0.094$, $\hat{\delta}_1 = 0.692$, we obtain the dynamic time paths of the unemployment rate that can be attributed to Labour and Conservative macroeconomic policies by simulating (11.7) for G_t held at $+1$ and -1, respectively. Figure 11.8 depicts the unemployment time paths for regimes lasting 20 quarters (five years). The steady-state values of ± 0.31 percent are fully realized after about 16 quarters or four years.

An interparty difference of just over 0.6 percent in government-induced unemployment levels may seem small by American standards, but, evaluated against Great Britain's average postwar unemployment rate of 1.67 percent, it is by no means trivial. Applied to the British civilian labor force, which has averaged 24.1 million workers during the postwar period, the effects graphed in Figure 11.8 translate into about 149,000 jobs. Since British unemployment data are

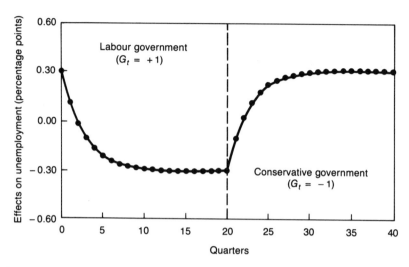

Figure 11.8.   Simulated net effects of Labour and Conservative governments on the unemployment rate.

compiled by the registration method, the measured unemployment rate tends to be biased downward relative to that of the United States, which is based on labor force survey data. Adjusting the British data to the American definition permits more accurate comparisons with the U.S. experience. Myers estimates the adjustment factor to be 1.51.[33] Applying this to the British data yields an interparty steady-state difference of 0.94 percent, or about 226,000 jobs.

Nonetheless, the estimated effect of Labour versus Conservative macroeconomic policies on the equilibrium level of unemployment is perhaps smaller than one might have anticipated from the earlier discussion of left-right cleavages regarding various economic goals. Indeed the ideological distance between the Labour and the Conservative parties on the full employment issue is undoubtedly not as great as that implied by the general scheme introduced previously in Table 11.1. Throughout the postwar period the Conservatives have made great efforts to disassociate themselves from the mass unemployment of the 1930s by repeatedly emphasizing their commitment to the full employment goal, although in practice it was sometimes viewed as necessary to induce increases in unemployment in order to fight infla-

33. R. J. Meyers, "The Unemployment Problem: What We Can Learn from European Experience," in Joint Committee of the U.S. Congress, *Measuring Employment and Unemployment* (Washington, D.C.: U.S. Government Printing Office, 1963).

tion. However, it should be recognized that, unlike the United States, Great Britain is very much an open economy and the macroeconomic policies of both Labour and Conservative governments have been severely constrained by the necessity of maintaining a satisfactory external trade balance. Political authorities of both parties had to ensure that the country's inflation rate did not exceed that of its principal trading partners, in order to maintain the competitiveness of British exports in world markets. In view of the international economic constraints facing all British governments, the estimated interparty difference of 0.62 percent (0.94 percent adjusted to U.S. concepts) does not appear quite as modest in magnitude.

The U.S. Unemployment Model

The impact of Democratic versus Republican administrations on the U.S. unemployment rate is also estimated by developing an ARMA intervention model. The model-building procedure is the same as that outlined in the British analysis. Figure 11.9 shows the sample autocorrelation function for seasonally adjusted quarterly observations on the U.S. employment rate for the period 1948:1–1972:4. The autocorrelations exhibit mild oscillations and decay as the lag k in-

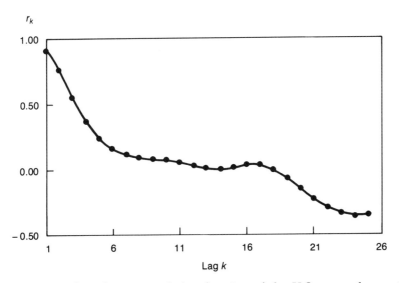

Figure 11.9. Sample autocorrelation function of the U.S. unemployment rate data, 1948:1–1972:4.

creases—properties that are characteristic of a low-order autoregressive process. Partial autocorrelations (which are not reported here) are significant for $k \leq 2$; therefore, I propose a second-order process for the stochastic component of the intervention model:[34]

$$U_t = \theta_0 + \phi_1 U_{t-1} + \phi_2 U_{t-2} + a_t,$$

$$\text{or} \quad U_t = \frac{\theta_0 + a_t}{1 - \phi_1 L - \phi_2 L^2}. \tag{11.8}$$

Adjoining (11.8) to the intervention function introduced in (11.1) yields the estimating equation:

$$U_t = \frac{\beta}{1 - \delta L} G_{t-1} + \frac{\theta_0 + a_t}{1 - \phi_1 L - \phi_2 L^2}, \tag{11.9}$$

where U_t = the percentage of the civilian labor force unemployed in the U.S. quarterly 1948:1–1972:4,
  G_t = +1 during Democratic administrations, −1 during Republican administrations,
  and other terms are as previously defined.

In its present form, the model in Equation (11.9) is unlikely to provide a very good estimate of the net effect of Democratic versus Republican macroeconomic policies on the U.S. unemployment rate. An important omitted variable, which is not likely to be captured by the autoregressive terms in the model, is American intervention in the Korean and Vietnamese civil wars. The enormous fiscal stimulus to the domestic economy (not to mention the sizable number of young men withdrawn from the civilian labor force) generated by American participation in these conflicts shows up clearly in the steadily declining unemployment rates during the war years. (The same can of course be said about the contribution of World War II to the recovery from the Great Depression.) Indeed the United States experienced its lowest postwar unemployment rates during the peaks of these wars. Since American involvement in the Korean and Vietnamese conflicts occurred during (covaried with) Democratic admin-

34. Eq. (11.8) is nearly identical to the model developed by C. R. Nelson for quarterly U.S. unemployment data for the period 1948:1–1966:4. Nelson's model, incidentally, outperformed the MIT-FRB-Penn econometric model in short-term forecasting experiments. "The Predictive Performance of the MIT-FRB-PENN Model of the U.S. Economy," *American Economic Review*, 62 (1972), 902–917.

Table 11.3. Estimation results for the U.S. unemployment rate model (Eq. 11.10).

	Parameter estimates	Standard errors
G_{t-1}	$\hat{\beta}_1 = -0.071$	.020
	$\hat{\delta}_1 = +0.974$	.017
W_t	$\hat{\beta}_2 = -0.179$	.145
	$\hat{\delta}_2 = +0.513$	.320
Autoregressive	$\hat{\phi}_1 = +1.49$	.072
	$\hat{\phi}_2 = -0.718$	.071
	Residual variance, $\hat{\sigma}_a^2 = .085$	$R^2 = .94$

istrations, it is necessary to include an additional "war" term in the model in order to disentangle the party effects of interest from the war effect. Therefore, an additional variable W_t takes a value of $+1$ during the Korean and Vietnamese wars and a value of 0 otherwise. The revised model is:

$$U_t = \frac{\beta_1}{1 - \delta_1 L} G_{t-1} + \frac{\beta_2}{1 - \delta_2 L} W_t + \frac{\theta_0 + a_t}{1 - \phi_1 L - \phi_2 L^2}. \qquad (11.10)$$

The specification of the W_t term in (11.10) is identical to that of the G_t term, except that the war variable appears without a delay or lag. The revised model therefore allows the economic stimuli accompanying American intervention in Korea and Vietnam as well as non-war-related interparty differences in macroeconomic policy to alter gradually the level of unemployment.

Estimation results for the U.S. unemployment model of Equation (11.10) are presented in Table 11.3.[35] The coefficient estimates associated with the administration term G_{t-1} ($\hat{\beta}_1$, $\hat{\delta}_1$) and the estimates of the autoregressive parameters ($\hat{\phi}_1$, $\hat{\phi}_2$) are substantially larger than their respective standard errors and thus easily satisfy the usual criteria of statistical significance. However, the coefficients associated with the war term W_t ($\hat{\beta}_2 \hat{\delta}_2$), though larger than their respective standard errors, are not significant by conventional standards; therefore,

35. Since the unemployment data did not exhibit a trend over the observation period, all variables were deviated from their means and the model was estimated without a constant term. θ_0 therefore does not appear in Table 11.3.

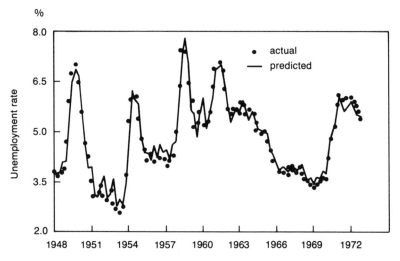

Figure 11.10.   Actual and predicted values from the U.S. unemployment rate model (Eq. 11.10), 1948:1–1972:4.

we cannot place very much confidence in these parameter estimates.[36] In view of the collinearity between W_t and G_t noted earlier, it is not surprising that $\hat{\beta}_2$ and $\hat{\delta}_2$ exhibit relatively large variances. However, since our primary concern is to secure an unbiased estimate of the net response of the unemployment rate to interadministration differences in macroeconomic policy, the war term should be retained in the model to ensure that the administration effect is not confounded with the war effect.

The actual and predicted values of the unemployment time series are graphed in Figure 11.10. The fitted values track the actual data very closely, and errors do not appear to exhibit any systematic pattern. The residual autocorrelations reported in Figure 11.11 confirm this observation. Except for $k = 8$, all of the $r_k(\hat{a}_t)$ fall within ± 2 standard deviations from zero, suggesting that the a_t are indepen-

36. Both the t ratio of $\hat{\beta}_2 = 1.23$ and the t ratio of $\hat{\delta}_2 = 1.60$ are insignificant at the .05 level. Computation of the implied dynamic response of the unemployment rate to American involvement in the Korean and Vietnamese wars is therefore problematic. Robert Solow has suggested to me that since the effect of both the war term and the administration term work through the actual tax expenditure and monetary actions of the government, a better way to specify the model might be to constrain $\delta_1 = \delta_2$. However, estimates obtained by imposing this constraint did not appreciably alter the results reported in Table 11.3 and graphed in Figure 11.12: the war coefficient remained insignificant, $\hat{\delta}_1 = \hat{\delta}_2 = 0.969$, and $\hat{\beta} = -0.091$.

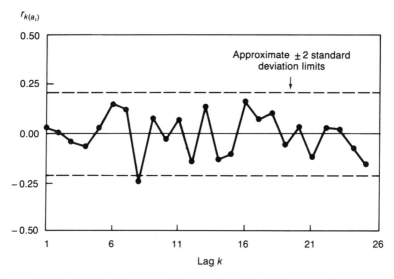

Figure 11.11. Residual autocorrelations from the U.S. unemployment rate model.

dently distributed random variates.[37] Finally, the average of the residuals is $\bar{a} = -0.034$ and the estimated standard error is 0.030, indicating that the residual mean is not significantly different from zero.

Having established the overall adequacy of the model, we focus on the substantive implications of the administration parameters $\hat{\beta}_1$ and $\hat{\delta}_1$. The estimates reported in Table 11.3 give strong support to the basic hypothesis: Democratic administrations appear to engineer downward movements in the U.S. unemployment level, whereas the

37. The negative residual autocorrelation at $k = 8$ $[r8(\hat{a}_t) = -0.253]$ indicates that there is a modest negative two-year (8-quarter) dependency between U.S. unemployment rates. This is compatible with the political-electoral business cycle argument of Nordhaus, Tufte, and others, in which unemployment tends to fall before presidential elections and to rise thereafter in response to administration efforts to engineer favorable economic conditions just before elections and to postpone austerity measures until after elections; Nordhaus, "The Political Business Cycle"; Edward Tufte, *Political Control of the Economy* (Princeton: Princeton University Press, 1978). If this pattern was strong and more or less uniform across four-year presidential administrations, we should observe a sizable negative autocorrelation at $k = 8$ (two-year intervals) and a positive autocorrelation at $k = 16$ (four-year intervals). Although the focus of this chapter is on long-run patterns in macroeconomic policies and outcomes that distinguish left- and right-wing regimes, attempts were made to build an electoral unemployment cycle of this sort into the model. However, elaborations of the model along these lines did not yield significant results.

reverse is true of Republican administrations. The estimation results indicate that the steady-state effects are on the order of ± 2.73 percent, that is: $\pm \hat{\beta}_1/(1 - \hat{\delta}_1) = \pm 0.071/(1 - 0.974) = \pm 2.73$, which implies an interadministration difference of about 5.46 percent in the long-run, equilibrium level of unemployment. In view of the fact that the (seasonally adjusted) U.S. unemployment rate has varied between 2.6 percent and 7.4 percent during the period 1948–1972, an interadministration difference of this magnitude is simply not plausible. However, this is a steady-state figure; that is, it gives the implied net difference in unemployment levels if one and then the other party were to govern nationally for an indefinite period. Since the dynamic adjustment parameter $\hat{\delta}_1$ is estimated to be .974, convergence to equilibrium is very slow and would not be fully realized until a given party had held office for more than 100 quarters, or twenty-five years.[38] However, since neither political party in the United States has held the presidency for more than two successive terms during the postwar period, it is sensible to restrict the interpretation of the estimation results to 32 quarters, or eight years.

Figure 11.12 shows the dynamic time paths of the unemployment rate implied by the G_t component of the model for Democratic and Republican administrations, respectively.[39] After 32 quarters (two presidential administrations) the estimated administration effects are on the order of ± 1.18 percent; hence the interadministration difference in government-induced unemployment levels is about 2.36 percent. This estimate is much more compatible with the postwar U.S. experience than is the long-run, steady-state difference of 5.46 percent reported earlier. Comparison of the U.S. results in Table 11.3 and Figure 11.12 with the corresponding results for Great Britain in Table 11.2 and Figure 11.8 also indicates that the ultimate impact of an administration on the rate of unemployment accumulates much more slowly in the United States than in Great Britain. In other words, the results suggest that the effects of government macroeconomic policies on the unemployment rate are processed much more quickly through the British system than through the American system. These inferences are entirely reasonable in view of the fact that the political and

38. This is readily confirmed by evaluating the expression $\hat{\beta}_1 \Sigma_{i=0}^{\infty} \hat{\delta}_1^i G_{t-1-i}$ over the index i for fixed G_t. The U.S. results contrast sharply with the British results, which implied convergence to steady state after only 16 quarters.

39. The results graphed in Figure 11.12 were obtained in the same way as described earlier for the British case, that is, by simulating $U_t = \hat{\delta}_1^t U_0 + \hat{\beta}_1 \Sigma_{i=0}^{t-1} \hat{\delta}_1^i G_{t-1-i}$ for G_t held at $+1$ and -1 over regimes lasting 32 quarters (eight years).

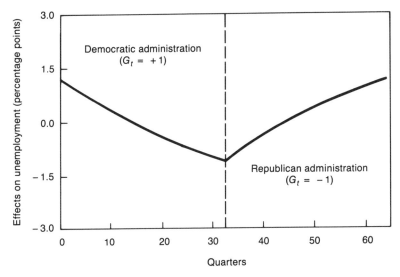

Figure 11.12.   Simulated net effects of Democratic and Republican administrations on the unemployment rate.

economic environment facing macroeconomic policymakers is considerably more decentralized and heterogeneous in the United States
than in the parliamentary system of Great Britain.

Discussion

Perhaps the best way to illustrate the estimated interparty difference
of 2.36 percent in the unemployment performance of Democratic versus Republican administrations is to contrast briefly the macroeconomic policies of the Eisenhower, Kennedy–Johnson and Nixon administrations. The principal economic goals of the Eisenhower
administrations were a balanced federal budget and a reduction in the
rate of inflation.[40] Despite repeated contractions in aggregate economic activity (the "Eisenhower recessions"), full employment and
economic expansion never became primary goals. Indeed the emphasis on price stability and a balanced budget was so great that federal

40. See, for example, O. Eckstein, "Economic Policy in the United States," in *Economic Policy in Our Time*, vol. 2, ed. O. Eckstein et al. (Amsterdam: North-Holland,
1964), pp. 1–88; and especially H. Stein, *The Fiscal Revolution in America* (Chicago:
University of Chicago Press, 1969), Ch. 11–24.

expenditures were actually decreased during the 1953–54 recession and budget outlays only barely exceeded receipts during the recession years of 1957–58 and 1960.[41]

The excessive caution exercised by the Eisenhower administrations in dealing with recession and the great weight placed upon price stability were of course roundly attacked by liberal Keynesian economists, organized labor, and others. In his memoirs of this period Eisenhower responded to such criticism by noting that "critics overlooked the inflationary psychology which prevailed during the mid-fifties and which I thought it necessary to defeat. . . . The anti-inflation battle is never-ending, though I fear that in 1959 the public was apathetic, at least uninformed, regarding this issue."[42] The consequence of this never-ending battle against inflation chronic economic stagnation and an unemployment rate that regularly exceeded 6 percent.

The Kennedy–Johnson administrations' posture toward recession and unemployment stands in sharp contrast to Eisenhower's. The most significant manifestation of the greater importance attached to full employment and economic expansion by these Democratic administrations was the 1964 tax cut. First proposed publicly by Kennedy in June 1962, introduced in Congress in January 1963, and signed into law by Johnson in February 1964, the Revenue Act of 1964 injected $10 billion into a sagging economy. This represented a clear break with the budget-balancing ideology of previous Republican administrations (although the rhetoric of the balanced budget lingered on) and, in view of the economic outlook at the time and the historical periodicity of U.S. recessions, undoubtedly helped prevent a serious economic contraction in 1964–65 and thereby contributed to the prolongation of the longest expansion in postwar U.S. history. Johnson defended government initiatives to reduce employment by arguing that "the number 1 in priority today is more jobs. This is our dominant domestic problem and we have to face it head-on."[43]

---

41. Many analysts argue that Eisenhower's fiscal policies not only did little to combat the economic contradictions of the period but also were important causes of the 1957–58 and 1960–61 recessions. See W. Lewis, *Federal Fiscal Policy in the Postwar Recessions* (Washington D.C.: Brookings Institution, 1962); and Stein, *The Fiscal Revolution in America*.

42. D. Eisenhower, *Waging Peace 1956–61* (Garden City, N.Y.: Doubleday, 1965), pp. 461, 462.

43. Cited in F. R. Dulles, *Labor in America* (New York: Cromwell, 1966), p. 394.

The basic economic priorities associated with the Eisenhower era were reestablished during the Nixon and Ford administrations. Although Nixon-Ford macroeconomic policies were more interventionist than those of earlier Republican administrations, high employment was again sacrificed for the sake of restraining inflation. It is generally agreed that the 1970–71 recession was deliberately induced by the Nixon administration to check inflation, though this policy was later jettisoned in an attempt to stimulate a preelection boom. In most respects the short-lived Ford administration was a replay of the Eisenhower years. The macroeconomic policy called for running the economy at considerable "slack" to reverse "inflationary expectations," and repeated attempts by the Democratic Congress to pass measures promoting a more rapid economic expansion were vigorously opposed.

Macroeconomic outcomes, then, are not altogether endogenous to the economy, but obviously are influenced to a significant extent by long- and short-term political choices. Perhaps the best way to determine real winners of elections is to examine the policy consequences of partisan change rather than simply to tally the votes.

Index

51; inflation variable, 51; Phillips curve, 51; simple log trend in, 58, 59

Time-series (ARIMA), 13
Tobin, James, 125
Trade union(s): and market wage, 70–71, 72; and wage inflation, 72, 78–79; recruiting drives, 95; mobilization, 95–96; Communist, 96n; cooperation, 113–114; British, 261
Trade Union Congress, 114
Truman, Harry S., 173
Tufte, Edward, 174, 187–189

Unemployment, 194; and inflation, 6–7, 10–11, 119–123; 292–295; public opinion regarding, 7–8, 11, 120–123, 127–141, 294–295; and politics, 11, 171; natural rate of, 13; and strike activity, 49; /wage ratio, 78–79; /price ratio, 101; and cost of inflation, 123–127; and leftist politics, 291; and national income distribution, 291. *See also* Employment and employment models; Phillips curve; Political support model, unemployment variable; Strike activity model, unemployment variable
United States: inflation in, 5–6; 113; politics and economics in, 6–10; strike activity in, 21, 39, 48, 54–58, 64, 66,

67, 68; GNP, 66; wage and price stability in, 78–79, 110; wage elasticity in, 92; price expectation model for, 100; economic performance in, 218, 222; unemployment in, 291, 297, 299, 301, 314; unemployment model for, 302, 304, 313–319. *See also* Political support model

Vietnam War: as variable in political support model, 112, 117, 148, 153–156, 162, 172–173, 202, 203, 222; as variable in unemployment model, 314–315
Volker, Paul, 185
Voter response. *See* Political support model

Wage(s): adjusted to prices, 5, 93, 100, 124; /profit ratio, 18; and strike activity, 39, 50, 78; elasticity, 90, 92; target, 91; inflation, 94–96; "key industries" theory of, 104; acceleration, 108, 111–113
Wage model, strike-augmented, 108
Watergate scandal as variable in political support model, 148, 153–156, 157–158, 162, 202, 203
Welfare state, 63, 64–66, 70, 71–76
Wilson, Harold, 41, 213, 258, 273, 278